The Eton Miscellany Volume 1

THE

ETON MISCELLANY.

VOL. I.-II

BY

BARTHOLOMEW BOUVERIE,

NOW OF ETON COLLEGE.

June—July, 1827.

——— Sive ego pravè
Seu rectè hoc volui, ne sis patruus mihi.
HORACE.

ETON:

PRINTED FOR T. INGALTON.

SOLD ALSO BY

E. WILLIAMS, ETON; KNIGHT AND BROWN, WINDSOR; R. S. KIRBY,
PATER-NOSTER ROW; AND W. ANDERSON, WATERLOO PLACE.

L. C. HANSARD, Printer, Great Turnstile Press, London.

TO THE

MANY-HEADED MONSTER!

An Epistle,

Dedicatory, Explanatory, and Conciliatory,

BY BARTHOLOMEW BOUVERIE.

———

WITHOUT doubt, the first question of my reader
will be, "Who is Bartholomew Bouverie?" In
this age of auto-biography, Bartholomew shall
answer for himself. To begin, then, "ab ovo:" I
was hatched at the house of my parents, Jeremiah
and Rebecca Bouverie, on the day which was
signalized by the victory over the French at
Corunna; from which event my mother drew
omens of my future greatness, probably forgetting
that whatever chance of success I might derive from
the auspicious circumstances of my birth, was to
be shared in common with at least five thousand

other children, who had precisely as sufficient grounds for anticipations of prosperity and honour. The first thing that I can remember in my childhood is, that I early acquired a taste for poetry; and I have still in mind some of my juvenile effusions, which my mother often rewarded with sugar-plums, but my father with birch. My chief delight was in the "Poet's corner" of a newspaper; but I considered a Review by no means contemptible reading. At length, in order to check this propensity to poetry, which my father considered at best a very useless accomplishment, he determined on sending me to school. Long and eloquently did my mother plead for at least a respite for her dear Bartle (for so was I called for shortness); powerfully did she urge that proper care was not taken of the little darlings; and movingly did she expatiate on the change they must undergo when separated from mamma: to all which my father briefly answered, " that he hoped I was no chicken," and ended this part of the dispute by quoting

"Home-keeping youths have ever homely wit:"

upon which, my mother, having an infinite respect for the authority of Shakspeare, immediately withdrew her opposition.

The next point, and that of no inconsiderable importance, was, to what school I should be sent : my mother proposed the Charter-house; but whether that I might be in the vicinity of my namesake, the Fair, I will not take upon myself to determine. But my father being resolved that, in his family at least, the Salique law should remain in force, asserted his prerogative, and resolved upon sending me to Eton. Now it so happened, that my mother had a perfect horror of Eton, for the following reasons, In the first place, she had a particular dread of my sleeping in damp sheets, which she thought must be the case in so low a situation. To this, objection the first, my father only answered by an emphatic "Pshaw!" The second objection was against the fagging system ; in discussing which, my mother enlarged upon the tyranny of the upper boys, whom the microscopic mind of Mr. Mortimer, the curate of the parish, had magnified into Neros and Domitians. My father was about to answer this objection, by saying, that it was common to all public schools, when he was interrupted by an exclamation of "Oh, and the water too !" coming from my mother, who was so carried away at the thoughts of this most terrible of terrors, that she

could no longer arrange her arguments in system-
atic order, but, as is usual in cases of hydrophobia,
gave vent to what was passing in her mind by convulsive starts and sudden ejaculations : " Oh, and the
water too !" cried she. " And the boats!—and the
bathing ! To bathe—to swim—perchance to drown !
Oh, Bartle ! Bartle !" After the first paroxysm was
over, she appeared to be sinking into a state of torpid
quiescence, upon which, my father, fearing lest she
should faint, imprudently discharged a glass of
water in her face : a relapse instantly took place ;
the former exclamations were renewed with increased
violence for the space of ten minutes, after which
time they gradually sunk into an angry expostulation with my father, on the cruelty of exposing his
child to the gulphs and whirlpools of the Thames.
At length, my father seeing affairs in this state,
ended the discussion by leaving the room, and in
about two hours, a post-chaise drove up to the door.
My mother had by this time learnt resignation, and
dismissed me with an injunction, which, in the
excess of her affection, differed little from the Irish
caution, " that a man should never go into the water
till he can swim." In short, I came to Eton, where
I have now continued five years ; and, in answer

to the objections of my mother, I can say, with
gratitude, that Mater Etona has been no step-mother
to me ; that I never yet encountered a miniature.
Nero, or Caligula; and that I hope shortly to be
able to show, that I can "keep my head above
water" in more senses than one.

But in my present undertaking, there is one gulph
in which I fear to sink ; and that gulph is Lethe.
There is one stream which I dread my inability to
stem—it is the tide of Popular Opinion.   I have
ventured, and, no doubt, rashly ventured,

> "Like little wanton boys that swim on bladders,
> To try my fortune in a sea of glory,
> But far beyond my depth !"

At present, it is hope alone that buoys me up ; for
more substantial support I must be indebted to my
own exertions; well knowing that, in this land of
literature, merit never wants its reward : that such
merit is mine, I dare not presume to think ; but still,
there is something within me that bids me hope
that I may be able to glide prosperously down the
stream of public estimation ; or, in the words of
Virgil,

> " —— Celerare viam rumore secundo."

With hopes like these, however they may be

founded, I, being minded to secure for myself
eternal fame, do hereby declare to the world my
determination to take up the trade of authorship.
If Grub-street is redolent of the Muse's odours—if
poets crowd the sacred haunts of St. Giles's—if the
soil of Birmingham is fertile in the flowers of
eloquence—if Manchester spins cotton and poems,
or, according to the ancient fashion,

     " *tenui* deducta poemata *filo*"—

why may.not I, being at least nurtured in a more
happy climate, and under more favourable circumstances, follow the example of my forefathers and
predecessors, of Griffin, and Grildrig, and Courtenay
—tread in the path which they have trodden—take
upon myself the part which they have acted—though
I cannot boast of the same excellencies, or hope for
the same commendations ? Surely when the trio of
the Lakes inundates Great Britain with the creatures
of their imaginations—of all sorts, and of all sizes
—prose and verse—(much more prose indeed than
poetry)—most formidable in appearance, and by no
means less so to the luckless wight who attempts a
closer examination—surely, I say, I may venture
forth, in a moderate size and a humble dress,
pledging myself, if I meet with a discouraging

reception from the public, never again to intrude myself on their attention. I will retire to my humble cell—I will indulge my visionary fancies in privacy alone—and show at least that I respect the rod which inflicts so severe, though, it may be, so deserved, a punishment.

I have here put the question, " Why should I not write?" Should some wag reply, " Why should you?" I can only repeat what a much wiser man has said before me, " *Semper ego auditor tantùm ?*" or, if that be deemed an unsatisfactory answer, acknowledge that I, among others, have been infected with the " *cacoethes scribendi,*" and content myself with expressing a humble hope that my mania, however much it may injure me, may be productive of some benefit, or of some amusement, to my fellow citizens.

For the better furthering and advancing the purpose which I have set forth, I have taken to myself certain coadjutors from among those around me ; in selecting whom, it has been my sincere wish, and my earnest endeavour; to make application to all those who might, from their talents or acquirements, from good-will or from connexion, prove best adapted for assisting my undertaking. These I

may, or may not, at some future period, as it may,
or may not, appear proper, or expedient, or necessary, have the pleasure of introducing by name to
the public.   In the mean time, as they will have a
little of their own way, they sometimes usurp my
appellation, and sometimes my power ; sometimes
address me as humble correspondents, sometimes personate me as real *bonâ fide* Bartholomew
Bouveries.

Having now, perhaps somewhat clumsily, performed a task, necessary indeed, but extremely
irksome to my natural modesty—that of introducing
myself to the public—having likewise informed
them that they may, in time, if they order me
plentifully, and pay for me liberally, become
acquainted with more—I can only proceed to
assure them, that we shall always remain their most
faithful and obedient servants, from this, the period
of our literary birth, to the time when the Fates
shall put a close to our existence.   May they avert
the day ! or at least grant that our life may be happy
in its nature, though brief in its duration.   But now

>   " ——extremo sub fine laborum
>   Vela traham, et terris festinem advertere proram——"

If any humble efforts of ours can contribute, in

the slightest degree, to add credit to the name of that foster-mother, whom we regard with affection and with reverence, let her enjoy the honour—let her receive the reward. But if our impotent attempt should recoil on ourselves, and bring disgrace on those with whom it may be supposed to have originated, then indeed on us alone rest the blame and the responsibility. If we have, like Icarus, ventured into regions in which we can neither sustain our burden, nor direct our course, let us perish in the oblivion which we have deserved; and let the boyish levity which was the cause, be also the excuse, of our failure. For those, under whose tuition and care we have passed so many happy years—years which are now fast drawing to a close, and which we begin to appreciate, as we begin to lose; with regard to them, let not their care of, and solicitude for, our welfare, make them answerable for whatever childish presumption, or sudden caprice, may incite us to attempt; or bring discredit on them, if we be found unequal to the task which we have gratuitously, and perhaps foolishly, undertaken.

If it be allowable thus to afford an opportunity to our fellow citizens, of displaying those embryo

abilities which may hereafter shine in a far wider
sphere, and to increase the innocent relaxation
and enjoyment to which it should be our wish, as
it is our duty, to contribute ; if these be objects of
legitimate ambition—it is at these alone we aim.
Fame we cannot, we dare not aspire to ; indulgence
we may presume upon ; and we commit our humble
offering to the world, with the hope and the
confidence, that those will be found both among
our fellows and among the public at large, who will
be so just as to praise the merits which may, and
so lenient as to pardon the faults which must, be
found in THE ETON MISCELLANY.

ETON MISCELLANY,

No. I.

THE PARGUINOTES FAREWELL.

AND must we leave our native sands,
  Our native rocks, to despot sway,
To learn the tongues of foreign lands,
  And moulder in a foreign clay?
    Yes! we depart in stern disdain
    Of those who crouch beneath the chain.

The sun-set gilds our Ocean's breast
  As softly as in days of yore;
The plumes of snow on mountain crest
  Are shining as they shone before.
    Where is that soul, by which alone
    Our fathers call'd this land their own?

We hail this calm and holy hour
  Responsive to our last farewell;
Yet, ere we go, the song shall pour
  A tribute to the brave who fell,
    When the red flow of Sunium's wave
    Incarnadin'd the Persian's grave.

Oh, for that spark of living fire,
  Whose stirring impulse rais'd the cry,
When Greece, resistless in her ire,
  Rush'd on to conquer or to die:

Hark ! how they answer to the shock,
The echoes of the island rock.

Those hearts are still'd for ever now,
Those hands have moulder'd in the sod ;
While Greece can see the myrtle bough,
Yet tremble at a tyrant's nod.
Dost thou forget, Athenian slave,
What foliage wreath'd the hero's glaive ?

Our fathers bones are on the shore,
Our fathers met a hero's doom :
We go—to view this land no more,
And dare we leave a hero's tomb
To foes who wield o'er land and sea
A sword to crush the brave and free ?

No—light the pile, to wrap in flames
The relics of our glorious sires ;
This land will not forget the names
Of those who fell ascend ye fires,
And flash defiance, as we go,
Upon the traitor and the foe.

MALEK.

ACCOUNT

OF THE

PROCEEDINGS OF THE ETON DULL CLUB.

Dulce est desipere.—Hor

The second meeting of the Eton Dull Club was held on Monday last. Mr. Ignoramus in the chair

The Chairman having called over the names, began the business by stating, that, in compliance with

the wishes of the Club, he had written to the
Heralds' College to request to know what arms the
Club might be permitted to take; and that he had
received the following answer :

"The Eton Dull Club are at liberty to take for
their coat of arms, what is technically called *virgatum sagulum;* bearing on the dexter chief, two
rods sanguine; on the sinister, two blocks proper;
in the base, three numskulls void, on a field sable,
with a bar sinister containing three plummets; for
the crest, an ass-head braisant. The motto may be
left to the choice of the Club."

While this was being read, looks of astonishment and doubt were exchanged by the members
of the Club; but chiefly with regard to the expression of *virgatum sagulum,* which nobody could
entirely understand, though all the members agreed
that they had been long enough at Eton to learn
that " virga" meant rod.

Mr. Stultze said, he could not imagine why an
ass-head brazen was chosen, in preference to any
other metal.

Mr. Duntze said, that he had been to France,
and that he was almost sure *braisant* meant the
language of donkies.

The Chairman called Mr. Duntze to order for
displaying too much knowledge, but congratulated
the rest of the Club on their superlative qualifications as members.

The House then proceeded to choose a motto.

Mr. Sloman proposed,

.   " Duller should'st thou be than the fat weed
      That rots itself at ease on Lethe wharf."

Upon being asked where his motto might be found, Mr. Sloman professed himself entirely ignorant, but said that he had heard it from a fifth-form boy, who was fishing at Perch-hole; and he had some idea that Lethe was another name for Eton College.

The Chairman being asked his opinion, protested he knew no more than the dead what Lethe meant.

While the House was in hesitation upon this point, Mr. Lernill rose, and said, that as the former motto appeared to be too difficult, he could supply them with one from Gray, which they could all perfectly comprehend, and that was, " Ignorance is bliss."

The Chairman agreed that the motto was good, but called upon Mr. Lernill for a fine, for having read Gray.

Mr. Lernill protested that every Etonian had an absolute right to read Gray's Ode on Eton College; to which the Chairman assented, but denied that it was legal that any member should remember what he read.

The fine was then paid, and the motto was received with acclamation, by all but Mr. Dolton, who denied that it held good in the case of a boy not knowing his lesson, and getting flogged in default.

The Chairman then proceeded to read the rules of the Club, which were these :

1. That the name of this Society be the Eton Dull Club.

2. That no member be admitted into the Club without producing a certificate of his having been flogged.

3. That any member who has been flogged three times in one day, shall be entitled to certain immunities and privileges, and shall receive a triple crown of birch.

4. That a room be provided looking into Barnes' Pool.

5. That no member shall presume to appear at the Club without a night-cap; on pain of sitting three hours in a chair without a back.

6. That loud talking be considered disorderly, and that any member (the Chairman excepted) who shall wake another, shall be subject to a fine of two-and-sixpence, unless he can lull him to sleep again in five minutes.

7. That any member convicted of a pun, shall drink salt water.

8. That all solid and all light subjects be equally avoided, and that all questions brought before the House resemble the night-mare, in being heavy without substance.

B

9. That it be considered illegal to play at cricket,
or to row, and that the only legal exercise
be a walk to the top of Windsor Hill and
back, with a cigar in the mouth, to prevent
conversation   -   ,   ˋ
10. That no member do more than his number of
verses, for fear of spoiling the masters.
11. That a book-fund be established for·the purchase of old verse-books.

Note.—It had been the intention of the Club to
buy a collection of Translations, comprising Smart's
Horace, and other similar works; but the Chairman
having heard that a person of the name of Hamilton
had given his sanction to this method of instruction,
thinks that it will not be expedient to pursue the
plan, for fear of rendering the Dull Club a dead
letter, by diminishing its stock of ignorance. · The
same observation applies to writing down the
English word over the Latin or Greek, which is expressly forbidden.

12. That the members of the Club use no other
than Pote's edition of the Classics.
13. That it be considered highly honourable to
eat, drink, and smoke, all day, and to sleep all
night.

Note.—That as it is creditable to sleep also in
the day, if nature is unwilling, a narcotic draught
may be taken from the " Eton Miscellany."   ,

Note also.—That in the event of the " Eton Miscellany" not being continued beyond the present fortnight, the Chairman is empowered to provide such a stock of poppies as shall to him appear sufficient.

14. That an annual dinner be provided, on the 15th of November, to celebrate the Institution of the Club; and that the dishes be Stewed Tench, Calf's Head, and Goose; succeeded by Whipped Cream, and a Trifle; and that the liquors be Black Strap, and Ramsbottom's Table Beer.

15. That no member shall drink Champagne, Claret, Ginger Beer, Spruce Beer, or Bottled Porter, and that it be laudable to be dead drunk, but penal to be merry.

RESOLUTION. That a deputation do wait upon Mr. Bartholomew Bouverie, to invite him to become a member of the Club, in consideration of his having shown qualifications of the highest order.

The Chairman then ended the proceedings with the following speech:

Gentlemen;—I hate what's called cleverness, and I know you do the same; whenever I see a clever boy, I kick him, and I hope you do the same. I would have all clever boys kicked, because they don't get flogged, or if they do, they feel it. Now I would have none of your tender-skinned varlets: give me a buffalo-headed, and a buffalo-hided chap, with a skin and a skull that can bear the brunt of

buffets and birch ; he's the man for the Club. Now,
you see, gentlemen, that it is not every man that's
fit for the Club, so you ought to be proud that you
are : it is not every one that can come to the block
in the cool, gentleman-like manner that you can :
so call *for another gallon of beer.*

P. S. *by Bartholomew Bouverie.*

In inserting the above communication, I am well
aware that there will not be wanting those who
will crack their small wit upon me, by bidding me
go to the Club; and on that account, as Addison
says, I beg leave to put in a caveat against that
joke. With regard to the invitation of the Club, I
shall beg leave to decline it for the present, while
I aspire to a higher honour, that of receiving Mr.
Ignoramus's toe.

LLAN EGWEST ABBEY.

Pensive Nymph, who lov'st to dwell
By waving wood, and winding dell,
Where grass and wild flowers mingling spread
Around the lonely fountain-head,
Marking oft the purple streak
Of evening tinge the distant peak.
Chiefly, Nymph, thou lov'st to stray
By Llan Egwest's old Abbaye,
Watching, with a tearful eye,
Where its fallen honours lie,

And heath-bells blow, and briars wave,
O'er many a monk's forgotten grave.
Then, on Memory's dewy wing,
To her shadowy realms you spring,
And times its holy towers arose
Amid the trees, in calm repose ;
Echoed then the sylvan Dee
" O miserere Domine !"
And oft you gently paused, to hear
The solemn organ pealing near,
Stealing on the ear of night
Like the heavenly song of the sons of light,
Till rock, and stream, and wood, and plain,
Seem'd living in the holy strain.
But time, and war's destructive brand,
Have rent its towers with reckless hand,
And steel-clad fanatics have trod
And trampled on the house of God.
And now, like blighted hope, it rears
Its mouldering pile of other years,
So sadly fair, we scarce can deem—
We will not own it as a dream—
A fleeting shade in Time's dark river,
That passeth soon to fade for ever.

GLENARTNEY.

Credidimus generi, NOMINIBUSQUE tuis.

Historians are, generally speaking, so intent on tracing home to a fine-spun philosophy of their own creating, all the wonders, and changes, and revolutions of the world, that they totally omit to mention those smaller circumstances which a plain man would consider as the main-springs, or very nearly so, of

human action. There are many such omissions;
but that which I shall venture to enlarge a little upon,
is certainly of the most paramount importance—I
mean, the constant neglect with which these over-
weening gentlemen treat the *names* of the heroes
they describe. " What's in a name?" said a wise
man—I forget, at the present moment, his own; but
that is not essential. " What's in a name?" I may
be asked by a hundred voices in a breath—by the
would-be philosopher, who would cut the throat of
the officious friend who should advise him to render
practical his high-minded system, by publishing it
to the world *without his name:* by the fevered politician, who would sacrifice health, fortune, life itself,
and all but that reputation without which life were
a bubble, to tack on Right Hon. *to his name:* by the
learned fair one, the bright azure of whose eyes is
far outdone by those stockings, so "*darkly, deeply,
beautifully, blue;*" and, lastly, by the sentimental
novelist; who, however she may bravado it to me,
would perish sooner than change Sir Marmaduke
Glenmore into *Giles Gibbs*, or her fondly cherished
Selina de Cleveland into plain *Susan Jones!*

Whoever, then, you may be—novelists, philosophers, place-hunters, or blues—whoever, in the teeth
of all that is sound in criticism, and true in nature,
persist in affirming there is nothing in a name, I,
Bartholomew Bouverie, who, thank heaven, was
never yet ashamed of any one of the seven liquid

syllables that set me together, throw you the gage of
defiance! Think you the Grecian democracies,
turbulent and anarchical as they were, would have
been any thing better than a rope of sand, had it not
been for that soft, musical, and inimitably flexible
language, which threw a spell over the most insig-
nificant places, and illuminated the poorest characters?   Again, when *Alexander* and *Darius* went
forth to battle it at Issus and Arbela, think you the
dominion of Asia was the only thing at stake? Nonsense! I, Bartholomew Bouverie, tell you, it was the
mighty strife between the *Trisyllables* and the
Quadrisyllables, that wound up to so fearful a pitch
the attention of the world! To come to more modern
times : reflect on the glorious career of the Protest-
ant hero, Frederick the Great: and I should like to
see the man, woman, or child, that would have the
face to tell me, that, had the name of that great man
been *Timothy*, he would have exerted the same
energies, and attained the same glory! Why,
Timothy's tactics would have carried rout and confusion in the very title! What is the reason *Jack
Straw*, or *Hob Carter*, so egregiously failed in their
attempt to overthrow constituted authorities, and
equalize the peasant and the noble?—why, on the
other hand, have *Mirabeau*, and *La Fayette*, revolu-
tionized their country, and upset Europe, with all
the facility imaginable? I confess I know of but
one really good reason, the superiority of these

French names to those English. Who can wonder,
provided he has never seen the inside of Bedlam,
that such a man as *Napoleon Buonaparte* won the
fields of Austerlitz and Marengo? not, assuredly, by
his sharp sword, or his sharper wit—these would be
the conjectures of weak minds—but by his unheard-
of, pleasing, pliant, melodious, Tuscan name!

I shall not put myself to any further pains to prove
what, perhaps, after all, my readers may think required no proof, but shall content myself with setting before them the pathetic complaint of a luckless correspondent, which will, I doubt not, excite
the same sensations of pity in their bosoms (especially amongst the gentle sex) which it moved in
mine.

. "Dear Mr. Bartholomew Bouverie,

"I am one of those unfortunate beings, whose
peace of mind has been utterly destroyed by the
lack of "*my good name.*" Do not mistake me : my
reputation, as an attorney, has never been attacked,
even by the bitterest sons of calumny : I abhor all
radicals, Papists, and smugglers, as well (modesty
alone forbids me to say better) as the best
Christian in England : but, Sir, when I tell you my
name, my abominable baptismal appellation, you
will see what it is that grieves me, and will, I am
sure, sympathize with my affliction. I am, Mr.
Bouverie, of an old Roundhead family—the more's

my sorrow; and it has been from time immemorial
the custom of our branch of the *Stubbs's* to christen
every second son by the outlandish and rebellious
name of *Bring-the-King-to-the-Block!* In the innocent days of my childhood, when I was greeted by
my brothers and sisters, with the pretty, harmless,
abbreviation of *Blocky,* which my father, when in
a drunken, or grumbling humour, used frequently
to improve into *Blockhead,* then was I contented,
because I was ignorant!

'Oh happy days! once more, who would not be a boy!'

"But too soon I arrived at years of discretion, and
as my father (heaven rest his soul!) had saved
enough money to procure me a liberal education,
forthwith I found myself in the vicinity of Eton
Playing-fields; where, alas! I was soon made sensible of the horrible nature of my prænomen, by the
jeers of my more fortunate comrades. I will not
detain you by enumerating the various modifications
of my name, which clung to me, like so many phantasms of a night-mare, during my long and laborious
passage from the *Nonsense* to the *Upper Division.*
Had I been a scamp in my conduct, or a leveller in
my political opinions, I might have borne with
patience this series of unprovoked mortifications;
but ever since I read Mr. Southey's Laureate odes,
the poetic feelings of a Stubbs have stedfastly attached me to Church and King: nor shall I ever

forget the solemn warning given me by my godmother, when I first stepped blubbering into the Eton
Tally-ho, " that though there was many a text in the
Bible which talked of the holy prophets anointing
kings in Israel, she had looked twice through, with
her spectacles on, from Genesis to Revelations,
without finding that they ever anointed a Republic !"
I am now a respectable attorney ; but my unfortunate name has deprived me, to my certain knowledge, of many a fee.   Pray, Mr. Bouverie, as,
from the moment I saw your elegant name in the
newspaper, I was sure you were a kind old gentleman, can you point out any mode of relief ?

Believe me your devoted

(Would I could say anonymous)

Servant,

BRING-THE-KING-TO-THE-BLOCK STUBBS.

E. L.

THE DOCTOR.

Quod medicorum est
Promittunt medici.—Hor.

I ONCE knew a doctor, of credit and skill
In mixing a potion, and gilding a pill,
Though he kill'd half his patients, yet praise he ensured,
For the dead went to nature, himself took the cured ;
He was fam'd far and wide in the neighbourhood round,
For curing the healthy, and healing the sound ;

Than this, his pretensions to skill went no further:
If you ask me his motto, 'twas "Killing no Murther."
I sent for him once, and he came in a trice;
His chin was well shaved, and his periwig nice.
He enter'd the room with a sour grimace,
Machaon and Galen were both in his face.
I gave him my wrist; "A slight fever, I see;
Hem! purging and bleeding, and camomile tea:
A draught and a bolus, the blood to refine,
To drive off the ague, a dose of quinine.
You'll be better to-morrow: I'll see you again,
And send you twelve draughts that will last you till then"
    The Doctor departed, and presently came
Six draughts black as coal, and six draughts red as flame.
A label to each, with "The draughts, Mr. White,
The red for the day, and the black for the night."
    The draughts on the chimney-piece quietly lay,
Till the Doctor return'd on the following day:
He came with his lancets, in case there were need,
(That's to say if I'd let him) his patient to bleed.
As soon as he saw me: "Why, bless us," he cried,
"In a week, at this rate, you'll be able to ride;
In a fortnight you'll walk, in a month you'll be well;
But you're still very sick, I can perfectly tell.
But none in their senses can ever compare
To your health, Sir, to-day, what you yesterday were:
'Tis the draughts that have done it; I know them of old,
They're the true panacea, the essence of gold."
    Just then at the door came a thundering knock.
"O master! O master! quick open the lock!"
Cried a blubbering urchin, that stood in the street;
And told his sad story to all he could meet;
With his cries and entreaties he set all the boys on;
And the street soon resounded with "Poison! oh, Poison!"
The doctor aghast, by his conscience accus'd,
Felt terrors arising the more that he mus'd;
The ghosts of his patients appear'd in his sight,
All clutching the phials that sent them from light.

At length the poor Doctor, his reverie o'er,
Screw'd up resolution, and opened the door.
" O master ! O master !" the blubberer cried,
" We are lost ! oh, the poison !—has any one died ?—
I mixed, by some horrible folly of mine,
Of arsenic ten parts, to one of quinine."
" Zounds, sirrah !—but, soft, bring the stomach-pump quick,
And hark, some emetics to make the man sick."
    The Doctor returned to my chamber, and said,
" You are number'd, alas! my dear Sir, with the dead ;
For poison was mix'd in the draughts, and I grieve
No hope is remaining."   I laugh'd in my sleeve.
The stomach-pump came, and the Doctor was stout ;
He pump'd long and strong, and some liquor came out :
" 'Tis arsenic all , oh, what horrible stuff."
" Hold, softly," cried I, " we have jok'd long enough ;
Count the draughts on the chimney, you'll find just a dozen :
I'll expose you abroad for a cheat and a cozen.
Get out, or I'll kick you myself from my gate,
With your ratsbane and stomach-pump flung at your pate ;
And I'll hire the beadle, and set all the boys on,
To hoot at your heels, " That's the vender of Poison."

WILLIAM WHITE.

NOTHING.

" Nihil" est ab omni parte beatum.—HOR.

Dear Mr. Bouverie ;

In my present frame of mind, I am induced to
think that " *nothing*" is the subject, of all others,
most appropriate to my feelings, and best suited to
my capacity : I do not remember any authors, with

the exception of the celebrated Earl of Rochester,
and Mr. Gregory Griffin, who have given the world
the benefit of their lucubrations upon this important
subject. This has always been a matter of no small
surprise to me, since there have uniformly existed
a great many individuals preeminently well qualified
to write upon it: for although few are candid
enough to permit their writings to go by their real
name, yet I feel confident you will agree with me,
that there are many Law Reports, many poems,
many cumbrous dissertations upon misunderstood
points, which ought to be designated by this comprehensive word : and it is chiefly owing to the
vanity of mankind, that they are so tenacious of their
talents, however small, as to call these productions
" treatises," " plays," " reflections," " dissertations,"
" essays," " criticisms," &c. &c. Were I to attempt
to mention the names of any of the works which I
think ought to be thus designated, such an endless
variety of authors would be presented to my view,
that the selection would be no easy task. You are,
of course, well aware, my dear Sir, that I am a
very extraordinary being, and that my tastes and
propensities are as peculiar as your own. A love
of paradox has uniformly been the distinguishing
feature of my character, and although the old saying, that " *nothing*" can arise out of " *nothing*," has
been held, and is still held by some, a sound and
undisputed maxim of philosophy, I have always

had some doubts upon the subject, and questioned the practical application of this maxim to the ordinary affairs of life : whether my doubts are rational or ill-grounded, I leave you to judge; but I will endeavour to refute the above-mentioned, and prevailing maxim—to prove the truth of Horace's remark, that it is by no means impossible

"——Ex fumo dare lucem ;"

and to show, that from what is by the generality of mankind denominated "*nothing*," spring all the most important events which daily take place around us. If I ask what took place at the House of Commons last night, the answer is, "*nothing.*" If I ask, "Has any thing been done at Court," the answer is the same. If I ask, "Is there any news at the Stock-Exchange, Foreign-Office, in the City ?" I receive for answer, "*nothing.*" But is this a correct representation of what has been actually taking place ? I think not : armies and fleets have been equipped—and those armies and fleets, though they have gained no great victories, though they have imprisoned no kings, have, notwithstanding, kept formidable armies at bay, and have contended with them for the sovereignty of the world ! *And is this "nothing"?* Look next at the city—Is there no avarice displayed there ? or is it "*nothing*" ? Are there no frauds committed ? no extortions practised ? or are all these things "*nothing*" ? Is there no stock-jobbing ? no hypocrisy ? is this "*nothing*" ?

Falsehoods are disseminated : this is " *nothing.*"
Malicious stories are propagated : this is "*nothing.*"
Scandal is hatched : this, too, is " *nothing.*"   Numbers were ruined yesterday ! numbers are ruining
to-day ! and numbers will be ruined to-morrow !
Now, my dear Mr. Bouverie, if you think that this
is " *nothing,*" will you not allow that " *nothing*" is
accompanied by very important results ?   Will you
not allow that " *nothing*" originates quarrels ; that
" *nothing*" causes dissension ; that " *nothing*" creates
suspicion ? Do you not, in short, concur with me in
opinion, that " *nothing*" is the cause of " *every
thing*" ?

> " Quicquid agunt homines, votum, timor, ira, voluptas,
>   Gaudia ; discursus."

I am sorry to have given you so much trouble in
perusing this empty and good-for-nothing Epistle .
by the way, I call it *good for nothing ;* but whether
you will consider it in the usual signification of the
word, utterly worthless, or really GOOD, for nothing,
I am at a loss to know : but I am vain and presumptuous enough to imagine that my letter is actually *better than* " *nothing.*"   As I have " *nothing*"
more to communicate at present, if you will favour
me with the insertion of these few remarks in your
valuable publication, you will much oblige

Your sincere and faithful Friend,

LAWRENCE LOVENOUGHT.

P. S.—I have just been alarmed by hearing,

from a friend, that "*nothing*" is without an end ;
but on second thoughts, I find myself the more
strongly confirmed in my opinion, that my letter is
" *better than nothing*," since, as you will see, I have
already come to a conclusion. · L. L.

THE PREDICTION

'Tis night—in Guadalquiver's stream
The stars reflected wildly gleam ;
'Tis night—beneath the moon's pale ray,
So silent glide the hours away,
That the soft waters seem to grow
Louder and louder as they flow ;
You would not deem, to gaze on bowers
Of myrtle and the orange flowers ;
You would not deem that, by the side
Of Guadalquiver's gentle tide,
Scarce waiting till the day drew nigh,
Two mighty hosts were met to die ;
The sacred banner of Castile,
The very crescent seemed to feel,
    As they floated idly there ;
How ill agreed that lovely night,
How ill those distant isles of light
    With the war-shriek of despair,
So Roland felt, while all around
Lay hush'd in slumber so profound,
    That he could not bear to know
That those who drew the careless breath
Must yield to Sleep's stern brother, Death,
    'Ere another sun was low.
The youth was brave as ever knight
    Who couch'd in rest his spear ;
He waited for the morrow's fight,
He waited with a fierce delight,
    To run his first career,

But yet he felt a solemn thrill,
As he recall'd the doom of ill
Foretold him in that hour of dread
By one arisen from the dead,
    The demon of his race :
That spirit of the grave, who came,
With brow of night and eye of flame,
To usher all who bore that name
    To the tomb's cold embrace.

Awhile he gazed with flashing eye,
That seem'd the crescent to defy,
    And shook his plumed crest ;
He grasp'd the sabre by his side,
His press'd lips quiver'd with the tide
    That boil'd within his breast.
Awhile he gaz'd—one murmur broke,
While his brow blacken'd as he spoke,
Then starting from his troubl'd dream,
His dark eye lost its savage gleam,
And on he rush'd to bid farewell
To her whom he had lov'd so well.

The lady sat within her bower,
And strove to while the passing hour
    With music's holy strain.
There, as she, graceful, swept the strings,
The airy gush on echo's wings
    Seem'd floating to remain—
The splendor of the changing cheek,
The eye's dark lustre seem'd to speak,
And every gesture serv'd to tell
What varying passions rose or fell :
'Twas now that calm and holy fire,
    That mildness of the dove,
By which the gods are won from ire,
    And soften'd into love.

C

Yet, when the voice of glory spoke
  In music's lofty swell,
A nobler spirit then awoke
  And kindled like a spell,
Till her young heart had caught the flame,
And felt the echoing thrill for fame.

And Roland, as he stood beneath
  The foliage of the waving trees,
And caught the music's floating breath,
  Upon the light wing of the breeze,
Mus'd deeply as he stood alone
On joys which might have been his own,
But yesterday, with flashing eye,
And heart where glory's thrill beat high,
While his blood rush'd in buoyant tide,
He thought upon his promis'd bride ;
He thought in victory to feel
His father's spirit guide his steel.
But the dark form had come between
The triumphs of the fancied scene,
While on the battle-field stood Death,
To crown him with the victor wreath,
Awhile he gaz'd in mute despair,
While recreant nature trembled there.
Till his proud spirit rose, at length,
And struggled with convulsive strength,
And wrestled down each vain regret,
And bade him every tie forget,
It bade him, bound by honour's laws,
To perish in his country's cause.

" Well, be it so ; I'll couch my spear
  With a bold and fearless soul,
Which, rushing on its bright career,
  Shall spurn the base control.
Then, be it so, when shouts are pour'd,
  When ready glaives are flashing high,
Then first shall be my father's sword,
  Then first my father's battle cry.

He gained the bower—"Now, Clara, now
I come to claim thy parting vow;
When those green trees, which soon will wave,
In sorrow, o'er the young and brave;
When those green trees in rapture fling
Their odours to the breeze of Spring,
Forget not thou the lonely tomb,
Which wakes not with returning bloom,
And drop a tear upon the wreath
You weave for him who sleeps beneath."
The lady shriek'd: "Oh, say not so:
To-morrow, ere the sun is low,
The laurel-crown shall gird thy brow.
   My Roland, live for me."
"No, Clara, it were vain to tell
What omens urge this sad farewell
    To happiness and thee;
Yet will I snatch the vain relief
   Of sympathy and kindred fear;
Our joys are made for all, but grief
   Is sacred to Affection's tear.

"'Twas yesterday, that fearful form,
   Which marshals us to death,
Came riding on the midnight storm,
   To claim my forfeit breath:
I saw him raise that phantom brand,
In attitude of high command,
And point to where those green trees wave—
He pointed to a warrior's grave.
I saw then, as I see thee now,
The dark smile wreathe his pallid brow.
Yet, still in battle's angry flood
   I will not fall alone;
And vengeance waits my father's blood,
   Though purchas'd by my own."

The lady rose—no tears would flow;
The warm blood gush'd across her brow,
  E'en as she gather'd strength ;
Convuls'd in agony, yet still
She bow'd her torture to her will,
  And calmly spoke at length :
While the red flush, which gather'd there,
Fast faded into pale despair,
And the wan lips, and swollen eye,
Remain'd the signs of agony.
" Go, then," she said, in noble pride,
" I would not be a craven's bride ;
I'd give my bosom to the steel
To save the pang which I shall feel ;
Those lips scarce ting'd with hovering breath,
That soaring spirit chill'd in death !
Yet I would rather see thee dead
Than hide in infamy thy head ;
And blush in shame, when glory's voice
Had call'd the nation to rejoice.
Yes, when those trees for ever wave
In silence o'er my hero's grave ;
Still, still, shall live that soaring name,
Embalmed in a nation's fame.
Where better can those limbs repose ?
'Twas here he broke his country's foes
I'll see, with a sublime delight,
His grave the trophy of the fight,
And there lay down, in tranquil rest,
The relics of a bleeding breast."

" Clara, farewell ! the only tie
  Which binds me yet to life,
Clara, farewell ! I thus defy
  The danger of the strife.
I may not hope to quit the field,
Unless borne back upon my shield.

My father's hall is desolate—
A fitter emblem of *his* fate
  Who stands alone on earth.
I saw my castle's overthrow—
I saw the ruddy life-blood flow
  From him who gave me birth ·
In vain I sprung, like rushing flame,
  On him who struck the blow;
I fell, while calling on his name,
  Beneath a meaner foe ;
Yet vengeance dogs the Zegri lord—
My father's life-blood warm'd his sword ;
Yes—like the wave thro' bursting banks,
To dash upon the Zegri ranks,
  To win revenge in death ;
To wrench the truncheon from his hand
(My father's spirit guide my brand),
  And drink his parting breath,
Are all that now remain to me,
Except the thrilling thought of thee.
  It was not, love, to see thy tears
    I left the warrior throng ;
  It was not, love, from selfish fears
    That I disturb'd thy song ;
But that I could not couch my spear
With death prophetic on mine ear,
  Without one look from thee,
Or think that when the Zegri's glaive
Had sent me to an early grave,
·When heaps above my corse lay pil'd,
Unconscious Clara might have smil'd,
  Without a thought for me.
Farewell ! this rose from Clara's hair,
  To grace her own true knight,
Shall flourish whilst the bravest bear
  The thunder of the fight.
All that I ask is Clara's tear
To deck her Roland's early bier :

I may not hope to quit the field,
Unless borne back upon my shield."

'Tis morn : the sun is rising fair ;
He knows not what shall greet him there.
   The Moor is on his way ;
The Spanish chiefs, resolv'd to die,
Steadily watch Gonsalvo's eye,
      In their sublime array.

The Abencerrage chiefs advance ;
Each warrior waves aloft his lance ;*
Each snow-white courser waits the word,†
Proudly submissive to his lord.
The fetter'd lion shakes his mane,
And laughs to scorn the futile chain :
Despite that chain upon their shield
The Abencerrages never yield.
Each tameless Zegri draws a sword,‡
Less fierce and harden'd than its lord ;
For while in front, the snow-white throng
Exulting bore their lords along,
Those coal black steeds were fleck'd with foam,
In fierce rebellion to their doom :
Theie, too, from every shackle freed,
The wild Numidian urged his steed,
And well repaid that courser brave,
The confidence his master gave,
As he sprung past with flashing eye,
And knowledge of his liberty.
The squares are form'd, and murmurs rise
Of fierce impatience to the skies ;

* The Eastern nations did not couch their spears.
† The Abencerrages, a Moorish tribe, who always rode white
horses, the chained lion their device.
‡ The Zegri is another tribe infamous for ferocity, who rode
black horses.

The trumpet sounds—and on the blast are borne
The savage echoings of the Moorish horn.
　　Each warrior held his breath,
　　　　For a moment, and no more;
　　Then on they dash'd to death,
　　　　Like billows to the shore ;
While the free plumage of the brave,
Floated like foam upon the wave.
Then, as the sabre left the sheath ;
Then, as the firm earth shook beneath
　　The rush of human wrath ;
Then, as the voice of battle spoke,
The war-song of Castile awoke,
　　And peal'd in thunder forth.
Oh, who can tell, the pride of conscious might
The fierce ebriety of war's delight ;
　　And amid the crash of shivering spears,
　　　　The hot blood's maddening flow,
It were worth the life of a thousand years,
　　To be first for a moment now.

MALEK.

[To be continued]

THE MISERIES OF GODFATHERS.

It almost invariably happens, that men, with
wives and *small* families of thirteen children, have
attempted to cry down the situation of a bachelor.
They say that he wants the comforts of his cheerful
fire-side, his homely fare, his smiling wife, and
children climbing up the knees of their sire, and so
forth ; but it always appeared to me, that they never

had been able to hit upon the true cause of the
bachelor's misery ; for the touchstone of his misfortunes is the certainty of being solicited to become a
Godfather. Every unmarried man is sure to have
a regiment of Godchildren, and it is this, and this
alone, which drives so many men, at the sober age
of fifty, to the altar of Hymen, and the arms of a
cook-maid. Dr. Johnson, in his spirited poem,
" The Vanity of Human Wishes," says,

> " The teeming mother, anxious for her race,
> Begs for each birth the fortune of a ————,"

not face (for every child is like its mother, and
every mother handsome, in her own opinion ; the
child, therefore, has that accomplishment already),
but Godfather. Accordingly, every good-natured
man, who is unmarried, is pressed to stand Godfather to some squalling infant. I lately called on
a bachelor, and not finding him at home, I amused
myself, till his return, by prying about the room,
when I chanced to light on a manuscript, which I
now present to the public, as the genuine diary of
a Godfather :—

" *(Ten o'clock.)* A Godson called on me, previously to his going to school. Knew his tricks,
and determined to punish him. Slipped a shilling
into his hand, and said, ' Here, my boy, here's a
sovereign for you.' He looked like a child on a
washing-day, but I would not observe his blue looks,
or discover my mistake.

"*(Eleven o'clock.)* Four letters, in envelopes (double postage), requesting me to take long journeys to christenings.

"*(Twelve o'clock.)* A few two-penny post letters, with wafers, appointing christenings.—N. B. Two on the same day, and at the same hour. I cannot, not being a crowned head, be sponsor by proxy to a child whom I never saw, and whose parents I never heard of.

"*(One o'clock.)* Went out for a walk, and met crowds of my little protegés. Their little fingers dirtied my hands, and thereby prevented me from calling on a certain lady of delicate nerves, and exquisite sensibility.

"*(Two o'clock.)* Attended a christening.—N. B. A truant nail in the corner of the stool tore my pantaloons.

"*(Three o'clock.)* Ditto. In my hurry to go from one church to another, my hackney-coach knocked down an old man, who dying of age a week afterwards, the parish officers made me pay five pounds for his funeral obsequies.

"*(Six o'clock).* Dinner—forced to say that I saw the light of genius in the eye of a Godson who squinted. Heard from another Godson a long account of an usher at his school, and from another, that William the Third was surnamed the Conqueror, and Blue Beard meant Henry the Eighth. My little Godchildren, one and all, made rude remarks;

talked all at once, and broke glasses; I with difficulty, as in duty bound, forced a simper, which almost gave me the locked-jaw.

"(*Ten o'clock*). Went home, and to bed, could not· get to sleep for two hours. At last dosed, fancied that I was surrounded by my Godchildren, in the characters of imps of hell ; jumped out of bed, fell on the floor, cut my head, and was confined to my room for a week."

Here my friend came in, and we joked together, when he showed me a list of his Godchildren, which I at first supposed to be a manuscript copy of the new Army List.

If I were a bachelor, I would bilk all my protegés, and rather found an asylum, or leave sums for the maintenance of favourite pug dogs. We have heard of an old man, who constantly asked parents for lists of their children, as they thought to name in his will, but he unfortunately forgot them all. So would I act.

Most people have three names, a Christian, a Family, and a Surname. I remember a person who, like the man in the Vicar of Wakefield, liked to call a person by all his names, and when he called his son, addressed him by ten names, two God-fathers', a Godmother's, and the original. " Come here," said he, "John Richard Williams George Augustus Jackson Charles Smith Thompson Fubbs— Charles made from Charlotte, at the particular

request of an old female friend, who stood Godmother.   Appalled by this assemblage of nomens
and cognomens, I asked if he was practising for
Champion at the Coronation.

How can people be so mean! how can they
expect to reap advantage at such a distance? Few
people have their fortunes made by their Godfathers.
Why, then, do they not bring up their children to
some honourable profession, instead of lingering on
the unsubstantial food of expectation?   B.

Vos valete et ———. Ter.

[*Enter* Bartholomew Bouverie *solus.*]

Most Potent Public;

Your humble servant is in a most strange dilemma, and from no common cause: he is at this
moment racking his brain to find that "consummation devoutly to be wished for"—an ending.
That indispensable requisite to a book, a "*Jamque opus exegi*," is the cause of all his anxiety: in
short, Bartholomew Bouverie heartily wishes to put
an end to himself, till restored to life on the 18th
day of June.

It has been the practice of authors to prate on
the difficulty of beginning, and to quote

" Dimidium facti qui cœpit habet ;"

but to say Good Night to the public with becoming
grace, is, in my opinion, an infinitely more difficult
task.   What can be easier than to plunge at once
into the middle, without caring for a formal beginning, with an impetuous " Ruin seize thee, ruthless
king ;" or with a more modest, though not less
abrupt, " 'Twas night."   " It is in the power of every
man," says Dr. Johnson, "to rush abruptly upon
his subject, that has read the ballad of Johnny
Armstrong,

> " Is there ever a man in all Scotland ?"—

And with the same view, I shall quote an honest
friend of mine, who began one of his tales with the
explanatory sentence, " Now his parents was very
good sort of folk."   But to end is a very different,
and far more difficult task, and it is in this that Bartholomew will chiefly fail, though with the consolation that in the same point many great men have
failed before him.

It has always appeared to me, I know not how
justly, that in this point the Iliad is deficient, for I
have never been able to think that the single line]

"Ὡς᾽ ὅιγ᾽ ἀμφίεπον τάφον Ἕκτορος ἱπποδάμοιο,

is an ending of sufficient grandeur to suit the sublimity of what has gone before.   Pope seems to
have thought the same : for he has inserted in his
translation, or rather imitation, a whole line, of
which there is not an idea in the original :

> " Such honours Ilion to her hero paid,
> *And peaceful slept the mighty Hector's shade."*

In another instance, who has not been disappointed with the catastrophe in Hamlet, whether read, or acted on the stage ; when, after his imagination has been worked up to the highest pitch by the deep interest of the play, he sees the bungling development of the plot, the awkward artifice of the exchange of foils, and lastly, the spectacle of no less than four persons lying dead upon the stage. Here, I think, every one must agree with Johnson, " that in many of Shakspeare's plays, the latter part is evidently neglected.   When he found himself near the end of his work, and in view of his reward, he shortened the labour to snatch the profit. He, therefore, remits his efforts where he should most vigorously exert them, and his catastrophe is improbably produced, or imperfectly represented."

Now, I do not make these observations, taking to myself any pretensions to criticism, but merely to show, that where Shakspeare has failed, the failure of Bartholomew Bouverie will be nothing very extraordinary. For, possibly, while he hastens to an end of his labours, he may forget, or be unable, to make his bow to the public with all the grace and decorum they may expect ; but to run off without saying a word, like a tavern guest bilking his landlord, is

what the Editor of " The Eton Miscellany " cannot
endure.

  ˉWith this imperfect apology for all his errors,
and for all his frivolity, for whatever he has said
wrong, and whatever he has said foolishly, most
potent Public, Bartholomew Bouverie entreats you
to be content.   By the time of publication of
the next Number, he hopes to receive the assistance of those who have. hitherto stood aloof, from
fear of embarking in a vessel of whose sea-worthi-
ness they had no certain testimonial. But having
now established himself admiral of· the fleet, Bartholomew Bouverie begs all those who may join
his squadron to steer clear of those dangerous rocks,
Politics and Personality, and particularly not to
venture among the conflicting waves in the gulf of
Theology. . And it is hereby signified to those who
are willing to embark in the enterprise, who, by-the-
by, must have learnt tactics at Eton College, that
the rendezvous appointed is Ingalton Point, Eton
Road ; and it is particularly recommended to those
who have any doubts as to the success of the expedition, to provide themselves plentifully with the
anchors of Hope.

  I think it but fair to inform the public, though
it is probable enough they have discovered it already
without my assistance, that I am no very great
poet ; were it not for my outlandish friends, Malek

the Moor, and Glenartney, I fear I should but
little attract the votaries of the Muses. However,
I have followed the fashion, and have managed,
by dint of some labour, to compose the following

EPILOGUE.

Most courteous Public! all who sell,
And all who purchase, fare ye well!
The task is o'er, the race is run,
I bid you welcome Number One!
Go forth, my book, and leave thy sire, ·
And brave the storms of Fortune's ire;
Go, meet the critic's piercing eye,
Go, hear his keen and eager cry;
With wisdom please the old and sage,
With humour charm a greener age;
But chief let this thy dwelling-place
Behold thy form, admire thy grace.
Here, when the printer's subtle art
Hath multiplied thine every part,
Hath made from one, with skilful ease,
Above five hundred Bouveries;
Here, when the swelling trump of Fame
Hath sounded forth thy honour'd name,
Here be thy wit, thy glory sung,
The theme of every boyish tongue;
Here let the urchin leave his task,
Beneath the summer's sun to bask,
And Homer leave, and Virgil, too,
To glut his greedy eyes on you.
And if the birchen rod repress
His rash and daring eagerness,
He'll heal his wounds and feast his soul
On Sloman's dark Lethean bowl.
　　Humble my wish, confined its scope,
Yet fear is mingled with my hope : ——

I know not what of ire or hate
Is written in the book of Fate;
I know not what is doom'd to me,
In hidden Destiny's decree;
What is reserved for Bouv'rie's name,
Of joy or grief, of praise or blame.
Will Fame assign to me a place,
Beside the fathers of my race,
And crown me with triumphant bay,
Like Griffin, Grildrig, Courtenay?
Or doom my melancholy ghost
To join the dark Tartarean host,
With many a luckless author more
To wander on the Stygian shore,
While housemaids tear my sacred strains
To light their fires, and scrub their stains?
  Meanwhile, my friends, I promise new
And wondrous things in Number Two:
I promise an Express shall come
With news from Pandemonium:
I promise many a sober page,
To soothe the angry critic's rage;
Good things of all kinds there ye'll see,
" Quæ longum est præscribere."
  Come now, Conclusion! in a trice,
With sober, brief, and sound advice;
I bid ye ALL, both young and old,
Go where Bartholomew is sold:
To venders' book-shops hasten—fly,
And order Mr. Bouverie.

***

*** *Communications (post paid) will be received by
  Mr. Ingalton, Eton, from Etonians only.*

Number II. will appear on the 18th of June.

T. C. Hansard, Paternoster-row Press, London.

ETON MISCELLANY,

No. II.

INTRODUCTION.

ON returning to my literary labours, I cannot but see that the first duty incumbent on me is that of returning my thanks for past favours; the second, that of endeavouring to merit them for the time to come. I need not borrow from Atkinson's Bears' Grease, or Warren's Blacking, epithets to describe my feelings. When I recollect the indulgence which has pardoned my errors, and the munificence which has patronized my exertions—when I recollect that in Eton alone, within the space of three days, a hundred and eighty copies of my work were actually subscribed for, when nothing but the mere advertisement of my publication had appeared—when I recollect all this, I become painfully sensible how much gratitude my friends deserve, and how little I can give.

And not the least among the gratifications which I have experienced has been that of hearing, and of taking part in, the conjectures as to the individual who personates Bartholomew Bouverie. Often have I laughed in my sleeve, while listening to the timid conjectures of some, the bold assertions of others, and the "authentic accounts" of a third, and still more audacious, class of

my fellow-citizens : *all*, gentle reader, being equally destitute of foundation.   Had all been true, I believe more
than a moiety of the individuals in the school would
have had a claim, perhaps an equal one, to the authorship of The Eton Miscellany.

I shall now proceed to bring before the public some

New Members of the Cabinet.

Though my superscription is alarmingly political, I
can assure my readers that the contagion has extended
no further. I love, like some other people, to give to
my proceedings an air of importance : and those whom I
shall now mention are simply companions whom I have
admitted into *my* Cabinet to aid me in conducting those
weighty affairs in which I have been, am, and hope to
continue, engaged.

I feel that I cannot make any better apology for this,
my second, intrusion on the notice of the public, than by
a simple introduction and a short description of one who
was mainly instrumental in promoting my first.   And I
am the more induced to this proceeding, from a consciousness that he will be found by no means an unpleasant acquaintance ; and that if his character should
be found wanting in strength, vigour, or originality, it
will be owing to inability on my part, and not to deficiency on his.

The friend and coadjutor, then, to whom I shall now
endeavour to do justice, is a descendant of the old genuine and much-vituperated John Bull family.   Nor
does he at all weaken the force of the ancient maxim,

ἐξ ἀγαθῶν ἀγαθοί : he still retains the characteristics, and the merits of the true and original stock.

I do not think that I should be guilty of any disrespect to Mr. Martin Sterling, were I to place my coadjutor in the same rank with him, in point of steady principle and sound morality : and I am sure that Mr. Sterling's sense of right would make him voluntarily yield the palm to him in point of humour and invention. But I should not act a candid part if I omitted to state, that with the sincerity, and the physical force, he retains some of the prejudices of his ancestors, the Bulls : he cannot conceive how the air of London can foster those plants which an University is formed to nourish. Smoke and dust, he says, will defile the groves of Parnassus ; and no genuine votary of the Muses will deign to quaff his Heliconian beverage through the very dirty medium of a St. Giles's pump.

Neither is he at all behind his ancestors in his manly and uncompromising hatred of all that appertains to the Pope ; the phantasms of former days are still present to his imagination : nor would he disdain to exercise his Stentorian lungs in sounding the war-cry of the cause. I do not suspect him of timidity, in one sense at least ; but I believe he would rather keep company with a hyena than with a Radical.

I mentioned his lungs : to him, indeed, nature has given the

> " Mens divinior, atque os
> Magna sonaturum—"

and I think I am not going too far, in saying, that I feel

confident he will make a noise in the world, perhaps in more senses than one.

Most fully am I convinced of his frankness and sincerity : he would suffer no one whom he disliked, to remain long in intercourse with him, without an intimation of the feeling on his part; and he would be the last man whom I should suspect of either actively or passively injuring an absent friend, by slandering him himself, or by suffering him to be slandered by others.   Indeed, with regard to the expression of his feelings as they actually exist, I am not sure whether he has learned the rule which ought here to be constantly and carefully observed : the rule never to deny, or utter what may be reasonably supposed to imply denial, but at the same time to reserve to one's self the privilege of choosing the period, the circumstances, and the method in which it may be right to put forth the plain and unadulterated dictates of the heart.

But when I have allowed that he seems to perceive no difference between concealing and suppressing, I must add, that few indeed are those who have in this been able to perceive and adhere to the just medium ; and that if there must be an error, Bartholomew Bouverie will not seek for his admirers among that class of men who would not prefer this sincerity of disposition, even when carried so far as to overstep the bounds of propriety, to a mind, especially to a youthful mind, corrupted by the wiles of deceit, and seeking shelter amidst the resources of equivocation.

My coadjutor is moreover a steady friend and constant encourager of all those sports for which Eton has at all

times been so deservedly celebrated ; but remembering—
many, I fear, do not remember—how well and how
wisely it was said of old,

"Nec tua laudabis studia, aut aliena reprêndes,"

he does not join in the vulgar and inconsiderate clamour
raised against the less popular pursuits of those whom
taste, or associations, or peculiar circumstances, may
have induced to adopt a different, though, I would fain
hope, not necessarily an opposing line of conduct.   And
it may safely be affirmed that his merits in this particular have met with their reward ; that he has been one of
the few, who, in our little community, have been so happy
as to attach to themselves the good-will of all classes
alike : of the higher powers, in the first instance, and
of the various descriptions of his fellow-citizens, in the
second.

Having now arrived at the conclusion of a long, but, I
fear, imperfect account of the individual to whom I
already owe so much, and to whom I hope to owe a
great deal more, I beg to introduce him to the public by
a *nom de guerre* which he has chosen himself, that of,
Mr. Antony Heaviside.

The next person whom I shall venture to present to
the public, is Mr. David ap Rice, a gentleman with an
antediluvian pedigree, and a profound veneration for
toasted cheese.   He is a great stickler for the honour of
his country, and the honour of his ancestors, and would
offer to fight any one who should venture to speak against
the sublimity of Snowdon, or the merits of Cadwallader.

With regard to his temper, we may describe him in the
words of Horace,

"Irasci celerem, tamen ut placabilis esset;"

indeed, while we were settling the preliminaries of our
partnership, he fell out with me three times, and as often
offered me his hand with the greatest cordiality. The
chief fault that I find in him is, that he will on no
account give up his own opinion ; he is more stiff-necked
than the mountains of his country, for " huge Plinlimmon bowed his cloud-topt head" to the magic song of
Modred; but all my arguments have not been able to
procure me the same favour from Mr. David ap Rice.
His forte is poetry, in which his style is decidedly
national, seldom adhering to the vulgar restrictions of
rhyme, and occasionally o'erstepping the modesty of
reason.   It will no more bear comparison with the
standard of legitimate poetry, than the Song of the Goat
with the purer age of the Grecian Tragedy; but still it
has a native wildness, an artless irregularity, which cannot fail to please ; it has none of that elaborate diction,
or studied harmony, which delights some classes of
our readers, yet it bears strong traces of genius, and of
genius unassisted by art.   Its greatest fault is its
inequality, for it runs, as it were, the course of the comet,
at one time illuminated by the full effulgence of the sun,
at another lost in impenetrable obscurity.

Such is the coadjutor whom I have taken, but there
are a few other traits in his character which I may hereafter mention ; at present I offer him to the public, such
as I found him, a wild, inflexible, poetical Cambro-
Briton.

ON ENNUI.

With your permission, friend Bouverie, it is my intention to offer a few remarks concerning that most unwelcome of all visitors, that enemy to conviviality, that bane of all rational amusements and recreations, commonly designated by the name of ennui ; not for the purpose of inspiring you with those unenviable sensations attending it, or of throwing a melancholy dejection on that brow of yours, which beams with perpetual serenity and good-humour, and which never cast a repulsive or interdicting look on the most humble of your more submissive fellow-creatures. Far otherwise is my intention ; I wish only to give an insight into those many miseries, those restless and uneasy moments, those frequent yawns and eye-rubbings, those instinctive ejaculations of " Oh, dear ! what a heavy day it is !" and many others of a similar nature, all of which the generality of mankind entail upon themselves, by neglecting that proper regimen, calculated to resist its encroachments and to repel its attacks.

Now, the common query attending all professed loungers, and especially those whose superior rank in life gives them a title to a certain leisure and independence, denied to their more active brethren, is, " How is Time to be killed ?" You must be well acquainted with the vulgar opinion, that cats have nine lives . now, how many lives should you think Time had ? For my part, I should give him a triple proportion of both vitality and muscular strength, if we may reason from analogy ; for

no one has effectually been able to beguile many an interminable quarter of an hour, although armed with the
anodyne whiffs of an Havannah cigar, or the more
sociable, and certainly less odoriferous, contents of a
snuff-box, when held in thraldom by the shackles of
ennui ; and many a young Miss has repeatedly turned
over the leaves of a deserted album, or fumbled in the
unfathomable abysses of a reticule, without experiencing
the least respite or alleviation from her sufferings.

For the purpose of illustration, I shall make no scruple
of quoting the expressions, verbatim, of two votaries of
the shrine of Indolence and Inactivity, to which I was an
ear-witness not long since. "I say, Dick, I be very
unk-ed."—"So be I, Tom," is the emphatic reply. Now,
I think it unnecessary to explain the meaning of this
word "unkid," or unked (you may question the ortho-
graphy of the word, if you please), to you, friend
Bouverie, since I am aware that you are equally conversant with cottage eloquence, and with the more refined
and more sophisticated departments of literary jargon.
This elegant dissyllable is as descriptive of the internal
feelings of my two heroes, as any other I could possibly
have brought forward ; and by its sulky, ominous, and
sepulchral pronunciation, is a sure proof that ennui, by
some means or other, has insinuated itself into some
unguarded chinks and creeks, and taken possession of
their animal faculties, having fortified itself against every
attempt to dislodge it. As to the authority of the word,
I do not vouch for its appearance in the columns of Dr.
Johnson's dictionary, but I imagine that the privilege of
ὀνοματοποιΐα. or fabrication of words, will be granted to

my heroes, although not pretending to the same powers of imagination and invention as the Chian bard.

I should guess there were few nations so free from the annoyance of ennui as the Italians: whether from the purity of the atmosphere which they breathe, or from other physical causes, I do not pretend to determine; certain it is, that Italy is the land where those delightful feelings of independence, and the blessings of that *dolce far niente*, or, to give it its literal translation, the sweet nothing-to-do-ish-ness, are most fully appreciated and practised in their most enlarged and comprehensive forms. Few human beings can exist on as little mental sustenance as the Italian; a guitar, a voice, and sunshine, are all his wants: these alone, carry him through Italy, and through life. He can be luxurious when luxuries are before him, and fast when not better employed. He will nestle by the side of his mule on the Appenines, or on a straw-litter in the valleys of Piedmont; dreaming perhaps of the "plaudits of the Boulevards, or the golden showers of the Haymarket."

Happy would it be for us, friend Bouverie, for us Englishmen, were our spirits as buoyant and elastic as those of the Italian; but, as I have before mentioned, we are all inevitably doomed, at certain times and seasons, to paroxysms, more or less violent, of the much-detested ennui: and even Etonians, though placed in the midst of merriment and joviality, and surrounded by a large assembly of literary friends and miscellaneous contributors, are not exempted from occasional visits from their old occupant.

How frequently my dear Bouverie I sigh deeply at

the recollection of it)—how frequently has it fallen to
our lot to be a constituent part of a numerous company
of friends on a rainy day in the country! When all
perambulatory locomotion is put an end to, and our
straining eyes in vain try to discover some slight portion of blue sky, or glimmering of sunshine. These
are the trying moments, when our letters are all conned
over for the fifth or sixth time, and when we have
quaffed political beverage from the columns of a newspaper to its very dregs; when the billiard-room is
deserted, and the battledoors and shuttlecocks thrown
aside in disgust; when we have the pleasing prospect
of being scarcely able to support our exhausted faculties
till the hour of luncheon; then, perhaps, not in a state
to endure any thing more substantial than a biscuit and
a glass of water. These are the agreeable effects of
ennui; and it is lamentable to reflect, how frequently
the harmony of a "little musical party," or the socia-
bility of a "little tea party," has been marred by the
gloomy visages, and invincible taciturnity of our "unkid" guests. And many is the time when either a
copious libation of Epsom salts, a rose-coloured gargle,
or a pill surrounded with a most inviting envelope of
raspberry jam, has been prescribed to some unfortunate
individual, by an apprehensive mamma, under the plea
of bodily indisposition, when the true cause was merely
mental dejection, brought on, perhaps, by the recollection of a forbidden custard, or an interdicted sugar-
plum. Nor is this all: an emetic is not unfrequently
resorted to, and administered to the persecuted victim,
to remove a disorder, for which neither Machaon, Hippo-

crates, or Galen, nor the many thousand apothecaries and quacks down to the present day, have ever discovered an effectual remedy.

But I already perceive, friend Bouverie, sundry manifestations of impatience on your brow, sundry rubs of the eyes, yawns, and scratches of the head, and many a wistful ogle cast towards the conclusion of my paper; I shall not, therefore, detain you any longer, but promise to renew my attacks upon your mental faculties on some future occasion, when I see you more disposed to attend to my tedious and uninteresting lucubrations.   W.

ON THE DEATH OF A PATRIOT.

'Tis morn ; the sound of muffled drum
Tells that the dreaded time is come ;
Along the streets, a servile band,
The hirelings of the tyrant stand :
Their souls no sense of shame can turn,
No generous feelings in them burn ;
Fit instruments for despot lord,
His will, their guide ; their hope, reward
To these, upon this fatal day,
The charge is given to clear the way ,
These round the prison's gloomy gate
The coming of the patriot wait,
The victim of perverted laws,
The last, sole hope of Freedom's cause.
Ask you his crime ? could such a breast
  His country's wrongs forgive ?
Could such a spirit tamely rest,
  Till tyrants ceas'd to live ?
Could he crouch to a despot's yoke ?
No—sooner seek to bend the oak '
Him saw the tyrant : him he knew
To freedom and his country true .

He knew him proof against each wile,
Each haughty frown, each treacherous smile.
Vain was his sceptred pride, to tame
The breast which own'd a patriot's flame :
Yet ill the tyrant's soul could brook
The freedom of that manly look.
The mutter'd curse, the gloomy sneer,
Which spoke of deadly vengeance near ;
Ill could he bear those words of blame,
That told of Freedom's injur'd name.
Of broken laws, of trampled rights,
By him, and by his parasites :
These were the crimes for which the slave,
    By treacherous bribes suborn'd,
Dar'd to traduce the injur'd brave,
    Who proffer'd mercy scorn'd
Should he to despots bend a knee ?
Should he submit to tyranny ?
And lead a life of endless pain,
Beneath his master's galling chain ?
But now the neighbouring convent's tower
Proclaim'd the long-expected hour.
Forth from the gate the captive came ;
His step, his voice, his cheek the same,
Save, that of rage, a deeper trace
Was pictur'd in his glowing face :
And on his fetter'd arm each vein
With throbbing seem'd to burst its chain ;
While frequent heavings of his vest
Show'd the wild tumults of his breast.
And now the dreaded spot appear'd,
Where its sad form the scaffold rear'd ;
Where instruments of deadly fate,
The block, the axe, the prisoner wait.
Not e'en this new unwonted sight
Had power the patriot's soul to fright,
With eye unchang'd, with thoughts on God,
Firmly the fatal stair he trod.
Once to his lips the cross he press'd,
    And breath'd one prayer to Heaven ;
His wrongs forgave, his sins confess'd
    And bade the blow be given !

[I have received the following contribution from a correspondent, who chooses to use the editorial "we." I give it to the public as I received it.]

REMARKS ON GIFFORD'S "FORD."

We were always very partial to John Ford. He was, we believe, the last of those potent enchanters, who, in the days of Elizabeth and James, awoke the dormant spirit of our literature into gigantic strength. Happy, indeed, we must consider him, looking only at his early life, in the period to which he belonged : to have moved in the same hemisphere in which that great luminary of all that is graceful and beautiful in language, of all that is intense and vigorous in conception, WILLIAM SHAKSPEARE, was lord of the ascendant; to have seen *him* in the endearing intimacies of private life ; to have conversed with him, or rather to have listened with meek reverence to the rich flow of his conversation, and to the outpourings of that wisdom which seems to have been familiar to him from the very cradle ; to have felt in our old age the proud consciousness, that the recollections of Shakspeare were imprinted on our memory so deep, that nothing, *till* death, could injure or efface them, and so bright, that they would cast a cheering radiance over the agonies of dissolution : this is a lot which few, who either have, or pretend to, taste, can help envying; and to obtain which, for our own parts, we should be much inclined to surrender each and all of the advantages of the nineteenth century, the march of intellect, and the invention of steam-engines.

But it was not to the creator alone of our drama, that

we referred, when we said Ford's youth had fallen on
fortunate days. Bright and glorious, beyond all imaginings, as the flight of the Eagle was, yet many were the
pinions that could wing a separate course, and the eyes,
whose piercing lustre could bear undazzled the noon-day
effulgence of that sun, at which they kindled the energies
of their nature. Beyond all question, the pinnacle that
Shakspeare holds is far above that of the Jonsons, the
Beaumonts, the Marlows, and the Fletchers of his age.
But it is the *superiority of Chimborazo, to the Andes that
surround his throne !* And, we confess, we have often
amused ourselves with reveries of the pleasure we
should have felt in sitting round the table at the *Mermaid*, amidst the choice, and master spirits we have
enumerated ; listening to the wild exuberances of their
fancy, and the sportive gambols of their wit; yet, what
with us is a mere humour of the brain, a sort of Mac-
adamizing in the air, with Ford was actual truth. Of
his personal character, and of any events that might
interest us as bearing on his conduct through life, we
are, however, almost entirely ignorant ; nor has the
present edition done much to remove the obscurity in
which former biographers had left our author. The
few traditions that have been preserved, point him out
to us as of a reserved and melancholy temper : an old
doggrel couplet assures us, that

> " Deep in a dump John Forde was alone got,
> With folded arms, and melancholy hat."

He makes frequent allusions in his prologues to his
having early embraced the profession of the law; but
always coupled with anxious disavowals to his patrons

of permitting his dramatic labours to encroach on his
proper business.   The first fruits of his poetic vein was
an elegy in quarto! dedicated to the countess of Devon-
shire, and professing to bewail the death of her husband.   We shall not detain the reader any longer with
this unworthy performance, than to quote the following
exquisite passage :

> " Life? ah ! no life, but soon-extinguish'd tapers!
>   Tapers? no tapers, but a burnt-out light!
> Light? ah ! no light, but exhalation's vapours!
>   Vapours? no vapours, but ill-blinded sight !
>   Sight? ah ! no sight, but hell's eternal night !
> A night ? no night, but picture of an elf!
> An elf ? no elf, but very death itself !"
>
> *Fame's Memorial.*

That any one, who at twenty could write such execrable
stuff as this, should start forth at forty-three a fervid,
delicate, impassioned votary of the Muses, is one of
those phenomena which awaken the interest even of
the obtuser portion of mankind (because even to them
is held out the excitement of vanity), and serve to vary
the somewhat monotonous prospect of the literary world.
    His first play was published in 1629 ; and he retired
from his dramatic, as well as professional life in 1640.
" Faint traditions in the neighbourhood of his birth-place
" lead to the supposition, that having, from his legal
" pursuits, acquired a sufficient fortune, he retired to his
" home to pass the remainder of his days among the youth-
" ful connections whom time had yet spared him.   Nor
" were there wanting powerful motives for the retirement
" of one of Ford's lonely and contemplative mind, who
" watched the signs of the times.   Deep and solemn notes

" of preparation for a tragedy, far more terrible than
" aught the stage could show, were audible in the dis-
" tance; and hollow mutterings, which could not be mis-
" taken, told that the tempest was gathering round the
" metropolis with fearful acceleration.   It is possible
" that he may have foreseen the approaching storm,
" and fled from the first efforts of its violence.

> ' Apparent diræ facies, inimicaque Trojæ
> Numina!'

" The Covenanters were already in arms, and advanc-
" ing towards the borders; and at home the stern and
" uncompromising enemies of all that was graceful
" and delightful, were rapidly ascending in the scale of
" power."*

We do not know how we can better preface the few
specimens of our author's peculiar manner, which it
is our intention to lay before our readers, than by the
masterly delineation of its beauties and defects which
Mr. Gifford has given us in his Introduction :   " Much
" as has been said of the dramatic poets of Elizabeth
" and James's days, full justice has never yet been
" rendered to their independence on one another : gene-
" rally speaking, they stand insulated, and alone, and
" draw, each in his station, from their own stores.
" Whether it be that poetry in that age

> ' Wanton'd, as in its prime, and played at will
> Its virgin fancies,' ——

" or that some other fruitful cause of originality was
" in secret and powerful operation ; so it is, that every
" writer had his peculiar style, and was content with it.

---

* Gifford. Introduction, pp. 44, 45.

" At present, we are become an imitative, not to say a
" mimic, race. A successful poem, a novel, nay even a
" happy title-page, is eagerly caught at, and a kind of
" *Ombre Chinoise* representation of it propagated from one
" extremity of the kingdom to the other. *Invention*
" *seems almost extinct among us.* That it does not some-
" where exist, it would be folly to imagine; but it
" appears to move, comet-like, in very eccentric orbits,
" and to have its periods of occultation of more than
" usual duration. It may, and undoubtedly will, revisit
" us ; meanwhile, as the knight of the enchanted cavern
" judiciously advises, 'patience, and shuffle the cards !'

" I have been led into these desultory remarks, not-
" withstanding it may be urged that an exception to the
" subject of them may be found in Ford. He appears
" to have discovered, indeed, that one of the nameless
" charms of Shakspeare's diction consisted in the skill
" with which he has occasionally vivified it, by convert-
" ing his substantives into verbs, and to have aspired
" to imitate him. He cannot be complimented on his
" success ; nor, indeed, can much be expected, without
" such a portion of Shakspeare's taste and feeling, as it
" seems almost hopeless to expect. Ford's grammatical
" experiments take from the simplicity of his diction,
" while they afford no strength whatever to his descrip-
" tions. Not so with the great original ; in his conver-
" sions all is life. Take, for example, the following
" passage ; it is not a description that we read ; it is
" a series of events that we hear and see :

' The quick comedians
' Extemporally shall *stage* u ; and present

E

' Our Alexandrian revels ; Antony
' Shall be brought drunken forth, and I shall see
' Some squeaking Cleopatra *boy* my greatness
' I' th' posture of a whore.'

" With this slight exception, which, after all, may be
" purely visionary, the style of Ford is altogether original,
" and his own. Without the majestic march that dis-
" tinguishes the poetry of Massinger, and with little, or
" none of that light and playful humour which charac-
" terizes the dialogue of Fletcher, or even of Shirley,
" he is yet elegant, and easy, and harmonious; and
" though rarely sublime, yet sufficiently elevated for the
" most pathetic tones of that passion, on whose romantic
" energies he chiefly delighted to dwell. It has, as has
" been observed, its inherent beauties and defects ; among
" the latter of which may be set down a pedantic affec-
" tation of novelty, at one time exhibited in the com-
" position of uncouth phrases, at another (and this is
" Ford's principal failure) in perplexity of language :
" frequently, too, after perversely labouring with a re-
" mote idea, till he has confused his meaning, instead of
" throwing it aside, he obtrudes it upon the reader in-
" volved in inextricable obscurity. Its excellencies,
" however, far outweigh its defects ; but they are rather
" felt than understood. I know few things more difficult
" to account for than the deep and lasting impression
" made by the more tragic portions of Ford's poetry.
" Whence does it derive that resistless power, which
" all confess, of afflicting, I had almost said harassing,
" the better feelings ? It is not from any peculiar beauty
" of language ; for in this he is equalled by his contem-
" poraries ; and, by some of them, surpassed ; nor is it

" from any classical or mythological allusions happily
" recollected, and skilfully applied, for of these he sel-
" dom avails himself. It is not from any picturesque
" views presented to the mind ; for of imaginative poetry
" he has little, or nothing ; he cannot conjure up a suc-
" cession of images, whether grave or gay, to flit across
" the fancy, or play in the eye; yet it is hardly possible
" to peruse his passionate scenes without the most pain-
" ful interest, the most heart-thrilling delight. This can
" only arise—at least, I can conceive nothing else
" adequate to the excitement of such sensations—from
" the overwhelming efficacy of intense thought devoted
" to the embodying of conceptions adapted to the
" awful situations in which he has imperceptibly, and
" with matchless felicity, placed his principal characters."*

We shall not apologize to our readers for having set
before such of them as have ·yet in reserve the pleasure
attendant on a perusal of the original work, this accurate
investigation of our author's faults and merits ; couched,
as it is, in language far better than we can command,
and displaying a depth of research to which few, beside
Mr. Gifford, have had time or perseverance enough to
attain. Were we, however, so presumptuous as to set
our humble wits in opposition to so eminent a critic, we
should be inclined to doubt the propriety of the censure
passed in such unqualified terms on the imitative
character of modern literature.

We scarcely can credit the fact, that in the days which
Byron has adorned, and which Scott and Campbell are

---

* Gifford. Introduction, pp. 36, 37, 38

still adorning with all the energy that master-minds
can alone bestow, this should be made a subject of complaint by one, whose whole life, besides being (we
believe) that of piety in all its fervour, and of benevolence in all its purity, was in a literary view so gifted
with all that can enrich, and purify, and ennoble the
intellect of mankind. But assuredly we are too conscious of our weakness to do more than wonder, where
it would be presumptuous vanity to censure; and we
had rather suppose it is a fault in us not fully to comprehend his meaning, than that Mr. Gifford erred in
thus expressing his opinion.   E. L.

[*To be continued.*]

THE DEATH OF THE CHARGER.

Merrily echoes the fresh'ning morn,
With the clanging hoof, and the bugle-horn,
The crashing fence, the courser's neigh,
O'er hill and dale, as he bounds away:
But there is one in plunging pride,
A noble steed, yet none to ride:
With mouth unbitted, and feet unshod,
Wildly he spurns the flying sod.
    Away! yet, mark'd ye then
That sudden start of sick'ning pain,
As if a cloud came o'er his brain?
    He staggers: there!—again!
'Tis o'er! With one short desp'rate bound,
And ears that seem'd to drink the sound,
(As onward yell'd each straining hound),
    And quivering eyes, he fell.
Oh! many a year, thou gallant steed,
Has pass'd, since just thou prov'dst thy speed,

With arching neck, and flying mane,
Along the verdant fields of Spain,
And heard the bursting onset roar,
By thy wild banks, dark Bidassoa:
Those years have chill'd more hearts than thine,
    And many an eye, that gaily then
Glanc'd o'er each squadron's length'ning line,
    Has closed to open ne'er again.
They closed, when back proud Gallia reel'd
Upon Vimeira's broken field,
Or mid Vittoria's battle wave,
Found soldier's death and soldier's grave:
But thou still on, where'er, like flame,
Rush'd fearfully the British name,
As the river foams along its banks,
'Mong grim Busaco's charging ranks,
Though peal'd the shot, and flash'd the steel,
On wildly dashed'st with thund'ring heel,
Or shared'st the lonely bivouac,
When the mountain clouds lower'd dark and black,
And the lightning glar'd on the blasted trees,
Among the stormy Pyrenees;
Nor ended yet thy bright career,
Till France bent o'er her broken spear,
And proud St. George's standard flew,
Along the plain of Waterloo.
Farewell, thou gallant steed, farewell,
Free as the breeze that sounds thy knell;
The grass and wild flowers merrily wave,
And the stag is couching on thy grave;
For monument, an oak is there,
Bending its young stem to every air;
Yet, when three hundred years are fled,
Its gnarled trunk, and aged head,
Shall a wild shadowy glory shed,
Above the charger's lonely bed.

                                GLENARTNEY.

GREEK MANUSCRIPTS.

We beg leave to present our readers with a few short specimens, selected from some ancient and ingenious MSS. handed down from father to son, and from nurse to nursery-maid, from time immemorial, in the Bouverie family. There is strong reason to suspect that the "Musæ O' Connorianæ," so much and so deservedly extolled in the publication of our defunct predecessor, Peregrine Courtenay, Esq. is, in sad reality, basely and treacherously pilfered from this invaluable collection

" The cat and her kittens
They put on their mittens,
  To eat a Christmas pie.
The poor little kittens
They lost their mittens,
  And then they began to cry.

"' O mother dear, we sadly fear
We cannot go to-day,
  For we have lost our mittens.'
' If it be so, ye shall not go,
  For ye are naughty kittens.'"

" Γαλέη, σὺν τοῖς αἰλουριδίοις,
'Γριοπλέκτους χειρῖδας ἔδυ,
  Χριστογενεθλίου
'Ιροῦ λάγχιον κατεδοῦντες.
"Ωμοι ταλάνων αἰλουριδίων
"Ωλολε χειρὶς ἐριόπλεκτος,
  Τότε δ' ἤρξαντο στοναχοῦντες·

Ἆι, ἆι· μῆτερ, μῆτερ, δεινὰ δεδοίκαμιν
'Ουκ, οὐκ ἰτέον, σήμερον ἡμῖν·
  'Ουκ ἐμπόδιαι χειρῖδες·
Σῖγ' ὡς τάδ' ἔχει, σήμερον ὑμῖν
'Ου μὴν ἰτέον, σπέρμα πονηρὸν
  Σπέρμ' αἰλούρων κακοειδίς."

How beautifully simple are these lines , though, perhaps, the surly critic might, in the plenitude of his power and spite, demand why they should put on their mittens to eat the Christmas pie, and might presume to think that a good appetite and digestion might have sufficed without them. But what can be more easy than to silence this paltry objection ? For what else could they possibly have put on which would rhyme to kittens ?

And that something must have been put on is evident;
else it must follow, that if nothing was wanted, nothing
could possibly have been found to be lost; and thus the
whole pathos of the story would be destroyed.   But let
us turn from the invidious task of answering the objections which may be made, to the more inspiring one
of reviewing the beauties which actually exist—

> " The poor little kittens
> They lost their mittens,
> And then they began——"

What did they begin to do ?   Why they began—to cry !
Poor creatures ! What could be more natural, what more
affecting, than this catastrophe ?   They had lost their
mittens, without which (I say it in the envious critic's
teeth)—without which, in the present position of affairs,
they *could not eat the Christmas pie.*   But they, with
a resignation superior to all the misfortunes which fate
had imposed on them,

> " O mother dear, we sadly fear
> We cannot go to-day,
> For we have lost our mittens."

And how pathetic the Greek version—

> " Οὐκ, οὐκ ἰτίον, σήμερον ἡμῖν
> Οὐκ ἱμπόδιαι χειρῖδις."

I defy the most indifferent reader to pass over these
lines without a most overwhelming sensation of the
piteous situation of the kittens. The first οὐκ is pathetic enough, the second increases our sympathy,
but the .l, .l   . ·   ., ` +   ˙ 'ming.
The .· : ,   -   ,   ··   ' · uties :

we have no doubt that the author had in his eye, not
only the usual sense of " in our way," or " to be found,"
but also another meaning of " on our feet;" as the
kittens, not being endowed with hands whereon to place
their mittens, the said mittens must naturally be trans-
ferred to the feet.   Their mother, however, far from
receiving the unhappy kittens with the consolations
which their candour and resignation deserved, and their
situation called for, receives them with most unmerited
punishment and abuse—

> " If it be so, ye shall not go,
>   For ye are naughty kittens."

Indeed, she seems, from all we hear, to be most ill-
conditioned   as   a   cat,   and   most   unnatural   as   a
mother.   Here   the   story   breaks off;   we are   left to
imagine the broken hearts of the kittens at their rebuke,
and '(* " this was the most unkindest cut of all ") the
eating of the Christmas pie without them, and, no
doubt, the remorse of the mother at having so cruelly
maltreated them.   But we will pass from the beauties of
this poem (which, indeed, must be evident to the mean-
est capacity, not only from their own clearness, but from
the ink that we have shed, the pens we have spoilt, and
the paper we have blotted to. explain them)—we will
pass from this poem, to discuss another, which we
doubt not would be altogether as beautiful, if more than
the first stanza were legible in the MS.

---

* Let not the grammarian deride this line · it is Shakspeare's

" Poor little Dorinda,
Was burnt to a cinder,
  By falling in the fire.
Her nose became red
Before she was dead,
And each hair like a blazing wire."

" Δορινδύλη τάλαινα
Φλογηροῖσιν ἠνθρακίσθη
Χώνοισιν ἐμπεσοῦσα
Ἡρυθίατι μυκτὴρ
Πρὶν ἢ παύσατ' ἔρρειν
Καὶ Θρὶξ ἔλαμψ' ἑκάςη
Ὡς μέρμις αἰθαλοῦσα."

This last fragment is as good a specimen of the sublime and terrific, as the other is of the soft and pathetic. The awful idea of her nose becoming red before she was dead, strikes us with wonder at the genius which could have conceived an idea so "magnificently terrible." And the original simile of the end of each hair being like a blazing wire, bears evident marks of the same stupendous talent. But we will now leave the *gentle* reader duly to chew the cud of reflection on the wonders which we have pointed out; and for Zoilus, if he attacks the English verses, we, in Scott's words,

" Bid him defiance stern and high,
  And give him in his teeth the lie."

But if he prefers attacking the Greek, we beg leave to say that the Greek, which was written before Bentley, Dawes, Porson, &c. &c. had revived or invented their myriads of canons, cannot be so perfect as in these golden days of literature it might be expected to be.

STANZAS TO * * * *

I lov'd thee long, I love thee now,
  In agony and gloom,
Whilst others, with unruffl'd brow
  Pass by thy silent tomb

I felt no hope, I felt no fear,
   No love like other men ;
It was enough to see thee near,
   And I was happy then.

The dream soon fled, thy marriage broke
   The visionary spell ;
No tear I shed, no word I spoke,
   My secret grief to tell.

I hate the wretch who set the seal
   Of death upon thy brow ;
I hate the wretch who could not feel
   The tears he caus'd to flow.

I saw from that fair cheek, thro' him,
   The colour pass away ;
I saw that beaming eye grow dim
   In slow but sure decay.

Oh ! 'tis a sad and fearful thing
   To watch the fading flower,
To see it, e'en in youth's first spring,
   Grow weaker every hour.

And years have past—and they forget,
   Forget that you are gone ;
Though time has banish'd their regret,
   One breaking heart loves on.

                    MALEK.

ON AUTHORS.

"Hæc placuit semel, hæc decies repetita placebit."—HOR.

It has been the frequent observation of many wise
and able men, which the experience of all ages tends to
confirm. that every man who writes is more or less fired
with ambition and that his object is not so much to

promote the pleasure and instruction of his readers, as to obtain for himself admiration and fame. But it may be, and perhaps is, justly considered, that to please and instruct, is one of the most certain channels to fame, and that it is somewhat unjust to suppose that every man, in sending forth his work into the world, is actuated by selfish motives, and that he does it solely with a view of gratifying his ambition : but where, I would ask, is the author, who has not been secretly incited by a desire to display his abilities, and who, notwithstanding the haughty and ostentatious beginning, the elaborate preface, and well-meaning titles of such as, " A Dissertation upon Moral and Sentimental Philosophy," "Hints on the Practical Parts of Education," &c. &c. has not looked upon his own aggrandizement as an object of more paramount importance than the wish or consideration for the improvement of mankind ? I am aware that to prove every author guilty of such ambition would be no easy task, as there are many diurnal writers, who, under fictitious names, send to the press their ephemeræ of learning, and in this secret manner delight to level their poisonous and calumnious darts against those individuals, who, either by their good fortune, abilities, or perseverance, have obtained an unrivalled pre-eminence, and rendered themselves objects of envy. Yet, it must be confessed, that, to such authors, it is no small gratification to see the objects of their raillery and calumny writhing under the sting they have received from an unknown source, and their reputation blasted without any possibility of reparation It has, indeed been generally acknowledged, that to write a work the the to the capitivate for the moment, or afford a merely temporary pleasure to its readers, but which may be able to undergo the ordeal of investigation, is, perhaps, one of the most difficult undertakings which can be imagined. Arduous, however, as it is, and insuperable as the obstacles may appear which every man must encounter on his road to fame, they have been found insufficient to damp the ardour, or lessen the expectations of an aspiring mind; nor have the innumerable examples of unfortunate authors been more effectual in blackening the prospect, who, sallying forth with self-assumed arrogance, have, after undergoing all the censure of ridicule, been at length compelled to retire into obscurity. Swift computed the authors of London at several thousands, and although common observation may convince us that this cannot be an unreasonable computation, yet it is difficult to imagine what can induce so great a number to trust to the slippery path of fame, many of whose works must necessarily be neglected, whilst the authors themselves live unrewarded, and die unknown. Every man, indeed, thinks his own pretensions to literary honours unquestionable, and himself entitled by merit to every laurel which fame has to bestow; but however gratifying it may be to indulge this "chimerical ambition of immortality," as it is termed by Johnson, it must be acknowledged, that it is of a nature too dangerous to be encouraged, as a too eager desire has often been considered as enthusiasm, and enthusiasm as the effect of inspiration; while the unfortunate individual who has deluded himself with vain hopes, has, on the first disappointment, been reduced to despair.

The comparison made by Horace, of poetry to a picture, will, I think, hold good with regard to every literary composition: there are many works which, though of no intrinsic merit, have, from one or two happy expressions, well adapted to the caprice of the times, caught at the moment the *aura popularis*, and obtained for the author undeserved rewards.

> " Inter quæ verbum emicuit si fortè decorum,
> Si versus paulò concinnior unus et alter,
> Injustè totum ducit, venditque, poema."

These, however, as their merit is built on no solid foundation, have never been found able to bear the brunt of critical investigation, but have soon met with the neglect which they deserve, when, after a closer inspection, their faults have been detected, and their follies exposed. If, then, such an unusual share of praise is given to those who least deserve it, what portion of admiration ought we to bestow on those whose works, instead of affording us a temporary pleasure, are a perpetual source of entertainment and instruction; the frequent perusal of which, instead of leading us to detect faults, only compels us to discover new beauties. Perhaps, among the many authors whose works are held up to the admiration of mankind, and whose names shine conspicuously in the annals of the world, I cannot do better than select Homer for example, whose works, as being the first and greatest of the kind, have always been considered as the standard of poetry. I do not here intend to enter into any general dissertation upon the merits or demerits of Homer; such an attempt would be

useless, since his works have so long stood all the brunt
of inquiry, and caprice of criticism, and 'have raised
for him a monument which neither time nor envy have
been able to destroy. Critics, indeed, content themselves
with directing their ingenuity towards the discovery of
new beauties, which had hitherto escaped their observation. I think it may be acknowledged, without risk-
ing the imputation of any wish to detract from the
merits of Homer, that he is, perhaps, indebted to this
ingenuity for some beauties he did not intend. If,
however, we acknowledge this, it is, perhaps, the part of
the candour we owe him, to suppose that some beauties
are still unnoticed which he did intend. Many are the
verses which, from time to time, have been pointed out
to us as peculiarly demanding our admiration, some, as
excelling in the perspicuity and beauty of the composition, and others, as enabling the reader, by the rhythm
of the line, to form some idea of the action they are
intended to record. It is needless to repeat all these
verses, and I am sure the reader will excuse me this
omission, as I have no doubt that he is acquainted with
them. There is one, however, which, though apparently
of no great merit, is altogether undeserving of the
neglect with which it in general meets. This verse, I
allow, does not possess any of the extraordinary qualities
of the verses to which I have alluded, nor is it so remarkable for the loftiness of idea, as it is for its simplicity; the reader will probably imagine that I allude
to the well-known line—

"Τὸν δ' ἀπαμειβόμενος προσέφη."—κ. τ. λ.

(I have purposely forborn filling it up, as I thought
it best to leave that to the reader.) Could any thing
be more simple, and, at the same time, more elegant?
Could any thing be better adapted to enhance the
reader's estimation, and awaken his attention? Here
an interest is excited, our expectations are roused:
we look forward with eagerness to the answer of the
hero who takes his place at the end of the verse, while
we are amused with the pleasing variety of a πόδας ὠκὺς
Ἀχιλλεὺς, or a κορυθαίολος Ἕκτωρ. Nor is this verse only
calculated to give pleasure to those who take delight in
reading Homer; but others also, who look upon the
obligation to read it as a trouble, rather than a source of
instruction and amusement. Where is the individual, who,
being compelled to toil through thirty or forty verses,
and endeavouring to understand, with the assistance of
a lexicon, the meaning and derivation of the words, has
not received some little pleasure on meeting with this
line as with an old friend? But there is another merit
which this verse possesses, and in which no other line,
I think, will bear comparison with it; I mean the peculiar manner in which it is adapted to every hero in the
poem. Would it not (if I may be allowed to make the
comparison) baffle the art of a Stultz, or a Pulford, were
they to attempt to make a coat which might fit men of
different sizes? Yet, the poet has in the most masterly
manner, by one single effusion of genius, rendered it
conformable to the size and quality of every hero. And
we see the πολύμητις Ὀδυσσεὺς agreeing as well in point
of rhythm as the great Τελαμώνιος Ἀίας. Having gone thus
far in my observations upon the merits of this verse, it

would perhaps be unjust to omit observing, that the
heroes of the poem are not the only persons qualified to
answer the rhythm, nor have mortals the sole·right to
this verse, but immortals have an equal right, and the
νεφεληγερέτα Ζεὺς or λευκώλενος Ἥρη, shine as conspicuously,
and excite as·much interest as the greatest heroes in
the poem.   Indeed, both Greeks and Trojans, Gods and
Goddesses, take their place here with equal facility, and
without any rivalry in beauty.

FRAGMENT.

I.—*A View from Glén Aber.*

Between yon rocks, that wave with many a tree,
Burst the wild waters of the boundless sea,
And dash the billows in the sunbeam's smile
Round the black cliffs of Seiriol's lonely isle.
The distant roar, as bounds the breeze away,
The shadowy sails that flit along the bay,
And yon clear sky, that spreads its azure plain,
And beams in glory o'er the sparkling main,
All speak of joy, and rapt the spirit springs,
And soars in freedom on the morning's wings.

GLENARTNEY.

II.—*Sunrise.*

Dark roll the waves—yet on the horizon's verge
What line of brightness gilds the living surge !
What tints that shame the rainbow's every dye,
Blend all in one the ocean and the sky !
He comes : the sun, amid the ruddy dawn,
And man has liv'd to hail another morn.
Fast fly the shades, and hill and vale and stream
Burst into glory with the gladdening beam ;
While from yon rock, far beetling o'er the bay,
The eagle soars to meet the god of day.

GLENARTNEY.

PANDÆMONIUM.

Fuit vivis quæ cura——————
—————— eadem sequitur tellure repôstos.

As I lay awake the other night, I found it impossible to turn my attention from the publication of " The Eton Miscellany." I turned from one side to the other, and back again, with equal inutility; I tried to compose myself to sleep, by resorting to all the usual methods; I shut my eyes, and endeavoured to count the waves of the sea, but could think of nothing but the metaphorical launch. I endeavoured to repeat verses—I could think of nothing but the motto of "The Eton Miscellany." I endeavoured to count—I could not get beyond the number of copies. I soon gave it up in despair, and, *par conséquence*, in five minutes I fell asleep. As I had been considering what my defunct predecessor, Peregrine Courtenay and his merry colleagues would think of my presumption in setting up another periodical while their own laurels were yet green, it was but natural that my waking thoughts should still pursue me in my dreams; indeed, it would hàve been incredibly incorrect, and contrary to all the unities of Aristotle, if they had not. To cut the matter short, I had one of those convenient dreams, so common in books, and so rare in bed, the substance of which I shall rohtly relate to my readers.

I saw a little, hale, active old man, with wings on

his feet, the caduceus in one hand, and a roll of paper
in the other. " My dear sir," exclaimed I, " who are
you?"—" Sir," rejoined the stranger, " I am Mercury."
—" Mercury !" I repeated in surprise; "where, then, are
the ' *crines flavos, et membra decora juventæ*'? for, of
course, my dear divinity, you understand the *dead* lan-
guages. Where is that youthful appearance and radiant
beauty so celebrated in Virgil?"—" I cannot compliment
your politeness," said the god, " in reminding me of
their loss; but, to speak the truth, the gods of Olympus
are now getting—*of a certain age!* It is unreasonable
to expect that I should be the same Mercury that I was
nearly 2,000 years ago, and even then Virgil flattered
like a portrait painter: in short, it is some centuries ago
since I began to get very grey; and, as we must all
yield to time, Venus herself is beginning to wear rouge."
—" My dear sir," I exclaimed, " I have been sadly re-
miss: pray take a chair, and explain why I am indebted
to you for the honour of your visit." The god bowed,
and after three prefatory hems, opened his mission. He
informed me that he had brought the congratulations of
the deceased subjects of the King of Clubs, and their
entreaties to have a copy sent down to them. " However," continued the little. god, " their wishes will be
better explained by this printed paper, than by any
eloquence of mine. You shall have it directly." He
then entered into conversation, and made himself very
agreeable, mixing up with the real object of his visit
a good deal of entertaining scandal and useful information about Elysium. He informed me that there was a
new subdivision in that territory, called the *Scribentes*

Campi, where every thing was poetical; where there were rivers that ran by, murmuring the most beautiful tunes, and that the most celebrated of them was practising the "Huntsman's Chorus," in Der Freischütz, with great assiduity : where the ditches were filled with ink, the trees flowered with paper, and the birds, as they flew past, dropped ready-made pens, equal to those usually sold at 12s. per hundred; that bad and tedious poets were doomed to have their own poetry, the inferiority of which they at last perceived, continually read out to them, without the *power of going to sleep!* that Pluto had had a long conversation with his head-carpenter, on the expediency of fitting up an abode exclusively for the poets of *The Lake School*.

After a long conversation, Mercury rose hastily, saying that he should be too late for the tide, which waited neither for gods nor mortals. At the same time he held out the following communication from the other world. In snatching eagerly at it, I awoke, and found myself sitting up in my bed, with the mysterious paper in my hand. I have placed the original in the hands of Mr. Ingalton, bookseller of Eton, for the inspection of the curious.

N. B.—Those who take the trouble to examine it, are particularly requested to take notice of the patent sulphureous smell, which precludes imitation or imposture. If any lady or gentleman should be disposed to ask how it was printed there, &c. I must refer them to that respectable Mandarin, with a name that nobody can speak, and nobody can spell—the editor of " Napoleon in the other World," who, as he preceded me in his work, has a right to precede me in his explanation. At the same time I must say, that these doubts would but ill repay my labours, as the ghastly and unnatural paleness of the ink rendered the deciphering of the manuscript a task of considerable difficulty. I should advise those who wish to see it at Mr. Ingalton's to be quick, as it is soon to be sent off to the *British Museum.*

<hr/>

" Ἥκω, νεκρῶν κευθμῶνα, καὶ σκοτοῦ πύλας
Λιπών."   *Inscription on the MS.*

<hr/>

" *Scene.*—ELYSIUM.   PLUTO'S BOWER.

COURT OF THE KING OF CLUBS *

Peregrine Courtenay in the Chair.

" *Courtenay.* — ' Well, gentlemen, I believe we are all assembled. Bless me, where is Wentworth?'

" *Golightly.*—' I am sorry to say Sir Francis is in *quod.* Old Pluto is a high Tory; and Wentworth amused himself with haranguing the mob upon the iniquity of absolute power, and the necessity of a radical reform. Pluto does not at all fancy this theoretical principle; this notion of a perfect equality: though I cannot but think that the kingdom of *shades* would have been the best place for putting such a theory into practice [Hear! *from Mr. Sterling*]. Old Pluto, therefore, sent Cerberus and Charon to take him up, two strong arguments in favour of *non-resistance;* and so thought

<hr/>

* *See* Etonian, No. I.

Sir Francis, for he suffered himself to be led away very quietly : and now, gentlemen, since we are in no danger, suppose we pass round our visionary punch-bowl, with as much glee as we did its "*beau ideal*" in the little world of Eton.'

" The Chairman then pulled a dirty newspaper out of his pocket, and proceeded. 'As Mercury is rather a friend of mine, I sometimes employ him to procure for me the ghost of a defunct newspaper. Conceited puppy ! he is always thinking of himself, and will never bring any one but the MORNING *Herald*. This paper seems to have had a long life, and to have been much addicted to the reprehensible practice of frequenting tap-rooms. Faugh ! how it smells of tobacco !'

" *Mr. O'Connor.*—' Give it me, then. The savour of tobacco to a ghost, is as good as a cigar to flesh and blood.'

" *Courtenay.*—' No, never mind. As I was looking over the list of the new publications, being naturally anxious to discover what chance there was of the "*facilis descensus*" for them, my eye was caught by an account of *The Eton Miscellany*, conducted by *Bartholomew Bouverie* [Loud Cheers]. I have entreated Mercury to put down our names as subscribers to Mr. Ingalton ; but he says, it is not likely to visit Lethe for a long time. Still, could they not make us a present of *one* copy ? we should be thankful even for the loan of the first Number ; though, even, if that be impossible, I should still rejoice at the commencement of *The Eton Miscellany.*' [Cheering.]

" *Mr. Golightly* made a most eloquent speech, which the Secretary regrets his inability to do justice to. [Really the Secretary should have recollected this was something out of the common way!] He expressed his entire concurrence with the hon. Chairman, but begged to remind him, that lending a book to Lethe was like lending a Tory pamphlet to Sir F. Wentworth, or a glass of wine to Mr. O'Connor.

" *Mr. O'Connor* observed, that if it at all resembled the latter, he should be very much pleased with it. [A laugh.]

" *Mr. Rowley* inquired whether the new authors had the punch-bowl, and the beef-steaks, and Mr. Golightly's receipt for the liquor. He did not conceive there was any doubt that the dinners were much the best article in the *Etonian;* as a dinner, even in print, was superior to every thing else, by recalling past delights, and being, as Lord Byron would say,

' The morning star of Memory.'

" *Mr. Golightly* begged leave to know how Rowley could ask so foolish a question; as he well knew the punch-bowl was unreal and shadowy, and, as such, it had been brought down there.

" *Mr. Rowley.*—' Shadowy! a punch-bowl shadowy! Do you mean to insult me?' [Exit in a huff, running against *Mr. Burton.*]

" *Mr. Burton.*—' I have estimated, Mr. Chairman, the expenses of the new publication; and ———'

" [Here a loud cry of ' Pluto's coming !' completely

drowned Mr. Burton's estimate. Exeunt omnes. *Mr.*
Courtenay drops the newspaper in his hurry.]

Signed.   R. HODGSON,

. Knave of Clubs."

P. S.—This, reader, is a correct account of the debate
in Elysium. I am much gratified with the kindness of
my predecessors, but am afraid they must wait some
time for No. I. A friend of mine is going to Italy in the
Summer; I will intrust it to him, to drop into the two-
penny-post hole at Avernus, as I really know of no
other communication. In the mean time, with tolerable
assiduity, I think our prospect of success is good . as
even if our poetry, and our prose also, should belong to
the class, which neither " men, gods, or columns " are
disposed to allow, I shall still depend on the Ladies and
the Ghosts.   B. B.

THE POSTMAN.

I have this morning received the following letters,
which I present without comment to the reader.

Trumpington, Munday.

Dere Measter Bartlemy ;

This comes for to say, how glad I be, that you've
setten oop that ere Eaton Mizilany, seeing as how I
knows where to aplie for hinformashion, aboot Eaton,
where I means to send my son Jem, for the benefit of
hedication Now for the matter of that I be'ent over par-
tichler aboot Latin alters and hable fun-flam,

but wants Jem to larn casting, and rithmetick, and to
rite rinning hand ; and as for the pay, I'd just like to know
if so be as I might send part of it in kinde, instead of cashe,
seeing as how cashe is harde to come at, and summat
scairce, in our countrie.   Wuld ye just ax the measter for
me this here queshtion : " Wull ye tak my beeves at a fare
valuwation, to pay for my Jem's scholaring."   If so be
as he wull, tell him as how I'll send him a cheese next
making for his koindness.   And Measter Buverie, if I
sends Jem to Eton, might I ax ye to be koind to him,
seing as he is but a dellicate chap, and but seventeen
come next October.

Your humble sarvant,
GILES PLOUGHTAIL.

Does the boys weare ony partickler dress at your
hecademy, or does ony of em wear cordroys and leggins,
bekase my Jem does.

Sir ;
I am not fond of parting with my money, but I have
a wife (I am sure you will pity me) who is distantly
related to a family, a member of which, they say, was
once brought up at Eton.   Somehow the old jade has
heard of you ; she declares her cousin did just the same
thing some fifty years ago as you are doing now, or
intended to do it, and will have me buy your Numbers.
Now, though I know it will be waste of money, yet, for
peace, I have consented to do it, in case, on my making
the inquiry, you declare to me that The Eton Miscellany
has been written by those who are now Etonians alone.
I doubt it myself: first, because some of ye be amazing

dull; second, for the sake of my shilling.   But my wife
says I must take your word : so I remain

Yours till answered,
PETER SKINFLINT.

London, June 8, 1827.

I have the pleasure of being able to assure Mr. Skinflint, however unwelcome the news may be to him, that
the first and second Numbers of the Eton Miscellany
were composed solely by Etonians, and that no change
will take place in our arrangements on that head, without
our intimating it to our friends and the public.   B. B.

THE SPANISH EXILE'S SONG.

Fast from Hispania's shores the gale
Was urging on the exile's sail,
And Cadiz distant rock and bay
Were lessening in the watery way,
When o'er the wide Atlantic main
Arose the melancholy strain :
" Farewell, my home, farewell to thee,
" Thou land of vanquish'd liberty.
" While yet thy well-known shores I view,
" Receive an exile's last adieu ;
" Receive the tears, that innate pride
" In vain would bid me strive to hide ;
" In vain would anger's fiercest flame,
" That kindles at my country's name,
" Bid me not weep ; it cannot be.
" Must I unmov'd thy bondage see ?
" Must I see thine unhappy land
" Crush'd by the Gaul's invading band ?
" Must patriots' blood thy scaffolds stain ?
" Must priestcraft re-assume her reign ?

" It matters not—my race is run,
" My task of toil and pain is done ;
" Far from my native land I roam,
" To seek in Western shores a home ,
" There liberty's new rising star
" Gleams on the crest of Bolivar,
" And sheds that pure unsullied ray
" That harbinger of coming day,
" When despot's nod, and Europe's chain
" Shall seek to bind the world in vain :
" There must I go : perhaps my life
" May perish in that glorious strife ;
" Perish it may ! that death has charms
" For him whom patriot ardour warms,
" Let me but fall at freedom's shrine,
" Nor let Riego's fate be mine ;
" Let not my quivering limbs afford
" A sight to that degenerate horde,
" Who, deaf to all their country's cries,
" A perjur'd despot's favour prize.
" Grant me but this—it boots not where
" I go to breathe a freer air ;
" Whether 'neath Lima's burning skies,
" Oι where the snow-capp'd Andes rise,
" Or whether by Panuco's wave,
" The exile finds a lonely grave."

ON LYING.

"Ἴδμεν ψευδέα πολλὰ λαλεῖν."—HESIOD.

In this age of education, and national schools, it seems strange that no one should have established an academy for the instruction of young men in the art of lying with

a good grace.   While, however, I say this, I do not wish
to be understood as being either an admirer or a censor
of this noble art; but what I complain of is this, that
although so many Munchausens are daily attempting to
amuse us, they relate their marvels so clumsily, that
weak indeed must the person be upon whose credulity
they can impose.   To travellers, and those who say they
have changed horses at Timbuctoo, or supped with the
king of Ava, we should allow implicit faith; for small
must that man's stock of politeness be, who would deny
to such the privilege of embellishing their adventures as
they please.   But every-day liars should at least have
some tact in their stories, some small show of probability
in their improbabilities, that they may not be liable to
detection from the dullest auditor.   Take W——, for instance, who has always a stock of wonderful adventures
on hand, and who might really be a pleasant companion,
if one could believe a word he says.   It is the more
distressing to be compelled to listen to his not extraordinary, but absolutely incredible, adventures, as, being
by nature blessed with a strong arm, he might, like the
true Munchausen, be ready to fight with what weapon he
please the man who is bold enough to be sceptical on
any point of his narrative.   He will gravely tell you, " I
had an excellent dinner yesterday ; turtle, venison, &c.
&c. and walked home sober, after drinking four bottles of
claret." Now, for ourselves, although we may be pretty
sure that he dined on mutton and small beer, we should
have no objection to his using the long-bow with moderation, and might possibly have extended our believing
faculties as far as two or three . but at present. Quod-

cunque ostendis mihi sic, incredulus odi." I have another
friend who usually lies in the future tense, who will talk
largely of what he intends doing, will threaten to astonish
the world with some new equipage, and to keep I don't
know how many horses.   Mark the result ; three months
hence you see-him drive down Piccadilly in a hired gig
and upon commenting upon his extraordinary propensity,
are answered on all sides by " Oh, he is a good sort of
fellow, but you should never believe a word he says."
Upon these considerations, what, I ask, would be more
conducive to the welfare of all rising Munchausens, than
some few rules, which, by curbing their power of lying,
might enable them to practise on our credulity with
some chance of success? And if I, Bartholomew Bouverie,
were at any future election to supplant Mr. Ramsbottom,
and sit for his majesty's loyal borough of Windsor, the
first act of my power should be to move, " That, whereas
the noble art of shooting with the long-bow has, from the
use of excessive and unnatural exaggeration, so far dege-
nerated, that few of his majesty's subjects practising the
same, can obtain credit, a special committee be appointed
for the purpose of taking into consideration certain regulations, with a view to ordering the same, that it may no
longer be an object of disgust and ridicule at all.   And
that whereas the most marvellous stories are usually those
of gentlemen continually engaged in field-sports, any
person or persons alleging that he or they have indivi-
dually killed more than —— head of game, or have broken
a neck oftener than three times in a fox-chase, be declared
unworthy of credit, and be punished as the act may
direct."

ON NAÏVETÉ.

I have always considered affectation to be little more than an ill-regulated emulation, an attempt at imitating those qualities, or manners, which appear graceful and natural in another person, by engrafting them on our own dispositions. I shall at present confine myself to the affectation of originality, or rather, what the Ladies call " *naïveté.* " Now, what the precise meaning of this word may be, I will not pretend to say, as I am almost inclined to think that it is a quality of nature, merely created that it might be awkwardly imitated by the votaries of art. As far, however, as I do understand it, it appears to be a sort of guileless simplicity, which is naturally inherent in some people (particularly in the *heroine of a novel*), and is therefore frequently adopted, to captivate insidiously, much in the same way as the elegance of a studied dishabille is frequently preferred to the splendor of a full dress. However, it is but just, to hear what the naïve ladies will say. If you were to ask Laura (in the "Palace of Truth," of course), she would tell you, that it consisted in being gracefully ungraceful ; in running into a room full of company like a race-horse that has just bolted ; in throwing herself violently into an arm-chair, and sitting cross-legged [N. B. Laura has a very pretty foot and ankle]; in short, in every species of infantine simplicity ; yet Laura has been married several years : and is it possible that this frail charm, this ephemeral halo, which is represented as gilding seventeen, can have survived this protracted

intercourse with the world?—Certainly not: and as
Laura is a woman of sense and talent, I cannot conceive
why she persists in this course, unless she hopes, by
continual practice, to verify the proverb, "Habit is
second nature." Now, from what I know of Laura's
character, and hear of the character of naïveté, if it come
at all, it will come only with second childhood: yet, as
Laura is a very pretty woman, I am afraid it will be difficult to convince her that the continued agitation of a
light and symmetrical figure, and the display of a pretty
foot is not naïveté. Indeed, had I the same advantages,
I too would shut my ears against conviction, and be like
her, in spite of nature; however, as my masterly arguments
have convinced all persons with thick ankles or club feet,
that Laura is not naïve, we will proceed. The next
species is an affected modesty, and a retiring timidity,
which is exceedingly graceful, and must interest every
body who admires the delicacy of the sex; it is, moreover, easier than the first, and requires only a quick eye
and a quantum sufficit of impudence. Being, however,
easier and less hazardous than the first, it is of course
less brilliant, and indeed is generally used as an orna-
mental appendage to it. We will therefore pass on to
the third class; this consists in saying every thing you
think, or, more properly, in going out of your way to
say rude things. If you were to ask one of the lady
professors of this branch, in the same palace, the definition would be short, but emphatic—to be regularly,
systematically, actively, ill-bred. So much for *the naïveté
of candour*. I cannot forbear noticing in conclusion the
affectation of resignation in public, though it does not

exactly belong to naïveté, in which a person is continually making a pretence of misfortune, to be pitied for her sorrows, and admired for her patience: this, however, is never successful, nor would I recommend it, for it is very soon discovered that a young lady who is perpetually in the dismals, however pretty it may be for a time, infallibly becomes neither more nor less than a dismal bore.

.MALEK.

EPILOGUE.

Again my cares and labours cease,
Again I hail the hour of peace;
Again the fruits of toil review,
And bid farewell to Number Two.
If not more bright, yet wiser now
Than when I launch'd my slender prow,
And felt the mild and prosp'ring gale
Urge on my course, and fill my sail:
I saw the orient God of Day
Beam brightly o'er the wat'ry way;
I felt from far the Zephyr breeze
That kiss'd the ripple of the seas.
  Such was the scene of joy on earth,
Such was the day that saw my birth,
Such was each kind and smiling face
That bade me run a prosp'rous race:
Each hand prepar'd the wreath to give,
And bid my fleeting pages live.
Some brows were wrinkled, some were sad,
Some voted me, "in toto," bad,
Some struck me dead with meagre praise,
Some straight condemn'd my boyish lays,
And some, with meek indulgent love,
Thought practice would my muse improve.

But some there were whose kinder heart
More genial feeling could impart:
Some could discern a trembling lyre,
A glimm'ring of the poet's fire,
Take Mercy's wand for Judgment's rod,
And favour and acceptance nod;
And these were many: and to these
Again may artless Numbers please,
Again may pardon'd errors lie
Conceal'd in dark obscurity,
Again may boyhood's efforts raise ·
The shout of undeserved praise.
    But, hark! I hear a thund'ring cry
That bids my pleasing prospects fly—
" Where are your sober pages?" where
" Good things of all kinds?" light as air,
And fleeting as the breezes gone,
Descend to Styx and Phlegethon;
There let the furies' scourges try
The courage of your youthful fry.
    Go, Zoilus! I fear not thee,
I fear not all thine obloquy;
This will I bear, and more, far more,
To reap the meed I reap'd before.
An hundred adverse critics' spite
Would but enhance mine own delight;
An hundred friendly voices round
Shall bid me spurn *one* angry sound.
    Not yet defunct, I roam on earth,
Made ready for my second birth;
And, with your leave, my worthy friend,
I will not quite so quick descend:
Full soon thou 'lt see me gaily drest
In Calf—perhaps in Russia—vest;
Long, long, I trust, my sacred strains
Shall dwell in these terrestrial plains,
And, when the hour of death shall come,
Repose in soft Elysium.

ETON MISCELLANY,
No. III.

INTRODUCTION.

I HAVE been taught by experience, since I first addressed the public, that the condition of an author is not one of unmixed pleasure. Not long ago I met with a line in Euripides, which is peculiarly consolatory to me in my present frame of mind :—

οὐκ ἔστιν οὐδένι δία.τέλυς εὐδαιμονεῖν.

When I have heard myself abused on one side, and commended on another, and when all the resources of my natural vanity have been exhausted, I have made up my mind to share with patience the common lot of mortals, and to be contented—as well indeed I may—with the unmerited patronage, and the liberal praise, which have been bestowed upon me.

I shall here present to the public two metrical epistles on the subject of the merits of this publication ; as, if true, they deserve insertion, and, if unfounded, they will not injure me.

To Bartholomew Bouverie.

When first I spied thy title page,
    And read thine introduction,
I deem'd thee sober, grave, and sage,
    A dealer in instruction.

But soon the cloud spread o'er my eyes,
 The Sun of Truth did banish:
Soon did the weak and thin disguise
 Of feign'd discretion vanish.

Some of thy verse is good, I own,
 And some of it is fairish;
Some scarce can vie with burial stone,
 And sexton of the parish.

But oh! thou dry and barren stick,
 Thy prose is prose indeed, Sir;
'Twas form'd to make thy readers sick,
 And well does it succeed, Sir.

Then I will close, as thou did'st close,
 With sober admonition;
Thou'lt now perceive an author's woes,
 And mourn his sad condition.

Go where no self-dubb'd poet's tongue
 His fustian rant rehearses:
And, leaving all the scribblers' throng,
 Return to theme and verses.

Misographe.

To B. Bouverie.

Oh! for an hundred mouths to tell,
How gallant Bouv'rie fought and fell:
Oh! for an hundred Stentors' lungs,
To each an hundred hundred tongues:
Oh! for an hundred eyes, to read,
And urge my course with breeze-like speed,
To wade through every page of lore,
Each duller than the one before.
I've plumb'd the depths of Peter Bell;
Would I could fathom thine as well;
An innate "vis inertiæ"
Hath borne me on through all, but thee;
And till the Gods my prayers shall hear,
And, listen with benignant ear,

And stock me well with voice and tongue,
I may not rove thy tomes among :
I wish thee safe dismiss'd from light,
And bid thy ghost a long good-night.

SINGLETONGUE.

Having thus given utterance to feelings so hostile to me, I shall now, in pursuance of my declared intention of gradually removing the mysterious veils which surround and conceal us from the public eye, admit a ray of light in a hitherto concealed, but most important, quarter, and introduce to the public a third among the coadjutors whom I have chosen.

No one, unless endowed with a more than common share of penetration, would divine from the exterior appearance of Francis Jermyn, how much of what deserves and attracts our admiration and esteem lies concealed beneath a somewhat unpolished superficies. Talents the most various, and pursuits the most opposite, distinguish this extraordinary being : yet, with the qualities which embellish the head, he possesses, in an eminent degree, the affections which adorn the heart. What nature could possibly have intended him for, I am entirely at a loss to divine : if she meant him to be a philosopher—he laughs too much for Heraclitus—feels too much for Democritus ; he is too light for a Stoic, too civil for a Cynic, too lazy for a Peripatetic, and too sensible for an Epicurean. He is passionately fond of Newmarket and Parnassus, of the racer's turf and the poet's ivy ; a muse and a jockey hold about an equal place in his estimation ; and Pegasus himself is hardly on a par with Mamaluke or Gulnare. He once intended to write an epic on the celebrated Memnon : the genealogy

I 2

was to occupy the first department; the training the
second; and the whole of the circumstances attending
the Grand St. Leger, with the triumph of his hero, the
third : the whole interspersed with episodes concerning
the victories of his forefathers, and the histories of his
riders. The notes (for who writes books without notes?)
were to contain many curious and interesting documents,
elucidating several disputed points in the history of horse-
racing. He had great difficulty in choosing a metre;
but at last determined on the anapæst, as having most
affinity in sound, to a horse's gallop. The names of
Memnon's ancestors he made into patronymics : a most
spirited imprecation on the demon of black-leggism
figured in the beginning of the second book; and it was
only from the vengeance of the aforesaid spirit, that he,
being thoroughly disgusted by the result of inquiries
which he was forced to make among the black-legs themselves, for the purpose of procuring information, was
compelled reluctantly to relinquish his undertaking.

The habitation of my friend is strictly in character.
Not containing more than the three or four articles of
furniture which form the usual complement of an Eton
boy's room, it exhibits a singular mixture of Sporting
Magazines and volumes of Lord Byron; of prints of
racehorses, and scenes from Shakespeare. Here and
there the curious observer may detect some of his own
compositions; and they are usually such as, when discovered, amply to repay any trouble incurred during the
search. His poetry is such as would not disgrace many
a more experienced candidate for poetical honours : and,
whatever may be the fate of poor Bartholomew Bouverie's

compositions, I am confident that those of Francis Jermyn will find for him a road to fame, and secure him a situation far higher than any which he can enjoy in my company.

There are no weapons more dangerous to the possessors of them, than those of ridicule. There are none which require more skill to use, and more self-denial to refrain from using. While carelessness is the predominant failing, warmth of heart is the prevailing virtue of my coadjutor; and I do not hesitate to affirm that I never saw him use those powers which he possesses in an eminent degree, with the intention of hurting the feelings of any one. An unhappy constitutional risibility is, indeed, inherent in him, which occasionally places him in rather awkward situations; but no one can laugh at his own failings or mistakes with more perfect sincerity and good humour.

His carelessness is remarkable. Whatever nature did intend him for, it was not to carry messages. Fortunately his head is well fastened to his shoulders, or he would leave it behind him in some of his perambulations. He will wonder what he can have done with a book which he *is* holding in his hand; and will as frequently forget the want of one which he *is not*. Often and often does he stalk into school, so far from having prepared a lesson, that he has no idea in what author, or in what language, it is to be found. He sometimes has his attention pinned down to it by being directed to translate it, and if, while he is actually at work, he forms resolutions, when he has completed his task he forgets them. Were I to represent to him how serious the consequences of these apparently most unimportant deficiencies are, and how often homely and unfashionable qualities are found to have an incalculable weight in promoting the happiness of life, he would not feel any resentment on being lectured by one so much his inferior, but would smother a laugh, and recommend me to keep my philosophy for the next theme day.

If I may assume the character of a prophet, I shall venture to predict that my friend, should he be spared so long, about fifty years hence, will be a good-natured, spirited, and amusing old gentleman, a great favourite with his grandchildren, and the constant benefactor of all comfit-loving, bun-devouring urchins. If he retains the present features of his character, he will still have a high sense of right, and an unqualified hatred of equivocation; he will still have a warm heart, and an open hand; he will still be a friend to taste and wit, and on opening a newspaper will still look first to the betting department; and, on a retrospective glance on the past years of his life, he will dwell with pleasure on the days when he began to tune his youthful lyre, and became a warm, an anxious, and a favoured votary of the Muses.

ENNUI.

Having perused an article in your last number, entitled Ennui, I have been induced, though reluctantly, to intrude myself on your notice, my dear Bouverie, I assure you with the best intentions, and I think it right to premise that I come with no satirical vinegar in my countenance, or gall of criticism in my pen; .my sole object is to argue the merits of the case fairly and candidly, and to contra- · dict assertions which, though. perhaps not entirely destitute of foundation, are nevertheless tangible in a certain degree.   .   .

Now it would be an insult to the human understanding, to suppose that an effectual remedy for Ennui was to be derived from "the anodyne whiffs of an Havannah cigar," or the rusty looking contents of that useless appendage to a gentleman's pocket, a snuff box. Nor can I concur with your correspondent in supposing that any young lady, in whatever situation, can be so utterly destitute of resources, as to be fairly reduced "to angle for recreation in an album," or to endure the purgatory of perusing love sonnets and other trash of the same nature, for in such cases the remedy would be less tolerable than the disease itself. These are mere trifles, my dear Bouverie, unworthy of a place in our recollections for a single instant; it may be very convenient for us, when engaged in a social conversation, to derive a remedy for the stings of Ennui from such ridiculous and ineffectual sources; but it is an active and energetic mind alone, superior to those little casualties, which are apt to depress the spirits, and throw a languid dejection over the countenance, which is proof against Ennui in its most hardened and inveterate forms. Our rational powers must always be open to conviction; they cannot possibly be so perverted as to deny or even question this assertion, and hence we derive the information that whatever tendency towards Ennui we may experience, is entirely to be ascribed to our own dulness and torpidity, and wholly emanates from that impenetrable chaos which envelopes our mental system.

Your correspondent proceeds to favour us with an expression used by two ultramontanes of the lower class; now as they are seemingly antediluvian in their notions, some excuse may be urged in their favour. Though I myself do not profess to be particularly conversant in the provincial dialects of this country, I can perfectly comprehend the meaning of this word "unkid," am fully aware of its "sepulchral and ominous" nature, and am fully competent to understand the internal feelings of any one writhing under its influence. But, I ask, whence originate the feelings here pourtrayed? Solely from a want of activity and of energy, which produces a total stagnation of those vital springs which equalize the passions, and insensibly promote what we have most at heart, the success of all our undertakings.

Your correspondent next proceeds to descant upon the freedom from Ennui enjoyed in the salubrious atmosphere of Italy. Now, whether or not the Italian has those delightful feelings of independence, I am incompetent to judge, but at any rate if his happiness rests solely upon the possession of the "*dolce far niente*" or "sweet nothing-to-do-ish-ness," or in other words, if it depends upon the acquirement of unequivocal indolence, I should presume his situation, with all its luxuries, was by no means an enviable one. Now I ask, is not the Englishman who is entirely dependant for his subsistence on his own exertions, is he not, I say, a king when put in compe-

tition with the languid and effeminate Italian? Are not
his spirits far more buoyant and elastic, his feelings less
shackled, and his employments more satisfactory? His
superior notions and more comprehensive ideas disdain
a comparison with the degenerate and unmanly inactivity
which is the evident characteristic of the Neapolitan;
from which neither the fleeting and unsubstantial dreams
of future emolument, " the plaudits of the Boulevards "
or the " golden showers of the .Haymarket" can possibly emancipate him.   Can the spirits of an Englishman
possibly flag? . The very name contradicts the assertion.
Was John Bull ever accused of dulness and torpidity?.
Cast not, ye cavillers, such unwarranted aspersions on our
national character.   How can he be destitute of resources,
when the intellectual delicacies of a Locke or a Milton, or
the productions of an Addison, are within his reach?
Surely here is an ample scope for his imagination to
revel in; surely here is a method of alleviating, if not of
entirely removing, Ennui, even supposing it to be ten
times as powerful as it usually is.

Here, my dear Bouverie, is a stock of literature exactly
suited to a rainy morning in the country, which your
friend mentions with such horror and indignation; neither
requiring the superfluous aid of a newspaper or billiard-
room, nor the elegant volatility of a shuttlecock; they
are of a truly substantial and sufficient nature, capable of
bidding defiance to the combined efforts of " dumps" and
Ennui; will moreover enable your friend to enjoy his
"little tea parties," and "his little musical parties,"
unalloyed by the "unkid" and taciturn physiognomies
of those around him. · ..

Your correspondent, I think, concludes with a long
rigmarole, sensible enough, no doubt, respecting gargles
and emetics. Now, my dear Bouverie, I perceive that my
indignation against him has insensibly been wound up
to a most awful pitch, and I therefore think I had better
dismiss those delightful, those truly celestial beverages
without comment. At the same time, I wish to make
known to him my cordial wish that he may long enjoy
himself under their genial influence, and that he may
imbibe their fragrant and fascinating odours in his nasal,
and their anodyne streams in his guttural, receptacles; if
he has not sufficient strength of mind to derive some more
effectual remedy for the miseries of Ennui, from his own
individual exertions.

W.

THE SACRIFICE.

" The approach of night, though it delivered the dejected Spaniards
from the attacks of the enemy, ushered in what was hardly less
grievous, the noise of their barbarous triumph, and of the horrid
festival with which they were celebrating their victory. Every quarter of the city was illuminated, and the great temple shone with such
peculiar splendor, that the Spaniards could plainly see the people in
motion, and the priests busied in hastening the preparations for the
death of the prisoners."—ROBERTSON'S AMERICA, Book V

Slow sank the sun. The coming night
Forbad the fury of the fight
No more the war-cry's savage tone
Was mingled with the dying groan,
  But hush'd was every sound ;
Save where upon the blood-stain'd banks
Repos'd Hispania's weary ranks,
  In fitful slumbers bound.
There might you hear the soldier's prayer,
The sigh that spoke the heart's despair

While to his mind stern fancy brought
The agonizing sting of thought,
   Those dreams of doubt and pain, .
That o'er his sleeping senses cast
The recollection of the past,
   And bade him think on Spain ;
That bade his tortur'd bosom feel
The memory of belov'd Castile,
Of Douro's banks, and happier hours,
And of La Mancha's verdant bowers ;
While still before his weary eyes
Dangers in wild succession rise.
These are his thoughts, with these opprest,
Can slumber sooth his anxious breast ?
Fear bids him wake   One savage yell
Resounded from the citadel—
A moment's pause—a thousand lights
Shone on the temple's lofty heights: .
The banks, the gore-polluted stream,
Reflect the radiance of the beam ;
While to the Spaniard's host it shows
The vengeance of barbarian foes.

For there with hand's imbrued in blood,
The Sun's unholy priesthood stood ,
There, too, weigh'd down with many a chain,
Were seen the captive band of Spain ;
Cortez' last hope, his chosen few,
Must he their latest tortures view ?
Must he, to every groan awake,
Watch their last writhings at the stake ?
Yes, he must hear their shrieks, and see
Each dying captive's agony.
And mark those hands, which oft the sword
Had grasp'd obedient to his word,
When on the causeway's slipp'ry height
He dar'd provòk th' unequal fight,
Now sever'd from the lifeless frame, .
Feed the unholy altar's flame.
Meantime each Spaniard's eager eyes
Survey the destin'd sacrifice.

Each well-known voice they seem to hear,
Each dying groan finds echo there.
While broken walls, and towers, prolong
The conqueror's triumphal song.

" Mexicans, our task is done,
Rise, ye Children of the Sun.
May your father's hallow'd name
Impart some portion of his flame.
May the victims, as they die,
Appease the angry deity.
· By the invading blood we shed,
By memory of the mighty dead,
By your trampled country's woes,
By all the hatred of your foes,
Let not Spain's accursed host,
Yet pollute your sacred coast.
Burst the chain, each gallant breast !
Let valour plume the warrior's crest.
Think on your degraded state,
Think on Montezuma's fate !"   Q.

THE ART OF CONVERSATION.

Arbitrium, et jus, et norma loquendi.—HOR.

Mr. Bouverie, I am one of those silent beings, who,
being troubled with "mauvaise honte," and destitute
of fluency of expression, content themselves with listening to conversation, without venturing to take a part in
it. You may, on this account, think that I am a very
unfit person to write on such a subject as the Art of
Conversation ; I confess the justice of the remark, but
venture to presume upon your indulgence. For though
I seldom speak, yet I never fail to listen attentively, and

make my remarks according to circumstances; and having by nature a desire of conversing, though marred by an unconquerable timidity, my only resource is in the pen. Whether that pen be gifted with more fluency than my tongue, I am not a sufficient judge; but I am compelled to give vent to my ideas, like the barber's boy in the fable of Midas, not without fear that my paper may rise in judgment against me, and cry, "Taciturn has ass's ears."

But, joking apart, I have often wondered that no one has attempted to reduce conversation to a system, for the benefit of those whose ideas are not so unembarrassed, and whose tongues are not so glib as their owners could have wished. For want of a better, I have ventured to send you a scheme of my own, which has already been of advantage to me, and I hope may be so to others.

The Art of Conversation is divided into seven grand classes: The Dialectical or Argumentative: the Masticatory, or Table-talk: the Anacreontic, or Love-making: the Terpsichoric, or Ball-room talk: the Soirée, or Tea-and-turn-out talk; the Poluphloisbian, or Fustian talk: and the Pompholugopaphlasmatic, or Noisy-nonsensical talk.

Class 1.—*The Dialectical or Argumentative.*

The beauty and effect of this style consists in giving your opponent the lie without ceremony, as nothing tends so much to weaken his arguments as impeaching his veracity; the next point is never to confess yourself beaten; but when hard pressed, to shift your ground, and attack him at a new point. The usual subjects in this class are all matters relating to politics ; and this style should never be used without an accompanying bottle.

Class II.—*The Masticatory, or Table Talk.*

-, The chief point to be observed in this style is, that it should never be used to such a degree as to interrupt the more essential duty of eating ; consequently, that man may consider that he has made some proficiency who can talk with considerable volubility with his mouth full, for thereby he kills two birds with one stone.

Class III.—*The Anacreontic, or Love-making style.*

In this class four things are essentially necessary : the first, Flattery ; the second, Impudence ; the third, Pertinacity ; and the fourth, Self-sufficiency. Those who expect to be successful in this style, must take especial care to have always at their fingers ends a good stock of ready-made "Impromptus ;" each of which should contain upon an average, four sighs, one bleeding heart, three lilies, and a rose ; Cupid and Venus, to appear classical ; three "till deaths," to appear faithful ; and sixteen metaphors to appear poetical ; for of those three appearances, the last is the best.

N. B. To this class the language of the eyes is a very necessary adjunct.

Class IV.—*The Terpsichoric, or Ball-Room Talk.*

In this class the chief thing spoken is Nonsense ; and

to speak that gracefully is the only object in view. Subjects are seldom sought from a distance; since the music, the lights, the floor, and the faces, will generally last pretty well to the last bar of "Finale." In criticising the last of these, great caution is necessary, as if handsome, you will often excite your partner's jealousy; if ugly, you stand a chance of hearing that you have been inveighing against her sister.

Class V.—*The Soirée, or Tea-Table Talk.*

The subject of this kind of conversation is generally Scandal, and it is chiefly by means of these that malicious reports travel with telegraphic expedition. No person whatever should venture to attend one of these meetings without providing herself with the news of the day: how Lady F. flirted at the Opera with Colonel C.: how Mrs. R. lost two thousand at Ecarté, and pawned her diamonds to pay it; how a separation had been talked of between Lord and Lady D.; how Lady Rougenoir's complexion was owing to Atkinson's Circassian Bloom, and the colour of her eye-brows to Rowland's Tyrian Dye; with fifty other stories of the like stamp.

N. B. No story should be told without some little addition, which the ingenuity of the relater will readily suggest.

Class VI.—*The Poluphloisbian, or Fustian style.*

The grand principle of this style is Noise; and its merit consists in the use of big words where small would answer the purpose. The more recondite, and less intelligible the words, the better is the effect produced. A professor of this style will never say, " Pray snuff the candle ;" but " Vouchsafe to decapitate the supererogatory elevation of the luminary :" instead of " Brush my coat," he would say, " Administer purification to the pulverulent superficies of my habiliments :" in short, he will stretch his jaws, and our language, to the greatest possible extent, and think more of himself for discovering a high-sounding word, than if he had Squared the Circle, or invented the Perpetual Motion.

Class VII.—*The Pompholugopaphlasmatic, or Noisy-nonsensical style.*

To this style the old proverb applies, " More Sound than Sense." It is chiefly used by Hectors, bravos, bullies, and those dandies whose stays are unfashionably loose enough, to admit of its being used with effect. It consists chiefly of oaths, to render which expressive, requires great power and skill. With ordinary performers they degenerate into unmeaning expletives; but with first-rate swearers they cannot fail to convince all those, who have not their ears stopped by good sense, or their minds depraved by that vulgar quality understanding.

Having thus completed my classes, I beg leave to announce to the world, my intention of publishing by subscription, a series of cards, containing every requisite to the above styles. The cards on class the first, will contain all the arguments of coffee-house politicians, on both sides of every question, arranged according to the Socratic method ; by means of which those who wish to display the versatility of their genius may change sides at their pleasure.

The Second Series will contain a vast variety of original stories, jeux d' esprit with suitable introductions : also two general speeches of thanks, adapted to any person, toast, or dinner.

The Third will contain new and original Raptures, warranted to captivate.

The Fourth will be found abundant in criticisms on the last new Quadrilles; with remarks on all descriptions of faces, blonde, brunette, Madonna, &c. &c. drawn from nature expressly for this work. Also an Essay on Lemonade, and an extract from Jarrin's " Italian Confectioner," on the subject of Ices.

The Fifth will contain every requisite of an accomplished scandal-monger ; also an history of the Tea-plant, for a botanical coterie. Fictitious stories and false scandal will also be inserted; equal to true.

The Sixth will contain, "The Difficulties of Johnson," selected chiefly from his dictionary ; also a supply of Greek words, of the best quality and loudest sound, neatly anglicised, warranted to contain more letters than any yet published.

The Seventh will contain a collection of challenges, and as many apologies; directions for talking big, with a copious assortment of lies, oaths, and gasconades.

If you will be so kind, Mr. Bouverie, as to insert this Scheme in the next number of your Miscellany, you may be assured that I will find a tongue to praise you ; in the mean time believe me   Your devoted Servant,

TOBIAS TACITURN.

THE LAST OF THE CAMBRIANS.

Hark ! on the breezes borne along,
Loudly sounds the warriors' song :
Swift it passes o'er the waves,
Resounding from the mountain caves ;
While Snowdon's high and rocky shore
Reverberates the battle's roar.
   Now all is hush'd, as silent night,
     Save where the impetuous tide,
   Gushing from the craggy height,
     Thunders down the mountain's side :
Save where the rocks repeat the cry,
" We go to conquer or to die."

Now all is still ; now hush'd that strain,
Never more to sound again ;
While, beneath the mountain's gloom,
Young Edward proudly shakes his plume ;
He bids his squadrons from afar
Mingle in the din of war.
   Each felt, amid the mortal strife,
     A momentary dread ;
   But ere another instant pass'd
     Those craven thoughts were fled.
Lo, on the mountain's craggy side,
- Glowing with his native pride,
Pride of his race, Llewellyn stands,
And urges on his patriot bands.

" Sons of Liberty, awake,
The English despots power to shake.
And shall the offspring of the brave
To foreign tyrants be a slave ?
   No—your battle blades unsheath—
     Be to your country true :
   That freedom to your sons bequeath,
     Your sires bequeath'd to you :
And he who fears to meet the grave,
Let him live and die a slave.

" On Plinlimmon, from afar,
I saw the Genius of the war :
He bids us think of days of old,
Of those who in the grave are cold :
  He couches now his purpled spear,
    Lo, down the craggy height
  Haggard death and giant fear
    Ride onward to the fight :
Revengeful Hate and pale Despair
And Rout and Anguish follow there.

" Rush on, ye brave, at Glory's name ;
Kindle again your fathers' flame :
And let the English plunderers know
Our breasts with patriot valour glow.
  But now the hour of fight is near,
    The moon is waning fast ,
  And, if the tyrant foe prevail,
    Let this day be your last.

" Lo, what phantoms, bathed in gore,
Stand upon yon rocky shore :
Awaken'd from his icy trance,
Each spectre shakes his shadowy lance ;
Their ancient fire within them glows,
They burn to meet their country's foes.
  Lo, within yon gloomy cave
    The funeral feast is spread,
  And through the caverns loud resounds
    The war-song of the dead :
They sing the triumphs of the brave,
The warrior's death, the warrior's grave.

" Ere to morrow's sun be set,
Our kindred spirits will be met :
With them we'll weep o'er days of yore,
And drink to freedom, now no more ;
  Then on the billows, side by side,
    To yonder camp we'll go ;
  And riding on the night-wind's wings,
    We'll flitter o'er the foe.

With them, upon yon bloody plain,
We'll sing the praises of the slain.

" Lo, what visions of the night
Burst upon the victor's sight ;
His glaring eye and startled ear
Shrink aghast with thrilling fear .
The phantoms rising from the tomb
Stalk across the dreary gloom,
    Denouncing vengeance on his race,
        The vengeance of a foe ;
    He hears in the gale the shriek of death,
        He hears the shriek of woe.

" Yonder rock is red with blood
Reflected in the foaming flood,
Yet redder still shall be that stream,
Redder still that rock shall gleam ;
Ere to morrow's sun be low,
That sun itself with blood shall glow.
    Many on that fatal field
        Shall meet to meet no more ;
    Few among those foes shall live
        To see their native shore.
Each hero in his war-cloak laid,
Shall grasp in death his broken blade.

" There, beneath that foaming deep,
Bound in adamantine sleep,
Ye'll moulder in your country's clay,
Nor shrink beneath the tyrant's sway ;
Ye'll ne'er behold your country's fame
O'ershadow'd by eternal shame.
    Rush on—rush on—the foe to meet,
        Nor tremble at your doom ;
    The wave shall be your winding sheet,
        The ocean's cave your tomb .
Beneath the surge of yonder sea
Your spirits will again be free."

                            WINANDERMERE.

ADVERTISEMENTS.

Lost in the mighty ocean of matter that floods the newspaper pages, alas ! how unlike that rivulet of text meandering through a meadow of margin in the novels of the day, I look to you, Mr. Bouverie, for rescue from my watery grave.

It is not among political debates, dreadful occurrences, or fashionable movements, that I am to be found, but among those little oblong compartments on the first side of the paper, commonly called Advertisements.

The existence of this valuable community is endangered, in spite of their emphatic fingers and grotesque faces, pointing and grinning their merits into notice.   Merits, which the name of a Bish and Goodluck are alone sufficient to perpetuate. Amiable pair ! whither would their prospective philanthropy have extended, had not premature fate closed for ever our positively penultimate peeps of Peru and Mexico.

But what inexhaustible stores, what long-withdrawing scenes of bliss and pleasure, glowing in all the luxuriant language and descriptive imagery of my brethren, still remain " for the inspection of the public." Secure of satisfaction among such varied resources, let the individual look to us for assistance, who may have lost his wife or his watch, who wishes to clean his coat, or clarify his complexion.

How many desirable residences, and terrestrial paradises remain unenjoyed, in spite of those two emphatic monosyllables " To Let," that so earnestly challenge our attention, and so successfully disdain compliance with the tame rules of grammar. What quantities of happiness may be -"purchased at a fair valuation;" what convenient premises and undisturbed tranquillity "may be entered upon immediately."

In vain do we assure our correspondents, that health and beauty are at our disposal, that they may be conveyed into the country packed in separate boxes; nay more—that they may be returned, if they fail to meet with approbation—the "Ægis of Life" lies neglected on our counter, and much unappropriated immortality remains corked up in pint bottles.

Such pernicious prejudices could scarcely be credited, were we not convinced by the bilious complexions, and tedious coughs of next-door neighbours, who let our "occasional pills, and expectorating lozenges," so unaccountably slip through their fingers. Nay more—how many an obstinate old man commits felo de se at seventy-seven, from neglecting the "Balm of Gilead"; how many a full grown person is useless at a ball, for want of *three* lessons from a professor; monstrous beyond measure! Orpheus plays, but the brutes positively *wo'nt* dance.

In spite of the natural predisposition of mankind to be imposed upon, which has prevailed from the Phæa of Pisistratus, to the less romantic but equally flagrant impostures of the present day; to the proposed union of the Chalk and Cream, the Thames and Milk companies of the metropolis, a most dangerous principle is gradually gaining on the public mind. Men, Mr. Bouverie, are actually pretending to judge for themselves, and with unparalleled incredulity, refuse to believe every thing they are bid

If such innovation is permitted, and so pernicious a prerogative gains a precedent, farewell to the noble art which has spread so widely the imperative command of Turner, and the milder entreaty of Lardner.*

The flowery prose of a Rowland, and the pointed poetry of a Warren will be forgotten, and the obliteration of such illustrious names will involve in their fall, the humbler destiny of

Your obedient Servant,
PETER PUFF.

THE PREDICTION.

(Continued from page 39)

As the torrent strikes the rock,
Fell Grenada's thunder shock
  Fiercely swept along.
As the lightning rends the oak,
On the impetuous Spaniards broke
  Through the Moorish throng.
Yet though the Moors were backward borne,
E'en in the battle's early dawn,
The lion banner flouts the sky,
The Abencerrages fight to die,
The kings, the Zegris are o'erthrown,
The Abencerrages fight alone.
Aye, charge, though in the hour of slaughter,
Ye shed that noble blood like water,
And pile the dying on the dead,
To turn th' indignant river red
  With the life-blood of the brave ;
They, when the trumpet prompts the spear,
Are foremost in the wild career ;

---

* *Use* Turner's Blacking.—*Try* Lardner's

They, when against those crests of pride
O'erwhelming rolls war's angry tide,
Can still raise high the lion shield,
Can bear to die, but never yield
    To aught except the grave.
Then, as the Moorish war-cry rose,
And back upon their Christian foes
    The wave of battle flow'd,
To where those hero chieftains bled,
Indignant that he ever fled,
    The wild Numidian rode
There, as the foaming mass swept by
In their unbridled majesty,
With flashing eye, and waving mane,
Each courser seem'd to share the pain,
And on to death, in fierce disdain
    And eager fury, strode
Next, waving o'er the Zegri lord,
The banner of the bloody sword
    Plung'd in the dark affray.
In Ali's eye of glancing flame
Were mingling pride, and hate, and shame,
    In one unhallow'd ray,
As he rush'd past in angry mood,
To write the crescent's fame in blood
But Roland, when, through war's red tide,
He saw the Zegri chieftain ride,
Sprung fiercely on, to do or die,
With fury dark'ning in his eye,
While his soul reel'd beneath the shock
Of passions which revenge awoke.
Why does the Zegri's falchion fail,
And the red light of his eye grow pale ?
With his own name the battle echoes rung,
While through the war-dust Roland fiercely sprung.
In vain he nerv'd his arm, remember'd well
Upon his ear that voice in thunder fell
In vain he thought of former times,
'Twas but the memory of crimes,
The widow's curse, the orphan's tears,
He strove to wrestle down his fears

But could not spurn their base control,
For guilt sat heavy on his soul
Yet rising courage nerv'd the spear
To bear him on his last career.
They meet , the spear has pierc'd his side ;
In death arose a hero's pride ;
He turn'd in wrath, and with an angry glare,
Laugh'd the short laugh of resolute despair,
And met the flashing falchion well,
Although in just revenge it fell
Here where the eddying war-dust roll'd
    Like the billows of the main,
And the blue banner's ample fold
    Had caught a darker stain,
The life-blood of the brave who died,
To guard that banner's sacred pride
As war's wild scream in thunder broke,
The energies of man awoke,
And squadrons dizzy with delight,
Swept thickly to the rising fight,
        Forgetful of their care.
'Tis well for man in savage mood
To joy in battle's angry flood ;
'Tis well for man in war to die
Beneath the glance of honour's eye;
        But what does woman there ?
With trembling hand and failing breath,
To overlook the toil of Death,
Sat Clara, fiercely nerv'd by grief,
Alone to snatch the last relief.
Oh, gaze not on that brow so fair,
The paleness of the tomb is there :
Ye saw of late the tender light
Which stole through lashes dark as night,
Just shading with their soft control
The beaming shrine of Clara's soul.
Then turn away—ye could not bear
The ghastly contrast of despair.
Yet as she watch'd, her eye was fraught
With wild intensity of thought.

And now a spark of living light
Would flash, then all again was night.
Dark is the strife where fiery zeal
On both sides whets the angry steel :
And well is prov'd, by deadly deed,
How fix'd each army in its creed.
The hours roll on ; with darker rage,
The ranks, though thinning fast, engage.
That morning, at the trumpet sound,
Each heart, with one triumphant bound,
   Leapt at the fierce appeal ;
They thought the plain which lay beneath,
The field of glory, not of Death,
   And wav'd the ready steel.
But now long hours of blood are past,
That gallant spirit fled at last.
As with parch'd lips and failing hand,
They still wave high the blood-stain'd brand,
And darker grows the wave of fight,
In every eye gleams wilder light,
And every brow has fiercer grown
Beneath the blackness of a frown.
That morning, when the plumes wav'd high,
   And throbb'd the swelling vein,
Each chieftain's rising battle-cry
   Peal'd wildly o'er the plain.
That morning, in their rush of pride,
   The trumpet rung a thrilling knell
O'er every chief who bravely died ,
   And falchions, as they rose and fell,
Were gleaming in a track of light,
Like flashes on a summer night.
That spark of glory's living fire,
Which, noble in her wildest ire,
   Pointed the morning steel,
Was sinking, and at every stroke
A darker feeling now awoke—
   Not such as heroes feel.
Then, as each chieftain caught the flame,
   The falchion's angry blow,

With nearer, surer, deadlier aim,
  Fell silently and slow.
The trumpets o'er the battle wave
  Sent forth a shriller tone—
The Moor is breaking; on, ye brave,
  And make the field your own.
Each warrior rais'd his battle cry,
To swell the notes of victory;
And the faint echoes of the dying,
Who lay e'en death itself defying,
Peal'd solemn on each Moorish ear,
An omen of defeat and fear;
As o'er the field, with slaughter warm,
Each band array'd itself, to form
  The last exulting charge.
Vain was the Moorish breast of rock
Against the Spaniard's earthquake shock.
Away, away! in that wild course
Down went the rider and his horse,
  The helmet and the targe.
Yet onward swept that eager throng,
More rapid as it rush'd along,
Nor deign'd to cast one glance below,
On the red mass of friend and foe.
Where are the lion warriors now,
  The lords of the snow white steed?
Have they not met their country's foe,
  In their country's cause to bleed?
They have—the lords of the snow-white steed
  Lie welt'ring in their gore;
They lie, from care and danger freed,
  Who fought alone before
Their blood has dried on every glaive
That pierc'd the bosoms of the brave.
And Roland, who had borne away
The prize of glory in the fray,
Though the red gush of many a wound
  Foretold approaching death,
Had fought, unsparing all around,
  Until his parting breath

Had mingled with the shout which spoke
Redemption from the Moorish yoke.
They bore him from the glorious field;
They bore him on his victor shield,
Yet straining in a nerveless hand,
The remnant of his broken brand,
Which high above the ranks of war
Gleam'd like a red and angry star,
And first, though feebly, glimmer'd high
In the wild rush of victory
They laid him in his lonely tomb
Amid the depth of the forest gloom :
They buried with its hero lord,
The remnant of his broken sword,
That sword which cleft the galling chain,
That bound the Christian sons of Spain
And Clara saw the cold earth close
Upon the form that caus'd her woes—
She paus'd to see them raise the stone,
The monument of glories gone—
She paus'd to read the hero's fate—
And felt that she was desolate.

     *   *   *

And years have seen the sylvan gloom
   Wave o'er the turf below,
Wave o'er the hero's silent tomb—
   It is not lonely now.
Another stone has risen there
   To share its sacred fame,
And many a flow'ret scents the air—
   Ye need not ask the name.

                            MALEK

REMARKS ON GIFFORD'S FORD.

(Continued from page 68.)

We shall now proceed to redeem the pledge given to

our readers, by laying before them two specimens of
Ford's pathetic powers : not without the hope that those,
who, from accident or prejudice, have as yet never
enjoyed his beauties, will now be induced by this humble effort to atone for their former negligence.   Our first
extract shall be from that painfully-interesting play, which
stands second in the present edition.   We know few
dramatic chef-d'œuvres that possess so irresistible a
power over the feelings.   At first our indistinct knowledge of the dreadful tale acts upon us like a spell, we
shrink back as from the glare of a disagreeable picture ;
we are afraid to open the page which is to harrow up
our every sensation, and to familiarize us with horrors.
But when this first impression wears off, when the phantoms of the poet's creation begin to pass in array before
us, the bold fatalism of Giovanni, the bewildered tenderness of Annabella, the feeble benevolence of the old
friar, and the fiendish concentration of purpose which
marks Hippolita, then are we indeed spell-bound, but it
is with the genius of a mighty poet.   Then our attention
becomes fascinated by the gradual development of the
plot, and the silent workings of the heart begin to have
their full effect.   Then are we irresistibly transported
into the very midst of the situations he describes : we
are the creatures, and the playthings of the poet's will,
and gradually, but surely, his characters assume in our
minds the clothing of reality ; taking their place there
"without corrival" immediately after the Lears, the
Juliets, and the Othellos, which have twined round our
memory since earliest boyhood.   We shall select the first
scene, which the editor calls "replete with excellence

as a composition;" and that in the fifth act, where
Giovanni adds the last, and darkest, to his black catalogue
of villanies, by murdering his sister.

ACT I.—*Scene I.*

Friar BONAVENTURA'S *Cell.*

Enter FRIAR *and* GIOVANNI.

Friar. Dispute no more in this : for know, young man,
    These are no school-points ; nice philosophy
    May tolerate unlikely arguments,
    But Heaven admits no jest : wits that presumed
    On wit too much, by striving how to prove
    There was no God, with foolish grounds of art,
    Discover'd first the nearest way to hell,
    And fill'd the world with dev'lish atheism.
    Such questions, youth, are fond . far better 'tis
    To bless the sun than reason why it shines ;
    Yet He thou talk'st of, is above the sun.
    No more ! I may not hear it.
Gio.   Gentle father,
    To you I have unclasp'd my burden'd soul,
    Emptied the storehouse of my thoughts and heart,
    Made myself poor of secrets ; have not left
    Another word untold which hath not spoke
    All what I ever durst, or think, or know ,
    And yet is here the comfort I shall have ?
    Must I not do what all men else may—love ?
Friar. Yes, you may love, fair son.
Gio   Must I not praise
    That beauty, which, if framed anew, the gods
    Would make a god of, if they had it there ;
    And kneel to it, as I do kneel to them '
Friar. Why, foolish madman '
Gio.   Shall a peevish sound,
    A customary form, from man to man,
    Of brother, and of sister, be a bar
    'Twixt my perpetual happiness and me ?
    Say, that we had one father, say one womb

(Curse to my joy !) gave both us life and birth ;
Are we not, therefore, each to other bound
So much the more by nature ? by the links
Of blood, and reason ? nay, if you will have it,
E'en of religion, to be ever one,
One soul, one flesh, one love, one heart, one all ?

Friar. Have done, unhappy youth, for thou art lost.

Gio.   No, father, in your eyes I see the change
Of pity, and compassion ; from your age,
As from a sacred oracle, distils
The life of counsel : tell me, holy man,
What cure shall give me ease in these extremes ?

Friar. Repentance, son, and sorrow for this sin :
For thou hast moved a Majesty above,
With thy unranged (almost) blasphemy.

Gio.   O do not speak of that, dear confessor.

Friar. Art thou, my son, that miracle of wit,
Who once, within these three months, wert esteemed
A wonder of thine age throughout Bononia ?
How did the university applaud
Thy government, behaviour, learning, speech,
Sweetness, and all that could make up a man !
I was proud of my tutelage, and chose
Rather to leave my books than part with thee ;
I did so, but the fruit of all my hopes
Are lost in thee, as thou art in thyself.
O Giovanni ! hast thou left the schools
Of knowledge, to converse with lust, and death ?
For death waits on thy lust.   Look thro' the world,
And thou shalt see a thousand faces shine
More glorious than this idol thou adorest :
Leave her, and take thy choice, 'tis much less sin,
Tho' in such games as those, they lose, who win.

Gio.   It were more ease to stop the ocean
From flows, and ebbs, than to dissuade my vows.

Friar. Then I have done, and in thy wilful flames
Already see thy ruin ; Heav'n is just.
Yet hear my counsel.

Gio.   As a voice of life !

Friar. Hie to thy father's house, there lock thee fast
Alone within thy chamber ; then fall down

On both thy knees, and grovel on the ground :
Cry to thy heart, wash every word thou utter'st
In tears (and if 't be possible) of blood '
Beg Heaven to cleanse the leprosy of lust
That rots thy soul · acknowledge what thou art,
A wretch, a worm, a nothing . weep, sigh, pray,
Three times a-day, and three times every night
For seven days space do this ; then if thou find'st
No change in thy desires, return to me,
I'll think on remedy.   Pray for thyself
At home, whilst I pray for thee here.—Away !
My blessing with thee ! we have need to pray.

Gio   All this I'll do, to free me from the rod
Of vengeance , else I'll swear my fate's my god.   [*Exeunt.*]
             ' 'Tis pity she's a Whore."—*Act 1.*

Act V.—*Scene V.*

ANNABELLA *and* GIOVANNI.

Gio.   What danger's half so great as thy revolt ?
Thou art a faithless sister, else thou know'st
Malice, or any treachery besides,
Would stoop to my bent brows ; why, I hold fate
Clasped in my fist, and could command the course
Of time's eternal motion, hadst thou been
One thought more steady than an ebbing sea.
   *   *   *   *   *   *   *   *

Ann. Be not deceived, my brother,
This banquet is an harbinger of death
To you and me ; resolve yourself it is,
And be prepared to welcome it.

Gio. Well, then !
The schoolmen teach that all this globe of earth
Shall be consumed to ashes in a minute.

Ann. So I have read too.

Gio. But, 'twere somewhat strange
To see the waters burn ; could I believe
This might be true, I could believe as well,
There might be hell, or heaven.

Ann. That's most certain.

Gio.   A dream, a dream ! else in this other world
    We should know one another.

Ann.   So we shall.

Gio.   Have you heard so ?

Ann.   For certain.

Gio.   But do you think
    That I shall see *you* there ? You look on me ;
    May we kiss one another, prate, or laugh,
    Or do, as we do here ?

Ann.   I know not that ;
    But—brother, for the present, what d'ye mean
    To free yourself from danger ? some way think
    How to escape ; I'm sure the guests are come.

Gio.   Look up, look here ; what see you in my face ?

Ann.   Distraction, and a troubled conscience.

Gio.   Death, and a swift repining wrath :—yet look—
    What see you in mine eyes ?

Ann.   Methinks you weep.

Gio.   I do indeed ; these are the funeral tears
    Shed on your grave ; these furrow'd up my cheeks
    When first I lov'd, and knew not how to woo.
    Fair Annabella, should I here repeat
    The story of my life, we might lose time.
    Be record all the spirits of the air,
    And all things else that are, that day and night,
    Early and late, the tribute which my heart
    Hath paid to Annabella's sacred love,
    Hath been these tears, which are her mourners now !
    Never till now did Nature do her best,
    To show a matchless beauty to the world,
    Which in an instant, ere it scarce was seen,
    The jealous Destinies required again.
    Pray, Annabella, pray ! since we must part,
    Go thou, white in thy soul, to fill a throne
    Of innocence, and sanctity, in heaven.
    Pray, pray, my sister !

Ann.   Then I see your drift—
    Ye blessed angels guard me !

Gio.   So say I :
    Kiss me. If ever after-times should hear

Of our fast-knit affections, tho' perhaps
The laws of conscience and of civil use
May blame us justly, yet when they but know
Our loves, that love will wipe away that rigour,
Which would in other incests be abhorred.
Give me your hand : how sweetly life doth run
In these well-coloured veins ! how constantly
These palms do promise health ! but I could chide
With nature for this cunning flattery—
Kiss me again—forgive me.

Ann. With my heart.
Gio. Farewell !
Ann. Will you be gone ?
Gio. Be dark, bright sun,
And make this mid-day night, that thy gilt rays
May not behold a deed will turn their splendor
More sooty than the poets feign their Styx !
One other kiss, my sister.

Ann. What means this ?
Gio. To save thy fame, and kill thee in a kiss,
Thus die, and die by me, and by my hand. [*Stabs her.*]
Revenge is mine ; honour doth love command.

Ann. O brother, by your hand !
Gio. When thou art dead,
I'll give my reasons for it ; to dispute
With thy (even in thy death) most lovely beauty,
Would make me stagger to perform this act
Which I most glory in.

Ann. Forgive him heaven : and me my sins—farewell,
Brother unkind, unkind—mercy, great heaven ! [*Dies.*]

    " '*Tis pity she's a Whore.*"—*Act V. Scene V.*

Our extracts have not been of the shortest; but the
energy and pathos of the quotations will, we are sure,
bear us out in the estimation of our readers. The last
will remind the most superficial observer of the famous
scene in Othello ; the same desperate struggle between
love and distraction ; the same attempt to varnish over
an inexpiable deed of blood by the sophistry of doing

"*nought in hate, but all in honour ;*" but there stops the
resemblance.   The noble and ardent, but misguided
Moor is nearly as superior a being to the impure and
frantic Giovanni, as innocent Desdemona is to the guilty,
though not altogether abandoned, character who forms
the groundwork of Ford's drama.   That any audience
should have permitted such a story to have been represented, may well appear surprising ; but it is to be remembered, that the system of personating female characters by boys, which in our author's days was the constant practice of the stage, was the principal inducement
to men of uncontrollable imagination and commanding
intellect to grasp at subjects beyond the pale of our
natural feelings, and to luxuriate in the display of powers
which their audience scarcely knew whether most to
shudder at, or to admire.   That any actress, however,
should have taken up the part of Annabella, would of
course be pronounced incredible ; yet such is the influence of custom on the manners and peculiarities of
nations, that not only has one of the greatest poets of
modern times chosen a subject of a similar nature ; but
this very character of Mirra, performed by a female, is a
high favourite at such Italian theatres, as, in spite of
Austrian bayonets, and an enervating atmosphere, still
prefer nourishing the heart by bursts of tragic grandeur, to
cultivating the ear by the monotony of an opera recitative.

The Broken Heart has the advantage of being on a
less painful subject.   It is a tale of love, agony, and
death : original, we believe, as to the conduct, and singularly striking as to the winding up of the plot.   Although Mr. Campbell probably went too far when he

asserted that "Ford interests us in no passion, but in
that of love;" there can be no doubt, that in depicting
love he principally excels.   When we recollect, that with
the exception of Otway, no writer, perhaps, since the
Restoration has escaped the sickly infection of the French
love-scenes, with how much pleasure should we not look
back on Ford, as being in this respect the " *Ultimus
Romanorum!*" We shall not enter at length on the
merits of the question, which has so long divided the
most eminent critics—we mean, the probability of that
scene in which Calantha, in spite of the calamities which
are momentarily announced to her, continues the revelry
in which the court is engaged, and though her mind is
shaken to its centre, preserves the external countenance
of health and pleasure.   In this war of critics, *magno
se judice quisque tuetur,* Mr. Gifford, and Mr. Hazlitt, are
on one side: Mr. Lamb, and the Edinburgh Review, on
the other !   But, while we refer the curious reader to
their more elaborate arguments on this point, we shall
just observe, that it is rather too much to expect the
audience of the Globe, to pare down their likings and
dislikings to a level with those of a Drury-lane pit; or
that the merry critics of the Mermaid should sympa-
thise with the loungers in Mr. Murray's drawing-room!
Surely there is nothing absolutely unnatural in the supposition, that Calantha, fearing to drive her soul back on
its own resources, lest she should quail in spirit before
her arduous duties were performed, strives for a time with
the full rush of her grief, and calls in the aid of choral
revelry to combat those emotions, by indulging which,
her country might be ruined.   It is unquestionably a
terribly-contrived scene; but unnatural we cannot think

it: and it would shew equal unfairness and narrowness of mind, to judge merely by the standard of our more refined and feebler taste, of those terrible bursts of dramatic power, which were so frequently called forth by the fantastic genius of the older poets.

(To be continued.)

ON UTOPIA.

———— Arva, beata
Petamus arva, divites et insulas.—Hor.

What and where is Utopia? That dwelling place of all that is blissful on earth; that scene of more than human delight; that country which every enthusiast has peopled with the creatures of his own imagination, and given them occupations consistent with his ideas of felicity; what and where, I say, is that country, in which alone the *"summum bonum"* is to be found? Whether does it repose on the tranquil bosom of the Pacific, or brave the surges of the Atlantic; is it to be discovered amid the fervour of the torrid zone, or in the genial climate of the temperate? where shall we place, and how shall we define, this island of islands, this Paradise upon earth; where no wish is without its completion, and where no care can dwell; where all inclinations are alike satisfied; in short, where that true and perfect felicity, which, though continually sought, has never yet been found, exists in its genuine and primitive excellence?

What is Utopia? "Utopia," cries Lady Arabella Wilmot, "is a town where there is perpetual spring, so that nobody thinks of going into the country; where every body dines at sunset, and goes to bed at sunrise; where there are no vulgar people, that get up before noon, where every house has a ball and concert room, and where new novels are published every day."

What is Utopia? "Utopia," simpers Miss Selina Sensitive, " is a country where the trees are always clothed with the freshest verdure ; where Philomela pours forth her plaintive melody the livelong night; where Cynthia's orb is never veiled in clouds ; where the lambkins frisk along the grassy meads ; where all nature bears tokens of innocence and love."

What is Utopia? " Utopia," growls Mr. John Timon, " is a cluster of islands, with one inhabitant in each, and a sea so stormy between them as to prevent all intercourse; they are all well stocked with animals, particularly mastiffs, for they fawn upon none but those they love."

What is Utopia? " Utopia," swears Mr. Augustus Dashaway, " is a place where there are no duns nor blacklegs, where there are horses to which Eclipse is but a cart-horse, and Childers a market-woman's pad-nag : Where every body keeps up the honour of the turf; and where no one is invisible on settling day."

What is Utopia? " Utopia," grunts Mr. Gastrophilus Gourmand, " is an island on whose shores are turtle, and in whose forests are deer ; where French cooks constitute a great proportion of the population; and where the air is so pure, that one is never at a loss for appetite; where the wines are of the first quality, and where nobody eats fewer than seven meals per diem."

What is Utopia? Mr. John Simpkins affirms, that Utopia is a place where every body minds his own business, and leaves other people to mind theirs · where pro perty is secure without the precaution of bars and bolts; where debts are paid without the interference of a bailiff; where every thing is conducted upon the principles of fair dealing, and where no monopolies are allowed.

"Utopia!" cried Bombastes Fustiano. "Utopia is like the garden of the Hesperides; Utopia is like the groves of Elysium; whatever delights Nature from her heavenly treasury draws forth she loves to shower upon Utopia; joys interminable; pleasures ineffable; matchless, supernatural, irresistible afflations of sublime, empyreal rapture; these, these are the joys of Utopia; these are the emanations which gladden this seat of the blessed, this habitation of incontaminate felicity; this unimpairable, undefinable, undiscoverable Paradise."

"Utopia!" whispers Bartholomew Bouverie, "Utopia is to be found at home: to what purpose do we delude our minds with dreams of happiness, and think that in another climate those joys are to be found, which spring alone from a contented mind. Is it in the power of season or of place to change the affections of the heart; or, if it were, would it be for our advantage to be freed from those petty annoyances which give a double zest to the manifold pleasures we enjoy? No: in vain does that man seek for tranquillity who seeks it only in change of scene, and variety of occupation; while the greatest, the most important change, the reformation of his own mind, remains unaccomplished."

What, then, is Utopia? Utopia is that nurse of liberty, that empress of the world, whose name is *England*. In vain may we traverse the colures to find her equal; if happiness is to be found upon earth, assuredly England is her dwelling-place. The various scenes of the world

may afford gratification to the traveller; the discovery of
new lands may please the scientific; the sailor may view
with triumph the banner of his country waving over
islands hitherto unknown; but where is the man who has
not hailed the white cliffs of Albion as the boundary of
all that is dear to him upon earth.

But with the blessing of a contented mind, Utopia
may even be found in a desert. What child of Arabia
would change the sands of his country for the pastures
of Andalusia; or would quit the tents of his fathers,
might he inhabit the halls of the Escurial? So true are
the words of the poet:

> Such is the patriot's boast, where'er we roam,
> His first, best country, ever is at home.

THE BATTLE OF THE BOYNE.

Calm flow'd the stream, nor seem'd to hear,
Or sign, or murmur, boding fear,
Flash'd all around in bright career
    The Orange Standard's chivalry.
A monarch check'd his courser bold
One moment, where the blue waves roll'd,
And " On," he cried, " On, to uphold
    The Orange Standard's gallantry !"
An instant—and the cannons roar
Shook to its base each frighted shore;
Yet still aloft those warriors bore
    The Orange Standard's majesty.
Then throbb'd each soldier's blood with ire,
As blaz'd around the battle's fire;
And still they saw wave high, and higher,
    That Orange Standard's canopy.
The Stuart saw his bravest die,
The red light darken'd in his eye;
For flight and gloom foretold it nigh—
    That Orange Standard's victory

Morn show'd three kingdoms lost and won :
The steel is sheath'd—the strife is done ;
Right glorious 'mid the sunbeams shone
　　The Orange Standard's brilliancy.
Land of the hero and the sage,
England ! thro' many a hoary age,
When tempests swell, and whirlwinds rage,
　　That Standard is thy panoply !

ROLAND.

[We extract the following Stanzas from a Copy of Verses which we
　　have received from a Correspondent.]

SWITZERLAND.

Sweet are thy waters, sweet the glee
　　Of peasant's evening lay,
Who, gliding o'er the crystal sea,
　　Beguile their easy way.

　　　　　＊　　　　＊　　　　＊

Tho' sunny smiles, to nature dear,
　　May shed their happy light,
No rays can pierce, no beauties cheer
　　Oppression's gloomy night.

'Twas sweet, I said, thy *ranz de vaches,*
　　Borne the still waters o'er,
Scarce broken by the soften'd splash
　　Of some fair peasant's oar ;

Tho' always sweet, far sweeter now,
　　Now freedom is its theme,
I love to see that gen'rous glow
　　In ev'ry bright eye beam.

The chamois, as the zephyrs, free,
　　Bounds o'er the fairy dale—
That happy heart, that liberty
　　Shall Switzerland bewail.

　　　　　＊　　　　＊　　　　＊

THE POSTMAN.—No. II.

Mr. Editor—

On my return to Eton the other day, I received an agreeable surprise on hearing of your periodical work, and determined to submit to your perusal an account of my journey.

As it is useless to enumerate at length the minutiæ of travelling preparations, and their attendant inconveniences, you may imagine me seated inside of the Old Windsor Original ; our party consisted of five, including myself, and although not our proper complement, was equivalent to it; for a stout gentleman, with a gold-headed cane, occupied at least the room of two common-sized persons; my other fellow travellers, were a lady most fashionably dressed, and two other gentlemen, one of whom appeared totally absorbed in contemplation, the other a young looking fellow, whose appearance denoted him to be, what is vulgarly called, a shabby-genteel. Having examined with the greatest accuracy, the physiognomy of each individual, I determined, for the sake of amusement, to discover, if possible, their professions and pursuits, by attending to their conversation and actions.   We at first sat with that dislike which people not too good-natured usually conceive towards each other on first acquaintance.   The coach at length jumbled us insensibly into some sort of familiarity; we had not proceeded in our journey above four miles, when the lady addressed herself to me, " Really, Sir, our progress is excessively slow, we do not advance much above a yard in the space of a minute; but if, Sir, it is not an impertinent question, would you be so obliging as to inform me what ·

was the prime cost of that cravat you are wearing? I am quite in love with it, it is real Gros de Naples silk." I immediately concluded my fair querist was a *milliner*.

My attention was next directed to the contemplative philosopher, who, after a strict examination of the stout gentleman's features, had actually pulled off his brown bob wig, begging him at the same time ten thousand pardons for his rudeness, but that the love of science and research must plead as his excuse; adding, as some compensation, that he had the organ of *positiveness, or knocking down* very strongly depicted by a tumulus or mound on the occipital superficies. The old fellow, good humouredly replied, that all the technical phrases, tumulus, occipital, &c., were perfect Hebrew to him, and that if he knocked any thing down, it was always with a hammer. The speaker then relapsed into his former taciturnity, excepting that when the coach was starting, after having changed horses, or any other stoppage, he invariably exclaimed, "going, gentlemen— going— gone," at the same time suiting the action to the word, by knocking with his cane on the bottom of the vehicle; from which circumstance, and from his exclamations, I was induced to suppose he was an *auctioneer*.

The philosopher then addressed the young man who had just killed a fly on the coach window, examining his head at the same time very attentively. "Young man, the Organ of Destructiveness, or Murder, is strongly marked on your pericranium, and the unjustifiable cruelty you have been guilty of, plainly proves the truth of my assertion." The youth replied, in his defence, that the fly had merited its death, because it had turned out a *roarer*, owing to which circumstance it had lost a race with another of its species, and my right-hand waistcoat pocket has lost a sovereign, which was wagered against one in the left-hand pocket. The philosopher replied, that the alleged reason, in his opinion, by no means justified the murder, and why the poor insect should suffer death for *buzzing*, which he supposed was the meaning of the word roarer; or why buzzing, which was the innate faculty of the whole species, should at all prevent speed; he could not understand. I had just determined in my own mind, that the philosopher was either Dr. Spurzheim in propriâ personâ, or else one of his disciples, and that the young man was a black-leg on his road to Ascot, when a person genteelly dressed entered the coach; he had scarcely taken his seat before he launched out into politics, saying he was intimate with a certain great man; could not mention names; was personally acquainted with lord——and other ministers, and ended his harangue by asking my opinion concerning the new administration. I concluded he was a profound politician; but the next day, when I made an inquiry concerning him, I discovered he was a butler to a certain nobleman, and had only thought proper to ape his master's manners.

Perhaps, Mr. Bouverie, you will think these few observations worth inserting, as illustrative of the different characters of my fellow travellers; the first description of persons, owing to their natural simplicity of manners and conversation, discover their real condition in life; but the other by affecting to be what they are not, deceive, for the time, the superficial observer, but when they are detected, obtain a double portion of well-merited contempt: I am, Sir, &c.

T. G. K.

To Bartholomew Bouverie, *Esq.*

Mr. Bouverie ;

I am a young gentleman, but an old politician, and shall esteem it a particular favour if you will tell me whether there is any truth or not in the report, that a Debating Society has been established at Eton. As I was talking over affairs in general the other day with an old acquaintance of mine, having lighted on our old topic, *politics,* I happened to lament the very unconstitutional education which Englishmen receive at our public schools. As soon as any glimmerings of sense are perceived, the mind of the urchin is immediately crammed full of *As in præsenti, Propria quæ maribus,* and such like, in which the poor victim finds less *sense,* than his torturers do *poetry*—and that is saying a great deal ! Now if, on the contrary, he were to be properly imbued with the " *blessings of the Constitution under which we live,*" * * * [Here follows so much that is political, that we have been obliged to curtail our worthy correspondent's epistle, in the very part, perhaps, which he considers the most valuable]. I concluded with declaring I did not believe six boys at Eton knew who was Prime Minister, and that there was not one who did not look forwards with more anxiety to the event of the next *Derby,* than to that of the *Catholic Question.* When I had concluded, a few gruff mutterings, and half-frowns from my friend, who, being on the wrong side of sixty, has a little touch of the " Diable de Contradiction," ushered in the following characteristic speech : " They do, Sir ! You're quite out, Sir ! The very chicks, just out of the shell, chirp

politics! More shame for 'em! When I was a boy, I
never minded any thing but my book, and I didn't mind
that much! Sir, I tell you its a speculative age this!
Why, Sir, here's a letter from my nephew, Matthew
Jenkins—a fine boy, if he wasn't spoiled—just rising
thirteen—and, hark ye! what he talks about—Liberal
principles — progress of civilization — narrow-minded
bigotry—and then here's the varlet's finale—'In short, .
you'll excuse me, my dear Uncle, if I tell you, however well
you might have suited the world three hundred years ago,
you are positively quite out of place in *the nineteenth
century.*' An impudent vagabond! I used to take a
pleasure in having him to dine with me, and regularly
gave him a sovereign at dessert; but I'm afraid the scamp
would put arsenic in my plate now, just to rid the nineteenth century of a bigot, and would fling my money in
my face, and say, he was above corruption! .

. "An Eton Debating Society, too! Pugh! pugh! Keep
'em to book and birch, Sir, and leave their politics to take
care of themselves!" I was so much amused with my
old friend's account of the matter, that I determined to
give the heads of our conversation to the World under
the auspices of the *Eton Miscellany.*

I am, Mr. Bouverie,

your's, very dutifully,

QUIDNUNC.

To BARTHOLOMEW BOUVERIE, *Esq.*,

THE ETON PREMIER, &c. &c.

Sir;—Though I have never before had the honour of
addressing you, I have no doubt I may so far presume

on your good nature as to ask whether it is really fact, that a society now exists at, or in the vicinity of, Eton, for the purpose of encouraging the only thing that can render life valuable to a reasonable mind, I mean, of course, *talking politics*. I have, myself, the honour of belonging to at least one hundred clubs, unions, and societies, existing and flourishing throughout the united empire; and should, although a nurseling of Merchant-tailors' myself, esteem it as the highest of honors, could I but be admitted as an honorary member of an association, meeting, perhaps, on the very spot which Chatham, Fox and Canning, have hallowed for ever by the emanations of their genius. When I consider, Mr. President—I beg pardon—(the force of association is so strong, that my oratorical propensity finds its way into my very letters)—I mean, when I consider, Mr. Bouverie, that I am writing at this moment from the round table of the *Cockspur-street Union*—than the members of which a more highly-gifted assemblage is hardly to be found, though candour obliges me to confess their *cravats* are nine times out of ten inferior in brilliancy to their *eloquence*, and their *hands* stand no comparison in point of purity with their *principles!* when I consider that I made my début in the well-known Constitutional Club at the Seven Dials, amidst, what I may well term, *popular* applause; that I have, since my noviciate, been successively elected to a seat in the Grimstead Convention, in the Ballynaclough Company, in the Thames and Medway Reform Meeting, in the Newcastle Luminary, in the John o'Groat's Political Beacon—but I had well nigh forgotten that I am not writing to make a parade of my old honours, but to request the addition of new. I will then only add that,

like Petrarch in the good old days of the revival of literature, when he received, in the same day, a letter from
the king of France and another from the king of Naples,
both requesting him to confer on them the inexpressible
honour of receiving a laurel crown from their hands in
their dominions, so my unworthy self has this morning
received a letter from the Labrador Association, for the
purpose of republicanizing the Esquimaux ; and another
from the Burrampooter Imperialists, who have already
brought to maturity (of course this is *entre nous)* a plan
for restoring the Great Mogul to his hereditary throne !
I do not mention this out of vanity, but merely to shew
you it is from no deficiency of friends, but from a sincere
affection for Eton, that I address myself to you on this
delicate subject.   Believe me, ·

Your's, very truly,

CHRISTOPHER CHRONICLE.

My dear Public, what can I do with Christopher
Chronicle, how can I tell him civilly that I sadly suspect him of being a *hoaxer ?* (there is a more melodious
dissyllable in the language, but 'tis not one half so civil !)
How can I tell him, should he abjure the Munchausen
school, that no " one but an Etonian" can be admitted
as an honorary member of a Society, which we feel
happy in being able to acquaint Mr. Quidnunc, has existed here *for sixteen years ?* ·

ETON MISCELLANY,

No. IV.

———◆———

INTRODUCTION.

HAVING, after the fashion of the most approved stage-players, made a low bow to the public, in an engaging attitude, and with a graceful demeanor, in return for the plaudits which we will suppose to have greeted, and at this present moment to be greeting, my fourth appearance on the Eton boards, I must confess, though the Galleries hoot, and the Pit frown, and the Boxes alone hold out an encouraging aspect, that I am grievously deficient in my part, and stand in great need of a prompter. A prompter! the Gods have heard my ejaculation, and have immediately furnished me with one, yclept GRATITUDE. Gratitude shall supply me with abundant matter wherewith to meet the public expectation and satiate the greediness with which, I doubt not, they open this Number. —"Thanks for past favours" ... "undeserved patronage" ... "hope to merit continuance" ... "unremitting assiduity" ... "grateful acknowledgments"—all, and more than these phrases tumultuously rush upward to get possession of my tongue, and to find utterance by my mouth. No wonder, then, if my enunciatory organ be overwhelmed by such a weight and such a multitude of expressions, as to leave me absolutely speechless in the very face of my friends. Wherefore, since all imaginable modes of

K

acknowledging obligation have already been pre-occupied
—since they are as old as hackney coaches, and have been
used as vehicles by as many and as various descriptions
of people—and since I wish to find for myself paths to
public estimation which are

> "—— Nullius ante
> Trita solo ——"

I will content myself with showing my afore-mentioned
prompter, or promptress, to the public; and, having so
done, despatch her behind the scenes, till another occasion (which I hope may soon arrive) shall make me
require her assistance again : in the mean time, she may
remain ready with a few phrases culled from the huge
mass which she carries about with her for sale, in order
to help me on in case my "*torrens dicendi copia*" should
desert me.

I think myself bound, as in my Second Number
I informed the public, that I had been, and should continue till further notice, entirely ETONIAN, to let them
know that now, for the first time, I have admitted two
compositions, selected from a great number with which
I have been favoured, which are the work of those who,
although my contemporaries, are not at present to be
designated as "Eton boys." I mean those headed "Discovery of Madeira," and "Stanzas."

But, as I believe my character for veracity has never
been impeached, and I can make an asseveration, with
some chance of being believed—I take this opportunity of
declaring, that it is not weakness or deficiency here, that
has occasioned my taking this step. The fact is, that I,
a most extraordinary being, am composed of as many and

of as refractory limbs as the body in the fable, of which my
old friend Menenius Agrippa made so exemplary an
use.   The case is exactly parallel, and I only hope the
application may - have as good an effect as it is said
(*credat Judæus Apella*) to have had then.   In short,
my legs, occasionally, will not walk; my hand throws
down the pen in disgust; and even my head, though I
hope it never deserts me, frequently complains of being
muddled, or addled, or something to that effect.   My
eyes cannot endure the sight of a proof-sheet; and my
ears are grievously startled when the footstep of my right
trusty and well-beloved publisher is heard approaching
my room-door.   Now, all will be aware that besides the
general utility of having more than one string to one's
bow, it will, in my circumstances, be peculiarly convenient to have a corps de reserve of contributors; as, by
following the maxim—

" Divide et impera——"

I shall probably be able to play one set of them against
another, and thus keep all in good condition and due
subordination.

Inability ! Bartholomew rejects the idea with scorn:
he will remain game : he will fight till his last drop of
blood, and write till his last bottle of ink, be expended.
Though Mr. Rice should abscond, thereby removing from
me no inconsiderable portion of my physical powers,
and should wrap his head in impenetrable clouds—
though Mr. Heaviside should march off with one of my
legs—though Mr. Jermyn, partaking abundantly of the
irritability of his species, should claim to himself the
other—still, though cruelly mutilated and miserably

K 2

mangled, I will follow the glorious example of the hero
of Chevy Chase—

> " For when his legs were smitten off
> He fought upon his stumps."

When, indeed, my pen (made of the best patent metal,
warranted to last *for six months*) is worn down to
the stump, and my sword survives only in its handle; when
I, being now stout, portly, and healthful, am worn to a
skeleton, or battered into a mummy, then, indeed, I will
quit the scene of contest.

But this is a state to which I hope I shall never be
reduced : when the general voice cries, "Mr. Bartholomew,
we have had enough of you," I shall, as in duty bound,
put an end to my existence, even though thereby I may
run some risk of a verdict of *felo de se,* with some such
epitaph as this over me—

> Here lieth Bartle Bouverie :
> A merry soul and a quaint was he ;
> He lived for gain, he wrote for pelf,
> Then took his pen, and stabb'd himself.

My readers will perhaps say, that the fate of any one
will be miserable indeed who is doomed to have such an
execrable inscription graven on his tomb-stone—nor can
I deny it—but, as it is to the public that I owe my existence, it would be by no means fair in me to endeavour
to protract it, when they had shown a wish for my dissolution.   Till then, I shall strain every nerve to afford
satisfaction to my readers : and as long as my aforesaid
worthy publisher's shop is crowded with customers on
my mornings of publication, so long shall I endeavour to
work all my limbs in unison for the production of some-

thing which may not entirely disgrace the name of my foster-mother.

And when the time shall come, as come it must, I also must do my best to meet it with fortitude and resignation ; I also must strive to depart with decency and gravity. ‾ Whether my shade may flit around the scenes where I myself have lived so long, and enjoyed so many pleasures, I know not ; I cannot expect that

> "The Majesty of Darkness shall
> Receive my parting ghost ‧"

but, while I disclaim all indifference, and feel with fervour every tribute of approbation paid to me, there are some of gentle mould and merciful disposition who will, I hope, look back at least without displeasure on the era and the works of

BARTHOLOMEW BOUVERIE.

SENSE *versus* NONSENSE.

My dear Reader, which do you prefer ? May I hope, for my own sake, that you will not give the palm to the first ? A dull, dry monitor, that does nothing but curb your gaiety, and compel you to creep circumspectly along, where you might have blundered laughingly and happily through life. Fair reader, if you be fair, or female (which terms, of course, are synonymous), have you ever had, on the same ball-night, a sensible and a nonsensical partner ? You must have had both, or, if you have not, you, at any rate, will suppose for a moment that you have, and politely agree with me in your recollections of their behaviour. Did not your sensible friend go through the

quadrille, like an automaton, as stiff and as unentertain-
ing, only excepting that the clock-work would at least
have had the advantage of going through the figures
regularly ; whereas the other would, most probably, by
some awkward manœuvre, put the whole party in disorder? Indeed, in a ball-room, sensible and insensible
seem to me to be pretty nearly approaching to one
another. How very different the votary of Nonsense !
Did he not canvass the room, dancers, plays, operas, in
short, all the topics of the day, in such a way as to make
you laugh, if not with him, certainly at him ?

The superiority of Nonsense, however, does not by any
means stop here ; the amusing style of Nonsense is not
the only one which can be turned to useful purposes.
We have the bewildering and distracting Nonsense ; we
have the perplexing and impenetrable Nonsense; we
have the astounding and awe-infusing Nonsense.

The Lover, or Fortune-hunter, will be a very fair instance of the distracting and bewildering. He knows
how very little chance he would have of prevailing on
the beauty of his affections to accompany him to Gretna
with no other aid than sheer, downright, plain, common
sense. But Nonsense, sweet, charming, benevolent Nonsense comes in to his assistance, and strings together a
set of unconnected words, never-dying, inextinguishable,
heart-consuming flames ; presiding deities, devoted and
eternal constancy : jealousy, suicide, poison, the favoured
rival's death, are interspersed here and there with great
success. The inamorata is half frightened, half forced
into a kind of compliance ; this is seized as an unqualified consent ; raptures follow raptures, and nonsense,

nonsense : both are satisfied, one with the prospect
of a husband, the other with the prospect of a fortune, and, in short, the pair are linked in a week.
After marriage the husband does not think it necessary
to keep up the unintelligible strain which formed the
charm of his courtship. Sense intrudes and spoils all
that Nonsense had done for them; the wife grows discontented and reproachful, the husband surly ; the first,
because she finds that her fortune, not her person, was
the bait that tempted him ; the second, because he finds
that the possession of his wife's money hardly compen-
sates for the torments of his wife's tongue : they both
grow wiser, and, in proportion, more miserable ; whereas, if they had remained as great fools (or at least if one
party had) as when they married, they might, perhaps,
have lived perfectly contented with themselves and with
their yoke-fellows.

The Counsellor will be a specimen of the perplexing
and impenetrable Nonsense. " When I can't talk sense,"
said Curran, " I talk metaphor." What the " metaphor"
means is pretty evident, and to what so great a lawyer
confesses, we hope no other will give the lie. How
inadequate would Sense be to the task of subjecting a
witness to the ordeal of technicality ; of confounding one
question with another answer; of contradicting the witness and puzzling the judge. The least mistake, of
course, in the hands of an able practitioner, instantly
becomes an inexcusable prevarication, the prevarication
is improved into a perjury in a very short time, and the
witness's testimony is discarded. If the counsellor give
Sense the preference over Nonsense, O ! ye phantoms of

contradictory cross-examinations, of verbose, unintelligible speeches, haunt him, shriek in his ears, "Shame on the infamous ingratitude," and avenge the cause of the bullied witness.

But let not any ungifted person presume to think that he can be nonsensical in either of the ways which I have mentioned. Neither are to be attained without considerable natural talents in that line. In the first place, impudence irrefragable; in the second, fluency inexhaustible; in the third, a quick eye, and ready invention, to seize the moment of letting fly at the victim the full torrent of humbug.

The astounding and awe-infusing Nonsense, besides being appropriated by nature to German Romancers and Travellers, is in great request among the proficients at St. Stephen's. What is more common, than for a politician to preface his objections to a Railway-Improvement Bill with protestations of its ruinous nature to King, Lords, and Commons, and a dreadful enumeration of the stabs and thrusts which our happy Constitution will receive from it.

As the Counsellor and Fortune-hunter would have reason to complain if they themselves were tied down to common Sense, the usurers, stock-brokers, and tradesmen of most kinds, would not be less injured if other people were purged of their folly. What, too, would the old maid say, if every action, look, or word of her neighbours were kept under the guardianship of that duenna of duennas, Sense? she would be reduced from harmless embellishment to point-blank invention, by which her too tender conscience might possibly be afflicted, and, moreover, nobody, if sensible, would believe her.

Last, not least, in the tribe of Nonsense, the Etonian cannot deny her his most cordial and unlimited gratitude. How, without this resource, could he get through his verses and theme on a hard week? What would he say, to have every exercise torn over, which was not in strict concordance with the rules of Sense; to have his verses pared from a magnificent copy of sixty or seventy, to the concise brevity of his number?

Sense, perhaps, will lay claim to the philosophers and essayists; we will yield them to her, though more from easiness and good-nature than from conviction of the justice of her claims: but nobody can deny Nonsense to be the lady paramount of all novels and romances, and by far the greater portion of the poets. All Adelinas, Euphemias, Angelicas, and Aramintas, all midnight apparitions and haunted castles, all despairing Corydons and dying Thyrsises, all sonnets to Mary or Ellen, may pretty safely be appropriated to her. Indeed I myself had some idea of becoming one of the latter class of her partisans, solely and purely from veneration for our Patroness, and of chaunting her praises in "lofty rhyme," beginning, of course, with a congenial invocation to divine Nonsensia, and ending with a high-flown apostrophe to that division of Eton College, which, from her, has received its name.

THE SIEGE OF CONSTANTINOPLE

O'er Byzantium's leaguer'd walls
Calmly the light of morning falls;
And calmly shines the Crescent's pride
Red . . . . . n the Euxine's tide.

Hear ye the sounds that are borne on the gale,
The shout of joy, and the shriek of wail ;
      Hear the songs of the Faithful rise,
      And " God and the Prophet" rend the skies ;
      Hear, with cadence sad and slow,
      Resound the Christian's notes of woe ,
      So melancholy are the cries,
      They seem the city's obsequies.
The trumpets thrice the signal sang,
With "Alla" thrice the welkin rang,
      The Moslem's cry of might ;
The horse-tails in the breezes danc'd
As Anatolia's bands advanc'd,
      And mingled in the fight.
The strife begins. Amid the lines
Each Janissary's falchion shines,
As on they rush'd, with eager course,
To stem the charging Christian's force.
Then vain was Grecian sword and spear
Against the Moslem's wild career ;
As leaves before the breath of heav'n,
Back to their gates the foe is driv'n
But who is he, whose giant form
Seems like a beacon midst the storm ?
Who, through the war's conflicting wave,
O'erthrows the bravest of the brave,
And urges on his foaming steed
Obedient to his Prophet's creed,
Which says, through Christian blood is giv'n
The Moslem's surest path to heav'n
'Tis Hassan—he whom eager zeal
Bears through th' opposing front of steel ;
Who burns in fiercer fight to close
With those, the Crescent's deadliest foes.
He flies, where from the Grecian fire
Dismay'd the Turkish hosts retire.
Quick from his hand the reins he flings,
Quick from his charger's back he springs,
One bound he gave—unseen by all,
He gain'd the summit of the wall,
And midst a thousand hostile brands
Alone. yet undismay'd, he stands

One Greek alone has tried his might,
And dared the Moslem to the fight ;
Nor dared in vain.   In Hassan's eyes
The flames of anger sparkling rise ,
With flashing course his falchion sped—
The Greek is number'd with the dead.
But fiercer soon their vengeance glows,
Thicker the Christian squadrons close.
Still Hassan fights, until a dart
Has drunk the life-blood of his heart.
     Meantime each turban'd band appears,
And nearer gleam the Turkish spears ;
Then peal'd the cannon's echo loud,
Then widely roll'd war's sulphurous cloud,
As sword to sword, and breast to breast,
Upon the foe the Moslem prest.
But, like an ocean-beaten rock,
The Christians bore the hostile shock,
And firm remain'd, though myriads bled,
Until proud Genoa's leader fled.
" On, Moslems, on ! the Grecians yield,
" Justiniani quits the field.
" On, Moslems, on !" fierce Mahmoud cries,
" Alla has will'd to us the prize ;
" Feel ye that pure, that madd'ning zeal,
" Which none but Mussulmen can feel ?
" See ye the dark-hair'd Houris wave
" Their welcome to the slaughter'd brave ?"
But then was seen the Christian's rout,
Then peal'd the conquering Moslem's shout ;
While worthy of his former name
Amidst his native city's flame,
Deserted by his recreant bands,
The last of all the Cæsars stands :
With brow serene, unmov'd by fear,
He saw the victor's fierce career ;
Unmov'd he view'd the tottering wall,
Unmov'd he mark'd each soldier's fall ,
Then, dashing madly through the strife
Resign'd the worthless boon of life.

Q

REMARKS ON GIFFORD'S "FORD."

(Continued from page 133.)

Our limits will not allow us to be as lavish in our quotations, as the admiration we feel for genius, and the wish we have to communicate that admiration in our humble sphere to all those from whose libraries the early dramatists have hitherto been aliens, would prompt us to be. But, before we leave " *The Broken Heart,*" we must recommend to the reader of taste and feeling, the exquisite pathos displayed in the fifth Scene of the third Act, where Penthea bids a last farewell to " the stage of her mortality," and intrusts to Calantha, as to her executrix, the legacies of her youthful affection.

> *Pen.*   I have left me
>   But three poor jewels to bequeath.   The first is
>   My Youth; for tho' I am much old in griefs,
>   In years I am a child.
> *Cal.*   To whom that ?
> *Pen.*   To virgin wives, such as abuse not wedlock ,
>   May those be ever young !
> *Cal.*   A second jewel
>   You mean to part with ?
> *Pen*   'Tis my Fame ; I trust,
>   By slander yet untouch'd ; this I bequeath
>   To Memory, and Time's old daughter, Truth.
>   If ever my unhappy name find mention,
>   When I am fall'n to dust, may it deserve
>   Beseeming charity without dishonour !
> *Cal.*   How handsomely thou play'st with harmless sport
>   Of mere imagination !. speak the last ;
>   I strangely like thy Will.
> *Pen.*   This jewel, madam,
>   Is dearly precious to me ; you must use
>   The best of your discretion to employ
>   This gift as I intend it.

Cal.   Do not doubt me.

Pen.   'Tis long agone since first I lost my heart :
   Long have I lived without it, else for certain
   I should have given that too · but instead
   Of it, to great Calantha, Sparta's heir,
   By service bound, and by affection vowed,
   I do bequeath, in holiest rites of love,
   Mine only brother, Ithocles.

Cal.   What saidst thou ? &c.

" The Lover's Melancholy," though beautiful in parts, will stand no comparison as a whole, with the two splendid dramas which have hitherto engaged our attention. The comic parts are deplorable, and generally disgusting. . The character of Eroclea, however, is cast in the same mould. of feminine delicacy and purity, which Nature seems to have broken in despair when it passed into the hands of those who, under the enervating influence of a vicious Court,

 " Profan'd the God-given strength, and marr'd the lofty line."

Strada's charming apologue of the Nightingale, though frequently attempted, has never been rendered with so much grace and harmony into English, as in the opening scene of this play. To appreciate its merit rightly, we should remember that the original tale is not only cast in a narrative form, but designed as an imitation of a poet, whose great error was diffuseness : to preserve, therefore, the raciness of dramatic composition, without swerving from the easy elegance which characterizes Strada, was a task of no ordinary difficulty.

" *Perkin Warbeck* " is endowed with a very different, though far more pleasing, interest. It is, perhaps, the only instance on record, in which an historical drama, since Shakspeare, has not proved an entire and hopeless failure. So completely has our immortal bard mono-

polized that province of his art, that the very name of
an historical play has become inseparably connected in
our minds with the rich humour of Falstaff, the morbid
ambition of Richard, and the chivalrous gallantry of
Hotspur. We insensibly confound the powerful colouring of the poet with the less brilliant, but more sober,
tints thrown off from the pencil of the historian. The
period of time which these plays embrace, is to us con-
secrated ground : the darts of criticism recoil from its
portal ; it stands alone, unhurt, undefiled, either by the
sneer of the sceptic, or the plodding dulness of the
biographer. Those times were the times of discord, of
civil convulsion, of feudal tyranny, and unhallowed ambition : yet, where the scene was darkened by the sullen
gloom of the tempest, even there the spirit of Shakspeare sits " from verge to verge," like the Iris of the
cataract, and sheds the full effulgence of poetical genius
over the dim chaos of historical confusion. But, as with
Shakspeare that pleasing illusion appeared, so with
Shakspeare it must vanish. It is the bow of Ulysses,
which none but Ulysses could bend. Nothing accordingly can exceed the wretchedness of those abortions
which the vanity of new-fledged authors, or the pride of
older ones, has occasionally palmed on the expectation
of the public. And it is equally gratifying and unexpected, to find, as in the instance before us, a play, which
even by the veriest bigots of the Shakspearian school
must be perused with pleasure ; a play which, if it no
where presents to our view a masterly delineation of character, or a highly-wrought development of plot, yet
contains nothing which can fairly be blamed, and much
which must in justice be commended. What young and

generous mind will forget the devoted Dalyell? Where
the fastidious beauty that would refuse her pity to the
sorrows of Catherine? What critic will not admire the
skill by which the dignity of Warbeck, from first to last,
is preserved; never allowing him to drop a syllable in
mistrust of his own cause, and thus completely identify-
ing him with the prince whom he strove to counterfeit?
The speech of Warbeck before his execution has great
merit, and reminds one of Shakspeare's best historical
manner :

> *Oxford.* Look ye, behold your followers appointed
>   To wait on you in death '
> *War.*   Why, peers of England,
>   We'll lead them on courageously, I read
>   A triumph over tyranny upon
>   Their several foreheads. Faint not in the moment
>   Of victory ! our ends, and Warwick's head,
>   Innocent Warwick's head (for we are prologues
>   But to his tragedy), conclude the wonder
>   Of Henry's tears, and then the glorious race
>   Of fourteen kings, Plantagenets, determines
>   In this last issue male ; Heav'n be obey'd !
>   Impoverish time of its amazement, friends,
>   And we will prove as trusty in our payments,
>   As prodigal to nature in our debts.
>   Death ' that is but a sound, a name of air,
>   A minute's storm, or not so much : to tumble
>   From bed to bed, be massacred alive
>   By some physicians, for a month or two,
>   In hope of freedom from a fever's torments,
>   Might stagger manhood, here the pain is past,
>   Ere sensibly 'tis felt. Be men of spirit !
>   Spurn coward passion ! so illustrious mention
>   Shall blaze our names, and style us kings o'er death.

' The less that is said of " *Love's Sacrifice*," and " *Fancies,
Chaste, and Noble*," the better. With the exception of a
few green spots, they present a wilderness of bad taste.
The first is an unsuccessful mimicry of Othello, "*impar*

congressus Achilli:" the second, though with more beauties to redeem it, singularly clumsy in its plot. " *The Lady's Trial*" is liable to the same objection : but the characters of Adurni and Malfato are powerfully drawn ; and the purity of language, which Ford has put into the mouth of Castanna, bears the peculiar impress of his manner. " *The Witch of Edmonton*" is calculated to excite in the present generation, feelings of a very different nature from those which it called forth in the days of king James. Then, it was hailed as a drama containing some scenes that might move the hearts, but many more that would excite the mirth, of an English audience. Now, it is looked upon with feelings of disgust, arising, not from any inferiority in the composition, for it has many scenes of power and effect; not from any introduction of supernatural machinery, for the contemporaries of " Der Freischütz " need not gibe at *that ;* but solely from the unconquerable horror which we feel in 1827 for the system of espionage, cruelty, and blood-shedding, which, under the name of "Laws against Witchcraft," darkened with an inexpiable stain the statute-book of England. That the death of a poor woman, probably innocent of every real offence, and whose life must have been embittered by the superstition and rancour of all around her, should be the object of unfeeling laughter, strikes us as totally alien from the English character. Yet, that such frequently was the fact, we need not the testimony of this play to convince us. But it would be injustice not only to Ford, but to Decker, who assisted him in this play, not to give them the praise which is their due, for the more serious parts. The character of Susan, a faithful, affectionate, confiding wife, is one of Ford's happiest efforts, and would have done honour to a better subject. Nor, considering the audience with whom he had to deal, is the comic part such as was unlikely to secure that immediate popularity which must always be the first aim of the dramatic writer.

We have now discharged the task which our zeal, perhaps our vanity, has imposed upon us : how deficient our labours have been in point of ability, we are most ready to confess ; but they have been undertaken in the sincerity of admiration for those creative spirits who, in a literary view, have made England what she is. The Elizabethan poetry bears the same resemblance to that of the succeeding age, as the free and mountain torrent, exulting in the grandeur of its liberty, bears to the inclosed waters of the fountain, leaping but to a certain height, and recurring with an eternal monotony of sound to the marble basin which imprisons it. All the vivid energy, all the wild freshness of intellect, by which the real poet is stamped from his birth, as with Nature's seal, belong to the master-spirits of that day. They are the originals of that glorious order of poetry which dares to throw off the shackles of imitation, and gaze on the universe with the frenzied eye of inspiration : the order which Wordsworth and his fanatics have had sense enough to perceive, and blindness enough to pervert, but into which perhaps Byron alone has, of all modern writers, fully entered. He has taught us, in his own beautiful language, that

> " The beings of the mind are not of clay .
> Essentially immortal, they create,
> And multiply in us a brighter ray,
> A more belov'd existence !"

I

Upon the threshold, then, of this mighty temple, whose walls have the burnish of genius upon them, and whose shrine has been erected by all the great and good men whom England has gloried in possessing, we, too, venture to lay the tribute of our veneration : not, indeed, without trembling lest our presumption should be punished, but not without hope, that in our lesser world we may produce the same good effect, which has been already produced in a great degree on the public taste— that of exciting a wish to abandon the school of vitiated taste, whether it be displayed in the wire-drawing of Pope, which spoiled the genius of Darwin, or in the overacted Shakspearianism, which makes the Lakists a laughing-stock and a bye-word : but to return, on the other hand, to the fountain-head of all that is really excellent in our literature, and once more to drink from " the well of English undefiled," the Elizabethan poetry.

E. L.

DISCOVERY OF MADEIRA.

The account of the discovery of Madeira is romantic. A young man of the name of Machim, fell in love with an English lady, by name Anna de ———, of great beauty, and in birth and fortune superior to himself; his passion was returned, but the parents of the lady were averse to the match, and in order to put it out of her power to dispose of herself, married her to an old baron, who had a castle on the sea-coast.

As may be expected, the lovers ran away, intending to

fly to France, but the wind took them out of their course, and after ten days of storms, accompanied by all the extremities of want, and the constantly harassing expectation of death, the horrors of their situation being, no doubt, heightened by the recollection of their fault, landed them in that most lovely bay, which to this hour retains the name of its discoverer.

Imagine yourself on a precipitous mountain of rock, down which there is a winding path, now lost, now appearing, and which, if pursued, would lead to the beautiful and extensive valley which spreads in sunny richness below; opposite to you are lofty rocks overhanging the ocean; on the left, distant mountains rising in one wooded amphitheatre, from which descends a stream that glides through the middle of the vale, and meets the sea. Its waves are calm, and hardly ripple on the beach,

> "While towards the east, Lorenço's rocky chain,
> Spreads the far point, and stretches to the main."

The houses which are scattered near the shore are of the ancient Portuguese construction; the want of glass being compensated for by wooden pannels, which must be opened to admit the light.

There is a church said to be built on the spot, beneath which the lovers were buried, and a rude cross cut from the very cedar which was growing above their grave.

A FRAGMENT.

XXI.

The waves are silent in Machico's bay,
And bright the sun, and cloudless is the day,
As on that morn when, spent and tempest-tost,
Machim first landed on th' untrodden coast;

And blest the shore that, when e'en hope was past,
Bade him awake to life and love, at last.
Alas ! how blind is 'man to change and fate,
What pains unseen upon his pleasures wait,
That can Hope's visionary joys believe,
And most rejoices, when he most should grieve.
Thus gladden'd he to view the lovely strand,
The woods, the hills, and unexpected land,
Then from the bark his beauteous Anna bore,
Sav'd from the sea, to perish on the shore.
Oh ! false deliverance ! too late to save !
That only snatch'd her from a darker grave
Here o'er her tomb one cypress wreath he wove,
The last sad tribute of ill-fated love ;
Then wild with grief, and frantic with despair,
Press'd the fresh turf, and droop'd and perish'd there
Oh ! hapless pair !—yet just this awful close
To lawless love, and violated vows ·
Yet blame not these, but rather blame the pride
That made the daughter an unwilling bride,
That tore the tender bonds of love apart,
That gave the hand, but could not give the heart
Then blame not, ye who pass their bridal bed,
But drop a tear of sorrow for the dead ;
Let pity most by man to man be given,
Vengeance belongs—and mercy too— to Heaven.

XXII.

They laid him in his lowly grave
  Beside the form he lov'd the best,
No more to hear the billows rave,
  At length together, and at rest.
No storied urn, no pillar rose
To tell their names, their loves, their woes ;
  But the dark mantling moss
Spread o'er their tomb its sad array;
And 'neath the cedar where they lay
 .Was plac'd a rustic cross,
To tell to all, who wander'd near,
That Christian man was buried there.

XXIII.

And they have left that lonely isle,
   And they are on the stormy deep ;
All is as hush'd and still awhile,
   As those two lovers where they sleep
All unregarded, silent, lone,
With none to mark, and none to moan,
   Their inauspicious love ;
Murmur the billows to the shore,
The wild flowers blossom as before,
   Bright is the sun above :
Oh ! Nature mourns not man's decay ;
He but returns to native clay ;
   Nor when a monarch dies,
Does one bright flower that decks the glade,
One leaf decay, one blossom fade,
Save those that on his bier are laid,
   Or grace his obsequies.

XXIV.

While prouder monuments arrest the eye,
We view, admire, and praise, and pass them by ;
Nor longer dwell intent upon the spot,
Seen for a moment, and as soon forgot :
But this, their simple tale, will aye impart
A spell that twines around the gazer's heart ;
Their memory mingles with the scene around,
Lives in the air, and sighs in every sound ;
And, as we tread above their ashes, moves
A silent sorrow for their hapless loves.

    *   *   *   *

ON FALSE FRIENDSHIP.

From the innumerable complaints of the faithlessness
of man, which fill the writings of those whom a bad
temper or bilious constitution may have rendered misan-

thropical, we might almost conclude, that friendship is
like the philosopher's stone, something merely ideal,
utterly unattainable by our degenerate race. Notwithstanding this, we give the name of " friend " to every
one who, during our acquaintance, may either have
benefitted us, or received a favour at our hands. The
man is as much a friend who lends us a horse for a day,
as he who supplies us with a thousand pounds in our
utmost distress. He who, by attending us as second to
the field, has assisted in endangering our life, claims
this hacknied title in common with the man who, at
the risk of his own safety, has delivered us from destruction. I should wish, therefore, disowning any idea
of treating of that perfect friendship, concerning which
so many poets have raved, and philosophers dogmatized,
to consider the nature of that common every-day in-
timacy which the world calls friendship.

We have long been taught that female friendship consists in filling foolscap sheets with—far be it from me to
say what. Of this kind of friendship I shall say no
more, not being qualified from experience, to expatiate on
such a subject; and those of my readers for whom it has
any interest, I shall beg leave to refer to the " Sorrows of
Adeline Schwartzenberg," or any equally sentimental
novel of the day. The *ne plus ultra*, it is said, of some
old ladies' friendship is in tea-drinking and scandal, in
abusing their absent friends, for the entertainment of their
friends who are present. Perhaps these worthy personages may think with Falstaff, that in dispraising any
one before the wicked, they act the part of a careful
friend. Whether such be a sufficient apology for scan-

dal, or this be real friendship, it would be impertinence
in me to decide.

Who is a good friend? Ask the gourmand and regular *diner-out*. His answer will be, "the man who gives
good and frequent dinners." That man is indeed an
invaluable friend; but let him reform his establishment,
and dismiss his man-cook, and, in the opinion of many,
all his good qualities will vanish: without his *piquant*
dishes, his wit will no longer please, and he himself will
be voted a bore. Who is the statesman's friend? The
man who supports him in every measure; " whose voice
is still his patron's own;" who looks up to him as the
sun of the political system from whom all the surrounding satellites are to receive light and benefit. While in
this mind, he is a friend; but let him disagree with the
minister on a single measure—let him for once have an
opinion of his own—and the severe taunts he will undergo will scarcely be palliated by the honied appellation
of *my honourable friend*.

It would be almost impossible to describe the qualifications necessary to obtain the friendship of the man of
the world; an honour as easily to be lost as gained. His
superior in rank and public estimation is to be courted,
while he whose wit and ridicule are objects of dread,
must be encouraged. He regulates, however, his choice
of friends, as well as his dress, by fashion; and while
he follows those whom the general voice pronounces
worthy intimates, he would blush to be seen with a man
whom, to use his own phraseology, *nobody knows*. If,
by rank, wealth, or any other qualification, he acquires
sufficient notoriety to influence the opinions of others,

he may then be at liberty to choose his own friends; but this is a distinction which few are permitted to attain; and the man of the world must generally be regulated in every thing by the authority of the fortunate individual to whom it has been allotted to become what the Morning Post would term a *distingué.*

, An old proverb says, " Friendship cannot be bought for money." The truth of this I, for one, doubt; and think few can deny that friends are to be bought in some of those towns which, enjoying what they call their rights and privileges, rail at rotten boroughs, and exult in the profits of a free representation. " Gentlemen," says the member, " I think I may call you all *my friends.*". He may, indeed, for what a man has bought belongs to him; and we all must admire this universal and indiscriminate philanthropy which buys friends, like sheep, at so much a head. Romantic friendship age *may,* and the dictates of common sense *must,* dissolve; the detected back-biter can no longer be a friend; opposition will alienate the minister, and reason disgust the man of the world; but while you continue to be the best bidder, you will ever be considered *a friend* by a corrupt and shameless populace.

ON PEDANTS.

There is nothing more commonly shunned than the character of a pedant; and from that very reason, there is nothing more commonly misapplied, or more commonly misunderstood; so much so, that we frequently

have occasion to consider those who value themselves
principally on their total abhorrence of that dreadful and
undefined being, to be more uselessly and finically pedantic than any scholiast who ever thundered forth his
anathemas against an inadmissible note of interrogation,
or execrated the stupidity of a commentator for eradi-
cating a favoured particle, whether it be $\delta\iota$, $\gamma\epsilon$, or $\tau\iota$. It
is true, indeed, that the most common and received
opinion is, that a pedant must of necessity be a scholar,
which those who seek excuses for their ignorance have
conveniently interpreted (by the aid of a certain figure
which, if I were one of the proscribed class, I should
call metathesis), that a scholar must of necessity be a
pedant. But before we grant even the first proposition,
let us consider what constitutes pedantry; is it the
knowledge, or the absurd display of that knowledge for
the gratification of your vanity, in the sense of your
superior acquirements? Most decidedly, the display;
and why, then, should the imputation of pedantry be
confined to the display of classical knowledge? why is
not my friend Francis Jermyn a pedant, when, in answer to the agonized inquiry of some novice (who has
been unwisely induced to risk his last half-crown)
whether the horse which he has backed is a good one,
receives in answer, the pedigree up to king Herod, and
the consoling assurance that he is well bred; who inter-
rupts a discussion on the Catholic question with an
account of the entry for the St. Leger, and answers the
breathless inquiry of his brother politicians upon the
fate of a bill with, "Oh, it was carried in a canter—none
of the opposition made any play;" who drowns the

conversation on the death of the emperor Alexander with
the performances of Smolensko, and ruins a debate on the
Slave-trade with the triumphs of Mulatto. This is pedantry of another sort, equally foolish, and more dangerous; there is the same vanity in displaying his knowledge of the "Racing Calendar," the same "boast of
heraldry," though it be but the heraldry of horses, as
in the man who is proudly conscious of having rectified
the punctuation of a Greek chorus, and of knowing
every coat of arms which was used under the walls of
Thebes. What, then, can be said for the politician who
would tell you the name of every member who voted
in the majority or minority of any question that was ever
brought before the House, from the emancipation of the
Catholics to the formation of a road, or the establishment of a turnpike; who numbers in his library more
political pamphlets than his brother pedant does sporting
magazines, and discusses the trivial questions which
may arise, with all the ceremony, and nearly all the eloquence, of Parliament. Does not this arise from the
same feeling as would have produced, if directed that
way, an elaborate treatise on the metres of Æschylus,
and unanswerable arguments about the Cretic foot?

Is not the man who can talk upon pictures, lights,
shadows, back-grounds, &c. for hours, and yet, when
forced to abandon this fertile subject, must remain as
silent as a statue—is not he a pedant, and a pedant fit
for nothing but to sell catalogues under the windows of
the British Gallery? is not the soldier who never opens
his mouth but to talk of battles; the sailor who can
speak of nothing but his own ship—are not these pedants

in their line as great, or greater, than any man who ever quoted Greek? Why, then, is the person who is obliged to listen to these, and such as these, till his head turns round, and the answering monosyllables flow out without order or direction, why is the suffering person denied the gratification of branding him with the mark of pedantry in return, as well as the poor man whom destiny or inclination has unfortunately directed to the acquisition of the Classics?

PENGANDER.

AN ELECTION DINNER.

Si te propositi nondum pudet, atque eadem est mens,
Ut bona summa putes alienâ vivere quadrâ, &c.—

Quamvis jurato, metuam tibi credere testi.
Ventre nihil novi frugalius.   JUVENAL.

Is it still thus? And have you still no shame,
O Trebius, in the poor-fed voter's name?
Will you still barter rights that make you free,
For an Election dinner and a fee?
Have you no qualms of conscience when you toast,
In meagre wine, your empty-headed host?
Does not the fish-bone rankle in your throat,
As you recall your prostituted vote?
And tho' strong beer awhile can stifle thought,
Yet not the less, O Trebius, you are bought.
　　Fain would I try to think a ten-pound note
Is worth a true-born Briton's honest vote;
Or that a smile from him, the great bashaw,
Outweighs the charter of our English law.
He calls you friend, nor doubt his friendship true,
In seven years' time he'll call you friend anew.

See where those diplomatic smiles encase
One humble candidate's obsequious face ;
While the hand, press'd upon his grateful heart,
Performs alike its ever ready part.
Himself the while in broken words declares
Your voices load him with unwelcome cares ;
And begging his refusal may be heard,
Trembles lest you should take him at his word.
Thus to the public eyes he seems a man,
Such as men were when first the world began
A man who scorns to cringe and condescend ;
A man in pow'r, yet still his country's friend.
O vain to think in these degen'rate days,
When sordid int'rest ev'ry bosom sways,
When Honesty would hide her head for shame,
But that not one acknowledges the name ;
And patriotic sentiments are lent
To rogues, who want a seat in parliament .
O little wise, to deem there might be found
A truly honest man on British ground .
When twice five pounds can silence patriot tongues,
And a bad dinner quell the stoutest lungs.
But lest the age, perchance, should think I write
With bitter envy, or concealed spite,
And doubt my gen'ral censure to be true,
I'll pause, and give the devil all his due.
Oft have I seen a burgess's sound mind,
Fraught with his schemes of good to all mankind,
Determin'd that the man who has his vote,
At least shall have his apophthegms by rote ;
Be true to his constituents, who all
Expect, at least, those dinners and a ball.
But have you seen this man of sentiment,
Though humble, honest, and though poor, content ›
Have you seen him, the bold reformer, stand,
As one who pitied, and would save the land ›
Have you seen him, firm, confident, and true,
Pocket his virtue and a ten-pound too ?
Grant that the Catholics, at least, may share
That which the member tells him is but fair ,

And stifle in his neckcloth sundry gibes,
Which come not well from one who pockets bribes.
If this be honesty, ye Gods, I'll eat my pen,
And grant that truckling rogues are independent men.
　　Suppose then, Trebius, that the day is won,
The hubbub silenc'd, and the polling done ;
Sit we invited at the member's board,
And for once dine and revel with a Lord :
For Horace rightly sings that wine alone,
Can alter e'en the smooth dissembler's tone ;
In short, that after dinner ev'ry speech
Comes from the heart, which only wine can reach ;
And that the well-coin'd lie, and polish'd tale,
Fly from the gen'rous grape, and mighty ale.
Listen then, Trebius, whilst the worthy man,
Of public good details his sapient plan :—
" My friends, I rise—mine is no easy part—
" Your independence—and my grateful heart—
" I reverence your worth—I love this town—
" And drink the mayor's good health "—and so sits down.
Gesticulation, and this eloquence,
Atone full well for want of common sense.
Wild with delight, the list'ning crowd applaud,
And with the clatter shakes the festive board ;
Whilst the dull burgesses admire their guest,
Robb'd of the little sense they once possess'd.
More wine is drunk ; each stands, or tries to stand,
Each would deliver the enslaved land,
And compliments, and toasts, and songs abound,
And some few fall to sleep upon the ground
Now mark the dancing eyes, the tripping tongue,
The glasses ring, and all the bells are rung ;
The candles give a triple light, the mayor
Is multiplied, and now and then a chair
Remov'd whilst some one saw'd the empty air,
Beneath the table brings his portly weight,
And the wide wig deserts his toppling pate !
Enough of this ; the member, far too wise
To hazard the detection of his lies,
Has slipt unnotic'd from the chairman's seat,
And sought his safety in a sure retreat ·

Unseen he flies ; the chair fills up his place
(As good a member for so wise a race),
And hears, unconscious, from the drunken throng,
Full many a silly speech, and murder'd song :
At length sleep comes upon their closing eyes,
And in his rank each, like a Spartan, lies.
And thus it is, a bribe, an empty phrase,
That independence and your conscience pays !
Away then, Trebius, nor dare complain,
Suppose your member's word be giv'n in vain,
And with repentance, but too late, you rue
The oaths forgotten, which he swore to you ;
And the high-minded, independent man,
Truckle to all, and pocket all he can—
Nor wonder you, if by a gen'ral cry,
(Save his alone, who dar'd your rights to buy),
The house disfranchise so corrupt a place,
And those the world thought only fools, prove base.

                                        ZAMIEL.

ON MUSHROOM GENTLEMEN.

Licet superbus ambules pecuniâ
Fortuna non mutat genus.—Hor.

Among the many obnoxious characters that are to be
met with in society, a purse-proud man is certainly not
one of the least. While other persons are in some measure
excusable in forming an high opinion of themselves on
account of literary attainments, or mental superiority,
the character I have mentioned is odious and intolerable
to all ; for his pride is not founded on any merits of his
own, but on the favour of Fortune, or the caprice of a
testator. Is there any one that has not at some period of
his life been disgusted with one of these supercilious

pieces of vulgarity? If there is, let him congratulate himself that he has escaped the contact of a creature scarcely less contemptible than the ground upon which he treads.

Far be it from me, while I thus inveigh against this class of persons, to deny to persevering industry the hard-earned enjoyment of its gain; but I blame those who think that a lucky hit in the Lottery, or a successful speculation in the Stocks, entitles them to start forward as gentlemen, and to move in an higher sphere than that for which nature and their education had adapted them.

The first method that is adopted by these aspirants to gentility, is improvement in dress; as if the distinguishing marks of a gentleman were the cut of his coat, or the arrangement of his cravat. I confess that these are accessories which few are willing to neglect; but it argues a weak and narrow mind to rely more on the lustre of a shoe, than on elegance of manners, or politeness of conversation. Yet it is on this that the soi-disant gentleman prides himself; and if he shall have had the good fortune to meet with a scientific tailor, and a dexterous clear-starcher, he will forthwith be a fashionable man. Thus gold, tailors, and washerwomen, can make or unmake gentlemen, with all the facility in the world.

But the candidate for consideration soon discovers that it is not dress alone that constitutes a gentleman, and consequently begins to imitate his manners. In this attempt his failure is more egregious than before. You may often detect him labouring to introduce an elegant expression, or throw his body into a graceful attitude; he will endeavour to interlard his conversation with French,

of which he knows-just as much as is sufficient to enable
him to murder it; if he happens to dance, he will pirouette
and caper. with considerably more energy than grace, and
will affect to like music, although, with his utmost dis-
crimination, he can scarcely distinguish " Money-Musk"
from " God save the King."

But let us view the converse of this character, I mean
the good man deserted by Fortune. How modestly he
shrinks from the society of those who were formerly his
equals, but now his superiors, at least in point of fortune;
how unobtrusive are his manners, as if he knew, that in
the estimation of the multitude, he is degraded; but how
contented is his look, how unbroken his mien, which
shows that in his mind he despises the vicissitudes of
Fortune! From his homely garb you would mistake him
at a distance for a menial, but the delusion vanishes as
you approach, for then appears that indescribable charm,
that perfect elegance of demeanour, which, under any
disguise, will still characterize the gentleman. He is
affable to his inferiors, for he feels how uncertain are
the distinctions of rank; he can sympathize with the
mourner, for he himself has tasted of affliction; he
can relieve the distressed, for he is conscious that the
tenure of riches is vain and unsubstantial.

Such is the man against whom the malice of Fortune
falls powerless and dead, the man whom wealth and
possessions could never induce to think more highly of
himself, than if he were the humble inmate of a cottage;
for he feels that though the stocks may rise and fall;
though ships may be wrecked, and lotteries be won, yet
man's intrinsic value remains still the same; and that all

the gifts of fortune, and all the appendages of state, cannot add one jot of real importance to the degraded and worthless characters who are too often found as their possessors.

" Nec verbum verbo curabis reddere."

Dear Sir;

Wishing, to the best of my power, to contribute to your Publication, I inclose a short Translation for your notice. You cannot be so unreasonable as to expect it should bear much resemblance to the original.

Like yours,
> *" Fear is mingled with my hope"*—

Like Horace,
> *" Si me Lyricis vatibus inseres*
> Sublimi feriam sidera vertice."

Your obedient Servant,

C. B.

CHORUS

From the " Hecuba" of Euripides, v. 444.

STROPHE I.

Gentle breeze, that fann'st the sea,
As the surge thou ruisest, free,
That bearest o'er the swelling foam
The way-worn sailor to his home;
Whither, o'er the billows wild,
Wilt thou bear the Trojan's child?
Whither shall the child of woe
To chains, and grief, and anguish go?
On the Dorian's distant shore,
Or where the Phthian rivers roar?
Where, sire of streams that lave the earth,
Enipeus gives his waters birth?

ANTISTROPHE I

Shall Boreas bear my mournful flight
To some far island's rocky height,
Where the first-born palms expand
Their treasures on the Delian strand ?
Where the bay-tree's hallow'd shade
Saw Latona's burden laid ?
Where the damsel minstrels raise
The hymn of chaste Diana's praise,
The golden wreath, th' unerring dart
That pierc'd the sylvan hunter's heart ?

STROPHE II

Or on the fertile olive plains,
Where virgin Pallas dwells and reigns,
Join the coursers to the car
Of her who loves the race, the war ?
Weave the car and weave the horse,
Bounding on in rapid course,
With many a tinge and many a hue,
Weave them for the Virgin's view ?
Or Titan's bold and giant band,
That dared the Thund'rer's red right hand,
Hurl'd from the heavens highest steep,
And hush'd in everlasting sleep ?

ANTISTROPHE II.

Woe, woe is me for those I bore,
Woe for my sires, and ravag'd shore;
Behold the flames in fury rise,
Behold the Grecian's sacrifice !
'Tis mine to lie on foreign strand,
No more to see my native land—
No more to see my country, save
To see her to her foes a slave :
And change the soft, the bridal bed
For the dark chambers of the dead.

APPEARANCE OF VIRGIL IN THE UPPER WORLD.

Somnia, terrores magicos.

Sir;

Being one of the very few individuals who, in this degenerate age, adhere to the practice, and maintain the certainty, of dreaming, and having seen in your second Number an account of an interview which you had with the sheep-stealing vagabond, Mercury (it was fortunate for him that there were no assizes in his days), I take this opportunity of informing you of an encounter which I had with Virgil some nights ago, in which the proceedings were far from pacific, and, indeed, we had almost come to logger-heads. He shook his hand at me in a menacing attitude; but by passing my little finger through it, I convinced him that his rage was impotent, and reduced him to a tolerable state of tranquillity.

I first heard him muttering, in a very sepulchral tone, but with an amazing nicety of accent, something which I supposed to be Latin, but it certainly was very different in sound and quantities from that which we work at here. The substance of his invectives, as far as I could understand them was, that he had been grievously mutilated in the Upper World, and having taken an opportunity when Cerberus was employed in eating his meat, he had played truant for the purpose of stating his calamities, in hopes of having them remedied.

"What, my dear Sir, are they?" I exclaimed. "Depend upon my willingness to assist the author of the Georgics in any legitimate enterprise."

"In the first place, I have to complain of the Delphin Editor, and his interpretation, and of the circulation which my execrable tormentor enjoys in this country." [Of course I translate for the benefit of ladies and country gentlemen].

"True enough," I replied; "but what expedient can you propose?"

"Only to burn the publisher's house, and so cut up the evil by the roots."

"You would have the Bow-street officers after you immediately, and, shade as you are, I defy you to slip through their fingers."

"Well, even if they did catch me, and if the worst came to the worst, they could but send me back to Tartarus, where my habitation has now been fixed for my flattering Augustus, and stealing so much from Homer. Alas, alas! it is but too true .—

> "———— Læva malorum
> Exercet pœnas, et ad impia Tartara mittit"

"Then I suppose Rhadamanthus, if your account of him be true, charged the jury with some severity."

"'Infandum jubes renovare dolorem.' We have no Court of Chancery there; for judgment is pronounced without hesitation, and executed without delay."

"And who pleaded your cause?"

"I wanted to get Cicero: but he remembered the cutting off his head by my friend Augustus, and would

have nothing to say to me. I am now sorry that I did not
mention him in my works. I was forced to put up with
a common hack. But, to return—another thing which
I wish to complain of is, the miserable manner in
which you murder me by your vile pronunciation. I
mean to indict you all for it when you come down, I
assure you."

"You impertinent fellow! why what shall we have next,

"—— Audent cum talia fures ?"

Here it was that his rage boiled over. However, in a
short time, he told me that we pronounced short syllables
long, and long syllables short; that we confounded accent
and quantity; that *amor* and *clamor*, *nomine* and *domine, pedes* and *sedes*, *desero* and *resero*, were all the
same to us : by which, and many other reprehensible
practices, his verses were deteriorated, and his reputation
injured.

I in vain endeavoured to confute him, by appealing, as
I thought triumphantly, to the testimony of my Gradus.
He laughed loud and long at the idea, and said that the
ear was the standard by which the correctness of sounds
ought to be judged, and that it was preposterous to make
little marks govern what they were only intended to
facilitate.

I confess I was rather puzzled by what he said, on this
head, of which I have only given you a very small part :
but the authority of a Gradus cannot, in my humble
opinion, be shaken :

"Ille, velut pelagi rupes immota, resistit."

"And what is become of the '*animæ dimidium tuæ*,'
Horace?" said I, feeling myself on rather ticklish ground

on the subject of pronunciation, and wishing to change the subject.

"Horace," said Virgil, "was doomed by Pluto to become a scullion in his family for his Atheism; but Mercury made interest for him, on the score of the Ode beginning with "*Mercuri, facunde nepos Atlantis,*" his having given such a genteel name to his robberies, &c., and succeeded in getting him appointed to the office of butler, which my friend likes amazingly, as he never gives Pluto a bottle of wine without performing the office of taster previously. When old Bentley arrived in the shades, he began to propose new readings in the names of our heroes: he thought the name of Charon very inappropriate, as it might be derived from χαίρω, to rejoice: he thought Chaon, from Χάος, would be decidedly preferable, as it contained an allusion to the confused nature of the old man's discourse, as displayed in Lucian. He innocently proposed this to the old man, as he was ferrying him over; at which he was so incensed, that he immediately struck him on the head with his scull, and tossed the ghost of his wig into the Styx. He was one day going to Pluto's mansion with a humble petition to be permitted to see Phalaris, on the subject of his Epistles; but he unhappily had the door opened to him by Horace, who said, he recollected his mutilations, hated a commentator as much as a dun, and a Doctor as much as a Stoic, at the same time kicking poor Bentley down stairs, the unhappy victim in the mean time producing passages without number in support of his emendations.—My compliments to Mr. Bouverie, and I think he might quote me a little now and then, as well as Horace:

I know the Eton boys hate me, because I am difficult to learn.   But hark ! the cock crows—I am gone."

> " Dixit : et in tenuem ex oculis evanuit auram."

I am sure it is now time for me likewise to withdraw ; and I beg to subscribe myself your obedient Servant,

PHILOPHANTASM.

STANZAS.

Ah ! fare ye well, my boyish years,
 For ever flown away !
And childhood's hopes, and childhood's fears,
 When I could still be gay.

The aspirations I had then
 Have vanish'd into air,
And I have learn'd me among men
 To wrestle with Despair.

The malice of the world has pass'd
 Upon me like the wind ;
But 'twas not like the Autumn blast
 That leaves its trace behind.

Ah ! fare thee well, my youthful love,
 Once all a world to me ;
But with the softness of the dove,
 Thou hadst the wings to flee.

The busy world around to me
 Is but a wilderness ;
Whatever face on earth I see,
 I meet with none to bless.

Then, fare ye well, my early years !
 For ever flown away ;
And yet I would not dry my tears,
 Nor—if I could—be gay.

F. W. J.

IMITATION.

O Imitatores servum pecus!—Hor.

The value of that innate spirit of Imitation, which acts
as the main-spring of all our actions, there can be nobody
who will deny. This is the principle by which we follow
the footsteps of all the great and admirable characters
who have gone before us; by this we emulate the fame
of the illustrious, and the worthy character of the virtuous.
It is too much to be regretted, however, that we are as
frequently inclined to imitate the failings and defects, as
the virtues and good qualities, of those who attract our
admiration. This subject has occupied, and will occupy,
the pen of many who are better suited for the task by
authority and talents, and to such let it be resigned. It
is my intention to confine my views of the subject to the
almost absurd degree of imitation practised in what the
booksellers call "the literary world."

Within the last fifty years, the mania of writing, from
the increase of education, has risen to an extraordinary
height. Hence it follows, that the number of authors
has marvellously increased, and the consequent dearth of
subjects has given a greater impulse to the spirit of imitation. In some unhappy hour auto-biography was planned,
and for a time succeeded, since which, the press has absolutely swarmed with the lives and reminiscences of almost
unheard-of characters, written by themselves for the sole
purpose of proving that he or she could write and spell.

From the interest also taken in voyages and travels, there is scarcely a man who goes out of the beaten road pursued by every-day tourists, who does not publish his travels. . We are, no doubt, indebted to this source for much valuable information which would otherwise be wanting, and many have been rewarded with success sufficient to compensate all their labours. But, incited by the example of these, how , many publish tours, with neither matter to render them valuable, nor talent to embellish them. For the proof of my assertion, read the advertisements that daily deluge the papers ; witness the " Residences in the South of France," the " Tours in Germany," the letters from all quarters of the globe, that, after their appearance, having been duly noticed in the Literary. Gazette, are heard of no more.

. But it is in Works of Fiction that this race of authors find the best field for the exercise of their imitative powers. Let one work of this description be successful, and, within a year, fifty imitations will appear. Who, for instance, while Mrs. Radcliffe held undisputed sway over the novelists of the time, ever thought of writing, or even of reading, any thing but German castles and sentiment, the softness of the skies, and the ferocity of the Italian banditti. Her works, as incomparably the best of the kind, had some claim upon our admiration, but her followers (and they were many), who had not even elegance in their style to compensate the want of originality, were fully worthy of the oblivion into which they have at length fallen. By the multitude of romances in this style, the public taste was for a time so vitiated, that we allowed the most absurd and improbable fictions to be forced down our throats by the aid of horror and mystery. In fact, after a potent dose of this kind of reading, we scarcely dared to walk across the room from dread of ruffians concealed behind the curtains, or open an old box lest we should find a mouldering skeleton, with the necessary accompaniment of a rusty dagger, sufficiently stained with blood to satisfy the imagination of the most romantic.

We have lately abounded in works of a very opposite nature; namely, those which, drawing their characters and scenes from private life, in some measure satirize the reigning follies and fashionable vices of the day. Those which first appeared, unquestionably had merit, and, in some measure, were a revival of the school of Sir Charles Grandison, except that, for the stiff civility and ceremonious bows of the baronet, they substituted the easy manners of the modern man of the world. But this seemed too easy a ground to remain long undisputed by the imitative tribe, who threaten to deluge us with books, which, while their sole claims to favour lie in the high-sounding names of their dramatis personæ, give a false picture of the scenes they pretend to represent, with neither spirit in the dialogue, nor wit in their attempts at satire, to recommend them to notice. It might be amusing to trace the adventures (though not so numerous as those of "A Guinea") of a book of this nature, from its first announcement as a true description of the manners of "High Life;" after being attributed to Lady S——, or G——; after being applauded by some, and criticized by more, Reviews, to its final fall into its proper sphere, the circulating library of a watering place, where it vainly attempts to dispel the ennui of those whom chance may drive to such an unprofitable resource.

THE POSTMAN.—No. III.

Dear Mr. Bouverie ;

I can assure you that your new Publication has given rise to some of the most ludicrous and unfounded opinions that the most ingenious and oldest practitioners in the art of fiction could possibly have circulated : you are represented in a pleasing variety of ways, manners, and shapes, by a crowd of wondering readers ; and, which is the most amusing of all, no two of them corresponding with each other ; indeed I think it is a problem very likely to baffle the endeavours of so many inquisitive and prying dispositions : the destination of an armament equipping in the ports of France or Spain could not have set the arts of imagination more completely to work than they are at this moment, nor would it be possible for a more unfathomable mystery to conceal their purposes, than that attached to the proceedings of Bartholomew Bouverie.

Constant applications are made to Etonians from their friends, all anxious to know who Bartholomew can be ; and to give you and your readers some idea of the sensation which your Publication has excited, permit me to send for your perusal the following correspondence which passed between a young Etonian and his mother.

" Dear William ;

" No doubt you are in full possession of all the particulars concerning your new Publication, entitled *The*

Eton Miscellany, conducted by Mr. B. Bouverie, which I should conjecture to be a feigned name, but we have heard so many, and opposite reports, that I determined to write to you to clear up all doubts concerning the matter : your father, my dear William, delights in the very idea of Eton again giving to the public what, some few years since, gained such universal satisfaction ; and as you well know him to be a patron of literature, especially where Eton is concerned, he has desired me to tell you to order *The Eton Miscellany* to be sent down to us regularly, as the Numbers come out ; and to give us a full and just description of Mr. B. Bouverie. I hope my dear William, that in process of time, and with proper application, you will, in your turn, be an ornament to Eton, not only by performing the routine of school business, but, like your predecessors, by showing yourself capable of advancing the interests of Eton, and securing your own praise ; all which, my dear William, I most sincerely hope for, and

" Believe me to be

" Your very affectionate Mother,

" *Langford Hall, June 20, 1827.*   M. MORLEY."

" *Eton, June 22, 1827.*

" Dear Mamma ;

" You are very much mistaken if you think I know who Bartholomew Bouverie is ; I do assure you it puzzles me more than the hardest lesson I have learnt since I came to Eton ; and even if I had any suspicions, I scarcely dare speak them, for it would be thought great impudence in

me to determine what nobody else seems to know; I
have been told of several boys very high in the school
being concerned in it, but when I have ventured to say
any thing of the kind, I have always been contradicted
by those who are much more likely to know than myself,
so I have given up troubling myself about him : I have
ordered it to be sent down according to your desires, and
I thought Ingalton, the publisher, might know who he
was, so I ventured to ask ; and the answer I received
was, ' that it was Mr. Bouverie, of Eton College, who
wrote the Miscellany ;' but I am quite certain there is
no one of that name now here.   You may tell Papa that
he must rub up his old Greek and Latin if he wishes to
understand it ; and, as for you and my sisters, I will
answer for it, you will not be able to understand one half
of it.   I am afraid it will be a very long time before I
shall be able to write any thing half so clever ; but I am
determined to try my best, if it is continued till I am
high enough in the school.   Give my love to all at home.

"I remain, dear Mamma,

"Your dutiful Son,

"WILLIAM MORLEY."

"B. D."

Mr. Bouverie ;

I am a very respectable bachelor, studying in the
Temple, and should, I believe, be very happy, were it
not for the constant intrusions of an importunate young
fellow, who, having the misfortune to have nothing to do,
and liking my company (which is rather more than I do

his), is always interrupting my studies. If I am alone,
he considers himself fortunate ; if I am engaged, he presumes that it is nothing private, and that, consequently,
his company is not unacceptable. I think, Mr. Bouverie,
you adverted in a former paper to a " *cacoethes scribendi.*"
Now, Sir, this fellow is not exactly possessed with that
mania. By-the-bye he once sent me a composition of
his own for my correction, before it went to the press ;
but it was so full of bad spelling, that I had some difficulty in understanding it, and upon my hinting that fault
to him, he told me that (like the man in the Spectator),
he spelt like a *gentleman,* and not like a *scholar.* I have
not, however, been often troubled with these compositions ; it is a kind of a " *cacoethes loquendi* " that I have
particularly to find fault with. Having a good fortune,
he considers himself qualified to talk on every subject,
and that his money must give weight to his opinion.
But here I would wish to observe on a peculiarly ingenious method he has of getting out of any difficulty
into which a wrong calculation or unfortunate ignorance
might lead him ; should he happen to be in such a
dilemma (which is frequently the case), he can confi-
dently assert that he had it from the best authority, and
can establish his assertions by such apparently well-
authenticated evidence, as to remove from the mind of
any impartial hearer every doubt. I have often been,
owing to this, in very uncomfortable situations : indeed
the other day, when I happened to make some remark
on *Dr. Johnson's* Rambler, I was assailed by the most
unqualified sarcasms, and received the most unaccountable
pity for my ignorance in not knowing that *Addison* wrote

the Rambler ; and upon my still venturing to doubt, he
told me that Dr. Johnson was a most intimate friend of
his *grandfather*'s, who had expressly told him upon Dr.
Johnson's authority that Addison was the author.—Indeed so greatly was I confounded by this overpowering
evidence, and so satisfactory did it appear to the company, that they looked upon me with astonishment, and
I myself began to entertain some doubts as to the author.
Now, Mr. Bouverie, if you will only have the kindness
to hint that unsubstantiated authorities are no proof, and
falsehood no argument, you will greatly oblige

Your humble Servant,

J. PLEADWELL.

An Epilogue,

IN QUINDECASYLLABICS,*

SPOKEN BY

DAVID AP RICE, ESQUIRE,

*In appropriate costume: a large leek in his hat; a lump on his head,
unhappily occasioned by a tumble from the top of Plinlimmon;
the arms of the Principality engraved on one huge seal, and those
of the Rices on another, appended to his watch-chain by a ring
made in the year of the World III.*

A descendant of Cadwallader, and skill'd in Modred's lore,
I come upon the stage, my friends, to publish Number Four ;
Mr. Bouverie is tired, and Mr. Heaviside is dumb,
Mr. Jermyn's gone to Tattersall's—so here I come !
" A very pretty substitute," some roguish wag may cry,
" With the leek that's in his hat, and the leer that's in his eye :"
I throw my martial gauntlet down, and dare the grinning band,
To show an older family in all this merry land :

---

* Mr. Rice is notoriously irregular in his metres, therefore the reader must not
be alarm[...] at the [...] deficiency of a syllable [...]

Ten hundred hundred years before *your* father Adam came,
The Rice's stock was flourishing, it flourish'd on the same.
This coat was once a jerkin, and was worn by bold Glendower,
When with many a drop of English blood he ting'd his native shore ;
This hat belong'd to Mrs. G , his spouse , for hats were then
Made use of as they ought to be, by women, not by men ;
The shoes my uncle Merlin bought, he bought this very pair,
And left them in his family to hand from heir to heir.
Perhaps you may expect that I should make a humble bow,
But 'tis forbidden to my family to bend their heads so low ·
This neck was never flexible ! 'tis firm as any bull's, ·
When fastened to the stake he roars, and shakes himself and pulls ;
And till Plinlimmon hearkens to another Modred's song,
No Rice may bend his haughty head before yon motley throng.

    I lay upon a mountain once, I dream'd a golden dream ;
I dipt my feet in Helicon, and drank the sacred stream ;
And the sighing maid, Melpomene, had grasp'd me by the hand,
And straight was I encircled by the fair Pierian band ,
Thalia brought a leek, and Polyhymnia some cheese—
" I'd rather have it toasted, madam—toasted, if you please."
Thalia brought the laurel, and Melpomene the bays,
And " Sacred be to us," they cried, " O David Rice, your lays .
" For we are Welch , in Wales, too, our Pegasus was bred ;
" And Jove is Welch, and Neptune Welch ; and he that rules the dead ;
" And when old Chaos was, where now are fields and hills and dales,
" They'd sun, and moon, and pedigrees, and toasted cheese in Wales !"
    Yes, and I found my limbs were drench'd, in waking from my
        dream ;
But ah ! 'twas not in Helicon, but in a mountain stream ,
For cruel Fate had roll'd me to the roaring torrent's bed,
And the weeds that grew around it were the wreaths that crown'd my
        head ;
The Muses were some mountain maids, that long had tried in vain,
To rouse me from my lethargy, and make me wake again.

    'Twas thus I slept—and fellow-feeling seems to make you sleep,
For many an eye begins to wink, but none, ah ! none to weep ;
None mov'd with pity hear the sad recital of my woes ;
But a fortnight more will give my limbs some quiet and repose :
Then hail ! all hail ! my friends around, may all in gladness thrive,
Till Bouverie appears again—to publish Number Five.

                                   [Curtain falls.

_____

ETON MISCELLANY,

No. V.

INTRODUCTION.

HAVING already, in my former Numbers, presented to
the public a sketch of the characters of three of my coadjutors, I shall proceed to delineate a fourth; who, though
he has taken no very active part in the furtherance of
my work, is held in considerable estimation amongst us.
There are few who possess the singular propensities and
inclinations of Mr. Frederick Willoughby. He is one of
those peculiar persons who, having a good understanding,
can prefer the society and approbation of a few to the
most enticing popularity. From this singularity of habit
and inclination, he has never been induced to mingle in
the popular pursuits at Eton, and takes more interest in
the leading article of a newspaper than in feathering an
oar, or handling a bat. The principal thing which occupies
his attention, and affords him amusement, is politics : the
speeches of Pitt and Fox are much better understood by him
than Homer or Virgil. He knows the arguments *pro* and
con upon most bills that have been passed from the time of Sir
Robert Walpole to the present day. His memory is the most

peculiar I have ever known. He can accurately repeat
many celebrated speeches, which he retains in his memory
for a long period of time ; whilst he would forget in three
minutes any passage in Horace, unless, perchance, it had
been used in the shape of a quotation by some distinguished statesman. In addition to the singularities I
have already mentioned, a particular dislike to all exertion which is not absolutely necessary is, I think, somewhat remarkable : I have often known him remain within
doors on the most beautiful day in order to write out the
lists of the majority and minority on some question. If,
however, he is induced to make a perambulation, it never
can be extended beyond the limits of Salt Hill, where he
generally regales himself with a melon and some strawberries and cream. It would be unjust to Mr. Willoughby to omit mentioning the grand theatre of his
action—the Eton Society—which, in a former Number, I
acquainted my readers had existed here for fifteen years.
It is here that his talents are displayed to their best
advantage, and I will venture to assert, what indeed is
very generally acknowledged, that he is, in this respect,
much superior to his companions, though they may surpass him in other pursuits. One of the principal failings
which my friend possesses (if it deserves the name) is, a
natural timidity, which frequently prevents him from
openly asserting his opinion ; indeed, I know of few
things which would tend so much to diminish (I will not
say weaken) his arguments, as an opponent rendered formidable by broad shoulders or a powerful arm. With
all these singular propensities, which may bear the appearance of eccentricity in this our lesser world, he has

qualities, which, the more you know of them, the more
you can appreciate, and which render him both an
agreeable companion, and a valuable friend. When in
the presence of those, whom, from the difference of their
pursuits, and inclinations he may consider as not well
disposed towards him, he maintains a somewhat reserved
manner, but with his friends he assumes quite a different
character, and does not hesitate to give his opinion upon
any subject. He makes no scruple in pointing out any deficiency which he thinks he can discover on your part, but
one can easily overlook these ingenious discoveries; indeed,
the undeviating good humour he preserves, and in which
spirit these discoveries are generally made, is more calculated to excite a laugh than to provoke your anger.
As he has a happy command of language, to which is
joined a competent knowledge of history, he is enabled
to talk freely on any subject; indeed to so great a
degree does he excel in this, that I know not whether
the volubility of his tongue or the generosity of his heart
is most pre-eminent. Mr. Willoughby has now been at
Eton three years; still has the same propensities and
inclinations; and still maintains the same somewhat
eccentric character. He lives, comparatively speaking,
rather secluded, and is considered as the political phenomenon of the day; he has often been censured for his
seclusion, and praised for his eloquence; but, however,
though he may not possess the substantial qualities of a
Heaviside, the pedigree of a Rice, or the poetical talents
of a Jermyn, he has qualities which, if sufficiently exerted,
and properly directed, may enable him to distinguish himself, perhaps in no inconsiderable manner, in after-life.

THE FORCE OF HABIT.

That our lot in life is cast by chance and confirmed by habit, is a frequent and obvious remark.

But few are willing to apply the full force of this truism to themselves; few are ready to admit that the tone of their character and tenor of their pursuits have resulted from other causes than the free choice and natural inclination of their mind. Still less is it flattering to the vanity of any one, to confess that he has casually entered upon the pursuit of objects, to the attainment of which his best endeavours and fondest hopes are now directed, and that he has blindly touched the spring which now gives an impulse to his energies, and points out the motive of his exertions. Yet it must be owned, if we proceed to examine the extent and influence of this principle, that the pursuits and profession of future life are generally decided at an age so early, as far to precede the development of character, still more the possibility of free choice, in the individual whose course is thus pre-determined.

The mind of youth, while yet pliant and susceptible, receives impressions too deeply traced, and on too clear a tablet, to be easily obliterated; it sees through a foreign medium, appropriates to itself the hereditary opinions and perhaps prejudices of its forefathers, and often closely copies the peculiar features and characteristic colouring of those minds in casual collision with its own.

Reared in such a soil, and trained by such culture, the youthful plant, when arrived at maturity, and capable of self-support, will make use of the vigour of its shoots and beauty of its blossoms, solely for those purposes pointed out by the hand which guided its infant growth. No doubt, many benefits arise from this all-pervading system; without it the unaided power of reason would perhaps be inadequate to the task of impressing on the rising generation a due respect for the memory, and obedience to the institutions, of their fathers. If, then, these barriers to innovation were removed, to what an extent would the established harmony and organized principles of society be endangered. On the other hand, a venial doubt may be entertained, whether mere partial respect for antiquity may not sometimes induce us to cling too closely to its institutions, and oppose with too narrow a jealousy, the introduction of those improvements which the extended views, or pressing exigence of the time may suggest. On such adoption of principles and accommodation to circumstances, rests the welfare and indeed existence of every community, no less than the pureness of the ocean depends on the fluctuation of its waters.

It may perhaps be objected, that the different usages of society are originally suggested by the dictates of nature, and regulated by the peculiar character of their respective climates, and that consequently the customs handed down from early, and held in respect by succeed_ing, ages, would have been equally observed, had posterity been left to follow the unbiassed impulse of their genius. But if among the imperceptible revolutions and progressive expansion of the mind, such a principle were to become prevalent, who could analyse its powers, or who

could appoint the limits of its action? Where must we
fix the boundary, within which, it would merely tend
to confirm the natural tenor of our energies, but beyond
it, would prove a fatal obstruction to the spirit of enterprise and improvement?

But are national customs always the offspring of
nature, harmonizing with the temper and complexion of
their climate? Do the banks of the Niger enforce any
indispensable necessity of the tattoo? Do the forests of
Germany inculcate the use of the segar, or the summer
skies of Constantinople that of opium? Has oriental
scenery alone superinduced that elaborate barbarism, that
immutable bigotry to their own and abhorrence of foreign
institutions, which has for ages rendered China the
historical phenomenon of the world? All-powerful, then,
as that feeling appears to be, which has reconciled the
captive to his dungeon, and the Indian widow to the pile
of her husband, with what daring and capacious energies
must those master-minds have been endowed, which,
throwing off the shackles forged by chance, and rivetted
by habit, have pointed, from time to time, the path of
progressive improvement—a task, for which even their
powers would perhaps have proved inadequate, could
they not have called to their aid that love of novelty,
which induces us to turn from happiness at our door, to
pursue those visionary prospects, only bright from their
uncertainty.

. To this latter passion may be ascribed the evils of
licentious innovation, as well as to the former those of
narrow-minded bigotry; while from a just amalgamation
of the two, that tranquillity may truly claim its origin,

which is ensured alike from the over-bearing tyranny, and
the violent subversion, of established custom.   F.

RICHARD CŒUR DE LION;

Bright beam'd the sun on England's smiling land,
Calm flow'd the waves to kiss the silent strand;
St. George's banner floated high in air,
And many a gallant band was marshall'd there,
And England's monarch England's children led
The pathless waste of eastern shores to tread.
Yes, many a youthful heart is beating high,
And valour beams in many a youthful eye:
But darker soon the beaming eye shall glow,
And hotter yet the life-blood's current flow,
When England's sons ten thousand glaives unsheath,
To stem the Moslem in the strife of death.
    Oh, could'st thou check that dark and mad career,
Rein the hot charger, break the glitt'ring spear,
Bid the wild clamours of dissension cease,
And taste the joys of harmony and peace—
But no—the clouds have gather'd in the sky,
The lightning gleams, the thunder rolls on high;
And that dread bolt's unseen, unheeded, stroke
Must blast the glories of the British oak.
    That flashing eye and heaving bosom tell
How stern the voice, how potent is the spell
That bids thee leave thy kingdom and thine all,
To lend thine ear to mad Ambition's call.
Fair was the semblance, fair the accents sound,
When Richard's voice in thunder peal'd around.—
    "Oh, if for you the Lord of Glory bled,
And sought the regions of the silent dead:
If He, Omnipotent to slay or save,
Lay cold and torpid in an earthly grave;
By His pale brow and agonized eye,
By His deep-drawn and quick-returning sigh,

By all the tortures of a ling'ring death,
By the last anguish of His parting breath—
On, on, to dare the squadrons of the foe !
On, on, to lay the proud invader low !
Sons of the prophet, haste ye to the fight,
And meet the torrent stream of England's might '
Then who are they, whose craven bosoms quail '
They hear the howling of the distant gale ;
Go, servile throng · be ours the nobler doom
To seek the meed of glory, or a tomb :
Yes, be it ours to purge the holy spot,
By foes polluted, and by friends forgot :
To tread the desert and the pathless wild,
Speak aid and hope to Salem's weeping child :
On o'er the plains of yonder glitt'ring sea,
For God, for England, for St. George, for me."

 Yes, Salem's child laments her country's fate,
The gorgeous temple, and the Golden Gate,
Mourns for the relics of forgotten fame,
Mourns the sad day when Alla's children came :
Once led the dance, once join'd the choral band,
That sang the triumphs of Judæa's land,
That the proud courts of Salem's temple trod
To hymn the victories of Salem's God ,
Now fix'd in sadness, deep in grief and gloom,
With tears bedews the scarce more silent tomb :
No burst of rage, no furious torrents there,
But the dark, hidden, anguish of despair ;
In plaintive accents now her bitter wail
Sounds mid the rushing of the frantic gale :
Her home forgotten, and her harp unstrung,
And e'en the sad tale of her woes unsung
Unseen, unheeded, friendless and alone,
Heaves the deep sob, and draws the frequent groan.
Pale as yon marble from the Parian isle,
She knows not joy, she may not, must not, smile ;
Yet still, at times, her thoughts can upward fly,
And seek for refuge in the courts on high ;
Can bid the raging storm of anguish cease,
Can hush its billows to the calm of peace ;

Then Hope is there, and rays of heavenly light
Dispel the clouds of sorrow and of night.
She hears the footstep of th' avenger nigh,
She sees the fire that sparkles in his eye.
Loud rise the voices from the distant surge,
With " God, for England, Richard, and St. George !"
Again in fancy gleams the Christian spear,
And joy, and glory, and repose, are here.
Again the standard of St. George on high
Spreads all its splendors to the eastern sky,
And he, the hero of the Lion Heart,
Draws the bright sword, and hurls th' unerring dart.
Then the wild glow of exultation high
Can tinge her cheek, and sparkle in her eye:
" Yes, and again," in joy she cries, " again
Shall Salem echo to the victor's strain;
Again the long-drawn aisle and pealing choir
Shall hear the echo of the victor's lyre,
For lo, he comes : he comes to burst in twain
The iron links of slav'ry's galling chain :
New strength shall nerve the mighty hero's arm,
That shields the chosen of our God from harm;
That wars to cleanse that stain'd, yet holy, place,
And dash the hopes of Ali's treach'rous race.
And shall it be ? and shall my list'ning ear
Again the music of our fathers hear ?
And this enfeebled and emaciate hand
Strike the glad string, and lead the virgin band ?
Ah, me ! the prophet's sons are dark and wild,
Their hands are drench'd, their swords in blood defil'd ;
And never, never can their countless host
Yield the proud tenure of their native coast ·
And none may see the haughty crescent fall,
The cross triumphant rising over all.
Ah, me ! ye are but victims more and more,
Swift as ye sail from far Europa's shore ,
Ye are but victims for the Moslem sword,
In battle vanquish'd, yet in death ador'd !"
  Yet Richard comes : th' opposing blast in vain
Hath rous'd the stormy billows of the main :

Yes, thro' the tempest's roar, the thunder's peal
The hero lifts on high the beaming steel ;
And the loud fury of the whirlwind's ire
But fans the blaze of Richard's darker fire.
   Who foremost now the deadly spear to dart,
And strike the jav'lin to the Moslem's heart ?
Who foremost now to climb the leaguer'd wall,
The first to triumph, or the first to fall ?
Lo, where the Moslems rushing to the fight,
Back bear their squadrons in inglorious flight :
With plumed helmet and with glitt'ring lance
'Tis Richard bids his steel-clad bands advance ;
'Tis Richard stalks along the blood-dy'd plain,
And views unmov'd the slaying and the slain ,
'Tis Richard bathes his hands in Moslem blood,
And tinges Jordan with the purple flood.
Yet where the timbrels ring, the trumpets sound,
And tramp of horsemen shakes the solid ground,
Though mid the deadly charge and rush of fight
No thought be their's of terror or of flight ;
Yet 'times a sigh will rise, a tear will flow,
And youthful bosoms melt in silent woe :
For who, of iron frame and harder heart,
Can bid the mem'ry of his home depart ?
Tread the dark desert and the thirsty sand,
Nor give one thought to England's smiling land ?
To scenes of bliss and days of other years ;
The Vale of Gladness—and the Vale of Tears,
That, pass'd and vanish'd from their longing sight,
This, 'neath their view, and wrapt in shades of night ?
   Yet, hark ! the battle's harbinger from far
Sounds on the breeze, and summons to the war
To many a warrior doth that trumpet's breath
Tell the swift doom of horror and of death.
But e'en the craven's breast in ardour glows,
When England rushes on her Moslem foes :
When he, the hero, leads the thick'ning charge,
First in the clash of helmet and of targe :
And Vict'ry, riding on the breeze's wings,
Loud the glad hymn of Richard's triumph sings

Nor he inglorious, that with tarnish'd crest
Fled from the hardy children of the west :
No, as the bow, receding, can impart
A swifter passage to the winged dart,
So he awhile, in cautious flight, can yield,
Too soon to triumph on that blood-stain'd field,
Too soon on Salem's walls again to raise
The banish'd trophies of victorious days ;
Too soon in glory and in joy to see
The victor bands, the victor monarch flee.
 Few suns shall rise, few sink in ocean's wave,
Ere Fortune back shall take what Valour gave ·
In vain the foe shall hurl the vengeful dart,
It may not pierce the Lion Warrior's heart ;
But Envy's shafts can inly wound the breast,
And Malice break e'en that unbroken rest
Lo where the steel-clad sons of haughty Gaul
Back from the field of war's red harvest fall .
Unaided, undefended, and alone,
Still Richard proudly calls that field his own '
Sad is the day, of anguish and of gloom,
That sees him leave the unredeemed tomb :
Then fly the visions of ethereal light
That pierc'd the thick'ning gloom of Salem's night ;
E'en Hope, the last that cheer'd them, vanish'd then,
And all was dark and desolate again
 But he must seek in grief his native land,
O'er many a threat'ning sea and hostile strand
Forget the splendors of a monarch's throne,
And all he fondly had believ'd his own,
That shines to perish, glitters to decay,
And is but valu'd as it flies away.
Full soon the giant limbs, the mighty hand
That wielded once the high-uplifted brand,
Shall bear the captive chain, the chain of woe,
To some sad dungeon of despair shall go.
While all around the birds in freedom play,
Breathe the free air, and see the light of day,

And while the billow of the stormy main
Roars on the strand that bounds it, in disdain .
He of the open hand, the valiant soul,
Sees days and months, and years, in slav'ry roll;
Yet still unbroken and unaw'd can rise,
Still fraud, and guile, and treachery defies;
Still can unmov'd the snares around him see,
In body conquer'd, yet in spirit free.

   Lord of the chace, and monarch of the wood,
That reign'st o'er all the sylvan solitude,
Like thee, exulting in his conscious might,
Did Richard hasten onward to the fight;
Like thee, he dash'd the squadrons of the foe,
And laid the hapless few that dar'd him, low ,
Like thee, he bade the meek and lowly live,
Like thee, he knew to conquer and forgive
And tho' a brother point the hostile dart,
And aim the death-blow at a brother's heart ;
Tho' many a gift and many a grace from thee
But fix the traitor in his treachery—
Yet thou can'st lull his slavish fears to rest,
And clasp the deadly viper to thy breast.

   Yet vain the thirst of glory, vain was all
That bade thee listen to Ambition's call ,
Lo, where the hand is nerv'd, the bow is bent,
And the dread messenger of evil sent ;
Lo, where the victor and the hero lies,
Death on his brow and languor in his eyes ;
Those eyes that glanc'd in scorn or gleam'd in fire,
That brow that glow'd with more than mortal ire :
That hand is wan and pallid that in war
Oft hurl'd the fateful jav'lin from afar ,
All, all are gone ; and dark Oblivion flings
O'er Richard's giant form his dusky wings ·
All, all are gone ; and sternly conqu'ring death
Claims the last forfeit of his parting breath.
Ah ! was no mother there, to close the eye
That oft had seen the rush of victory ?

Ah ! was none there to tell of mercy given,
And turn the dying soldier's thoughts to heaven ?
None, none to shed the tribute of a tear
O'er the cold relics, and the silent bier :
But ye who oft had seen your hero lord
Head the glad charge, and draw the beaming sword,
Ye laid the warrior in his bed of clay,
Then turn'd ye from the mournful place away ,
Nor pass'd the mem'ry of that hour of gloom
Till death had call'd you to the silent tomb
    Deem not, proud man, that human tongue can tell
What doom is his, of heaven or of hell .
Ye know the path, the earthly path he trod,
Yet vengeance, judgment, mercy, are of God.
In silent wonder gaze, nor further dare ;
Pray to be spar'd thyself—thy fellows spare.

GREEK MANUSCRIPTS.

We again offer to our readers' notice a short extract from the Bouverie MSS., which we hope they will think worth the reading. We do not hesitate to pronounce this piece superior in plot, in incident, in the unexpected catastrophe, and in the preservation of character throughout, to the one before quoted ; as to the execution, the language, and the subordinate parts, we give them leave to judge for themselves :

1.

There once was a bear,
Who was kept at a fair,
    All dressed in green and gold ;
He made such a racket,
He soon tore his jacket,
    And his keeper began to scold.

α.

Ἄρκτος ἦν τὸ πρόσθ' ἀναιδής,
Ὃς πανηγύρει 'τετρίφθη
Πορφύρᾳ φανοῖς τε χρυσῷ
Σήμασιν παμποίκιλος;
Κᾆατον κυδοιδοπῶν τι
Αἶψα χλαῖναν ἐσπάραξε
Αἶψα δ' αὖ προπηλακίζειν
Ἦρξ' ὁ θηρίων ἄναξ.

2.

" My dear Mr. Bear,
" You are scarcely aware,
" Of the cost of your tailor's bill:
" If soon you're not quiet,
" I'll shorten your diet;
" How can you behave so ill?"

3.

The bear in a rage,
Jump'd up on the stage,
And bit off the keeper's head;
" A fig for your tailor,
" You stupid old gaoler,
" No bills are paid by the dead "

β.

Ἀρκτίδη* κάρα φίλιϛον,
Οὐ γὰρ ἔμπειρος πέφυκας
Οἷά σοι τὰ γραμματεῖα
Μαρτυρεῖ τὰ Στουλζίʊ.
Εἶγε μὴ ταχ' ἡσυχάζῃς,
Ἰσχνανεῖταί σοι τὸ δεῖπνον·
Πῶς γὰρ ἔϛθ' ὅπως παράσχῃς
Σαυτὸν ὧδ' ἀνάξιον.

γ.

Ὀξιώς δ' ὁ θὴρ χολωθεὶς
Ἰκρίων ἐφ' ἁρμογαῖσι
Ἧλτο κἀπίδηξε λύσσα
Τοῦ φυλακτῆρος κάρα.
Εἴθ' ὁ σὸς διαρραγείη
Στούλζιος, φύλαξ ἁπάντων
Μῶρε μώρων, οὐ γὰρ οὐδεὶς
Ἐν τάφῳ χρίους λόγος.

In the first place, we beg the critic to observe the beautiful beginning. There is no unnecessary "circum-bendibus," no senseless bombast, no worn-out invocation. We plunge at once into the story; but yet we are not so hurried along as to be called at once to feel for personages of whom we know no more than their names, if, indeed, so much. The exordium is at once concise, poetical, and to the purpose—"There once was a bear." The second line gives us a very necessary piece of information concerning his character, that he was kept at a fair. The third, and well does it perform its object, is given us to impress us with a becoming

---

* Vid. Lucian (Ἀλεκτρυὼν) section 14. Simon having got rich, changes his name from the vulgar Σίμων to Σιμωνίδης. Thus, as the name "Bear" does not in our language imply any very great compliment, it is rather softened off by the keeper, in the English, into Mr. Bear, in the Greek, to Ἀρκτίδης

respect for his dignity: he was "dressed in green and gold," or the Greek says, even in purple and gold! Was ever any thing more magnificent? Could a monarch have chosen more beautiful colours? But the bear seems, from his utter contempt of all external decorations, to have been pretty much of the Cynic persuasion. He tears his jacket! He tramples on the purple and gold like any Diogenes! And the keeper begins to abuse him; for what else could he expect after such a transgression?

However, a person of his consequence was not to be slighted with impunity, and of this danger the keeper (whom, as nothing is said of his character, we may conjecture to be much the same as keepers usually are, surly, but kept in order by a proper awe of the superior corporeal powers of the bear) seems to have had a just idea. He begins rather in a flattering and humble strain of expostulation, and only gently hints at the enormous expense which he is put to, to support the dignity of "Mr. Bear." But, carried away by the impetuosity of his temper, he goes to such lengths as to make an ill-timed threat of short commons, and concludes with a most touching appeal to his moral feelings—"How can you behave so ill?"

And here we must for a time divert our readers' attention from the English, to express our unfeigned and unbounded astonishment at the Greek. In the second stanza, and the fourth line, he will observe the word Στούλζιος, used in the sense of "Tailor." Now, we have looked over Lexicons and Thesauri of all sorts and sizes, and cannot even find such a word in the language, and the only relation which the Greek word seems here to bear to the English, is in a strong resemblance between that and the name of an eminent tailor of the present day: and how the author of this piece could possibly have known any thing of a tailor who flourished many years afterwards, we are at a loss to conceive. Nothing short of prophetical inspiration could have prompted this effusion; unless, indeed, as a learned friend suggests, an ancestor of the above-mentioned gentleman then exercised the same lucrative functions as those which his descendant at this moment embellishes, and had attained the same eminence in his art, as it would be an insult to the bear's taste to suppose for a moment that he, dressed as he was in green and gold, would stoop to employ a second-rate tradesman. We would certainly advise Mr. Stultz to make a most diligent inquiry on the subject, as he would by that means establish for himself a most noble genealogy, and if, through means of the keeper's untimely fate (dî talem avertite casum!) the bill was left undischarged, Mr. Stultz would, I should think, be in justice entitled to the amount of the bill, which was certainly a very large one, from the descendants of the keeper, or in case of his being unable to trace them, from those of the bear.

We have wandered too far from our subject; we beg pardon, and return to it again. We concluded our last criticisms with some remarks on the keeper's ill-timed rashness; ill-timed indeed it was, for the insult of shortening his diet was too great for so high-spirited an animal, and one who had such a lofty sense of honour, to pocket. He was wound up to the highest pitch of indignation, and at once throwing off all shackles of pity and moderation, he takes vengeance in the most summary and decisive way, by cracking the unfortunate keeper's pericranium between his jaws, and then, in a style of bitter triumph, which Homer or Virgil would have given their ears to have attained, apostrophizes the body—

> " A fig for your tailor,
> " You stupid old gaoler,
>   " No bills are paid by the dead."

This strong sarcastic exclamation finishes the poem; a spice of humour is thrown into it, to take off, in some measure, the melancholy which the tragical exit of the keeper must leave on every feeling mind; and the sublime and consoling truth of " No bills are paid by the dead," assures us of at least one advantage which the keeper gains by being thus soon dismissed from the stage.

THE WOES OF ERIN.

When in old Eblana's bay,
Pembroke's hostile navy lay,
And to Erin's hapless shore,
Back the exil'd tyrant bore,
From a cliff, whose beetling brow
Frown'd o'er the foaming surge below,
Loudly, on the ev'ning gale,
Were borne the minstrel's notes of wail;
And floated o'er the wave his song,
Prophetic of his country's wrong.
   " Erin, on thy sacred shore,
England's haughty squadrons pour,
Shall tyrant's force, shall stranger's wile,
Pollute the free and holy isle ?

Yes, so it is, the fates decree
Dooms lasting, endless misery :
Too sure these aged eyes can view
That heavy debt of slavery due.
Too true, alas, this anxious sight
Has pierc'd the gloomy veil of night,
And mark'd, through each revolving year,
New scenes of tyranny appear.
Low shall be Eblana's walls,
And strangers lord in Tara's halls ;
And to be born 'neath such a clime,
Shall be to Erin's sons a crime.
But, ah ! what tortures can assuage
The tyrant's and the bigot's rage?
In vain shall many a victim bleed,
The martyr to his Father's creed ;
In vain shall each polluted heath,
Be purpl'd with the flood of death,
And ruin'd temples widely spread
The marks of the Fanatic's tread.*
Thus I thy destin'd woes reveal,
Which fate forbids me to conceal,
I see no beam of cheering light,
To dissipate the shades of night :
Through unborn ages yet shall be
One course of endless misery."

PROTEUS AND JOHN BULL.

A DIALOGUE.

Proteus. Dear Mr. Bull, I rejoice to see the reformation which has taken place in your demeanour; you
are quite an altered man ; you have polished off all that

---

* The cruelties committed by the army of Cromwell will immediately present themselves to the mind.

brusquerie, as my pupils, the French, say, which used to be your characteristic, and are really becoming worthy to be enrolled in the number of my votaries.

Bull. Then I am to consider that I am indebted to you for this valuable reformation; forsooth, that as I was formerly as steadfast as a rock, so I am now as changeable as a weather-cock. Beware, good master Proteus, lest I find means to confine your boasted mutability; there are in England stocks and bonds, out of which you may find it difficult to slip, though you should even change yourself into an eel.

Proteus. Surely I misunderstand you; for nothing is more completely under my dominion than what you have mentioned: what is more variable, more fluctuating than the Stocks? what more changeable in its nature and its value than Chili and Colombian Bonds?

Bull. Positively, Mr. Proteus, you are enough to make a man hang himself for pure vexation.

Proteus. If your inclination runs that way, I can change myself into a tree for your accommodation.

Bull. The most useful change you can make is, to give up changing at all, and to become a steady kind of divinity, such as your friend Janus, who has eyes before and behind, that he may never be obliged to turn his head round.

Proteus. I am much obliged to you for the hint, but must decline taking it, in consideration of the great sacrifice I have made, in leaving my post of Head Keeper of the Sea-Calves, for the express purpose of taking care of those upon land.

Bull. What insolence is this? do you call the English, calves?   o 2

Proteus. Yes, and you the father of the herd, Mr. Bull.

Bull. Then I must say, that it is my hearty wish that you had confined your dominion to the sea; there indeed you were in your element; she has a disposition congenial to yours, being at one moment tranquil and unruffled, at another agitated with the fury of the tempest; and besides, whether, calm or tempestuous, she is still under the dominion of that most changeable of mistresses, the Moon.

Proteus. But pray, Mr. Bull, may I ask the reason of your antipathy to me? for I am perfectly unconscious of having injured you in any way.

Bull. Not injured me? then injuries were never known upon earth. Zounds, sirrah! if a man who has his whole fortune in good solid gold is compelled, against his will, to change it for the flimsy currency of a country bank, especially in the time of a panic, is not he injured? yet when I see my sterling and solid inflexibility, my pertinacity of the right stamp, and my native decisiveness of character, changed for fickleness, foppery, and Frenchification, I, forsooth, am not an injured personage!

Proteus. But what proofs have you that the national character of the English is changed?

Bull. Proofs indeed! proofs enough to stun the deafest man that ever used an ear-trumpet. Look at the Stage, to begin with; what does that pretend to do, but to hold the Mirror up to Nature? and truly it does hold it up with a vengeance, when a Pantomime is acted on its boards: then it is, that the people flock to see things as changeable as themselves, and the more changes there are, the better the pantomime. They delight to see a tawdry, parti-coloured, tinsel-wearing varlet change with his wand houses into stage-coaches, and sign-posts into turnpike-gates; and does all this show no fondness for change? O thou patron of harlequins, mountebanks, and courtiers!

Then again, my people are not satisfied with changing themselves, but they must change every thing that belongs to them : where are the substantial pavements that used to support the moving mass of the English population; alas! they are changed for an unsubstantial thing, that is either mud or dust, according as the caprice of that most capricious of all things, the weather, shall determine. Think you that I will be blinded, that I will be bespattered with impunity? think you that I will see the basis of the British, the foundation upon which they stand, converted into—Zounds! is there in England no orator

"To move the stones to rise and mutiny?"

Are there none to take pity on the forlorn condition of my pavements? There are none. Then may their flinty hearts be broken with hammers, to mend those roads of which they are the advocates.

Proteus. I can assure you, Mr. Bull, it grieves me to see you thus indignant; and as discretion is the better part of valour, I shall retire.

Bull. Retire, Sir, you shall not, till I have received satisfaction for the insults and injuries you have heaped upon me.

Proteus. That is easily given; at least, if you are the reasonable person which I have always supposed you to be. Nay, calm the severity of your brow, and listen to sober reason. That the English are imbibing a fondness for change, is most true ; that they are giving up those prejudices in favour of established customs which were formerly their characteristics, is also true ; and happy it is that they are. Nothing has tended so much to perpetuate errors, as the pertinacity with which they have clung to the customs and manners of their forefathers, a feeling which has sanctioned abuse, and immortalized absurdity. In what particular were their ancestors better or happier than themselves, that they should look back with such regret on their condition ; in what particular were they wiser, that their institutions should be respected in the face of reason and sense ? Can it be supposed that, while all the arts and sciences have made rapid strides to perfection, the condition, wisdom, and energies of man have alone been retrograding ? If it can be proved that man was neither wiser nor better five hundred years ago than he is at present, how strange is this infatuation, which estimates customs and institutions, like wine, or black-letter books, simply by their age. That the English under Edward the Third were one jot better than the English under George the Fourth is, in my opinion, untrue ; and all the boasted superiority of olden time is owing to the simple reason, that men cannot bring their minds to be contented with the present. Of all evils, the present is always the greatest ; but with respect to good, precisely the reverse takes place. Thus it is, that the greatness of the dead, and the excellence of past times are exaggerated ; while living virtue, or present felicity, is too often undervalued. For these reasons, Mr. Bull, be not angry with me, if I advise

you to burst the shackles of custom, and to acknowledge the advantages of change.

ANTONY HEAVISIDE.

THE BRIDE OF THE LAKE.

Relic of fairy days—deep, blue Loch-lein, *
Whose waters kiss Creation's noblest shrine,
A mountain's purpled outline, where no rude
Invader tracks the pine-clad solitude :
How sweet to watch, ere yet his course be run,
The mellowing glory of that vesper sun !
While o'er the foam, that wreathes in smiles thy wave,
Varies the magic light his parting radiance gave :
And distant chimes, heard thro' the twilight's grey,
Swell the sad note, and mourn th' expiring day. †
How sweet to hear the light-breath'd serenade
In tuneful echoes melt along the glade ;
While choral voices seem to wake around,
Stealing on Night's dull ear with rapt'rous sound !
Ye, too, dark-crested pinnacles of might,
That from the giant grandeur of your height,
Fling a broad shadow to the lake below,
Where, silver-bright, the languid waters flow ;
Storm-children, hail !   On yon tremendous peak
The wheeling eagle rests him from the break
Of some unbridled tempest : by that scaur,
Which seem'd the centre of the thunder's roar ;
E'en there the monarch of the mountain gloom
Ceas'd his wild flight, and dropt the flagging plume !
Well do thy glories beam on Fancy's sight,
Loch-lein, by Memory's mild, reflected light :

---

* Loch-lein, the ancient name for the Lake of Killarney.
† Che paia 'l giorno pianger, che si muoja.—*Dante.*

The warring winds had soften'd to a breeze,
Mild as the musk-wind o'er Arabian seas ;
The waves were rippling round my bark's career,
And the light blossoms hail'd the vernal year,
Wafting their scents from Innisfallen's shore .
Then, as the boatman check'd his plashing oar,
Midst the calm slumber of that moonlight bay,
Broke forth the richness of his deep-ton'd lay,
That told of haunted stream, of fairy bower,
While Erin yet was Freedom's loveliest flower ,
And sang, how erst the Chieftain's arm of pride
Bore to the cavern'd halls his destin'd bride.

The Boatman's Legend. *

O wildly o'er the buoyant tide
    Floated the echoes of thy water,
When the dark chieftain woo'd his bride,
    Killarney's meek and lonely daughter

---

* To those who are acquainted with Moore's beautiful Melodies, it will
be unnecessary to call to mind, that the story of the Chieftain of the
White Horse, or O'Donoghue, as he is sometimes called, who, on the first
of May, returned to the upper world to claim a bride of exquisite purity
and loveliness, has furnished materials for four or five highly poetical stanzas in his collection   The story, however, which is related
above, is essentially different from that of Mr. Moore, who has made the
courtship entirely on the lady's part   "Among other stories connected
with this Legend of the Lake, it is said, that there was a young and
beautiful girl, whose imagination was so impressed with the idea of this
visionary chieftain, that she fancied herself in love with him, and at last,
in a fit of insanity, on a May-morning, threw herself into the Lake." Although, as the peasantry of Killarney will tell us, many years have elapsed
since the sound of O'Donoghue's unearthly music has been heard on their
waters, a remnant of the superstition still remains, and the waves, to
which a windy day gives, *me ipso teste*, a very formidable appearance, are
still called by them " O'Donoghue's white horses."

As the star that heralds morning
 On its brightly-gleaming way ;
As the rainbow, richly dawning
 Where the mountain haloes play ;
So shone her cheek's unfading hue,
While, deck'd with blushes ever new,
She shunn'd th' impassion'd gazer's view.
The maid has started from her bed
With Nature's own profusion spread—
For she was resting where the stream
Of cloudless Evening's crimson beam
Illumin'd banks of jessamine,
That on the hill's dark verge recline :
A· thousand mingling branches made
Her canopy of light and shade ,
And the lake's breezes sighing near,
Mildly fann'd her golden hair.
'Twas said, around that leafy grove
The lightsome fairies lov'd to rove ;
And well might spirits love, I ween,
The glories of that highland scene ;
Where arbutus, and lichen wild
Allur'd the steps of Beauty's child,
As light and merrily she flew
 Along that deep, fantastic glen,
To cull the wild rose, bright with dew,
 Far from the busy haunts of men—
Now has she started from the bed,
Where balmy flowers had wreath'd her head ;
And, kneeling on the fragrant sod,
She breathes the holy name of God,
In accents such as angels raise
With purity of sinless praise.
Then rising, towards those waters bright,
Glistening in the pale moonlight,
 She bent her lonely way :
Her blue eyes sought the western star,
Where, thro' the cloudlets from afar
 Trembles that magic ray. .

'Twas stillness all ; as in that hour
All nature felt her beauty's power,
And hush'd the grove, the lake, the air,
To gaze upon a thing so fair !
Slowly o'er that deep repose
   Steals a distant, distant strain :
Now soft it fell, now wild it rose,
   Like that blest song, that poets feign
Is heard among the rolling spheres,
That swim in light for endless years.
Far up the lengthen'd lake are seen
Those streamers of celestial sheen,
Which tell to all who watch them there,
That spirits ride the viewless air.
Full in the midst a steed of snow
Seem'd starting from th' abyss below ;
With heaving breast, and loosen'd mane,
And hoofs that spurn'd the liquid plain.
And who is he, that dares to ride
With eye of fire, and crest of pride ?
Hark ! by the sullen sounds that wake,
'Tis the dark chieftain of the Lake !
Tho' many a circling year is fled,
Since he was number'd with the dead,
Yet still in the bloom of early May,
Is heard his wizard roundelay,
As he seeks the bride, whose eye's blue languish
Will banish long-enduring anguish ,
O mild and pure that bride must be,
As snow-flakes on a waveless sea !
Now faster and braver he dashes on,
And the waters curl, where his course is run.
Faster and braver he makes for the shore,
And his glossy plume is spangled o'er
   With the white-crested foam
And now he checks his headlong speed,
And curbs awhile that panting steed,
   Near the maiden's woodland home.

    *   *   *   *   *   *

Another winged hour has broke
Upon the world ; and morn has woke
O'er the deep still of those cavern'd halls,
   O'er the distant music floating round,
O'er the cooling airs of the fountain falls,
   The blended rapture of light and sound :
All, all the same, as when the day
On Turk's proud summit died away : *
But where is she, whose lovely mien
With added beauty grac'd a scene
    So beautifully wild ;
Gave music to the tinkling rill,
Gave lustre to the fringed hill,
    E'en while the gloaming smil'd ?
Will not yon island's cavern lone
   Mourn o'er her loss with fond delay ?
Will not yon crystal fountain moan,
   And weep itself in tears away ?
They have borne her to an elfin green,
To see what mortal ne'er has seen ,
To watch the clouds of amber sailing
   Thro' the depths of heav'nly air ;
To live, perpetual balm inhaling
   From the wreaths that spirits wear ;
To bask in moonlight luxury
   Mid a thousand lakes, and a thousand isles ,
And still to watch with melting eye
   The spot that most like Erin smiles !
Such was her doom . like that proud star,
   Gleams on th' Egyptian maiden's rest †
But may not wheel his magic car,
   To glad the regions of the West.
So from her home, her country far,
   She walks the islands of the blest.
       [*End of the Boatman's Legend.*

---

* Mount Turk, the most picturesque of the chain which surrounds the Upper and Middle Lakes of Killarney.

† The Canopus, a star of great brilliancy, but never seen in European climates.

Harp of the Lake ! if now no spirits love
The emerald foliage of thy chequer'd grove ;
If now no more with music from afar
Thy fairy guardians hail the evening star ;
No more the waves in proud submission play
Around th' unearthly monarch of the May ;
No virgin bands their yearly tribute bring,
Strew the fresh rose, and welcome in the Spring :
If these be hush'd, and stern Oppression flings
The chain of Silence o'er thy voiceless strings,
Harp of the Lake ! forgive his rash career,
That gives to Erin one melodious tear, *
And for the halcyon days of Freedom's fire,
Weaves the wild wreath, and tunes the youthful lyre.

ROLAND.

LETHE.

Sir ;

I once, having a good deal of interest in the lower world, was favoured with a sight of the lake Lethe. The aperture giving access to it from the earth has of late been much widened; but the showers of books which incessantly pour through it are so thick and heavy, that the spirited proprietors mean to afford still more accommodation to the public, by yet further enlarging the space for admission. There seemed, from the noise above, to be a competition among the books for the privilege of first falling into oblivion. As, however, they got further down, the noise became less, and when they had reached the surface of the lake, it entirely ceased, and in falling in, there was neither splash, nor

---

* " Without the meed of some melodious tear."—MILTON, *Lycidas.*

sound of any kind. It received all within its unruffled
bosom, and it was indeed a shelter to the friendless.
Notwithstanding the immense bulk of matter (I forget
how many tons daily) thus thrown in, the lake does not
rise one inch higher on its banks ; whence I suppose
that the books are all dissolved and completely incor-
porated with the water, which, however, appears still
capable of receiving many more without saturation.

In the falling column I perceived a great number of
foolscap sheets of paper, some single, some double,
some in blue covers. These, I was told, came down
only for about three or four months in the year, usually
from February to June, and were Parliamentary Reports
and Proceedings, and other papers procured by divers
persons of motion-making notoriety in the upper regions. Besides these, however, there were immense
numbers of other descriptions, of which I can only
enumerate a very few. Newspapers of all kinds were
there in abundance : even as they fluttered downwards,
they were engaged in combat with one another; the
Courier was fiercely grappled by the St. James's
Chronicle, and the Times was at loggerheads with
John Bull ; but all alike, Ministerial and Opposition,
the factious and the servile, ended their deadly strife in
speedy dissolution. Among these came Cobbett's
Registers : I observed that they made common game of
these unfortunate productions, and attacked them in
every direction, though few were daring enough to meet
the terrific gridiron face to face. The Registers, however, no whit abashed or alarmed, returned most of their
buffets with interest. But, alas ! some papers, under the

same title, and of dates not widely different, were actually endeavouring to make prey of their own species,
and came in violent collision with one another. I was
surprised even to see some works with the names of
Shakspeare and Milton on them sharing the common
destiny; but, on examination, I found that those of the
latter were some political rhapsodies, which richly deserved their fate; and that the former consisted of some
editions of his works which had been burdened with
notes, and mangled with emendations by his merciless
commentators. In other places I perceived authors
worked up into phrensy by seeing their own compositions descending like the rest: often did the infuriated
scribes extend their hands, and make a plunge, to endeavour to save their beloved offspring; but in vain:
I pitied the anguish of their disappointment, but with
feelings of the same commiseration as that which one
feels for a malefactor on beholding his death, being
at the same time fully conscious how well he has deserved it.

Together with these, I saw one noble effort made, and
I rejoice to think that it succeeded. A bold and spirited
individual stepped forward and rescued some old and
almost illegible volumes in their fall, though not without
labour and danger, when they were almost immersed in
the waters. On investigation, I discovered that the
preserver was William Gifford, and the preserved no
less than Massinger, Jonson, and Ford. And though
he perished after accomplishing this glorious object, yet
I saw a smile of honest and cheering satisfaction on his
countenance; and I saw many, very many, of his coun-

trymen crowning his monument with the honours he had
so nobly earned, and so justly deserved.

I need hardly mention, that novels constituted a by
no means inconsiderable portion of the perennial stream
which I have been describing. I endeavoured for some
time to spy their titles, and catch a glimpse of their
contents, but found them so unsatisfactory, that I became more disposed to accelerate than to impede their
descent. Infinite was the variety of the tales of imagination which were doomed to Lethe; they extended from
the wildest flights of fable and romance, to the humble
fiddle-faddle of exquisite sensibility; from the unassuming appearance and moderate dimensions of a six-
penny pamphlet, to the magnificent array of type, and
majestic latitude of margin which figure in Mr. Col-
burn's shop, while the three volumes, and the awful
"One pound eleven and sixpence" inscribed on the back
terrify the greedy but penurious Novel-hunter, and put
the book far beyond the reach of those circulating
libraries which, as we are here informed, so effectually
promote the march of intellect all over your country.

With these were an immense number of political
pamphlets, of "Substances of Speeches," &c. which,
after making an amazing flutter and hubbub in the
upper regions for a brief space of time, all hastened to
their common destination.

I perceived that the art of Swimming was entirely unknown in this region; though one would think it would
be particularly easy, from the very density of the element itself. Indeed, among the more humble publications, I did see some with that very title prefixed to

them, which might, perhaps, have been useful to their surrounding companions, had not stern Fate irrevocably determined thus to check the overflow of genius, and drain off the deluge of literature.

Thus it is, Mr. Bouverie; *metam properamus ad unam.* With regard to my own case, I know not whether I am destined to find a Lethe for myself in one of the corners of your bureau, or whether it may be my lot to figure in the pages of your Miscellany : *that,* it would be treason to doubt, would be an effectual preservative, and would give me the right of making for myself a "Jamque opus exegi." Really however, Sir, considering the nature of the air I inhaled in the lower regions, I think it is wonderful that I have contrived to enlighten you with so much of what I perceived there, and have escaped uninfected by the contagion of forgetfulness.

Not having been myself an author till the present time, I looked on the scene before me with interest, yet without partiality ; but now, Mr. Bouverie, I too having, like others, a reputation to guard, I shall watch most narrowly the perennial shower, lest I should allow a Number of the "Eton Miscellany," containing my production in it, to slip by unperceived.

Believe me, honoured Sir,

Your sincere, though oblivious, admirer,

MANDRAGORAS.

It is scarcely necessary to inform the Reader, that I received this composition by the same channel as those of my former ones which contained Subterranean News. It was "Favoured by Mr. Mercury," who contrives to convey all communications from that quarter clandestinely into Mr. Ingalton's pocket, as he, good man, silent and pensive, hurries along the street, buried in reflections concerning the probable loss of reputation which he will sustain by having become the publisher of " The Eton Miscellany."   B. B.

LINES,

To a Young Lady who acted Helen, in a Charade.

May Fancy's art for thee, my fair,
  Her brightest wreaths entwine,
And may no lighter step be there,
  No lighter heart than thine.

When yielding all around delight,
  Amid the festive scene,
As Helen fair, as Helen bright,
  You personate the queen.

Then let no gem or gaud, my fair,
  Destroy the classic spell,
Wreathe myrtle in that dark-brown hair,
  Which suits a Helen well.

I see, I see, from that bright eye
  And ever-varying mien,
The kindred joy to others fly,
  And animate the scene.

Those flushing cheeks thy joy denote,
  While mingling in the dance,
'Tis heard in ev'ry soft low note,
  'Tis seen in ev'ry glance.

And ever may that voice so light
  Fall gaily on mine ear,
And may those eyes be ever bright,
  And bright without a tear.   MALEK.

Nec tua laudabis studia, aut aliena reprendes.

My dear Mr. Bouverie;

This is, perhaps, the last subject of all others upon which I should have ventured to address you, had I not felt convinced, that there is not a subject more misunderstood, nor a maxim more perverted at our public schools and colleges, than the one to which I allude. I will, in the first place, endeavour to prove the truth of my assertion; and in the second, to show that this maxim is too often departed from, and that, were it held in greater repute, much inconvenience, much pain, much ill-feeling, which are inevitably produced by it, would subside. Those, for instance, who form the majority in our community look down with contempt upon the more retired avocations of those whom different habits of thinking and of acting have led to take up different pursuits, and to be as much interested in them as their companions are in theirs; they frequently bestow undeserved abuse and calumny upon that minority, forgetting that by far the better course to adopt would be, to allow these little animosities to subside, and to prevent any pursuit from interfering with another; for it is idle to suppose that there is any irreconcileable difference between them, and that they cannot easily chime in with each other. On the other hand, I confess, my dear Sir, that I by no means think the conduct of the minority to which I have adverted (those, I mean, whose retired habits may have kept them aloof from

more popular avocations or enterprising pursuits) entirely unexceptionable in the line of conduct which they
pursue. They also, in their turn, are too much in the
habit of treating with a kind of reserved and implied
contempt, those who are not of the same tastes and
habits as themselves; and whilst they are too much in
the habit of arrogating the infallibility of their own
judgments, they call in question the utility of those
other pursuits, which they do not follow, and affect to
ridicule those other occupations, simply either because
they do not understand, or take no interest in them.
There are, indeed, a few, but very few, who steer safely
between the two extremes, and thereby conciliate the
good will and favourable opinion of both, which is no
easy task. I would, for all these reasons, recommend,
as it were, a cessation of hostilities, and that an end
should be put to those injurious and useless distinctions
between the different classes of our fellow-citizens which
tend only to exasperate one against the other, and discredit both. But there are those who, in their endeavours to ingratiate themselves with all parties, forfeit
the esteem and good-will of both : take, for instance,
C. How unenviable is his lot, and how unpopular his
character! he takes delight in prying into every one's
affairs, in giving his advice, which, though at all times
bad, is then, perhaps, particularly unseasonable; he
obtrudes himself upon your time, when you are most
deeply engaged, and is as loth to take his departure as
he is happy to torment you (though he does it uncon-
sciously) by his frequent visits; his conversation, though

shallow and unsubstantial, has, at least, the merit, or
rather demerit, of being incessant, and he leaves you
apparently satisfied that he has produced a favourable
impression upon your mind ; he knows enough of the
different pursuits of his companions, to imagine that he
is well qualified to become their most intimate and
valued friend; and yet, in reality, he knows too little to
be the intimate or valued friend of any . this, perhaps,
is the very worst of all characters. Let us turn for a
moment to the character of Mr. Theophilus Headstrong,
the leading features of whose character are, activity,
obstinacy, and ignorance.   His mind, being of the most
enlightened kind, naturally soars above all vulgar prejudices that books or book-learning are in any way desirable ; it embraces nothing but field-sports, for the
manliness of which, and for the folly, inexpediency, and
slavishness, of following any other avocations, he is a
most ignorant, obstinate, and furious, stickler.

My friend, Lorenzo Languish, falls into the opposite
extreme : he terms cricket nothing more than the knocking of balls about, and whilst he broods sulkily over
what he daily sees passing before his eyes, for his part,
he cannot help expressing his unfeigned surprise, that
any one should think it worth while to give himself so
much unnecessary trouble in a rowing-match, or heat
himself so violently in any bodily exercises.

There is also another class, who look down upon all ;
who are of opinion, that games, reading, and every
other avocation, are entirely beneath them ; whose powers
of conversation are extremely small ; who can converse

upon no subjects except the number of rich livings in the disposal of their families; the number of valets, butlers, grooms, &c. &c. which they keep. But it is an insult to our community to suppose that this is a common case. An example of this sort is Lord * * *, who appears to be incapable of conversing upon any topics of real interest : but though persons like him have not the good sense to escape this snare, the world either laughs this fault away, or, should it be too deep for that, they become intolerably disagreeable; but I am sure you will agree with me, that nothing can be more ridiculous, and that nothing can display more " mauvais ton," than to say presumptuous things of one's self; and even if there really is ground for self-approbation, does it not argue a sounder judgment, and a safer discretion, to repress the exultation which may be felt upon the shadowy and unsubstantial compliments of temporary friends ?

My only object in writing the above, my dear Sir, has been, to excite in your mind the same reflections that have been called forth in mine, and to suggest to you the propriety of employing some part of your valuable time in endeavouring to remedy this serious evil, and in throwing out some recommendations upon the subject to which I have alluded, to those among our fellow-citizens who would be so ready to receive them.

I am, my dear Sir,

Your obliged servant,

BENJAMIN BENEDICT.

THE CAPTIVE.

Ye mighty barriers, why do ye array
Your craggy pinnacles in proud disdain,
Pile beyond pile ? and think ye thus to bind
What neither tyrant's arm, nor torture's pangs,
Nor e'en these manacles I bear, coerced ?
Frown on; I spurn ye : never shall this free,
This adamantine, spirit crouch beneath
E'en Nature's yoke : it soars beyond the scope
Of human vision, toward those glorious realms
Polluted nor by filth, nor mortal dross
Degenerate : ye torrents of yon height,
I hail ye as congenial to my soul ;
Howl on, ye whirlwinds, through th' impervious glade,
And ye foreboding spirits, in the gloom
Shriek ominous ; your horrors I revere :
Let others serve, let others bend the knee,
And act the parasite ; degenerate herd,
Servile in body, and debas'd in soul,
Ye fawning sycophants, I here renounce ye ,
Ye neither feel, nor act, nor utter sounds
As honour dictates ; honour is a name
To you unknown, unsought for, unrever'd
This is your creed ; to this degrading faith
Ye cling enamour'd ; and in heart and soul
Cringe to that wretch ye tremble to disdain.
War has his victims, servitude her spoils ;
The first I courted, and the second gain'd,
My doom irrevocable ; nor from heaven
Beams the bright Sun, nor with his gladd'ning ray
These desolate, inhospitable, crags,
These emblems of captivity illumines ,
Yet I repine not—nor within my breast
Boils Indignation's too impetuous tide;
'Tis stifled by Contentment's aid divine ;
Foam, then, ye torrents, down your native heights ;
Flash bright, ye meteors, o'er the troubled sky ;
And ye eternal snows, engulf this frail,
This unsubstantial shadow in your tomb,
But still my spirit, undismay'd, at east,
Triumphant soars above Perdition's wave

THE CHARMS OF MYSTERY.

Dear Mr. Bouverie;

- I have lately been much discomposed by the circula tion of sundry whispers, intimating that a part of the mask, a corner of the veil, that at present screens you from vulgar eyes, is to be raised. You must know that I am much accustomed to picture to myself the exact locality of the scenes, and features of the characters, that interest me, and have consequently a lively idea of the face and stature of Hercules and Jack the Giant-Killer; can give you a correct ground-plan of the Castles of Udolpho and Torquilstone; and, aided by your works, have traced to my fancy, no faint out-line, but a highly-coloured portrait, of yourself. Often have I exclaimed, when a pensive figure in the twilight glade of Poet's-walk, or the retiring gloom of the Cloisters, has glided past my eyes, "It must be Bouverie!" This interesting idea naturally inspires me with the highest respect for your character, but I much fear it will cease, if you really prove to be a common cricket-playing, ab-sence-attending, animal like myself. Nor can I doubt that such a discovery will have wider influence; for, when did the potent spell of Mystery fail to fascinate? who has not felt "the icy scalp of fear" grow colder on his head at the bare recital of those dark tales never to be unra-velled by human knowledge? From what other source can we derive that all-pervading feeling of interest to which the Man of the Iron Mask owes the celebrity of his sufferings, his dearly-bought pre-eminence among the forgotten victims of coward Cruelty? Would not Junius, in spite of the bitter irony and energetic elegance of his Letters, have long since found his level among the political writings of the day, had not curiosity been awakened by ignorance, and cherished by the ingenious proofs of authorship brought forward in favour of those for whom that honour is respectively claimed?

It is needless for me to profess my conviction, that the Waverley novels require no adventitious aid to enhance their popularity; but who did not feel some little disappointment when that declaration, which confirmed the opinion of the public, totally extinguished the long-lingering hope of some interesting disclosure, some unexpected development, of the secret?

Such is the irresistible attraction that Mystery possesses—such is the illusive halo that hovers round the bright creations of fancy, giving brilliancy to the tints and magnitude to the proportions of that ideal picture, which, once conceived, attains its most powerful charm and its highest beauty. For, when could the tame reality, the actual presence of such scenes vie in interest with those glowing colours in which the imagination had invested them? Who has not seen those eyes overflowing in sympathy with the fictitious sufferings of the actor in the theatre, that have been turned in contempt from the homely, but too true, distress of the beggar at the door?

Such, Mr. Bouverie, were my last-night's speculations, and so narcotic was their nature—a quality, I fear, too likely to prove contagious—that my two chairs, nay, even my faithful bureau, gradually faded from before my eyes, and, instead of the contents of my narrow domicile, there appeared a spacious hall, thronged with well-known faces; and at the upper end, on an elevated dais or platform, were placed two figures, the celebrated authors of the "Microcosm" and "Etonian." But my recognitions among my school-fellows were shortly interrupted by the entrance of a figure, whose resemblance to the shadowy form that had crossed my evening path, as well as certain characteristic traits, corresponding with the mental portrait I had sketched, convinced me was Bouverie.—His countenance, as he approached, seemed to win the partial courtesy of the crowd, by its straight-forward and unassuming air, though not possessed of the intellectual dignity of the first, or the sparkling vivacity of the second, of those conspicuous figures who now kindly rose to welcome the new claimant to their honours.   Upon him, as he slowly ascended the platform, all eyes were now turned, when suddenly pausing on the fifth step, he raised his cloak, and from under its folds there issued a troop of pigmy scribblers, among whom, to my utter dismay, I recognized my own proper physiognomy.

But there was little time for reflection; the whole assembly was in uproar; in vain did Bartholomew extend to us the protection of his parental mantle, while amid the confusion I could distinguish such fatal, though unconnected, sounds, as,—" without any pretensions"— " what presumption"—" O! the hypocrite,"—" insufferable"—from the surrounding throng, who

> "   ——howled in my ears
> Such hideous cries, that with the very noise
> I, trembling, waked—"

but, Mr. Bouverie, as you have found by, I fear, woful experience,

> " Such terrible impression made my dream,"

that I determined to communicate it, together with my previous lucubrations to your notice; and the hope that they may suggest a single idea, or avert a possible prejudice, to your venerable self, will more than amply repay

Your sincere admirer,

PHILOMYSTES.

LINES TO CONTEMPLATION.

Pensive Nymph, whose beaming eye
Gazeth on the tranquil sky,
You do love to while away,
With thoughts on Heaven the livelong day;
Or hear the carol of the brook,
Resting in some lonely nook,
Where the hermit once did dwell,
Tenant of the holy cell;
Or when the moon, pale eye of night,
Glimmers o'er the waters bright,
There to think on time gone by,
Lull'd by gentle Phantasy;
To see the fairy's mazy dance
Lightly o'er the green-sward glance,
Or by the ocean's waves to go,
That sweetly murmur as they flow,
And listen to the rising gale,
That swells the bosom of the sail;
Or when the angry billows moan,
When the seaworn caverns groan,
You catch the drowning seaman's cry,
His shriek of dying agony.
I've seen thee mid the deserts wild,
Weeping o'er thy well-lov'd child.

. . . Pouring on thy Milton's bier,
The mournful tribute of a tear :
He was the voice of thunder, he
The eyeless light of·Poesy.
And I've seen thee in the grove,
List'ning to the tale of love,.
Which the turtle, mid the trees,
Warbles to the fragrant breeze,
Lovely mourner of the spray ;
Weeping joys now flown away,
Her plaintive notes thy feelings lull,
So musically sorrowful.

ON PATRONAGE.

Mankind, when they consider the poets and philoso
phers who have flourished under the encouragement of
a Patron, are induced to think, that any deficiency which
one particular age or individual may bear with respect
to another is rather owing to a difference of cultivation
than any want of natural talent. This leads us to regret
that more encouragement has not always been given to
rising genius, and that more attempts have not been
made to call forth the powers of the soul. Many, indeed, have been the tyrants who, though blessed with
all the opulence which might qualify them for the office
of patrons, have preferred spending their time in the
false enjoyment of luxury, rather than in the endeavour
to encourage genius, and to promote liberal knowledge.
If, however, we consider the many advantages which
must arise from such a patronage, the honour of the
patron, who, by connecting his name with the works of
the genius he has fostered, may be able to escape ob-

livion; and the aggrandizement of his country; we shall perhaps be surprised that more have not been induced to cultivate the rising buds of genius. It must, indeed, be confessed, that, owing to the want of encouragement, many have perished in obscurity; while others have consumed their life in indolence. -

Notwithstanding the acknowledged truth of this position, some have been found who, by dint of genius or perseverance, have overcome every obstacle, and burst the fetters, which poverty imposed on them. Nor, indeed, have the threats of a tyrant always been successful in preventing the exertion of mental capacities; and we see Juvenal neither over-awed by the unrelenting tyranny of *Nero*, nor the mean severity of *Domitian*. It is customary to instance the age of *Augustus*, as a specimen of the effects of patronage; but I am sure I need not recall to the memory of my readers the names of those illustrious poets who stand eternal monuments of the patronage of *Mæcenas*. But while we dwell with delight on those glorious times, we cannot but reflect on the different prospect which some ages present to us. Who can help lamenting that the profligate Charles II. expended the revenues of the state for the gratification of base sensuality; but which, had it been directed to the more useful cultivation of talent, would have conferred some honour on his name?

In considering the long night of darkness, in which Europe was enveloped, when the human mind was so fettered with superstitious ignorance, that it dared not exert its capacities, and all learning was buried in the cloisters; it may, perhaps, not be an unreasonable conjecture to suppose that there were many, even in those times, blessed with all the talents which might have qualified them to shine but little inferior to *Homer* or *Virgil*, lost, however, in undeserved oblivion, from want of the favouring smiles of a patron. But it is painful to dwell on those dark and uninteresting ages, though it must be confessed, that there were some illustrious characters, who were able to shed a temporary lustre over the ages in which they lived; but that dawn did not open into perfect day until *Lorenzo* and *Leo* roused the human soul from its lethargy, and, by their example and patronage, called its powers into action; when we remember the venerable names which adorned that period; when we recall to our memory *Politian, Raphael,* and *Michael Angelo,* all flourishing under the fostering care of a patron, we may, perhaps, be at a loss to determine whether the genius most demands our admiration, or the patron our gratitude.

In descending into later times, we still find many great and noble patrons; and the names of *Anne* and *Louis XIV.* must be for ever dear to every lover of science; whom we see surrounded by a group of immortals collected by their cares, excited by their genius, and encouraged by their goodness.

THE DEATH OF HOFFER.

No lip was mov'd; from the inmost soul
  Rush'd forth that sound of ire,
When the death-bolt reach'd the fated goal
  Launch'd on its wings of fire.

On the despot's hearing sternly fell
  The echo's mountain breath,
Reviving, with a spirit's knell,
  That groan for Hoffer's death.

Disdainfully his patriot soul
    The tyrant's pow'r defied,
And scorn'd the death-peal's closing toll,
    In virtue's latest pride.

When first our free-born gales gave birth
    To the blast of a tyrant's horn,
The mountain spirits' bitter mirth
    Threw back the notes in scorn.

Then, as the mountain voice leapt forth,
    That blast was answer'd well ;
Then on the foe, in crushing wrath,
    The stony Lawine * fell.†

Prouder, when in the noon of night
    He was led forth to die ;
Then prouder gleam'd that eye's dark light
    In triumph's wildest cry.

As he had liv'd a hero's life,
    He met a hero's doom :
The wreath that was won in Freedom's strife,
    Shall wave o'er Freedom's tomb.

                                            MALEK.

CONCLUSION.

" Mox, ubi lusit satis abstineto
Dixit ————— "

I have been accused, and I fear with too much foundation for the charge, of levity without wit, and of flippancy
without spirit : while I plead guilty to the indictment, as
regards the past, I venture to promise, at least, less of

---

* The avalanche.
† The Tyrolese hurled down rocks on the French who were below.

the obnoxious qualities for the future; and declare that, as respects the present, I come before the public in sad and real earnestness of regret, to take leave of my indulgent friends for a longer interval than has as yet elapsed between my periodical renewals of acquaintance with them.

Would that, to aid me in the performance of my unpleasant task, I had, if not a sense of merit, at least a feeling of innocence: but I know that I must make my exit with many a fault both of omission and commission on my head, unless my readers be pleased to grant me a pardon in full for the past, and to trust to my honest, though humble, desires to serve them, for the future.

I need hardly mention that I have consulted my trusty friends, Messrs. Jermyn, Heaviside, and Rice, on the subject of my resuming my literary labours after the Vacation. Mr. Heaviside does indeed desert me: Mr. Rice may indeed meet an untimely fate in his roamings among the Welch mountains: Mr. Jermyn may break his neck in riding a race, or his heart in writing "Stanzas" on some cruel fair one: but still I feel within me the desire of a protracted existence, and cannot discover why, while my strength is spared to me within, and while I have friends to encourage and incite me from without, I should stop short in the race which I have ventured to run; and should wilfully put an end to my own pleasures, or disappoint my friends' expectations.

However, as my prudence inclines me to view my future prospects in an unfavourable, rather than in a flattering, light, in a grand council lately held at my palace, I left it to my friends to give encouragement, and contented

myself with starting objections. Mr. Jermyn was shocked
at the idea of desisting, and declared he would rather
become another Hercules, and let me play truant like
Atlas, than suffer the ponderous and majestic load which
it is my good fortune to bear, to fall to the ground un-
honoured and unowned. "Why, my good friend, what
will you write upon?" said I. "Upon paper, to be sure,"
retorted the irritated poet : — "What will you write,
I mean," I exclaimed : "Any thing," he replied, "rather
than a Last Dying Speech and Confession, before I have
been either arraigned or condemned at the tribunal of
public opinion."—"But would it not be prudent, Mr.
Jermyn ——"

"No, it would not, Mr. Heaviside."

"Hear me speak, at any rate, ——"

"It is just what I wish, and have been endeavouring
to persuade you to do.—Speak on, I say, and do not
bury yourself alive as you threatened."

"Would it not be well to retire before the public get
tired of us?"

"By that rule, my good friend, you ought to eat no
dinner for fear of a surfeit, and never to go to bed at
night, for fear of not awaking early enough in the morning. Enough is as good as a feast : but in the name of
Apollo and the Nine Muses, let us at least go on with
our undertaking till we have had enough. In short, if
you are determined to be a Trebatius, I tell you that I
shall be well content to act the part of Horace in the
conference."*

I concluded by a classical, and as I thought powerful

* HORACE *Sat. II.* 1.

allusion to the rule laid down by Horace, wherein he fixes upon the number five, which I have now happily attained, as the boundary of a drama. But Mr. Jermyn retorted, that though a play could only have five acts, he really did not see why a Miscellany should not proceed to ten. He quoted his fusticular Majesty, of verberatory, glorious, and immortal memory, as an example and precedent for this most excellent number ; and declared he was sure that the redoubted Peregrine would have made use of the instrument from which he derived his title and his kingdom, to belabour the shoulders of any one of his subjects who had recommended an earlier application of the scissors of Atropos to the thread of his glorious existence. Loud cheering from Messrs. Heaviside, Rice, and Willoughby, followed the conclusion of Mr. Jermyn's address.

I rose to wind up the proceedings by a parting address to my friends :—

"To you, Mr. Heaviside, who are now about to desert us, at a period too early both for our pleasure and for your glory, I can only give my thanks and my good wishes :

> '——— I secundo
> Omine ———'

but I will still express a hope that your broad-shouldered ghost may even hereafter continue to haunt the favourite scenes of the real Antony ; may still watch over the interests, and aid the progress, of his friend Bartholomew.

"To Mr. F. Willoughby, with whom the public have been acquainted so short a time, I recommend less political reading, and more Miscellany writing : and though an Essay on the British Constitution would unhappily be unfit for the pages of our publication, yet an Ode to Salt-hill, or a Dissertation on Strawberries, would be by no means unacceptable.

" From you, Mr. David ap Rice, I expect at least three ' Legends of Snowdon,' Lines to Welch Nymphs, and Elegies for Welch Heroes, without number.

" To you, Mr. Jermyn, I could give a long lecture, but that you would laugh in my face in the middle of it. Do not employ your thoughts on the St. Leger, but on the Miscellany; and be more anxious about hard writing than hard riding. If you must bet, be sure to lay odds on Bouverie.

" This, then, is the plan which I have sketched out, and which, if I am spared, it will be my earnest endeavour to execute. Looking forward to the winter as the probable termination of my existence, I hope again to appear in print on the Eighth day of October; from that time to proceed as heretofore.

" Although the vacation does to my limbs as Medea did to those of her brother,

' Dissipat in multis invenienda locis ——'

yet, in whatever parts of the globe I may be discovered, I hope that all parts of me will be found exerting themselves in unanimous industry and indefatigable perseverance."

CON-

CONTRIBUTORS

TO

"THE ETON MISCELLANY,"

VOL. I.

————

The names of the Authors of the remaining Articles will not be
divulged, at least, at present.

INDEX

INDEX

END OF VOL. I.

T. C. Hansard, Paternoster-row Press, London.

ETON MISCELLANY.

VOL. II.

THE

ETON MISCELLANY.

VOL. II.

BY

BARTHOLOMEW BOUVERIE,

NOW OF ETON COLLEGE.

October—November, 1827.

——————— Sive ego pravè
Seu rectè hoc volui, ne sis patruus mihi.
HORACE.

ETON:

PRINTED FOR T. INGALTON.

SOLD ALSO BY

E. WILLIAMS, ETON; KNIGHT AND BROWN, WINDSOR; R. S. KIRBY,
PATER-NOSTER-ROW; W. ANDERSON, WATERLOO PLACE; AND F. CLARK,
3?, 1?.

T. C HANSARD, Later-noster-row Press, London

ETON MISCELLANY,

No. VI.

INTRODUCTION.

IN defiance of the Autumn, the south wind, and
Libitina, I am again at my post to resume my humble
labours : and by way of advertising the company which
I have secured for supporting my performances, I will
venture to introduce to my readers a couple (at this
season of the year I ought perhaps to say, a brace) of
my allies, hitherto concealed from the public eye : concealed, perhaps, on the principle by which the more
lowly hills are manifest to every observer, while those
whose proportions are more grand, and whose elevations
are more lofty, assert the privilege of their superior rank,
by involving their summits in the mist and the cloud, till
the beams of the sun dispel their coverings, and display
their grandeur. The morning of my existence has assuredly passed : the evening must soon approach : what
remains therefore to suppose concerning my present
state, save that I am now actually basking beneath the
beams of the sun of prosperity and indulgence, neither
hidden in a cloudy sky, nor chilled by a wintry atmosphere?

Oliver Quincy is by no means the least singular of those somewhat extraordinary beings who have come upon the stage of literature hand in hand with Bartholomew Bouverie. Extravagant in some of his opinions, yet sober in all his actions : in theory, an embryo demagogue, in practice, every way qualified to be an useful, an estimable, and a distinguished, member of society, there are few whose sentiments on certain subjects are more at variance with the formation of their minds and the tenor of their lives.

From his very cradle he has worshipped Freedom. The Cap of Liberty he would have preferred to the less conspicuous appearance, yet equally sure protection, of a hat. Still he retains the recollection, still he venerates the shades, of all those who at any time, and in any country, have vindicated the "rights of man," and shaken the thrones of their " tyrannical oppressors." From his conversation, it might be supposed that patience was the object of his detestation, passion and resentment the darling idols of his heart: yet none can endure with a better grace, none can forgive with more readiness of will, more sincerity of heart; none are more susceptible, none more worthy of, affection.

Incendiaries of Rebellion are, in his eyes, the best friends of Freedom; and the haranguers of mobs the regenerators of mankind. No martyrs can occupy a more distinguished place in his calendar than those assigned to the men who have felt the severity of laws making treason a crime, and obedience a merit: who have been unceremoniously decapitated, like Tyler, by the heads-

man; or who have received, in modern times, kicks
from the horses of the life-guardsmen, or cuts from the
sabres of the yeomanry. The summit of his wishes
(hope, alas! is now out of the question) would have been
to have fallen a victim to the good cause on the memorable Sixteenth of August: but fierce as he is in ideas,
and indomitable in theory, he cannot either point with
heroic exultation to a limb maimed by a musket-shot,
or boast of having broken the staff of a single constable,
or the head of a single exciseman. So passive is his
zeal, and so inert his principle, that his name is never to
be found among the speakers, or rather brawlers at
meetings convened for the abolition of church-wardens,
churches, and all other public nuisances: for refining
sugar-boilers into orators, and for filtering scavengers
into statesmen: for the vindication of natural rights
which are, in effect, unnatural wrongs: for embodying
a phantom which never was seen, and for establishing a
" primitive equality," which never was known. His
spirits are not sublimed to such a degree of phrenzy,
that they are incapable of returning to the ordinary form
and consistence of human faculties; and though his imagination flies off like water in steam, when indulged in
the excursions of fancy, and stimulated by the flames of
Freedom, yet when exposed to a more frigid atmosphere,
when in contact with more substantial objects, it disdains not to return to its natural element, and to re-assume its legitimate functions.

Yet in visions like these there is one consolation to the
unvisionary and matter-of-fact portion (a very small one,
it is to be feared) of mankind, that while the form is

too aerial to be detained for investigation, the texture is too flimsy to be adopted for use : that in exact proportion to the wildness of its features, will be the brevity of its duration : that its vehemence will exhaust its energies, and its improvidence preclude the possibility of their renovation : that thus every phantom inevitably cuts short its own existence, and adds to its former enormities that of closing its career by becoming a *felo de se*.

Yet many worse symptoms may appear in the opening mind of youth, than such as I have here described. Far more dangerous, and far more ill-omened, are those hidden evils which lurk like the adder in the grass; whose bite cannot be avoided, because it is not foreseen : which, as vigilance cannot perceive, nor prudence ward off, so also the time of their approach is ever to be dreaded, and the remedy for their poison always to be sought. On the contrary, these extravagances are the weeds which a generous soil alone can produce: which, while by their native rankness they show its exuberance, by their verdure and their vigour, they bear equally sure testimony to its fertility. Hence it is to be trusted, that the hand of experience may remove them, and plant in their stead shoots of a more worthy origin, and a more benignant growth.

Both my compassion for my already wearied readers, and my own incompetency to give an exact or a minute delineation of my second ally, will certainly induce me to shorten my sketch of his character. Modesty and reserve, much more, I believe, of the former than of the latter, prominent features in his character, alike preclude a lengthened detail.

As remote as possible from any indulgence in the visionary dreams, or any participation in the undefined notions of Mr. Oliver Quincy, he abhors the name of politics; takes up the Classical Journal with far more interest than the Edinburgh Review, or Blackwood's Magazine—but here my comparison fails, for these latter, I believe, he avoids like the touch of a viper; he would certainly listen with delight to a discussion of the principles of accentuation,* but with impatience to one on those of government. The Utopia of the one is in the land of—" Freedom, Equality, Higgledum-piggledum," &c. while the other revels in feasts of commentaries, and wanders over whole realms of annotations. His intellectual food might be, Porson for breakfast, Elmsley for dinner, and Bentley for tea: Parr might serve for a mid-day luncheon, and Monk or Gaisford for an occasional snack. Surely it is more glorious to reform an author's text, than—a nation's government: and more creditable to the patriotism and public spirit of an individual to replace an ejected particle in its station, than an ejected monarch on his throne ! Obsolete statutes are at best no better than antiquated editions: and if Mr. Huskisson makes laws to regulate the manufacture of silk, why, Professor Porson makes laws to regulate the manufacture of Iambics; and the one lays as many restrictions *on* British poets, as the other takes *off* from British traders.

Such, perhaps, or nearly such, may be his method of

---

* A Sceptical Correspondent impertinently hints, " If there are any"— If there are any ! !

comparison between our Political and Literary Go-
vernors : and I must do him the justice to say, that if he
has not troubled himself much about the allegiance he
owes to the former, of the latter, at least, he has been a
most active, dutiful, and exemplary subject: both eager
in acquiring, and successful in attaining, copious stores
of Classical Erudition.

I believe, that Mr. Philip Montague is gifted with an
amiable disposition, and a kind heart. He has, assuredly,
suavity of manners, and a most entire freedom from all
affectation and self-consequence, to recommend him to
those with whom he is in intercourse: and high as his
estimation of the importance, and his knowledge of the
nature, of classical learning is, his esteem is free from
affectation, and his knowledge from pedantry. It is
both delightful and advantageous to have to do with
those, (and few they are,) who have learned to be obliging
yet not officious ; and who are always as ready to afford,
as unwilling to intrude, their valuable services.

Thus having feebly endeavoured to describe my two
coadjutors, I will dismiss the subject, in the hope that
they will be as acceptable to our readers as they have
been useful among ourselves. If in the estimate of their
characters I have not sufficiently applauded their abilities,
it is because the heart, in my humble opinion, must go
before the head : and because it would be presumptuous
in me to affect to point out, what he who runs and reads
will, I believe, not fail to perceive.

ANCIENT AND MODERN GENIUS COMPARED.

Illi alternantes multâ vi prælia miscent.

On entering into a field so widely extended, and so magnificently variegated, as that which is to be the scene óf my present labour, it may be proper, in the commencement, to state the boundaries by which it is confined, and the portions into which it is divided.

It is fit to exclude from such a comparison as this all consideration of the Holy Scriptures. It is not for me to discuss the nature, the limits, and the provinces, of human genius and Divine Inspiration. The sublimity of Job, and the pathos of David; the raptures of the prophet, and the precepts of the sage, are subjects on which I must forbear from expatiating. It might be difficult, it might be impossible, to find parallels for these and for their fellows, even if the footing on which they were to be placed had been clearly ascertained: but these topics, and such as these, if they are to be approached and handled at all, are to be approached with reverence—to be handled at once with delicacy and with power; with more power and more delicacy than it ever has been, or, I fear, it ever will be, my lot to possess.

Beginning with Homer (a venerable name, whether it was used to designate the real and sole author of the Iliad, or not), and the fathers of Grecian literature, the comparison will be drawn, chiefly, between each two of the four great and splendid periods which, divided equally as to number by the intervening ages of darkness and barbarism, have usually been assigned respectively to Ancient and to Modern times. Those ages indeed, during which the gloom of the cloister was the only remedy for the violence and barbarism of the world at large, situated as they were between civilization on either side, were like an ocean raging between two fair and fertile continents; where few, indeed, are enabled to pass from the one to the other; where those who would avoid the rage of the winds, and the turbulence of the waters, must be sheltered from the contact of the wrathful elements in a gloom and a confinement, by which alone their force can be defied, and their entrance forbidden.

Against the Grecian and the Augustan will be placed the age of Leo the Tenth, and that which we usually call by the name of Queen Anne; our continental neigh-bours, by that of Louis the Fourteenth. It would, how-ever, be both unjust and impolitic to exclude from our account those who, on the side of the moderns, will have a material influence in casting the balance, the many brilliant names which frequently before, and con-stantly since, the period last mentioned, have decorated the annals of this and of other countries. Had each link of their uninterrupted chain been perceived by men unconnected with the splendid series, the time in which it was formed would have derived from it the stamp of superior merit, and the pledge of lasting reputation. We boast, and justly boast, the age of Queen Elizabeth; and we might, too, bring forward that of the Common-wealth and Charles the Second, when we had Massinger,*

---

* It is, perhaps, hardly fair to introduce Massinger, but the far greater name of Newton might be substituted, as he belongs more to Charles the Second than to Queen Anne.

and Waller, and Cowley, and Denham; Rochester and
Roscommon; Hobbes, Harrington, Selden, and Chil-
lingworth; Usher, Davenant, Clarendon, and Dryden;
Harvey, and Wren, and Wallis; Stillingfleet and Bur-
net; Temple and Butler; and, above all, the immortal
Milton. Great must be the literary force of that country
which does not place even a period like this among its
most brilliant and conspicuous ornaments. Such assem-
blages as these were rare among the ancients; but with
us, the series has been, for centuries, unbroken; and
the abundant fertility of the soil has given birth to a fresh
growth, before the preceding one has been fully reaped.
Hence no limit has been clearly marked, whereby, of the
last hundred years, any single year, or period, might be
celebrated above its successors, which, following it in
the course of time, have usually equalled or excelled it
in the records of distinction. A Gray, a Beattie, a
Johnson, a Churchill, and a Goldsmith, rose up, without
intermission, to occupy the proud stations of Pope,
Addison, and Swift, in the ranks of literary eminence.
When those luminaries were on the decline, together
with no inconsiderable portion of merit in poetry, there
appeared in the British Senate such a constellation of
oratorical genius, as the whole world had seldom or
never paralleled; and at once might be seen, on one side,
Pitt and Burke, Canning, Windham, Dundas, and
Grenville, opposed to worthy adversaries in Fox, and
Sheridan, and Erskine. After these came Gifford, Byron,
Campbell, Scott, Moore, Southey, and their illustrious
contemporaries of the present day. Hence it is, that
each of these sets of men, who might well have con-

ferred, if separated, a distinct and individual honour on
their respective eras, now enjoy, though an equally solid,
an assuredly less brilliant, meed of renown.   They are
looked on as parts of a splendid whole, instead of being
splendid but isolated portions of a whole which does not
merit the appellation; the one being as the rare oasis
amidst the expanse of the desert; the other, like the
glorious but homely spectacle of an unbroken range of
cultivated country.

In the consideration of such a subject as this, we feel
like men wandering in Fairy-land, surrounded with all
that can engage the eye, all that can attract the inclination, and all that can captivate the intellect; we are
bewildered by the extent and variety of the prospect;
we are staggered by the brilliancy of the objects on either
side, but it is a bewilderment of delight, and a doubt
which only enhances our admiration of the illustrious
subjects.   Wherever genius appears, we must feel an
interest in her destiny and condition.   When we see her
struggling with difficulties, and overthrowing obstacles,
and coming to light in the wild and unpolished effusions
of Orpheus and the early bards ; or when we behold her,
in more recent ages, again rising with renewed vigour
from the ruin with which barbarism had overwhelmed
her—again to struggle, again to captivate, and again to
shine—she must, and she *does*, interest the kindly feelings
of the human heart.   In any of her innumerable garbs
we admire and love her:

Mille habet ornatus, mille decenter habet.

And though I cannot but fear that both a want of

judgment, and a want of research, and *no* want of prejudice, may rénder mé a lamentably inefficient and unsatisfactory essayist on a subject of such magnitude, yet,
having assured my readers that I have endeavoured to
lay aside entirely the last of these uninviting qualifications, I must plead the interesting nature of the question
as my excuse for attempting it, notwithstanding my consciousness of the existence of the two first-mentioned
obstacles to the success of my undertaking.

In addition to the difficulties, therefore, which necessarily attend the execution, my design in the present case
renders it peculiarly formidable. It has been asserted
by Dr. Blair (who allows, however, that Milton and
Shakspeare are inferior to no poets of any age), that we
find "among the Moderns sometimes more art and
correctness, but feebler exertions of genius," than those
of the Ancients. The names, too, of Boileau and
Dacier, who in the controversy in France during the
reign of Louis the Fourteenth, supported the cause of
olden times, may be considered as more illustrious and
authoritative than those of their opponents Perault and
La Motte. The latter worthies, will, however, have an
auxiliary, such as he is, in the person of Bartholomew
Bouverie, though he has not the honour of any further
acquaintance with them, than is constituted by the knowledge of their names, and the opinions they supported.

While we discuss the general nature of the subject,
we shall, I think, find analogy, often so beautiful and
useful, a guide to aid us in forming an opinion. We
may do well to compare human nature to human life,
and the growth of the mind to that of the body. We

see youthful genius abounding in vivacity, and often
almost rank in its luxuriance ; but when the calm maturity of manhood has succeeded to the brief and fleeting
spring of life, that genius remains, deprived, indeed, of
its exuberance, but retaining its fertility; possessing,
instead of a crude and undigested mass, an arranged and
solid substance to work upon : still calculated to astonish
by the grandeur, it has also learned to please by the
propriety, of its efforts : it has lopped off from itself the
" ambitiosa ornamenta," but it preserves and improves
the true and original stock.   Dr. Blair, himself gives a
hint of this comparison, which goes so strongly against
his own opinion.   For surely as in the form and nature
of man both body and mind possess most vigour when
the rawness of youth has given place to the plenitude of
strength in manhood, so, in the course of ages, mankind
has gradually become more adorned with learning, more
replete with intelligence, and more abundant in ability.
The efforts of the young may be lively, spirited, and
bold ; but manhood exhibits that liveliness chastened
into true wit; that spirit curbed, and governed, and concentrated ; that boldness freed from its audacity, yet
replenished in its vigour; the whole joined in harmonious union, and assuming the appearance of the lofty
fabric where the magnitude of dimension is equalled
by the justness of proportion.   When a young man
exhibits proofs of talent, do men consider that he has
reached the boundary of his labours, the summit of his
fame?   Do they suppose that nothing more is to be
expected from him, save the lees of the goodly wine,
the refuse of exhausted excellence ?   Nay, they rather hail

the first-fruits of the fertile soil as the harbingers of mightier efforts, and the forerunners of a more abundant and more timely crop.   Was Milton young when Paradise Lost was produced?   Nearly sixty.   Are not the learned and the lofty tragedians mentioned in Horace mentioned as " senes ?"   And who that has pictured to his imagination the form of Homer (supposing, or allowing, that such a person did exist, and did write the Iliad), has not figured a venerable sage, rather than a sprightly youth?   Virgil, too, died at the age of fifty-one, still engaged in the Æneid; and Æschylus published his best plays when upwards of sixty years of age.

Often has it been asserted, but never proved, that knowledge is hostile to genius; that civilization in its progress retards the growth of the human mind! and that what we have been wont to look upon as a blessing and a privilege, has, in fact, deprived us, in great measure, of the ground-work of all that can render a man eminently great, by instructing and delighting his fellow-creatures ' Most unhappy, then, is our situation; wisdom bids us to dissolve the frame of society, and return to the wood, the hill, and the cavern.   Genius, it appears, like sleep, can only dwell

> " ———— in smoky cribs,
> Upon uneasy pallets stretching her,
> And hush'd with buzzing night-flies to her slumber."

Modern writers have, indeed, learned to avoid many of the conceits, much of the hyperbole and confusion of the Ancients ; to cast away what was useless, to eradicate what was faulty : if these are losses, who would not be poor ? If these be genius, who would envy its possessor ?

What can be more preposterous than Andromache's
giving, in the very midst of her most bitter wailing,
" a circumstantial account of her birth, parentage, and
education?" Why, she might rival a Scot in her
genealogical skill! The only parallel for this exhibition
which I can remember is, the account which the worthy
Baillie Nicol Jarvie in " Rob Roy," gives to Helen
M'Gregor of their connexion, tracing it through Mac
Farlanes, Mac Nabs, &c. &c., and, by its various ramifications, endeavouring to establish the relationship which
might possibly save his life. But Andromache had no
such sensible object in view. Then, if we are, with
Pope, to believe the lines genuine, she feelingly proceeds
to complain that Astyanax will lose his dinner! No
doubt it is very dignified to compare a hero to a fly—nay,
a host of flies, round a carcase! and to give the account
of a certain poor fellow who tumbled on his nose in a
certain race, and filled, not only that, but several other
receptacles, with a certain substance which shall be
nameless. No doubt the repetition of ὁ λοα δρᾶν, ὁ λοα λέγειν,
a dozen or a score of times is wondrously pathetic! and
yet more so are three or four lines together composed of
the singularly affecting monosyllable ἲ! It would be
unjust to Phædra, who might have been wife to one of
the seven wise men of Greece, to omit mentioning the
admirable morality which she pours out wholesale *in
Euripides*, when, *in reality*, she would have raved like
a Bacchanalian. But in spite of the unassuming ἆ ἆ, and
all exclamations, even up to the grandisonant ὀττοτοῖ—
in spite of Phædra's wisdom, and Andromache's folly,
great and powerful geniuses were the authors of the Iliad

and the Hippolytus.   But greater still, in my humble opinion, were those of Paradise Lost and King Lear.

Certainly the Moderns have enjoyed great and manifold advantages, but these could not, as certainly, diminish their genius.   They increased their opportunities, they gave additional facilities for exerting their natural powers ; but surely those natural powers were not thereby *diminished*.   The animal that drags his weary burthen over hill and dale, would possess the same physical powers if he performed the task on a level road ; and the man whose genius can effect great things, and overcome great difficulties, surely can perform still greater things when the difficulties are less which attend and impede the performance.   Such reasoning as I have here endeavoured to combat has always appeared to me most unnatural.   Knowledge it is, assuredly, which forwards intellect ; and, therefore, if this knowledge be unfavourable to genius, the more we multiply obstacles, the more splendidly shall we achieve success ; the more ignorant we are, the more clever we shall be ; and the brilliancy of our genius will be in exact proportion to the deficiency of our intellect !

Let us adopt a more clear, a more liberal, a more sound opinion.   Let us not, at this time, and in this country, raise our voices, feeble as they are, in support of doctrines so pernicious, and theories so unfounded : rather let us hold that in animate as in inanimate things, the moral government of God is beautiful in its consistency ; that knowledge is to the mind as cultivation to the earth ; it fosters and increases genius itself by the extraneous aids which it lends to it ; it calls into exist-

ence, into growth, into maturity, by fertilization of the
soil, those latent seeds which, in other circumstances,
might have perished unobserved and unassisted : and
as in the benignant bosom of the well-tilled and fertile
field the seed springs up to renovated and expanded
life by the ten—aye, by the hundred fold multiplication
of its own consistence and form, so, in the mind which is
cultivated by knowledge, and tempered by civilization,
the nobler and more glorious seeds of genius lie, soon
to spring up in matchless beauty, and to enrich us with
a more benign, a more copious, and a more luxuriant
harvest.

[*To be continued.*]

THE TEMPLE OF JUPITER OLYMPIUS, AT ATHENS.

Oh! Athens, Athens, when the last sad ray
That gilds yon sinking ruins shall be thrown
From the pure lustre of the cloudless day
O'er thy spoil'd temples, where th' encrusted stone,
Torn from its mother rock, so thick is strown—
Alas! Alas! we then shall weep for thee—
Thy marble columns, and thy golden crown
Of radiant glory, on that boundless sea
Whose wave thro' time and space rolls on eternally.

Then, then, perchance, each eye may drop a tear,
That views thee slowly, sullenly repine—
Proud of thine ancient splendor—views thee rear
Thy turreted Acropolis—and shine
With smiles amid thy sorrows—and decline
By the slow crumbling touch of envious age ;
While through each widow'd hall, and mournful shrine
Howl the contending tempests, fierce t' engage
With stormy-footed winds and elemental rage.

Thro' Time's dark mirror do we view thee yet,
Of past—of future—and of scenes we see—
In the deep gloom of cold despair hath set
Each hope to conquer, and each wish to be
What once thou wast, "The Glorious," and "The Free."
While thro' the cypress-waving lonely tomb
Of Gods—of Heroes—and of Liberty—
(Oh! fate too cruel, and too hard a doom!)
The fitful flashes strike, and all the shades illume.

And thou, proud fabric! o'er whose crested neck
Black ruin hangs—decaying and decayed;
And ye! last fragments of th' immortal wreck
That must for ever flourish, whilst ye fade!
E'en mid yon towers, that crown each beauteous glade
Along th' Ægean's island-tufted shore;—
Alas! within ye hath the night-owl made
Her ivy-mantled nest, from whence to pour
The sad ill-omen'd scream, "Proud Athens is no more!"

And is her race to endless shame condemn'd?
And 'neath her towers shall foemen spur the steed?
And hath no hand the mighty torrent stemm'd,
Which, rushing with impetuous haste, decreed
Her noblest sons, her bravest hosts to bleed?
Whose ravag'd country, and whose roofless home
The boast of whirlwinds lie! Was this her meed?
Haste, haste, Athena, on the blue sea's foam
To seek for other realms, thro' distant climes to roam!

All o'er thy sacred hill the birds of prey
Brood on those ivied walls—fair Science' reign—
With restless hootings ushering in the day
That wakes them from their slumbers—while the plain,
No longer joyous with its golden grain,
Lies idle! View thine own fam'd Parthenon!
Disfigur'd with the trace of years—the stain
Of Athens' blood! Not thus thy Phœbus shone,
With bright illumin'd face encircling Marathon!

Far different were the sounds of joy, that then
Harmonious echo'd thro' yon vocal shrine—
When Greece was glorious, and her sons were men !—
When thou, Olympian Jove, in peace didst shine
On thy devoted temples, and the line
Of Heroes which hath vanish'd ! Lo, the tear
Of Heaven bedews the fane, which once was thine !
No voice to utter—and no power to hear—
For they have perish'd long thro' many a rolling year !

View 'mid yon broken pillars—Oh ! how true
Is Desolation's symbol !—where the foe
Hath made thy squadron thin, thy children few,
Hath whet his sabre on thy stones, to mow
Whole patriot armies by one fatal blow—
Where thy brave sons of nobler faith have kneel'd
Upon their parent soil—while rivers flow
Of blood-ensanguin'd hue, yet scarce can shield
From that dread wrathful blade which furious tyrants wield.

But Athens, thron'd upon her firm-fix'd rock,
Must last thro' long, long, years of misery—
Must feel the Moslem's soul-despairing shock,
Whilst "Allah !" breathes on his departing sigh,
The curse upon his lips—and in his eye
Defiance ! Sworn not e'en thy babes to spare—
The perjur'd, bloodstain'd son of cruelty—
Men, heroes, all, thy heart-felt griefs must share,
And worse than Death itself, the fellness of Despair !

Then, Athens ! if thou still hast life, ascend
The loftiest turret of thy mouldering wall—
And swell thy trumpet, that its voice may rend
The vault of Heav'n—and, girt with Terror, call
The Freeborn Sons of Liberty to fall !—
Where Immortality itself were pain,
Death—that ye cannot fear !—Or from yon hall
Plant thy first standard—wipe away the stain—
And lead, thy sons to fame, thy chiefs to arms, again !

Oh, by the hands that rais'd thee from the ground
To Honour's empire, and to Glory's height !—
Oh, by the gracious Power that yet hath crown'd
Thy walls with lambent splendor, while the fight
Hath rag'd with all the virulence of might :—
Turn thee, ah turn thee, and thy fame restore
To purity—to vigour—and to light !
Be thou the Queen of Nations, as before,
Be thou bold—brave—triumphant—as thou wast of yore !

Oh, Athens ! Athens ! then shalt thou be great—
Then shall no Infidel thy fanes defile—
Great in the paths of Glory, and of Fate !
Then shalt thou rest from ev'ry grief awhile,
Beneath Heaven's blessing, and thy country's smile !—
She lives !—where heroes deep below the sod
Lie coffin'd—and throughout that sacred pile
Are holier pavements than her Patriarchs trod—
She lives, to light—and life—to glory—and to God !

HESPERUS.

THE LEADING IDEA.

"——Huc propius me,
Dum doceo insanire omnes, vos ordine adite."

No one who has read the Satire from which I take my
motto can be ignorant of the overwhelming judgment
of the Stoics by which they pronounced all mankind,
with the exception of the philosopher, irretrievably mad.
Although I cannot entirely concur in this sentiment, yet
I think that if we examine the lives and conversations of
men, we shall generally find some leading idea, by which
(that I may not enter too deeply into the abstruse doc-

trines of ideas) I mean, that every individual has some peculiar point in his character, which acts as his distinguishing mark, and frequently leads him into such absurdities as may almost entitle him to the name of madman. Even Don Quixote, as egregious a madman as any inmate of Bedlam, was mad but on one point; he could talk sensibly on almost every subject; but his leading idea, knight-errantry, acted as a spark upon an inflammable pile of insanity, which, when in full blaze, no arguments or reason could stifle. Although perhaps too strongly coloured, the character itself is naturally enough drawn, and if *their leading idea* does not act so forcibly on most men, as on the knight of La Mancha, if they do not mistake a windmill for a giant, or a bason for a helmet, yet it is often sufficiently powerful to render them ridiculous and troublesome.

Mr. Triptolemus's chief idea is Farming; that of Dr. Orbilius lies in Education. The one, during half an hour's conversation, will fatigue you with agricultural details, and discussions on the good qualities of Swedish turnips; while the other will engage with you in a controversy respecting the comparative merits of a Scotch university, and a public school, or confound you with political economy, and metaphysical questions as unintelligible as uninteresting. Why does the poor half-starved weaver, while he plies the shuttle, rave about " the rights of man," and neglect his business to descant on the beauties of science? Why? but that all his ideas are concentrated into one, by those levelling doctrines, which have made philosophy synonymous with Jacobinism and Blasphemy.

If, as frequently happens, we see a man, whose sole aim is to be thought superior to fear, taking pleasure in doing those rash feats at which a prudent man would shudder, if we do not consider him altogether mad, must we not, at least, with honest Sancho, conclude, "that he is exceedingly brave?" What makes the virtuoso rave upon seeing a coin with an obliterated inscription, or an illegible manuscript? Why does he consume his fortune in the purchase of old pictures, and the erection of new lodges? Is not his conduct prompted - by the wish of being thought *un homme savant ?* Is it not his sole ambition to place after his name the three magic letters F. R. S., which at once pronounce him a man of taste and genius?

But this too great indulgence in one pursuit, this habit of allowing the mind to be engrossed by one object, may be productive of more serious results. What during the darkness of the middle ages induced men, sometimes the most conspicuous for their learning, to waste their time, labour, and wealth, in the unprofitable study of Alchymy? In these more enlightened times, the absurdity of such an undertaking seems self-evident, yet then we find those who were superior in science to their contemporaries, the most ardent pursuers of the philosopher's stone. This must have arisen from permitting the mind to revel too freely in the mazes of fancy, and with too sanguine hopes to indulge in speculations which would never be fulfilled. We might here expatiate on the danger of such an indulgence; we might observe the pernicious effects of suffering our leading idea or, passion to influence all our pursuits, and give a peculiar character to our lives and actions. We might say this and more, but such a style would scarcely become us; and those who might be included in our censure, would laugh at the Lilliputian moralist who could so audaciously attempt to reform them. It is better for us to assume the character of a Democritus, and to smile at those follies, which we have not authority to censure with any probability of success.

TO MARY.

Oh! tell me not that dark abyss
   Is closing o'er the form I love;
Ah! no, in worlds more pure than this,
   Thy lovely spirit roams above;
And leaves the realms of grief and care
To wander o'er the fields of air.

Midst happier hearts, and brighter hours,
   I did not sing of themes like these,
Where clustering vines, and azure flowers,
   And every charm which once could please,
In ripening bloom, were wont to shine
Along the fairy banks of Rhine.

But where are they! and where art thou,
   My Mary? in the silent tomb
Decay has mark'd thy marble brow,
   Thy lovely cheek has lost its bloom,
And every heart is far away
Which made those joyous hours more gay.

Lo! yon bright orb withdraws its gleam,
   No star is mirror'd on the wave,
And nothing, save the raven's scream,
   Is echoing near thy lowly grave;

While gathering clouds, with black'ning gloom,
Roll darkly o'er my Mary's tomb.

And round me lie the silent dust,
    Of hearts as gay, and forms as bright,
The eyeless scull, the mould'ring bust,
    Shine ghastly by the glowworm's light;
And yet the hour is far more dear
Than friendship's smile, or beauty's tear.

Ah! whither flits thy fairy form,
    My Mary! if in yon bright star,
Which shines amidst the rising storm,
    Thy lovely spirit roams afar,
Oh! leave thy place of blissful rest,
And soothe thy lover's aching breast.

Fair as the vapoury forms which glide
    In rapture o'er the poet's eye,
Even now methinks my earthly bride
    Floats lightly o'er the low'ring sky,
And beck'ning, points to that bright star,
Whose radiant beauty shines afar.

In vain! in vain! yet if thine ear
    Is listening to thy lover's lays;
If seraphs e'er bestow a tear,
    For joys which flew in earlier days,
Oh! Mary, let one thought of thine
Still linger on the banks of Rhine.

ON COCKNEY POETRY.

Hac rabiosa fugit canis, hac lutulenta ruit sus——

Tu me inter strepitus nocturnos atque diurnos
Vis canere——

Sir;—

I am convinced that nothing is more deserving of your

notice and reprobation, than the unmerited abuse which, even in this little world, is showered on the head of the innocent and persecuted Cockney.—Cockney! The very name seems to carry on its face the most bitter insult. They and their productions are branded by one sweeping denunciation, as more dull and heavy than their own smoky atmosphere.—Now, I having a sort of sneaking kindness for this abused race, and having by deep study armed myself cap-à-pie for the contest, do hereby throw down my gauntlet to the world, and most strenuously take up the cudgels in behalf of the reviled : and not only am I prepared to defend their dialect, but moreover to assert their claim, in the highest degree, to poetical merit.—I might, with great advantage to my cause, set forth, as in my motto, the myriads of inconveniences, under which the Shoreditch poet labours, and the muddy and smoky paths through which he must wade to Helicon, with fifty other excuses of the same *genus ;* but I disdain all such subterfuges, and fearlessly stand forth the champion of " the Cocknaye."

Imprimis, then, let us, quietly or belligerently, as the reader pleases, discuss his style of poetry. Now he seems more peculiarly to shine in the "tale of disastrous love ;" in relating with the strongest pathos, and in the most touch- ing language, as how William (Cockniacè Villiam), Jenkins was ever a faithful lovyer to Sally Brown ; as how Villiam took a Sunday jaunt on the water, was over- turned, and then, after having said something wond'rous pretty and sentimental of his mistress, was " drowned :" and as how Sally Brown, being " the very *moral* of faith," went dead for grief: Or in case she forgets the quondam favoured, and consoles herself with a new one, a most soul-harrowing scene of " ghosteses," skeletons, smoke, and sulphur, ensues.   Old Raw-head-and-bloody-bones, maugre all shrieks and kicks, enfolds the fair one in his most delectable embraces, and *exeunt* in thunder and lightning.   The company (for of course the aforesaid Raw-head takes the occasion of a dinner party) are for the moment rather astounded, or, to use the Cockney's own expression, nonplushed ; however, after making one or two suitable reflections on this most unceremonious finale to Miss Sally's sojourn here below, they resume the more important office of discussing the good things before them.   And then, then, comes the beauty of the poem, in the shape of a moral, kindly informing us why this most offensive operation was performed on the culprit :—

> This here did happen, evermore
> A warning for to be, et cætera, et cætera.

The Cockney, however, sometimes soars far, far above his established style, and disgorges an " Arma virumque cano," he tunes his lyre to lofty deeds of war,* and breaks forth,

> General Wolfe was brave,
> Uncommon brave pertik'lar,
> He scrambled up rough rugged rocks,
> Well nigh perpendiklar.—

After such a specimen as this, who can doubt for a moment the ability of Bow Bells to chime to heroic as

---

* I never heard that this was Cockney; I dare say, however, that it is ; at any rate, your readers will receive as great edification from it, Cockney or no Cockney.

well as to pathetic strains? Perhaps, indeed, in the two
first lines the pleonasm is in a slight degree greater than
is entirely necessary; however, the writer seems to think
it so very essential a point, to impress the reader with a
just conviction of the General's courage, that he considers
nothing as lost, which may add, *tant soit peu*, to this
trait in his character: thus "uncommon brave pertiklar,"
serves, as he thinks, to heighten our opinion of the hero;
and certainly all faults in this phrase are entirely venial,
as rising from a redundancy in the author's genius. As
pent-up water, the instant that the smallest opening is
made in the dam, rushes forward, and carries every thing
(again to use the Cockney's expression), higgledy-piggledy
before it; thus the moment that our author puts his pen
to paper, a most terrific eruption of ideas bursts into the
poem, in a most awful array, though perhaps not exactly
in the same order as that in which a more regulated, but
at the same time, less inspired, genius would dispose
them.—The beauty of the third line consists chiefly in
that concordance of sound with sense, in which Homer
must now, for the first time, confess himself beaten. I
myself have ventured to add an Editor's mite to the
rough-ruggedness of the line, by substituting "meo
periculo," scrambled for climbed, as harmonizing somewhat better with the three following R's, though perhaps
scrambling is rather derogatory to General Wolfe's dignity. The same *eruptiveness* and zeal for his hero's
character is remarkable in the last lines, as in the first;
while our veneration for the achievement, and in consequence for the achiever, is at least trebled in proportion
to the eulogist's judicious use of three epithets.

Enough, however, of this subject, and let us turn now
to the defence of his dialect, in the which I hope to prove
to my reader's full satisfaction, that our protégé bears the
palm from his scoffers, both in classical elegance, and in
the force of his expressions.   In the first place, his more
polished ears being unable to bear the W of the vulgar
tongue, he kindly extends his protection and patronage
to the persecuted but classical V.   And whereas we
change vinum to wine, vidua to widow, and vasto to waste,
he restores the ousted letter, and throws in our teeth vine,
vidow, and vaste.   But perhaps you will say that the
Cockney forfeits all claim to indulgence on the score of
classic elegance, by turning out V in several instances, to
make way for W :   now this we agree is a most grievous
accusation, but I rather think that my friend having none
of that uncompromising hardihood, with which a defender
of right against might ought to be gifted, bends somewhat weakly to public opinion, and wishes in some
measure to compensate W for the losses which it has
endured, by introducing him to some places which he
has never before experienced.   But, after all, a thorough-
paced Cockney will seldom or never commit this heinous
fault; a few illiterate pretenders have thought, that as W
had given place to V, V, per contra, ought to give place
to W.   A lameish conclusion, to say the best, and only
calculated to entail disgrace on themselves, their de-
fenders, and their heirs and successors for ever.   And
now I hope my readers, if they get thus far awake, will
own themselves infinitely inferior to the Cockney, at least
in that point, and show themselves nobly impartial in the
rest of the discussion.

"First and foremost," then, the double negative is
so notoriously Greek, that it is scarcely necessary for me
to enlarge upon that subject. The Cockney would think a
denial, in which there was only one of these little parti-
cles, a weak and shuffling kind of evasion; he would
hardly believe you, were you simply to say that you knew
nothing of some rascally business which had lately taken
place; but if you were to adorn your phrase with the
appendages of some half-dozen negatives, as "I don't
know nothing about it no-hows," you would scarcely fail
of making in his mind an indelible impression of the
truth of your denial.

·The double comparatives, more better, more agreeabler,
lesser, and worser, are again, as our Greek Grammar tells
us, drawn from the same root : in blasphémous too, and
contráry, for blásphemous and cóntrary, the Cockney
stands forth, and restores to the injured syllables their
paternal rank and consequence.   Not that this valorous
redresser of grievances confines his feats to the single
province of deposing usurping letters, and re-enthroning
the legitimate possessors ; he has studied Horace, and
there learns that he ought not only to revive obsolete
words and sounds, but to invent new ones : he accordingly sets to work, but, it must be confessed, does not
succeed here quite so well as in his other office : instead
of introducing to the world original words, he, after
manifold travail and labour, only ejects some well-known
faces with new significations tacked to them; thus our
old friend aggravate comes forth with the new meaning
of irritate; thus I have heard of a person being dragged
in the stirrup, and not being able to rise up, till his ankle

was "dislocated." I, even I, Mr. Bouverie, their most ardent patron, was for a time puzzled to know how the dislocation could possibly assist the poor man, till I found that that word in the Cocniac dictionary, had somehow adopted the quite new meaning of extricate.*—Over one word I believe he may claim paternal authority, and a most magnificent word it is ; viz. " rumbustical ;" if the reader has never heard of this most energetic expression, let him know that it bears the same meaning as " obstropolous :" if he wilfully shuts his eyes, and (which I can hardly believe possible) denies also all knowledge of " obstropolous," I will inform him, that the Cockney has, for harmony's sake, promoted that to the place of the now defunct, at least as far as he is concerned, obstreperous.—That A, which formerly, first of five syllables, shed lustre round the head of apothecary,

> " A the great and A the good,"
> Is now " by too severe a fate,
> Fallen, fallen, fallen, fallen,
> Fallen from his high estate,"

and not quite " weltering in his blood ;" but debased to the senseless task of lengthening out monosyllables and dissyllables, " a-dry, a-hungry, a-going, a-gone."—The never-enough-to-be-regretted i has fled from curous, and takes refuge in sitiation, from whence the exile u flies to add harmony to " stupenduous," " tremenduous," &c. All figures and licences of poetry are

---

* I am not clear whether " siscrary," too, is not originally one of his progeny.

employed to render our language more palatable to his
nicer judgment : to crowd is, by the united aid of Pro-
thesis and Paragoge, metamorphosed into "scrowdge,"
squeeze becomes "squeedge," vulgarity is dissolved into
wulgularity, and perpendicular and particular are changed,
by a most Attic contraction, as above, into partiklar, per-
pendiklar. Every one must instantly see how much the
Cockney has improved upon all of these words, how
much more emphatic scrowdge and squeedge than their
predecessors, how far more terrible the idea which they
convey, and, at the same time, who would think of using
vulgarity when the more melodious "wulgularity" lay
in his way, unless overawed by that monster of monsters,
custom. But as the matter stands at present, I am rather
afraid that "rumbustical" will have to experience many
hardships, and often to totter on the brink of death before
it is admitted as a standard word into the English language : that potticary, stupenduous, scrowdge, and
squeedge, will sink unnoticed into the oblivion from
whence they sprung, and that no man will be public-
spirited enough to hurl W from its vantage ground, and
to hold up the despised Londoner as the model for
poetry, pronunciation, dialect, and, in short, for every
thing belonging to the British language.

> I remain, Sir,
>
>> Your obedient servant,
>>
>>> METROPOLITAN.

SONG OF THE VAUDOIS WOMEN.

Farewell to the land where each spot that we trod
Was hallow'd by freedom, and sacred to God;
Farewell to the shades where the Vaudois have dwelt,
And the shrines of our faith, where our forefathers knelt.

Farewell to our mountains; no more shall we raise
The suppliant pray'r, and the anthem of praise :
Too soon will our altars, and snow-cover'd heights,
The Monk, and the Bigot pollute with their rites.

But, say ; shall we tamely bow down to the stroke,
And writhe 'neath our tyrants' and conquerors' yoke ?
No. We fly to the hills, but our husbands will bleed
For their hearths and their homes, for their rights and their creed.

'Tis for these ye contend ; 'tis for these be ye brave ;
May the God of our Fathers his votaries save.
May he be the guard of his once belov'd home,
From the priest-ridden despot, the vassal of Rome.

In vain are these hopes; yet we lingering stand,
To snatch one last look on our dear native land ;
And to gaze on those roofs, which envelop'd in fires,
Shall gleam on the slaughter of husbands and sires.

O fly, sisters, fly ; do we tarry to feel ·
The tyrant's revenge, and the priest's bigot zeal !
Approach, ye invaders ! afar will we flee,
But, God of our fathers, still kneel we to thee !

FROM SIMONIDES.

When round the vessel's varied side,
Roar'd the blast, and stormy tide,

The mother, o'er young Perseus sleeping,
    Cast her arms and fostering vest,
And, pale with grief, and wan with weeping,
    Thus th' unconscious child address'd :
" Sleep, my child, thy careless slumber,
    All my grief thou canst not know,
Fears and sorrows without number,
    Haunt me in this house of woe ;
Think not that the stormy deep,
Rocks the cradle of thy sleep.

" Thou carest not that wind and storm,
    Sweep in gusts around thy pillow ;
Thou carest not that o'er thy head,
    Dashes swift the foaming billow ,
Rolling o'er thy prison bark,
Cold, and comfortless, and dark—
Thou the while in purple vest,
Dreamest at thy mother's breast.

" Hush ! my child, lie still and sleep ;
    Would that my unmeasur'd woe,
Would the winds and swelling deep,
    Could be hush'd and slumber so.

" Jove, to thee I raise my cries,
    Hear me in my sore distress,
Baffle all my enemies
    In their hate and wickedness.

" Calm—if ever thou didst love me,
    Calm the storm and ocean wild ;
If the Mother may not move Thee,
    Hear ! Oh ! hear me, for my Child."

R E C I P E S.

I. *To make a Watering Place.*

Take a fishing-town on any part of the coast, and build
some twenty or thirty houses in the form of a crescent,

the walls of which should not be thinner than four inches;
then take some covered carts, similar to the portable
habitations of the gipsy tribe; dignify them by the name
of bathing-machines, and set them on the beach, attended
by a band of Nereïdes, vulgarly denominated bathing-
women.   Next to be procured are, a physician, an apothecary, and an author; after which, an attorney will drop
in spontaneously, and the settlement will be complete.
The physician must analyse the air, the apothecary the
waters; in the former there must be an extraordinary
proportion of oxygen, the latter must be most medicinally
chalybeate: the author must write a Guide; he must extol
the extent of the sands, if there are any; if not, there may
even be found a panegyrist of shingles.   If there are
trees, as at Worthing, let him praise the salubrious
shades, in which the valetudinarian delights to inhale
the balmy fragrance of the chequered grove; if there
are no trees, as at Brighton, let him dilate on the free
circulation of the air, on the absence of damp, and on
the invigorating properties of unconfined respiration.
In the next place, let a billiard-room, ball-room, and
circulating library have their complement of cues, fiddlers,
and romances; and lastly, let the Morning Post hold out
some such bait as this: "*Fashionable Movements*—Lord
Funguston, and the Honourable Augustus Champion, for
the Royal Marine Hotel, ——, for the benefit of the
waters."

II.   *To make a Novel.*

Take of extraordinary adventures, a quantity equal to
a large pill; of doubts and difficulties, five scruples; of

love, two hearts-full; of sense, three grains; of nonsense, an unlimited quantity; of moral, a very small quantity for fear of nausea; of wit, one salt-cellar full; of puns, a gross; of marriage, *quantum suff.* Let these ingredients be well mixed, and spread upon tissue of plot.—N. B. To be used immediately, as they will *not keep.*

III. *To make a Gothic Story.*

Take of the best lambent blue flame, as much as will not be extinguished by a gust of wind through a dilapidated corridor; of mouldering skeletons, well dried and blanched, a vault full; of rusty daggers, one haft and two blades; of hair-standing-at-end, one wig; take also as many tremulous moon-beams as will discover the above; add divers mysterious noises; and a few ghosts with bloody fingers, or wounded hearts, or sable shrouds; place the patient in the middle of these, and if the story is not sufficiently Gothicised, add a little more of the blue flame, two chains clanking, and a band of robbers.

IV. *To make a Speech.*

Take a score of figures of all descriptions, tropes, metaphors, similes, &c.; make them into sentences, and let those be rounded as nicely as possible, for in that form nonsense is more easily swallowed and digested, and affords no handle for an opponent. Add on the question under consideration, as few words as possible, for though in the hands of able practitioners, that is useful and salutary, yet he will be more secure from failure, who makes use only of the drug called "general ideas."

A. H.

ON CHEPSTOW CASTLE, MONMOUTHSHIRE.

Within yon turret's moated walls,
Within yon castle's mould'ring halls,
How chang'd that scene, that stately. tower,
That princely court, that lordly bower !
Who can view without a tear,
All that rests and slumbers here ?
Where oftentimes, in days of old,
There feasted many a baron bold,
   The flow'r of English chivalry ;
But now neglected and forgot,
Beneath yon chancel's roof they rot—
   And hush'd the sound of revelry.
But many a fleeting day has sped,
Since these were number'd with the dead ;
And many a change these towers, I ween,
Of masters and of times have seen ;
Full often has that massy door
Repuls'd the fury of the war ;
Oft has the soldier's-bugle horn,
That usher'd in the smiling morn,
   The conqu'ring foe defied
The boatman, at the break of day,
Hath sped in fear his wat'ry way
   Along the silver tide.
On yonder hill has Cromwell stood,
And bade the plain be red with blood ;
And bade the cannon's fiery breath,
Launch the swift messengers of death.
And hark : Rebellion's trumpet-call
Is answer'd from the castle-wall ;
But now no drum, or trumpet's swell,
Is heard along the winding dell,
   Where the mighty met their fate ;
No warrior's cry, no charger's tread,
Disturbs the slumbers of the dead—
   Yon camp is desolate.

No sound is heard o'er hill or dale,
Save the sound of the passing gale ;
But e'en this solitude has might
To charm the mind with stern delight ;
But though all warlike sounds have fled,
Here sleep the ashes of the dead ·
For yonder tree with ivy crown'd,
Spreading a fearful shade around,
 Just serves the spot to show,
Where, beneath the unhallow'd soil,
Resting from his warlike toil,
 A soldier sleeps below.
The peasants oft, with silent dread,
O'er yon meadow quickly tread ;
And as the evening shades advance,
Cast around a fearful glance,
For many a dreadful tale is told,
Of deeds of blood in days of old ;
And often, in the raven's moan,
Deems that he hears a dying groan
 That oft was heard before ;
The boatman, as he passes by,
Views the place with fearful eye,
 And thinks of days of yore.

ON GOOD WRITING.

My dear Mr. Bouverie ;

As every thing which takes place in this, if I may so
call it, our little kingdom, is of particular interest to me,
whether we surpass our adversaries in cricket, whether
we are celebrated for hard pulling, or whether, though
last, not by any means the least, in my estimation, we
are renowned for good composition, both in prose and
verse ; I have taken the liberty, after having perused
with the strictest attention every paper in The Eton Miscellany, and likewise being most earnest in my wishes for

its success, of addressing the following hints to you,
which, if you think them worthy of insertion, are perfectly at your disposal; and I can only humbly hope
that they may be of use to your more regular correspondents.   Without, therefore, any further explanation,
let me briefly give you, what I consider to be the more
essential rules of Good Writing.   In the first place, in
my opinion, the characteristics of a perfect composition,
whether it be an epic poem, or merely a familiar letter,
are, just sentiments, regular order, and elegance of style.
Secondly, every thought must be properly adapted to
the subject, and contain something as new and ingenious,
interesting and important, as possible.   These last, however, are qualities in which, I am afraid, writers too often
fail, their composition, in too many instances, being unequal ; at one time rising into superior merit, at another,
suddenly falling below mediocrity, either the expressions
being too flippant, or the detail too elaborate.   As I
said before, therefore, every thought should contain
something new and ingenious, interesting and important; besides which, our remarks should be acute, rational,
and judicious : our arguments, logical and conclusive.
Thirdly, as we are continually disgusted by those injudicious writers, who confound and promiscuously crowd
words and phrases together with more than poetical
licence, and do it in violation of correct style, even where
the expressions ought to be clothed in the clearest and
purest language, and where the judgment ought to confine itself to the most accurate and explanatory discri-
mination of those ideas which are susceptible of the mi-
nutest ambiguity   As this is too often the case   a regu-

lar method, or what is called by Horace " lucidus ordo,"
must be strictly observed in the arrangement of our ideas.
Our sentiments and observations must follow one another
in regular gradation ; that is, the latter must confirm and
illustrate the former, and throw additional light on the subject. Confusion often, too often, arises from the want of
a methodical arrangement of our ideas, which alone is sufficient to condemn a book ; for the mind, if it has to labour
to find out the direct meaning of every sentence, becomes
wearied and fatigued, and rejects, perhaps, a valuable
work, because it is deficient in perspicuity, the first and
most essential beauty of style. If our ideas are promiscuously thrown together, the whole composition must
inevitably become nothing better than a confused inco-
herent rhapsody ; it will resemble an edifice which,
although consisting of the best materials, can never be
pleasing to the eye, if wanting in proportion, regularity,
symmetry, or any of the important requisites of architecture.
Fourthly, the last essential ingredient in good writing is
elegance of style. There must be no ungrammatical expressions, no obscure or embarrassed sentences, no mean or
vulgar remarks (which always disgust the reader), no pompous or pedantic phrases , but every thing should be written easily, naturally, and gracefully. The inimitable Mr.
Addison perfectly agrees in the opinion, that elegance of
style is that which adorns and recommends good sense,
where he observes that there is as much difference between
seeing a thought expressed in the language of Cicero,
and that of an ordinary writer, as there is between viewing an object by the light of a taper, and the light of the
sun.

Having made these few observations, I again hope that you will pardon the liberty I have taken, and my boyish presumption. I beg leave to subscribe myself, my dear Mr. Bouverie, a well-wisher of your's,

CANDIDUS.

SKETCH.

A merlin small she held upon her hande,
With hoode and jesses gallantlie bedighte,
But little did he need or hoode or bande,
Could he but gaze on her, full safe were he from flighte.
Old Ballad.

Oh! she is young, that maiden gay,
  Nor yet within her tender heart
  Hath thought, or care, for aught had part,
Save thought, how that the present day
May gladly, gaily, pass away;
Save care, that when she slip the string
Her hawk be sure and swift of wing.

Her cheek with youth's first blush is glowing,
  Her eye with new awaken'd light,
And o'er her neck the tresses flowing
  By art untaught, yet soft and bright,
Woo every breath of summer-air
To nestle, all enamour'd, there.

Her step is full of grace and life;
  While the glad eye, that ever strays
  Intent on nought that meets its gaze,
  Proclaims a mind as bright and free,
And ignorant of passion's strife,
  Unhurt by aught that might alloy
Its innocent serenity—
  All, all is youth and careless joy:

Nor need is hers of gaud or dress,
    For fair enough without is she,
    Yet aye, as lovely maid should be,
Unconscious of her loveliness.

Her thoughts o'er pleasant fields are straying,*
    Or in the depths of hidden groves,
Or where the noisy streams are playing
    Amid the scenes her fancy loves :
The sun is warm, the earth is gay,
    The flow'rets spring, the skies are bright ;—
With her, too, life is in its May,
    And all with her is young delight ;
And summer comes—seek not to know,
    Light maid, the season that shall follow ;
I would not see that sportive brow
    Clouded by dream of future sorrow.
Still touch thy lute, and gaily sing,
    Thy voice will blither measures move ;
Not yet hath spoke the trembling string,
    The hopes, the fears, the pangs of love.

ON DINNERS.

" Νῦν δὲ μνησώμεθα δόρπɛ."—HOMER.

Dear Bouverie ;

Although it has been generally considered, and I
believe not without justice, that the partaking of what
is usually termed a Good Dinner tends to diminish not
only the acuteness of appetite, but that also of the human
intellect; yet the people of the present day either hold

* Circum virentes est animus tuæ
Campos juvencæ.—Hor.

an opinion of a very different kind, or discover the most striking inconsistency that can easily be imputed to the human race.

You, Mr. Bouverie, may question the veracity of this assertion; but I will, nevertheless, affirm it to be decidedly inconsistent for any one to think a " good dinner" hostile to the exercise of a clear judgment and sound discretion, and at the same time, to make it the most fundamental, perhaps the most alluring, object in the performance of business which would essentially call for enlightened judgment, and demand perspicuity.

We frequently see a company, whether from interested or philanthropic motives, insuring the lives and properties of their fellow-creatures against the destructive effects of fire; much business is to be transacted, many calculations are to be made, many things to be resolved by the company: when and where are they all performed? I answer, in the London Tavern, over a well-dressed dinner. On the other hand, some persons discover a new science—suppose, for instance, Political Economy: surely, you will say, " the feast of reason, and the flow of soul," are sufficient for Scholars and Economists. I answer no. notwithstanding the old adage, " Enough is as good as a feast," these scientific gentlemen require another, and a more substantial feast, united with the flow of Bacchus, to discover the definition of value, or discuss the alarming propositions of M'Culloch, or the explanatory expostulations of Malthus, in the shape of a well-dressed Dinner.

An University is on the eve of being established in a wealthy and populous city: with what zeal do its managers form, plans of the future education of their youthful posterity? Why, with the cheering and soul-inspiring zeal borrowed from a " good dinner."

Alas! how many Cow and Dairy Companies, how many Mining and other Associations would be objects comparatively unimportant to their Directors, had not those directors the pleasing recollection, the comfortable assurance, that they should, at all events, occasionally meet, to enjoy a " good dinner." And, dear Bartholo-mew, permit me to conclude by inviting you, should a favourable opportunity at any time offer itself, to honour me with partaking of a private, though I hope a well-dressed, Dinner.

Your's, truly,

IMPRANSUS.

AN EVENING VIEW OF

CÆSAR'S HILL,

NEAR THE COAST OF SUSSEX;

SUPPOSED TO BE THE SITE OF SOME OLD ROMAN ENCAMPMENT.

Oft has the muse in plaintive accents sung
  The charms of many an ever-hallow'd spot,
Where once the bow, but now the lyre is strung,
  Once loved by many, now by all forgot.

Thus, when the breeze among the summer-leaves
  Disturbs that sleep, refresh'd with evening dew,
Then a dark amber cloud the Moon receives,
  And veils the crescent from all mortal view.

Reclining oft where glow-worms rays illume
  The verdant mead, I pour my humble lay
To thy dark majesty, amid the gloom
  That ever dims the closing eye of day.

O while such haughty blood with fervent glow,
  Unceasing throbs in ev'ry Briton's veins,
Say, what invidious, or what treach'rous, foe,
  Shall madly dare t' invade thy native plains ?

Now, all in vain thou court'st the wind to swell
  The stormy concert of their martial song,
And call'st the playful fairies of the dell
  To join the chorus as they sport along.

No more is heard the threat'ning din of war,
  But 'tis the liquid flute's melodious sound,
Which, borne by gentle zephyrs from afar,
  Breathes its soft charm and harmony around.

Lo, from the ocean-wave thou seem'st to rise,
  And thine own honour proudly to proclaim,
By stretching forth thy summit to the skies,
  Where live the records of thy former fame.

HENGIST.

THE LONDON UNIVERSITY;

OR,

THE MARCH OF INTELLECT.

Mr. Bouverie ;

A great revolution is at hand. The giant Intellect, that has long slumbered in the shades of Isis and of Cam, has roused him from his lethargy, and is marching

with seven-league strides to the arena of Smithfield, and
the classic fountains of Fleet-ditch. Is it that he has
come to visit his brother giants at Guildhall, or his
chronometrical brethren at St. Dunstan's? Gog and
Magog frown from their pedestals, and the satellites
of St. Dunstan strike their clubs in contradiction.
Wherefore comest thou hither, Intellect, child of Perfection? The grey fog of the house-top is around thy
head; the dun smoke is wreathed on thy temples. I
see thee on the mist-enveloped Monument! thy form is
as the sun in an eclipse; thy step is like the tramp of
the war-horse—it rattleth on the pavement of Cheapside;
thy hair distilleth ambrosia; the apprentice-boys catch
it in their caps. Hail! thou harbinger of refinement;
hail! regenerator of man: Ignorance trembles on her
throne; Dulness wraps her head in murky darkness;
Stupidity flies at thy approach, like the mist before the
sun of the morning.

Citizens of London, rejoice! your greatest glory shall
no longer be this, to be members of the Skinners' Company, or to have the freedom of Fishmongers' Hall:
new and more noble titles shall be yours: anticipate
with exultation the splendid appellation of Master of
Arts, though ye be but journeymen mechanics after all!
hail with rapture the prospect of being able to subscribe
to your names the envied addition of LL.D.; but beware,
lest those letters may with justice be read, Little
Learning Dangerous; for, as Pope says,

> " A little learning is a dangerous thing ;
> Drink deep, or taste not the Pierian spring."

Rejoice, ye assistant apothecaries! no longer shall a

physician's prescription be to you as unintelligible as
an hieroglyphic; Latin shall be current in London, from
Temple Bar to the Minories. Woe to the vernacular
idiom of the Cockneys ! woe to the ancient licence of
w and *v*, and the cherished mal-pronunciation of *h*.
But still long will it be before those time-honoured
barbarisms shall be abandoned; long will it be before.
these recruits to Latin and Greek will understand, in the
one language, that their favourite letter must be abandoned; in the other, that the distinctions of aspirate and
lene must be observed.

But still, whatever be thy consequences, hail Giant of
Intellect! thou, from thy bounteous horn showerest down
upon London Latin and Greek, Physics and Metaphysics,
Literature and Science, Attics and Mathematics. Where
is now the tailor so mean and so unscientific as to take
a measure in the common way? Let him imitate his
brethren of Laputa, and clothe his customers, not
secundum artem, but *secundum scientiam*. Hail, wide-
ruling science! soon shall thy dominion be confessed
in the chamber of the Royal Society, and in the stall of
the cobler !

Where is the man that is so barbarous as to affirm,
that learning is not salutary, even to tradesmen and
mechanics? Who would not be pleased to hear, instead
of the vulgar invocation of "'Prentices! 'Prentices!
Clubs! Clubs!" the classic war-cry of

"Arma, viri, ferte arma !"

I myself shall hail with rapture the day, when in Smithfield shall be heard the Virgilian query of

"Dic mihi, Damœta, cujum pecus ?"

when the gentlemen of 'Change Alley shall be as well acquainted with sesterces and denarii as with pounds, shillings, and pence; when those sounds shall be heard in the streets of London which have not been heard there since the era of the Cæsars.

Citizens of London! Cockneys! Countrymen! in whichsoever appellation ye delight, Awake! 'tis the voice of Intellect that calls; the voice of Intellect, which, like the neighing of Chanticleer, bids you rouse yourselves from your sleep of apathy and ignorance to welcome the dawn of improvement which glows in the chambers of the East.* Widen your alleys, that the sun of literature may penetrate the murky recesses of Pudding-lane and Pie-corner, and vivify the embryo germ of talent. Sound the curfew, lest the smoke of your fires quench his rising beams; Macadamize your streets, that Intellect may march at his ease. Who can say, that under the mist and smoke of the city smoulders no spark of intellectual fire? I, for one, will venture to predict, that hereafter some civic Byron shall arise, who, though nursed in gloominess and night, with the sound of cart-wheels for his lullaby, shall start forth into lustre and renown, and shall be able to do that which Homer and the Gas Companies alone have yet accomplished,

"—— Ex fumo dare lucem."

Then shall be displayed the glory and magnificence of the metropolis; no longer shall civic ceremonies be dishonoured by the doggrel of Grub-street, but shall glow

---

* *Query*—East End of Town?

with all the fire of poetical description. The Lord Mayor
and Aldermen, swan-hopping on the Thames, shall be
more celebrated than Cleopatra in her barge upon the
Cydnus; and all the banquets of antiquity shall yield
to the courtly magnificence of a Lord Mayor's feast.
Then shall the luscious turtle, the "*grata testudo dapibus*"
(as Addison has it), float in Lyric measure; the lordly
haunch shall be borne along in the majesty of heroics,
and the portly convexity of an Alderman shall swell the
pompous Alexandrine.   How great will be the revolution, when science shall have been diffused through the
inmost recesses of the metropolis; what works of interest
will emanate from this hitherto unenlightened portion
of our countrymen; works of the deepest interest and
importance to civilized society, works of such moment,
as "An Analysis of the Waters of Cripplegate Pump,
showing the same to be Chalybeate, and relating the
right system of drinking them;" or "A Trigonometrical
Survey of Seven Dials;" or "A Project for making Shoes
of London Smoke, by condensing it to the substance of
Indian Rubber;" or "A Conchological Account of some
Fossil Shells, found under the Pavement of Billingsgate;
showing the same to be the remains of Antediluvian
Oysters;" or "A Metaphysical Disquisition on the reasoning Faculties of Swine;" or "An Anatomical View
of the internal Conformation of a Flea."   These, and
perhaps works of even greater interest shall be the
gigantic efforts of minds, whose sole attention has, perhaps, been hitherto applied to the mending of galligas-
kins, or the measuring of calico; for, it must be observed,
that the absence of genius is not to be argued from its

non-appearance, when it has slumbered in obscurity, owing to the want of those springs of action, which are now about to be applied, by the foundation of the London University.

Welcome, then, to the halls that are prepared for thee, O Spirit, that bringest civilization in thy train. By the hecatomb that is sacrificed in Fleet-market, by the libation that is poured out at Meux's, by these I adjure you, O Giant Intellect, that stalkest round Granta and Rhedycina, march on to enlighten the benighted inhabitants of London, and, if the prayers of thy votaries be heard, march on in double-quick time !

I remain, dear Sir, your's, faithfully,

ANTONY HEAVISIDE.

NOTE BY B. BOUVERIE.

With all due deference to the opinion of my venerable friend, I must beg to enter my protest against such sweeping denunciations of the abilities of Mechanics. I cannot help recollecting, that from them, vituperated as they have been, have proceeded almost entirely those improvements in practical Science, to which England owes a great portion of her present wealth and power; and that Watt, Arkwright, Telford, and Rennie, once belonged to that most useful and most enterprising class of men.

ETON MISCELLANY,

No. VII.

———————

INTRODUCTION.

MY wish to introduce two friends to the Public, and my compassion for the eyes and understandings of my readers, prevented my extending the commencement of my last Number beyond a simple delineation of some of the principal features of those characters, which I there endeavoured to pourtray. Nothing of great moment has occurred during the intervening period, to constitute an era in the literary lives of the conductors of The Eton Miscellany. It may possibly be worth my while to reveal a few of the cabinet secrets to my friends, and to give them some slight specimens of the various habits of thinking and acting belonging to my coadjutors, curiously exemplified as they have been in the different channels of exertion into which, during the late reasonably long release from severer studies which they have enjoyed, their individual inclinations happened to direct them.

Immediately after my return, I hastened to Francis Jermyn's apartment. It was, if possible, in a more primitive state of chaos than usual. The poet was a-sleep,

but it appeared that his mind was not disposed to partake of that rest in which his body, for a considerable
number of hours, had been recruiting itself, as his tongue
was by no means idle. His sleeping, like his waking,
thoughts, appeared to be divided between his Betting-
book and his Album. His exclamations at one moment
appeared directed to the sights which he had witnessed;
at another, to the plans which he had meditated. Heroes
and heroines were singularly mingled with race-horses
and their riders; and, on awaking, he said the substance
of his dream had been, that he was riding a favourite mare
in a match against time, which he had engaged to do with
pen, ink, and paper in his hands; and, at the same time,
enjoying a most Parnassian fit of inspiration, and disem-
boguing odes and sonnets, heroics and epics, with un-
exampled rapidity.   On the judges' stand were Gregory
Griffin and Peregrine Courtenay, who both cheered and
waved their hats to him as he rode the race and came in
some seconds within the time, with an innumerable
quantity of lines written down, but the paper and his
vestments somewhat blotted !

    " But, my dear Sir," quoth he, " I have here for you
an ' Ode to Matilda;' and ' Consolatory Verses to
Mamaluke;' and ' A Visit to Doncaster;' and ' A Legend of the Turf,' or,"——I broke off his narration at
this point, and assured him that the only race which he
was now called upon to ride, was the race of Reputation;
which he, having now a fair opportunity of winning,
might never again be so happy as to be engaged in.

    I next repaired to Mr. Montague. He produced im-
mediately a formidable roll of paper, which I hoped was

a Tale of Olden Times. No : it was entitled " Strictures on Porson's Preface;" and was backed by a
"Synopsis of Greek Metres, with the Possibility of
Transferring them to the English Tongue considered ;"
a "Genealogical History of Expletives ;" with "The
Loves of the Anapæsts, a Classical Poem." I struck my
forehead in Melpomenean fashion, turned on my heel
with cothurnian swing, and retreated in utter dismay.

Mr. Quincy, thought I to myself, will have been guilty
of none of these vagaries. However wild are his theories,
his practice is domesticated enough. Judge of my surprise, when, on his table, I found nothing but compositions of this and a similar nature : " Account of the
Antediluvian Rebellions;" "Principles of Government
of the Hottentots considered ;" "The late Insurrection
of the Esquimaux, with some Account of Kilotsopa, its
Leader ;" " Ode to the Shade of Wat Tyler ;" "Lines
written in the Broadway, New York."

Kind reader, might not your humble servant have gone
mad, after seeing such sights as these, with far more reason for so doing, than one half of the heroes or heroines
of plays, novels, and romances have often had, for pursuing and justifying such a line of conduct ? I had some
thoughts of it ; but on reconsideration, was disposed to
allow that the happy lot, which I here enjoy—that the
boundless indulgence, which, from high and low, I here
receive—that the unmerited approbation which good-
will alone has here bestowed upon me—constituted all together a very strong chain of argument in favour of Activity and Existence, *versus* a Convent, a Mad-house, or a
Tombstone.

2

ANCIENT AND MODERN GENIUS COMPARED.

(Continued from page 16)

Illi alternantes magnâ vi prælia miscent.—VIRGIL

Among the various inconsistencies and errors, into which the advocates of the superiority of Ancient Genius have fallen, one is, I think, peculiarly observable. These worthies have learned to blow hot and cold in the same breath. At one time they will tell us that modern, civilized, times do not admit of mighty expansion or exertion of genius ; that, by civilization, it is damped, and cramped, and pared down, &c. &c. ; and that in the early stages of society alone must we look for the most vigorous and magnificent efforts which human ability is capable of making. Yet so rapidly are they hurried on, so carelessly are they willing to investigate the subject, that one moment after this they break out into declamatory commendations of ancient authors for breaking down the barriers of barbarism and ignorance—causing their light to shine through clouds and darkness, and performing many other fine things. Now surely it is hardly fair, or consistent, to give *additional* praise to the Ancients, because they *had not* the facilities afforded by civilization ; and, at the same time, to detract from the merit of the Moderns, and to assign their *possession of those very facilities* as a main cause of their inferiority to their rivals.

It seems to me that there has been an equitable distribution of advantages and disadvantages on either side.

The Moderns have flourished under the fostering care of
Learning, and have been borne onward in their triumphant progress by the advancing tide of civilization.
They have also enjoyed the advantages of imitation; and
have had thereby the opportunity of avoiding the errors,
and still of aiming at the excellencies, of their predecessors. But the Ancients had one great advantage, which is
seldom, if ever, even touched upon. To them, every thing
was new—to us, most things are not so. The lover who,
in verse, first compared the cheeks of his Delia, or Julia,
or Chloe, to a rose, her neck to ivory, her hands to lilies,
had before him three very obvious, yet still *original*, images:
the poet who likened his hero, descending on the foemen, to a lion rushing on his prey in the sheep-fold, and
when pent up by his enemies to the wild boar of the
forest, at the time when he gathers energy from despair,
and turns in rage and wildness on the crowd of his pursuers, affrighted in their turn—then had before him two
very obvious, but *original*, similies. Far different has
been the condition of the Moderns. The paths, which
lay most open to their eyes, had already been trodden ;
the flowers, which grew on their borders, had already
been gathered. Ill would it have fared with them, if
they had only adopted second-hand the beauties of their
predecessors. But by this almost universal preoccupation,
their resources were narrowed, and their genius fettered.
Deprived of these simple and obvious stores, they had
imposed upon them the difficult task of travelling over a
wider range, and selecting, with a more studious diligence,
those ornaments necessary to their undertakings, acquired
with more difficulty, and distributed with less profusion.

Surely, then, when the materials which Nature afforded
had been first offered to the Ancients ; when from the
whole multitude of objects and mass of materials so many
had been selected, and those only left which were either
undiscovered or despised—surely Modern Genius has
herein suffered an incalculable privation, and been opposed by a mighty obstacle ; a privation which could not
have been repaired, an obstacle which could not have
been overcome, had not learning and civilization extended
its prospects, and stimulated its exertions—had they
not opened to it new scenes of wonder, and new
sources of wealth.

Many, however, among those who stand at the head
of the list of Modern authors have laboured under singular disadvantages. What situation could be more
unhappy than that of our own Shakspeare ? He had to
contend with prejudice, to expect contempt ; before him
lay

" Poverty's insuperable bar '"

Without friends, without experience, without instruction,
without learning, did this extraordinary man, by the
innate powers of his mighty mind, engage in the arduous contest, and achieve the splendid triumph. Formed
more to rule and govern the public taste than to receive,
through its capricious revolutions, popularity and renown
at one time, oblivion and contempt at another, he claimed
the admiration he deserved; he inscribed his name in
characters of everlasting brilliancy on the tablet of
Renown, and raised for himself an imperishable monument in the productions of his mighty mind—he left that

name the pride of Englishmen, and those works, never to
be touched by the ravages of time—never to be assailed
by the malignity of envy—

> "——— Non illud carpere Livor
> Possit opus,———"

but to remain through succeeding generations as the
shrine whereat the whole civilized world might combine
to lay down their tribute of praise and veneration.

Let the case of Milton be compared to that of Virgil.
The latter, having the model of the Iliad before him,
dwelling in the midst of ease, leisure, and tranquillity;
fostered by patronage, encouraged by applause, and not
scrupulous as to appropriating the property of others
as his own, possessed every advantage for research,
meditation, and composition. But John Milton spent
the best years of his life in the midst of the horrors of
civil war : and his pen had been long imbued with the
bitterness of party virulence, (as how few were not so
imbued, during that unhappy time?) before he proceeded to the execution—perhaps even to the choice—of
a subject for his splendid master-piece. And when he
had chosen and did execute—when he explored a new,
and a lofty, and an unattempted, road to the pinnacle of
Fame—when the secrets of Creation and the councils of
Heaven were the subjects of his awful meditations—how
little aid, comparatively speaking, could he derive from
watching the progress of the ferocity of Achilles, or from
following the milk-and-watery, yet savage, Æneas through
his long-continued wanderings. Were these the materials

on which he.worked, or were these the wings on which
he soared, when he cried, exulting,

"Into the Heaven of Heavens I have presumed,
An earthly guest, and drawn empyrean air ''"

Though . the auxiliaries which other countries can
afford are both numerous and powerful, our own must
bear the brunt of the battle. It would be unjust, however, to leave such men as Lope de Vega, and Cervantes,
of Spain ; Goethe, Schiller, and their fellow dramatists,
of Germany ; Petrarch, Tasso, Dante, Ariosto, and some
few more of Italy, and many French' writers, in ·the
shade. Many may not be brought forward, simply from
their not being required to establish my position ; and
many more will certainly be omitted from that feeling
of compassion and humanity towards my readers which
so often teaches me to lop the redundant luxuriancies
of my imagination. In numbers, if we looked to them
for victory, we are certainly most powerful ;· as either
England, Italy, or France, could, 1 believe, exhibit a
catalogue of authors, exceeding the whole sum of the
ancient writers. In some branches of the subject, the
comparison may be instituted between man and man :
in others, we must be contented with a more general
view. To find a parallel to Horace, I must select from
the works of several : yet the Odes of Dryden, Gray,
Collins, Byron, and other not despicable auxiliaries, may
match those of Pindar and Horace : and the latter, with
Juvenal and Persius, at least incur no disgrace by being
compared with such men as Pope and Dryden, Boileau
and Swift, Byron and Churchill, and Butler, and John-

son, and Gifford. But if we were obliged to have
recourse to such a method of retaliation as condemning
the whole of either side on account of the difficulty of
matching individuals, we might safely ask for an Ariosto,
a Chaucer, a Spencer, a Byron, or a Butler, among the
Ancients.

Few or none will, I apprehend, now be found prepared
to dispute the immense superiority of the Moderns in
political philosophy, and in general science. Such men
would be laughed at, more than argued with, for their
pains; and such, probably, do not exist. The sum of
practical genius now in operation in this country is
immense, in almost every branch of science ; and many
a one, whose daily labour now can but earn his daily
bread, would, in ancient times, have been hailed as a
prodigy, or worshipped as a god, for the skill he could
display, and the wonders he could work. And in those
branches of philosophy which the Ancients have touched
upon, who will compare for depth of research, sublimity
of conception, and soundness of reasoning, the vague
and futile systems of Aristotle, Plato, and Cicero, with
the truths established even to demonstration, by Newton
and La Place, Kepler and Galileo, Bacon, Locke, and
Boyle ? Extraordinary as was the ingenuity and ability
manifested by the ancient philosophers and mathema-
ticians, here, at least, we have been placed on an exalted
eminence—an eminence, an object of wonder to all, and
of admiration, it is to be hoped, to many. Let all the
institutions which have been formed, all the lights which
have shone, among us, THE ROYAL SOCIETY in particular, testify on how lofty a throne Science has estab-

lished her position among us. And it is glorious to
think, that she is still in her infancy; that others may
look back on us as we look back on those who have gone
before; that there are still new regions to be explored,
new secrets to be revealed, and new pleasures to be
enjoyed, by those to whom it is given to remove the veil
from the face of Nature, and expose her to the gaze of
men.*

Perhaps in History, even Davila and Guicciardini,
Hume, and Robertson, and Mitford, Gibbon and Clarendon, may, by some, not be considered equal to Herodotus
and Thucydides, Xenophon and Polybius, Livy and
Tacitus. But I really know not whether I should place
Herodotus in the list, or set his works in a separate
division, as a parallel to Robinson Crusoe and the
Arabian Nights; for one is nearly as credible as the
other. And if Xenophon actually was a romance writer,
sure I am that we have many better.

In that great branch of Poetry, the Epic,† Milton and
Dante may well meet Homer and Virgil. Tasso we will
give upon trust for Varius. The Lusiad, the Messiah,
and the Henriade may surely stand against Lucan and
Statius; and the poem of the Creation does credit to

---

* It has been remarked, that little has been done of late in this country
to facilitate the acquisition of mathematical knowledge, and that the
elementary works published at Cambridge seem more calculated to inspire
the learner with awe, than to relieve him from ignorance Some foreign
ones are considered much more clear · and, in many branches of speculative science, it is thought that France has, for years, much surpassed us

† It is in deference to the probable prejudices of the great body of my
readers that I do not adduce Ossian, or Macpherson, or whatever the name
be, as a very powerful auxiliary. such I cannot help considering him.

our literature, extolled as it has been by Addison, though the name of poor Sir Richard Blackmore has something ominously prosy in its very sound.

The Pastorals of Gesner and Pope may be matched with those of Theocritus and Virgil; and we have at least one Anacreon in Herrick, if not a second in Moore. In elegiac verse our Milton and Buchanan, with many others both of our own countrymen and of the Italians, have rivalled the Ancients in their own style and their own language, and attained the spirit and elegance of the Augustan age itself. In Didactic poetry, what antagonists can be advanced against such men (to select a few from many) as Beattie, Thomson, Goldsmith, Byron and Campbell? or where shall we look for one whose inborn genius, and unadorned simplicity, and vigorous conception, may render him a rival to Robert Burns?*

But it is in the consideration of the comparative merits of the Ancients and Moderns in the powers with which they have worked that mighty engine on the minds and manners of men, the Drama, that I look for one of our most brilliant triumphs. Remembering how many of the ancient plays have been lost, and regretting the want of the Merope and its companions most sincerely, I feel,

---

* Looking back, as I do, with veneration on my great predecessor, Peregrine Courtenay, whose throne I fill, however unworthily, and whose sceptre I wield, however weakly, I feel bound to apologise to his Majesty's shade for an insult offered to one of his Cabinet, or Club, in more appropriate phrase. His Majesty will perceive that I have not brought forward Messrs. Wordsworth or Coleridge to cope with the mighty men of old. It is, I can assure his Majesty, from a tender regard for their welfare, as they w   :   .   .   d   't   :

at the same time, bound to remember, that many of the
productions of our own dramatists have shared a like
fate.* But we can make allowance for all these. We
can give them Alfieri and Metastasio; the great Goethe
and his German brethren; the Chinese plays, and the
Indian nataks; we can allow to them the fabulous
twenty-three hundred, and the actual five hundred,
dramas of Lope de Vega, with those of his numerous
Spanish followers; Voltaire, Racine, Corneille, Molière,
will we yield; still fully and proudly confident,
that Massinger and Jonson, Beaumont and Fletcher,
Shirley and Otway, and Marlowe and Ford, and
Congreve, with the inimitable Sheridan, may sustain
the charge of the formidable phalanx formed by
Æschylus, Sophocles, and Euripides, with their light-
armed allies Aristophanes and Menander, Plautus and
Terence. But if neither kick the beam, the name of
Shakespeare shall descend into the scale with a weight
and a power like the sword of Brennus—a name which
alone might meet their combined force, and rival their
united excellency.

The seeds of eloquence do not usually spring into
existence, unless sown in the soil of Freedom, and reared
by the hand of Industry. But it is liberty, and not
licentiousness, which strengthens the machine of government, and invigorates the powers of a mighty nation.
Among ourselves, Lord Strafford was one of the earliest
orators. Lord Halifax, in the next reign, and Lord

---

* See Mr. Gifford's anecdote (in his edition of Massinger) of the forty-
nine plays used for covering pies by Mr. Warburton's cook-maid, &c.

Shaftesbury, were able speakers. After the Revolution,
however, commenced a brilliant series. Some among
Sir Robert Walpole's speeches—that on the Peerage
Bill, and that in his own defence, towards the close of
his administration, in particular, are very eloquent.
After him came Charles Townshend. Then there arose
the British Demosthenes, to utter in a British senate, the
sentiments of a British statesman; to protect the
oppressed, and to thunder on the oppressor; to rival as
an orator, and far, far to excel as a statesman, his great
prototype. Soon after came worthy and numerous successors; and great as were Cicero, and Hortensius, and
Æschines, they yield to Fox, Sheridan, Erskine, Grattan
—to Burke, to Pitt, and to Canning.

The critics I had almost forgotten. Here I shall
certainly give the preference to the Moderns, thereby
hoping to disarm the wrath and to secure the approbation
of any animal of the tribe who may deign to notice me.
If it have not this effect, in my very next edition I will
prove Aristotle, Longinus, and Quintilian superior to
Boileau, Addison, Johnson, and Gifford.

But it is not on superiority in those points, where there
is an actual and direct comparison alone, that the
Moderns may, I think, ground their claims to a favourable verdict. We have new stores yet untouched. We
have humourists, and essayists, and novelists; we have
the Spectator, the Tatler, the Guardian, and the whole
tribe—we have Cervantes, and Fielding, and Smollett
and Sterne—and greater than any, we have WALTER
SCOTT—whose splendid efforts and magnificent creations afford the surest and most triumphant proof that
the spread of civilization does not forbid, or impede, the

legitimate exercise of the inventive faculties. But yet
further—we have the venerable array of our pulpit
orators. Scanty and cold, or unmeaning and ridiculous
—aye, even too often execrable—was the devotion of the
Ancients—far, far removed from that fervent and animated
spirit of worship, which the Christian religion is so
eminently and so admirably calculated to inspire.* Hence
we derive our highest and our proudest claim : hence it
is, that wisdom, and power, and ability, and virtue, and
piety have been marching onward hand in hand : hence
it is that we are able to look back with joyful admiration
of the past, and to look onward with triumphant anticipation of the future : to look back on the great, daunt-
less, and invincible, supporters of that faith for which
Cranmer, and Latimer, and Ridley, endured with joy
the flames of persecution, and entered in triumph the
gates of death ; and to look onward to those who will
never be wanting to adorn and to defend it. Hence it
is, that we venture to declare that Newton, Shakspeare,
and Milton, stand unrivalled in the history of the world
—and to express our humble satisfaction at feeling able to
award to our country the prize of arts as well as of arms,
and to claim for her the pre-eminence in genius, which
she has so long enjoyed in virtue.

It would be both undutiful and unjust in me to conclude, without some reference to the part which Eton
has performed in fostering within her walls men who
have afterwards become the delight and the glory of
England. I need only select from a host the names of
Wotton and Sherlock, of Boyle and Porson, of Gray

---

* "Every thing like creative Poetry can only be derived from the inward
life of a people, and from religion, the root of that life."—SCHLEGEL

and the Walpoles, of Fox and Windham, of Chatham and Canning! Canning, over whom even now not Eton alone, but all England, and the whole civilized world are shedding the tear of heartfelt sorrow and merited veneration. But, alas! he is beyond the reach of calumny on the one hand, and eulogium on the other —in the cold and silent grave.

It is for those who revered him in the plenitude of his meridian glory, to mourn over him in the darkness of his premature extinction: to mourn over the hopes that are buried in his grave, and the evils that arise from his withdrawal from the scene of life. Surely if eloquence never excelled and seldom equalled—if an expanded mind, and a judgment whose vigour was paralleled only by its soundness—if brilliant wit—if a glowing imagination—if a warm heart —and an unbending firmness—could have strengthened the frail tenure, and prolonged the momentary duration of human existence, that man had been immortal! But nature could endure no longer. Thus has Providence ordained that, inasmuch as the intellect of man is more brilliant, it shall be more short-lived; as its sphere is more expanded, more swiftly is it summoned away. The ardent soul spurs on the harassed body to activity; for its unearthly and unseen substance neither demands nor admits of repose. We are fearfully and wonderfully made. And lest we should give to man the honour due to God—lest we should exalt the object of our admiration into a divinity for our worship—He, who calls the weary and the mourner to eternal rest, hath been pleased to remove him from our eyes. He hears not the splendid panegyrics of the great, nor the humble praises of the lowly. Assailed by the pitiless abuse of some, who forgot the period of his splendid services to their cause, that they might indulge in unlimited condemnation of one who, during by far the greater part of his political career, had fought the same battles with themselves—torn in mind and harassed in body—he fell, like his great master, Pitt, a victim to his proud and exalted station. Distant from all extremes—firm in principle, and conciliatory in action—the friend of Improvement, and the enemy of Innovation, England fondly looked to him for her peace and glory; who, *from first to last*, had been her faithful servant and her sure friend.

The decrees of inscrutable Wisdom are unknown to us : but if ever there was a man for whose sake it was meet to indulge the kindly, though frail, feelings of our nature—for whom the tear of sorrow was, to us, both prompted by affection and dictated by duty—that man was GEORGE CANNING.

Note.—On reviewing what has been written, I am somewhat fearful lest I should seem to have endeavoured to depreciate the Ancients. Such an endeavour, I am well aware, would recoil severely and deservedly on my own head and there its action would terminate. I am their devoted, though unworthy, admirer. But I admire the Moderns *still more* · and am only anxious to rescue myself from the imputation of an attempt, which would be equally insolent and feeble ; exactly as weak as regarded hurting their reputation, as it would be effectual in proving and commemorating my folly.

A D A.
A TALE.

Who has not dreamt a lovely dream,
    Before his Spring of life has fled,
And left him spirits, that but seem
    To hold communion with the dead ?

When all around, above, beneath,
Alike for him have ceas'd to breathe,
And, living for himself alone,
He deems all others chang'd to stone.
Who, after such a life of pain,
Would not delight to dream again ?
To live a new and fairy life
With every varied feeling rife ?
Secluded from the worthless world,
  A world I never lov'd too well,
From high Ambition's summit hurl'd,
  I learn in peace at last to dwell.
Adieu ! the hopes my boyhood sent !
Welcome, thou Winter's discontent !
If I may call my dreams my own
What boots it whither ye are flown ?
I ask not you, whose hearts are cold
To all that love or youth unfold,
To hearken to my tale of woe,
And bid the tear of pity flow ;
But you that still with transport cling
To the bright hopes of boyhood's Spring,
Whose youthful visions have not fled,
And left reality instead.

It was a lovely morn of Spring,
The joyous lark was on the wing,
And, borne with airy flight on high,
Had sung his carol in the sky.
There, in yonder shady bower,
Where blooms full many a fragrant flower,
Where noontide beams may ne'er intrude,
Fair Ada sat, in solitude.
With many a lovely flower entwin'd,
Wav'd her dark tresses in the wind.
That deep-drawn sigh, that silent tear,
Too well forebode some secret fear.
Does sorrow touch young Ada's heart ?
She knows that Raymond must depart.

Her sigh is hush'd, her tear is dried,
For, Raymond sits by Ada's side ;
Oh ! for a Raphael's pencil now
To paint that lady's beauteous brow :
The beaming eye—the heav'nly grace
That smiles on Ada's angel face :
'Tis only in her lover's mind
The living portrait is enshrin'd.
They have a language of their own
In Nature's book—not words alone.
They have a purer, lovelier sky,
Than seen by every mortal eye ;
A world of spirits—an universe
Untouch'd by the primeval curse :
The Serpent has not entered there,
Nor voice of sin, nor frown of care.
They look'd upon each other—now
True love is written on each brow.
He fixes on her hand a kiss ;
His love would ask no more than this.
Than this—Oh ! Heaven—is Paradise
A fairer thing than Ada's eyes ?
And many a time on a brighter day,
When morn had chas'd the dew away,
Had Raymond sought that lonely bower,
And cull'd the fragrance of the flower,
And many a wreath of beauteous hue
Had he twin'd for her hair, as their ripe lips grew
Into an innocent kiss, as sweet
As that which now doth Ada greet.
Ah ! can he think of parting now
While gazing on his Ada's brow ?
The big tear stood in Ada's eye,
While Raymond's bosom heav'd a sigh.
She seiz'd her lover's yielding hand—
" Thou goest to a foreign land,
" Where warrior's honours, fairer dame,
" May banish from thy mind my name :
" Yet never be this hour forgot,
" Whate'er may be thy future lot.

" O Raymond !—how I lov'd thee—how
" I love—thou didst not know till now ;
" This burning tear, this heaving breast
" Leave now no secret to be guess'd.
" I do not ask thee to resign
" All hope of fame for love of mine—
" I do not beg thee here to stay,
" I would not, may not, wish delay—
" With hapless Ada's prayer depart,
" Thou hast her love, then have—her heart.
" And when in some more blissful hour,
" Thou sittest in a lovelier bower,
" With softer maiden by thy side,
" Forget not in that moment's pride
" Thine Ada's love · forget not her
" Whom first in thought thou taught'st to err.
" The rest I may not, dare not, tell.
" One kiss—remember—Oh ! farewell !"

His steed is at the gothic door,
His bark is anchor'd near the shore.
An ancient serf is seen to wait,
With tearful eye, by yonder gate ;
With mantle o'er his shoulder flung
Upon that steed he wildly sprung.
One faint " Adieu, my love !" he cried,
Then fiercely spurr'd the courser's side.
Across the park to yon high wood,
He dash'd in sad and sullen mood.
He has outstript the dark-ey'd page,
Who check'd his gallant courser's rage :
He halted, gaz'd behind, " 'Tis well
That none be here my shame to tell—
'Tis well !—in stormy battle's field,
My Ada ! be thou yet my shield :
If when, around, the death-bolts glare,
Like meteors in the troubl'd air,
If ever in the fateful hour,
When death displays his giant pow'r,
If I forget thee—if I feel
A coward's fear upon me steal,

Ye lightnings' blast my withering frame,
And, Ada, be thy lovely name .
Remember'd but to speak my shame."

In silence then the two pursued
Their journey thro' the lonely wood.
They spoke no more, for Raymond's eye
With solemn sternness barr'd reply ;
And gentle Hugo dar'd not brook
His angry master's chiding look.
And ev'ry tree of varied hue,
That near with leafy foliage grew ,
And ev'ry path and ev'ry flow'r
Brought tokens of an happier hour :
Away, away, for many a league,
Their mettled chargers scorn fatigue ;
Until at length they reach the goal,
That cheers not Raymond's sullen soul.

The sunken eye, the vacant look,
The bloom that Ada's cheek forsook ;
The deep-drawn sigh but half represt,
The heaving of her tender breast,
Show Ada's thoughts are wand'ring far
With Raymond and the toils of war.
The song of birds, the bloom of flow'rs,
That sooth'd her solitary hours,
All, all, must yield to restless care,
Lost love, and maddening despair.
The purple sun has sunk to rest
Amidst the islands of the blest ;
Those glowing clouds that streak at ev'n,
The boundless realms of the lovely Heav'n—
Who that has seen the calm sun set,
That soft'ning hour can e'er forget ?
Then o'er wide earth, and wider sea,
The queen of night steals silently.
It is the hour when even grief
Finds in the stillness a relief ;
While o'er mountain, grove and vale,
Is heard the plaintive nightingale.
Seeks Ada now her fav'rite bow'r,
When silence tells 'tis twilight's hour '

Yes, she is there, unseen, alone,
Gazing on the cold gray stone,
With steadfast glance, all motionless,
A living image of distress ;
While slow and calm, the moon-beam falls,
And gilds the frowning castle's walls.

The whisper—that is half represt,
Can make the worst forebodings guess'd.
The silent sneer of bitter hate—
The heart that seems compassionate—
E'en that can still within conceal
The thoughts that fiends would scarce reveal ,
That proud, unmov'd by pity's call, .
Would triumph in a brother's fall.

'Tis her's to hear, the hapless maid,
To Raymond's charge what sins are laid :
The creature of a despot's sway,
'Tis her's to hear—and to obey.
Suffice it, that she wedded one,
  That never lov'd like him, who yet,
In desperation, has begun
  The vain endeavour—to forget.

But he is gone to his far home,
  O'er the blue waters of the sea,
Where she who lov'd him may not come,
  Where Peace, and Ada, may not be.
A wand'rer on the face of earth,
  A wand'rer on the swelling sea,
Despising fear, and hating mirth,
  With soul as air or ocean free,
He rush'd to glory, or despair,
He look'd not, knew not, reck'd not where;
Upon his dark and sullen brow,
No smile of pleasure lingers now ,
He lives on earth a guilty thing,
E'en in his own imagining.
He long'd for nothing, save the rest
Which dwelt not in th' unhallow'd breast

Poor Ada ! in thine earlier hour,
When like the dew upon the flow'r,
Thy tears but soften'd beauty's pow'r.
Then thou wert happy—art thou now,
With broken heart and broken vow ?
But, trust that in a brighter scene,
Thou wilt be blest as thou hast been ;
Blest in the realms of light above,
Of Peace—of Innocence—of Love !

FAMILY PORTRAITS.

Animam pictura pascit inani.—VIRGIL.

There is nothing which gives me greater pleasure at
certain times, than a stroll through a gallery of family
portraits. I love to trace the gradual refinement of
manners, from the successive changes in the costume of
the portraits in their descent ; from the armed knight, to
trace the stream of civilization as it flows downward,
through the judge, the great man of the family, the cour-
tier, and the improving country gentleman, down to the
modern general. But these considerations, though interesting in themselves, do not constitute the chief
attractions of the gallery. The successive generations
of beauties, whose figures adorn the venerable walls, are
to me a more pleasing speculation ; though a certain
feeling of disappointment is always awakened, as, in
turning from the contemplation of any beautiful features,
you are called upon by a sudden inward warning, to
recollect that those eyes are now closed for ever, and
that those lineaments have long mouldered in the grave,
forgotten in the halls which were once brightened with

their beauty. These reflections gradually create in you a kind of indefinable and unacknowledged, interest in the fate of the fair original. You conceive yourself able to understand, nay more, to enter into, all her feelings as, in all the pride of youthful beauty, she gazed upon the newly-finished portrait—feelings, alas, how different from those with which you now ,contemplate the features, which, though yielding slightly to the hand of time, are still smiling on in all the mockery of youth and loveliness, when the bones of the fair original have been laid for centuries in the unbroken slumber of the grave. It is under the influence of this melancholy train of thought that I love to watch until I almost fancy the expression of those eyes, as the young lady, with a slight tinge of natural vanity, not only pardonable, but even pleasing, from its exquisite gracefulness and good humour, prepared for conquest at her first tournament. I can see now, as plainly as if she stood before me, the slight flutter of her spirits, accompanied with a half-bashful peep into the large Venetian mirror, as she ventured to encounter the ordeal of so many critical eyes ; and the recovering smile of conscious beauty, as she took her place in the galleries, which were crowded with all that was noble and beautiful in the land, who assembled to overlook the mimic strife. I can see as plainly as if I were the Genius,. who, according to the Roman superstition, was associated to the existence of man, her mind gradually acquiring the fashionable indifference to the overthrow or wounds of the *preux chevaliers*, who broke their lances in behalf of her charms, and mingling in all the .pleasures of early life with the zeal of youth and beauty. So far the vision is pleasing. But it is too·

regular and connected- to continue, so the dark side of
the picture remains to be examined. I can still trace
her course in life ; but that fair and open brow is more
and more frequently overclouded, and those bright eyes
at length begin to overflow with tears. The picture is
painful, but I still must proceed, till I can fancy those
eyes closed in death, and her very name slowly, but
surely, vanishing from the hall of her fathers. It is but
too natural to follow up the same train of thought; and
to draw a fanciful parallel between the lady of the portrait, and one of the many fair forms who are now
dancing into life, " Heart on their lips, and soul within
their eyes," with the same feelings, the same disposition,
the same ignorance of evil, and natural eagerness after
all that bears the appearance of pleasure ; you have but
to substitute a ball for a tournament, and the graceful
lightness of modern dress, for the cumbrous magnificence
of the thirteenth century, and the parallel is . complete.
I see the one standing before me, in the living beauty of
nature, and the other represented with all the advantages
of art. There is the same smile playing upon the cold
features of the portrait, and glancing over the animated
countenance of its living representative. They appear
to be of the same age, but the contrasted effect of the
same expression; when proceeding from two such different sources, is frightful ; and the many years which
have passed over the head of the picture, have bestowed
an expression upon the faded features, which did not
originally belong to them, and blends a look of selfish
and malignant exultation, with the smile which plays
over the wasted lineaments, as if she rejoiced in knowing
that another spirit, cast in the same mould as her's, was

soon to experience the same disappointment in her imaginations of unsullied felicity, and like her, was, at no
very distant period, to pass away and be forgotten.

F. JERMYN.

THE DYING CRUSADER'S SONG.

This is no time for selfish fears,
    No time to think on man ;
Away—away—the Island spears
    Are in the battle's van ,
Although on her all swords are set,
Our Island banner lords it yet.

Oh ! who would change, for all that life,
    That love itself e'er gave,
The rapture of the holy strife,
    The martyr's holy grave ?
When kings to twine as proud a wreath,
Would rush into the arms of death.

Yet there are ties which bind to earth,
    Ties which will claim a tear ;
For though I left my father's hearth
    To die in glory here,
I could not tear the links apart,
Which bound my country to my heart.

I could have wish'd a brother near,
    To watch the soul's decline,
To tell thee, love, my latest tear,
    My latest sigh, was thine ;
Oh ' is there none to bear from me
A token of my truth to thee ?

Must I then close this glazing eye,
    My last sad thoughts unknown ?
E'en in this cause, 'tis hard to die
    Unaided and alone,
No eye to see, no ear to heed
The wishes of the brave who bleed.

I thought to lay my coffin'd head
   Where a hundred Barons lie,
Where a hundred choral voices spread
   The song for those who die !
Amidst the bravest of my race,
To find a fitting resting place ;

Where to the night-wind's freshen'd sighs
   The yews dark branches wave,
So that thy soft and radiant eyes
   Might look upon my grave,
Might drop a tear, in grief to see
How cold the heart that beat for thee.

But now, e'en in the grave's decay,
   A grave which many share,
No gentle hand will pluck away
   The weeds that blossom there ;
For one that would have planted flow'rs
Is safe within her own fair bow'rs.

And she will hear her lover's name,
   Now not unjustly dear ;
Those eyes which kindled Honour's flame,
   Will drop Affection's tear.
And I shall lie in stony sleep,
All heedless if she smile or weep.

When first I couch'd my father's spear
   On Judah's desert plains,
I swore by every temple here
   The Infidel profanes,
To see, let good or ill befal,
The cross triumphant over all.

I die—yet in the war-field's crash
   Like a sun burst from a cloud,
I see the Island banner flash
   Through battle's angry shroud ;
And mingling in the fateful fray,
My rising spirit soars away.

                  F. J.

Pandæmonium, Oct. 9, 1827.

MEPHISTOPHILES, alias BEELZEBUB, alias PLUTO;

To Mr. B. Bouverie, Greeting :—

Sir ;

I am very much scandalized at the impudent and reckless way in which my name is handled in your upper world, and amongst none more so than your Etonians. You cannot but feel, Sir, that it is impossible for me, in honour, to sit here and hear myself and mine talked of with impunity, in such a way as that with which my ears are perpetually insulted. Sulphur and Brimstone ! It is enough to make a man (much more then a devil) go stark staring mad. If any thing is ugly, mischievous, or has any bad quality about it, I am instantly made the climax of all rascality : a jackass, for example, is " as ugly and mischievous as the devil ;" a most flattering comparison for me, and well drawn ! Not that I mean to assert that, since horns and hoofs are not the reigning fashion, I am a perfect Adonis, nor do I mean to deny, that I may now and then have lent a hand to a spiteful trick or two ; but if I am not quite a model of beauty, how are you, as I presume I am no personal acquaintance of your's, how are you to know it ? Milton says, I am peculiarly handsome ; the Indians paint me white, and what grounds have you for opposing yourselves to these most respectable authorities, and for making me such a disgusting black brute as you generally do ? And granting my physiognomy to be none of the handsomest, is that any reason that you should perpetually be dinning it into my ears?—Well, then fruit is "as sour as the devil;" the weather is "as cold as the devil." Now, upon my honour, Sir, this last is a fault of which my worst enemies have seldom accused me: in fact, the inconvenience which is generally found in my climate is, that it is rather sultry than otherwise, so that to stand by your own notions of the matter, you do not say much for the coolness of a day in comparing it with me.—Indeed I cannot conceive what you take me to be, when you ring on me the changes of hot and cold, sour and sweet, sharp and stupid, in such an extraordinary manner as is your custom.

There is one point, however, which, if your actions came up to your words, would amply compensate me for all your libels, I mean your unbounded liberality; any thing which happens not exactly to meet your fancy is unhesitatingly and unconditionally handed over to me. What an accession both of subjects and treasures should I receive; what libraries of Virgils, Horaces, and Homers; what repositories of bats and balls; what fleets of boats would daily descend, if all your generous ejaculations were to take effect. But of this I am afraid there is very little chance; so, Mr. Bouverie, as a small recompense for the insulting comparisons of which I am eternally the subject, I think that you ought to try your hand at a panegyric. I have not had an Ode, Sonnet, or anything of the kind addressed to me since Burns's

> " O thou, whatever title suit thee,
> Auld Nick, auld Hornie, or auld Clootie,
> Come from thy mansions drear and sootie." &c.

And some even of this is not of the most complimentary kind; and really, Mr. Bouverie, I do not see why I should not look just as well at the beginning of a poem, as any of your heathen and unchristianlike Gods and Goddesses. You can stuff in quite as much bother about what name you shall call me, as you could with them, since really I boast a very tolerable catalogue; and, as for the Muses helping you, I doubt, most Heliconian Bartholomew, that I could do pretty much the same as they would. And now, having constituted you my poet laureate, I shall expect something pretty handsome in your next Number; and if I do not see any thing, you may depend on hearing from me again, and that not in the most conciliatory manner, though at present,

  I am,

   Your most obedient, humble servant,

     Mephistophiles.

EPISTLE FROM A PAIR OF OLD SHOES.

On looking into a small closet of mine the other day, I observed an old pair of shoes which had long been laid aside, trembling and shaking in a most extraordinary manner; I not well knowing what was the matter, took them up, and saw inside one of them the following eloquent Epistle :—

 Sir ;

We both agree in considering your behaviour to us as ungentlemanlike in the highest degree; in considering

it a most mean and ungrateful action, to let two faithful
old servants, such as we have been to you for time immemorial, pine away in neglected solitude. Solitude
did I say? No; fifty times worse than the worst of
solitudes, is the company in which you have dared to
place us!

We, Sir, who have supported you through thick and
thin for no less than a year; we, Sir, who have unshrinkingly borne the foot-ball of November, the shooting of
December, and the muddy leaping of January and
February; we, Sir, who have been forty-six times wet
through in your service, and as many times parboiled on
the hob, to " get the wet out of us;" we, who have been
four times soled, and twice patched, once left in a quagmire for six hours (at least my brother shoe had that
misfortune, I stuck close), three times sent floating down
the Thames, and now are better than new; we, Sir, are
the persons whom you insult by shutting us up in a hot
closet, with a pair of effeminate slippers, and another of
snipper-snapper pumps; a rascally pair of coxcombs,
who have never known what it was to feel a drop of
rain, and who would leak like a piece of muslin in a
minute's walking in a muddy street.

My very lining burns within me at the bare recapitulation of the insults I have received! Were I not
already jet-black with Warren's blacking, I should turn
so with rage and indignation. A pair of pumps! A
pair of jack-a-dandies!

    " Quos ego—sed motam præstat componere mentem."

and yet I'll have a kick at them.—Zounds! Sir, how
any one who pretends to be a person of any decency can

commit such an outrage! And then consider what a
privation it must be for one who has been used all his
life to spend his time in the open air, and to be well
bathed, at least, once a week, to be cooped up in this
accursed dungeon. And after the service I have gone
through, what a mortification must it be to see a foppish
pair of scoundrels put over my head, because they are
more *fashionable* than we are. Must a worthy and
estimable pair of shoes — yes, Sir, shoes — such as
deserve the name, must they be laid aside because they
happen to have round toes, or a patch or two in the
side? And then the things you wear at present! You'll
repent it, Sir! You may depend upon it.—I say no more,
Sir. You'll repent it. You'll repent it.

REFLECTIONS IN WESTMINSTER ABBEY,

October, 1827.

" How are the mighty fallen!"

Stranger, approach! approach, and lightly tread
Above the ashes of the mighty dead ;
Learn, awe-struck here thine home, thy dwelling learn,
'Mid the cold dust, or 'neath the storied urn.
  Can Jove's bright eagle, check'd in midway flight,
Descend, far swifter, to the shades of night?
Can darkness low'r o'er that all-gazing eye,
That loves to dare the splendors of the sky?
Yes, when the fateful Angel of Decay
Spreads his dark wing, and speeds his noiseless way,
In deadly silence dooms the murd'rous doom,
And calls his victim to the silent tomb.

Believe on this : and then believe, beside,
That Pitt was mortal, and that Canning died !
Death aim'd the stroke at him, at him alone,
Claim'd him, the first, the noblest, for his own :
Knew that, in Him, by one unerring dart,
He gain'd the fated goal, and pierc'd proud Britain's heart !
In more than eagle's flight he soar'd on high,
Yet soar'd to fall, and dazzled but to die !
'Mid the high Heavens dropp'd his mounting plume,
And fell, yet struggling, to the yawning tomb.
And was there none to aid, and none to save
His beaming radiance from the murky grave ?
Ten thousand voices, that arise in woe—
Ten thousand streams of Grief and Pity flow—
Ten thousand sighs are heav'd, and tears are shed,
Yet HE lies number'd with the silent dead.
The light, that glitters 'ere it flits away,
And casts its brightest radiance on decay ;
The sounds that soothe the mourner's thrilling ear,
The pomp and splendor of the tomb were here ;
Now all have vanish'd, and one, one alone
Sheds the salt tear above thy burial stone !
Yet 'times the hallow'd anthem's notes arise,
And waft the Christian's worship to the skies ;
Though pealing organ fill the swelling dome,
No sound may reach thee in thy lonely home
And 'times the wand'rer pays thy glory here
The sad and silent tribute of a tear ;
No voices round thee, nor the tear that flows,
Move thy calm slumber, break thy deep repose—
Burst through the iron fetters of the tomb,
Dispel its silence, and dissolve its gloom ;
Bid England's sun again in glory rise,
And shed his radiance on the low'ring skies
Ah no ! the beam his parting splendor gave
Hath set for ever 'neath the rolling wave :
The tongue is silent, and the lip is cold—
Yon pallid hand no more the helm may hold !
The soul, that rov'd unwearied, unconfin'd,
May Death's cold grasp, and icy fetters bind ?

    O Britain, weeping o'er his ashes, prove
How true thy faith, how fond thy ceaseless love ,
Yes, all combine . the tears of friend and foe
Mingle their streams in one, in one, unceasing flow !
    Brief is the tale the graven stones declare—
The name of him that sleeps and moulders there ,
No sculptur'd urn, nor pomp of breathing bust,
Proclaim his glory, and enshrine his dust :
No · 'tis to them, whose deeds might never raise
A living monument of deathless praise,
The fleeting honours of the tomb to claim,
And seek a meaner path, an humbler course to fame '
    But he hath rais'd his monumental stone
In Mem'ry's soft and hallow'd shrine alone ,
Hath writ, in characters of living flame,
On Britain's weal, on Britain's heart, his name.
Oft in the sculptur'd aisle and swelling dome,
The yawning grave hath giv'n the proud a home ;
Yet never welcom'd from his bright career
A mightier victim than it welcom'd here !
Again the tomb may yawn—again may Death
Claim the last forfeit of departing breath ·
Yet ne'er enshrine, in slumber dark and deep,
A nobler, loftier, prey than where thine ashes sleep '

ON EYES.

Eloquium oculi.

  · What a field for admiration is contained in those little
oval cavities which are called the Eyes ! it is there that the
philosopher may revel in examining the wondrous mecha-
nism of Nature ; it is there that the man of sentiment
may see beauty, in comparison with which, the efforts of
art must sink into insignificance ; it is there that the

lover may read the soul of his mistress, and perceive the first indications of reciprocal affection. How subservient to all the impulses of the mind, how prompt in expressing its internal movements, is the Eye : though the smallest and weakest of our organs, yet through it more ideas are conveyed to the seat of understanding, than by any of the rest. Except when closed in sleep, it never ceases from its functions, but is occupied in conveying images to the brain, in adding energy to our words, or in acting as an interpreter of the thoughts without them.

The motions and uses of this organ are so various and important, that I shall venture to speak of them under distinct heads. Let us begin with the Eye of the Poet.

> " The Poet's Eye, in a fine phrenzy rolling,
> Doth glance from Heav'n to earth, from earth to Heav'n."

Yes, it is the Poet's Eye that roams over the immensity of space ; that seems to penetrate beyond the bounds of human vision, and to draw inspiration from those realms of light which are spread in glorious majesty above. Such is Gray's description of Milton.

> " The living throne, the sapphire blaze,
> Where angels tremble while they gaze,
> He saw, but, blasted with excess of light,
> Clos'd his eyes in endless night."

The next position of the Eye, which I shall mention, is when it assumes a stern and fixed glare, to inspire awe in the mind of an enemy. Such is the glare of the hungry lion, when, crouching with his belly to the ground, he prepares to spring upon the traveller ; and such was the Eye of Marius, when fixing his countenance on the Cimbrian slave, that came to be his executioner, he exclaimed, "Man, hast thou the audacity to kill Caius Marius?"

The next is the Eye of Contemplation; with what devotion is it raised to Heaven ' while the mind,- forgetful of its care, and regardless of the joys or miseries of the world, holds sweet communion with the spirits that hover, unseen, around the dwellings of the virtuous, and is wrapt in the prospects of Eternity.

But whose Eye is that which is bent upon the ground, which seems unconscious of all passing objects? It is the Eye of Affliction; does it glisten with the falling tear, which speaks of a brother's or a parent's death, or is it fixed by that apathy which forbids the tear to flow? it tells of unpropitious love, of unrequited affection, of hopes annihilated by the grave.

What Eye is that which gazeth on vacancy; which seems ready to start from its socket; which glares with unearthly light upon the visions of a distempered mind? It is the Eye of Madness. Now rolling with hideous distortion it traverses the surrounding space, yet finds no object upon which to dwell; now it is fixed with phrenzied expression upon something which awakes the recollection of the past; at one time it roams through the Heavens with all the fire of frantic exultation, at another it is dimmed, and sinks to the ground with a look that tells of the despair that hangs heavy on the heart.

But let us turn from this contemplation, and gaze with rapture on the Eye of Love. That eye which Anacreon describes

ἄμα γλαυκὸν, ὡς ᾿Αθάνας,
ἅμα δ' ἱμερὸν, ὡς Κιθήρης

that eye which beams with a languishing lustre through the dark lashes that overshadow it; like the April sun, when he sheds his watery beams through the light clouds which partially obscure his brilliancy.. It is here that' Cupid, all armed, has placed the throne of his dominion, and has endued it with the fabled fatality of the basilisk, and the irresistible fascination of the rattle-snake. It is there the antic sits, the arbiter of happiness and misery, of life and death; one beaming glance of affection can raise the soul in rapture; one frown from that eyebrow can plunge it in the abyss of despair.

A truce to all mawkish sensibility, and let us look upon our favourite eye, the Eye of Fun. Those who have seen Grimaldi will know exactly what I mean; to those who have not, I fear it will be impossible to describe the roguish leer, the inimitable roll, the laughter-loving wink, that prefaces every joke, and inspirits every motion; the perfect independence of one another that is seen in his two eyes, as if they were determined never to act in unison: the vivacity and expression of the eye at one moment contrasted with its lack-lustre tameness at the next; all these together form a combination of ludicrous effects, at which he who looks must laugh, though he be Heraclitus himself.

A. H.

TO A YOUNG LADY COMING OUT.

There is a magic in thy smile,
  I shall not feel again,
Which melts into my heart the while,
  Like music's mournful strain.

Though light and gay that smile may be,
　　As the sun-beam on the waters,
It wakes a deeper spell in me,
　　Than the smile of Beauty's daughters.

If, then, that low and feeling tone,
　　That soft and graceful mirth,
Which seems a claim for thee alone,
　　To find all joy on earth :

If these, the youthful spirits balm,
　　Are threads which time must sever,
Oh, why did nature form the charm,
　　But to decay for ever ?

I know not, and I would not know,
　　What life prepares for thee,
I know not whether joy or woe,
　　Will change the soul I see.

The cherish'd rose may droop and die,
　　Or beam in Beauty's brightness ;
But its deepest blush can never vie,
　　With the rose bud's opening lightness.

　　　　　　　　　　　　　　　F. J.

ON STEALING.

Callidus quicquid placuit jocoso
　　　　Condere furto.

Among the many ways which fortune has pointed out,
as enabling a man to live comfortable and independent,
there is, perhaps, none more pleasant, and at the same
time more convenient, than that of putting your hand into
your neighbour's pocket. and easing him of what you

are willing to believe he can do without. It must, however, be confessed, that this is a somewhat dangerous
practice, and often attended with some little inconveniences ; though professors in the art have declared, that
to get hold of a very *necessary* thing " audacity," and to
be regardless of a very *unnecessary* one " reputation," is
all that is desirable to qualify a man for this undertaking.
Let him but regard himself, disregard others, consider
law as a thing only to be talked of, right and wrong as
unmeaning words, look upon all judges, constables, &c.
with contempt, and comfort himself with the pleasing
anticipation of a rope, as the very *acmè* of happiness,
and the only fair and just reward of his *honest* labours.
Much as this noble and honourable science (for such I
must consider it) has been depreciated; much as the
gentlemen who have made it their profession have been
stigmatized with the appellation of " thieves," by the
generality of mankind, it is difficult to deny that it offers
a life of ease and independence, and enables the practitioner to obtain many comforts, of which he must otherwise necessarily be deprived. Mankind, indeed, have
perhaps to regret, that more encouragement has not been
given to an art, which produces such inestimable benefits.
He who has been fortunate enough to have received an
early initiation into the mysteries of the science, and
equally so in not having felt any unpleasant tickling
about his neck, proceeding from something which might
check him in his career, has, from his long practice, obtained so extensive a knowledge, as to have no difficulty
in finding means sufficiently calculated for the attainment
of his object. Indeed, so well does this art appear to

answer the hopes and expectations of every man, so admirably adapted to the gratification of his pocket and himself, so well calculated to procure him every thing he wants (for I know of few things which cannot be either lawfully or unlawfully obtained) that I must confess I am surprised that no one has undertaken to reduce it to a system, or. at least to convert those motley assemblies, denominated gangs, into some respectable and regularly established institution. But, in addition to the many advantages arising from this art, the simplicity and facility of execution, and the certainty of constant employment, cannot, I think, be looked upon as any inconsiderable recommendations; as it is an established Hibernian doctrine, that as long as people do not go naked they must wear clothes, while it is almost as certain, that as long as they wear clothes they will have pockets, which may be open for secret examination. Now, could any thing be more pleasant, or more comfortable, than the assurance of perpetual employment, and inexhaustible resources? Here is the prospect of a life of little trouble and constant amusement, which, by the accidental, though convenient, mistaking of another man's pocket for your own, may be rendered easy and independent. Who is there, but would feel some sensations of pity on seeing any unfortunate man, who having by the most indefatigable industry obtained some little recompence for his exertions, has suddenly been deprived of the fruits of his labour, and plunged into the abyss of poverty and despair? Who, on the other hand is there, that does not admire the dexterity, and secretly envy the facility, with which an ingenious practitioner of this art is able to acquire

that which has cost another such labour to attain? But
it may.be hinted to me by the more serious part of my
readers, that there is a piece of wood called the " *Gallows*," which, though it may not be.considered as any
reasonable objection to the practice of this art, yet still
has such a formidable appearance, that one has considerable difficulty in reconciling the mind to the prospect of encountering it. I am aware that this is calculated to create some unpleasant reflections, and to cause
some little inconvenience, though, perhaps, it is better
to look upon it in the words of the famous Richard
Turpin, as a mere matter of form, and to consider it as a
reward rather than a punishment. Many, indeed, has
been the miserable fellow, who, from an unfortunate
connection, or more unfortunate circumstances, has been
compelled to suffer under an unjust condemnation ;
while the thief, though he may find the gallows equally
formidable, and the rope equally inconvenient, may at
any rate comfort himself with the pleasing reflection that
he has deserved it.

If, however, we take into consideration the various
branches of this science, and the various manners in
which the ingenuity of its professors enable them to
practise it, I own I am not without my suspicions, that
we shall find that the generality of mankind, in all ranks
and stages of life, from the accomplished gentleman to
the professional pickpocket, are, if not theoretically, at
least practically, acquainted with the benefits arising from
it. Pardon me, gentle reader (for I adhere to the established maxim of supposing, at least hoping, my reader
to be of a gentle disposition) I do not mean to insinuate

that you have actually picked any body's pocket, or that you have committed any crime, which would qualify you to take up your residence in Newgate; though at the same time, I must confess, that I see no reason to exempt you (whoever you are) from the imputation of being an adept in a science so generally understood and adopted. Where is the parasite, who has not exerted all his abilities, by insinuating addresses, or elaborate panegyrics, for the purpose of *stealing* the favours of his master, and surreptitiously obtaining that patronage which he could not otherwise hope to enjoy? Nor in truth does it only belong to those of a riper age to practise it successfully. It has often been considered as an advantageous acquirement to boys; indeed the dexterous performance in youth, has been thought a mark of ingenuity, and a proof of future excellence. But here I would wish to observe the improvement made by these youthful professors, in rendering obsolete the old verb "steal." Now, to *steal*, has something so formidable in the sound, and carries with it such unpleasant ideas, that one is apt to recoil with horror on being accused of indulging in so heinous a crime; and, although the sensations it is calculated to produce, must in a great degree depend on the substantive which follows it, yet it has never been fully divested of its original horrors; and it still remains as formidable as ever, and conveys to the mind a great idea of criminal depredation. To alleviate the misery of having so harsh a word applied to the most trifling theft, modern ingenuity has invented a word, which, though it may bear precisely the same meaning, yet is so entirely free from any thing formidable or unpleasant in the sound, that on the contrary it carries with it something humorous and agreeable, and generally enables you to form some idea of the dexterity of the performer. The reader will probably imagine that 1 allude to the word " *sharp.*"

. But while I am indulging in these insinuations against the generality of mankind, who knows whether I myself may not be accused of having *stolen* some hints on this subject from some unknown author, and thus deprived him of the merit (if any) to which he has a just claim? I can only say, for my part, that I am not aware of having committed any such depredation; and, as I prefer, so will I endeavour, to remain posted in Mr. Ingalton's window, to reclining in the most comfortable or best furnished cell in Newgate. G.

ON THE MORNING.

Lo! In yon orient eastern sky
  The varied tints of morn appear,
Her rosy blush and azure eye,
  Wash'd by the dewy ev'ning tear,
Whilst silent thro' the vault of day,
Pale Lucifer withdraws his ray,

And hark! the voice of Matin breeze,
Sweeps softly o'er the waving trees; `
The violet and the primrose fair,
Diffuse their op'ning fragrance there;
While thro' yon grove the purling stream
Sparkles beneath Aurora's gleam.

I'll raise me from the bed of sleep,
　And bend my steps to yon blue hill ;
And ás I climb the rugged steep,
　And listen to the murm'ring rill,
I'll watch the cloud's light silver fleece,
That sails above, and dream of peace.

And, onward as I eager tread,
　The lark shall leave the crystall'd mead,
And borne aloft, her warbling note
　Shall on the downy zephyr float,
As, bent to Heaven's high throne her flight,
She hails the glorious orb of light.

The sprightly warbler strains his throat,
　As perch'd on some tall beech, he chants
Responsive to another's note,
　Deep echoing thro' the sylvan haunts,
Whilst, all around, the joyous throng
Resounds the oaken boughs among.

Then as I muse in holy-trance,
Let woodland nymphs around me dance,
And contemplation o'er my soul,
Shall cast her dark sepulchral stole,
As thro' the woody depths I rove,
Shades dear to liberty and love !

'Tis thine, O Nature, to beguile
The mind with calm unruffled smile,
Thine to disclose the mighty power,
And picture hope on every flower—
Thine to relume the tear-worn eye
With prospects of eternity.

　　　　　　　　　　　THROCKMORTON.

THE POSTMAN.—No. IV.

[I have received some short letters, which I shall lay before my readers under this head]

From VINDEX.

Sir ;

It has often struck me, whether correctly, or not so, as a singular, though, I fear, irremediable piece of injustice, that Virgil has committed with impunity, throughout his works, literary thefts of an extent, a value, and a frequency, far, infinitely, greater, than those for which so many unhappy urchins are, under the auspices of *Mater Etona*, brought daily to the block.   Why, Sir, do the petty criminals receive punishment, and the great ones praise?   He who writes his twelve lines on the same *plan* as his schoolfellows, with certain incidental similarities, no doubt, and he who does the same in an affair of twelve books, are very differently rewarded : for the one is honoured by a sprig of laurel; the other, by a sprig of birch.   Your's, truly,

VINDEX.

I fear that my correspondent's complaint must stand over *sine die*; this will, however, serve my friend Philophantasm* as an argument, the next time he has one of his nocturnal visitations.

The following communication I can throw no light upon, as to the means of its composition, or the method of its journey to my hands. Lifeless, however, as our venerable Founder in the quadrangle appears to the vulgar eye, he has here shown with what propriety we may apply to modern sculptors the celebrated words of Virgil—

VIVOS ducent de marmore vultus.

---

* See p. 179, vol. I.

From the STATUE IN THE QUADRANGLE.

Often, Mr. Bouverie, have I seen you borne about in the hands of your school-fellows around and near my site. Much have I desired to see and peruse a copy of your work. But sellers are hard-hearted, and no one can buy without money. I have occasionally caught a glimpse of a torn leaf, and have also overheard sundry discourses relating to you, and others appertaining to myself.

No doubt, Sir, you have perceived how frequently I am struck, and how grievously bruised, by missiles, discharged from the hands of idle urchins who sport around me. Were I in full life, I should long ago have complained ; but, as my bodily pain has never been intense, I have hitherto deferred it. But how, dear Sir, can Eton be said still to adore

" Her Henry's holy shade"

while she suffers her nurselings with impunity to bruise, and indent, and disfigure, the substance of her Henry's not holy, yet harmless, substance ? Often do I find my sceptre crowned with orange-peel, stones resting quietly on my crown, and my robes bespattered with eggs instead of being adorned with ermine ! I am sure that a representation of my calamities will, by inducing your school-fellows to be a little careful, procure their removal.

I confess that I did not expect to have ever seen Eton boys turn authors in miniature. In my time they were more intent upon their playthings than their books, and would as soon have thought of a hangman as a publisher. In truth, it was then more easy to write than

to circulate;. but now it is easier to circulate than to
write. Then there were, perhaps, not so many copies
of Horace in England, as there are now of your Miscellany; may you stand the test of time as well as they
have done !

I observe that, once in every three years, when the
weather begins to get warm, a vast crowd gather in the
quadrangle around me; and, amidst loud music, a
number of youths, dressed like mountebanks, for the
most part; many like those monkeys which we see
touring through this country, march several times round
the square. Pray what may the purpose of this be ? I
am quite perplexed about the matter; and, if I had the
faculty of speech, should have made inquiry long ago
on the subject. For, Sir, the singular part of this affair
is, that all who are there seem discontented, and grumble.
One of these mountebanks, or monkeys (who in features
are not unlike the Eton boys), goes round with a friend :
he begins to rail at the superiors, to complain of the
weather, of the trouble he has undergone, of the vexation
he has suffered. It is hot, and he will faint; or it is
cold, and he will have an ague; or it is dry, and he is
parched; or wet, and he is drenched : his dress, also,
spoiled; his shoes pinch him, or his sword galls him;
he has lost his friends in the crowd ; he has had no food
all day; he is fatigued, almost to death. Such, Sir, are
the exclamations of these creatures; but, though they
look angrily at me, I can assure them that I am not to
blame in this matter, as I never founded any thing of
this sort.

Next come two women ; they have been squeezed into
mummies : or two tradesmen —they have had their

pockets picked; or two labourers—they came to see what was to be seen, and were stopped and robbed on the way. The ladies have ruffled their feathers, and the gentlemen their whiskers; those are stared at by fops, and these elbowed by clowns. In one corner, a family pushes about in search of their Willy; in the other, their Willy in vain seeks them. Round and round they go, keeping, of course, thus at an equal distance; and both sit down in despair at the same time, on opposite sides of the court-yard, each waiting till the other shall pass.

Now, as all seem wretched, and hungry, and fatigued, and ill-humoured, why in the world do they come there?

Should you be pleased with this communication, I may tell you more of what I see and hear. At present

I remain, your's,

With paternal affection,

HENRICI EFFIGIES.*

ON THE IMPERFECTIONS IN SCIENCE.

Sir ;

No doubt your scientific readers have observed, and often reflected on, the flaws in the theories of learning. The case of the twelfth axiom of Euclid, and of the multiplication of two *minus's* into a *plus* in algebra, are notorious. And scarcely less so is the defect in the geometrical propositions of Euclid, where he is compelled to have recourse to laying one figure on another to prove their equality. Now, Sir, herein it is proved, if at all, simply by an appeal to the ocular sense;

* Of course the spelling has been modernized for the use of my readers

whereas I conceive it is an essential property of perfect
theoretical science of that kind, that it consists in
appeals to the reasoning faculties alone.

, But, if so prosy a moral be not unacceptable, I would
venture to hint, that these imperfections have been most
wisely ordained by Him whose care is ever directed
towards the welfare of all his creatures. We all know,
young as we are, how strongly the heart of man is
inclined to imbibe pride from the consciousness of excellence in any art or branch of knowledge. In speculative
knowledge this is particularly the case : and the pride
of philosophy is notoriously prevalent, and as notoriously
dangerous.

Then how wisely has it been ordained, that checks
and restraints should be put upon the increase of this
evil affection! If, even when science is imperfect, we
are inflated by the consciousness of possessing her, how
much more so should we be if we could look upon her
as a monument of perfect and unsullied magnificence, designed and erected by human ingenuity!

Your's, respectfully,

PHILOMATHES.

⁎ Herewith I close my Seventh Number. The winter will, I trust,
neither freeze me nor my readers. I am, I hope, as truly grateful
for past, as humbly confident of future, indulgence.

In my Sixth Number were contained three pieces by Etonians, my
contemporaries, but not original contributors, or now at Eton, those
headed "From Simonides," "Sketch," and "Stanzas to Mary."

In the present number, "Ada" is the only piece which comes under
this denomination.

ETON MISCELLANY,

No. VIII.

INTRODUCTION.

FROM the sombre hue cast over this paper, my readers will probably discover, that the gloom attending the present season of the year has communicated itself to my spirits: whence it has crept, through the medium of my pen and ink, into my composition.

I have now arrived without accident or disturbance at the half-way house of my second volume. This domicile should, according to precedent, be gloomy and lonely, as half-way houses usually are. During their stay here, therefore, I shall edify my readers, or customers, with my reflections on the nature, and ruminations during the continuance, of solitude.

But as it is the part of a prudent landlord to examine the quality of his guests, such a part I have performed. The result of the investigation has been most flattering. I might indeed *boast* of having royalty itself enrolled among my friends and supporters, did I not feel, that I was not so highly honoured from any deserts of my own, but simply from that regard and affection for Eton, and all that belongs to her, which has before been so eminently

displayed by those, whom, as we are always bound by
station to respect, so we must now peculiarly be led by
gratitude to love.

There are some who feel the truth of the poet's affirma-
tion—

      " There is society where none intrudes"—

who love to seek that society within themselves, and to
spend in silence and in peace a portion of the hours
which others rather choose to devote to more joyous
pursuits. Who can deny, that he who is most accustomed thus to examine and to hold communion with himself, is far better fitted to relish the true pleasures of
rational society, than the man who seeks his enjoyments
in the illusions of voluptuousness, or his ease in the
torpor of sloth ?

They love—and they do not fear to assert that they
love—the solitude of the wood and the mountain better
than the crowded city : and the ripple of the lake, and the
whispers of the breeze, have more charms for their
unfashionable or uncultivated ears, than the din of human
turmoil, or the bustle of human activity.

To proclaim and support the cause which they adhere
to, I dedicate my present lucubration, although I have
received from two political friends most elaborate and
ingenious pieces on the great events for which this day
has been celebrated ; each eager to appropriate the interesting period to their own principles. Mr. Heaviside
has sent me " A Sketch of the Gunpowder Plot, and the
Blessings ensuing on its Discovery and Frustration ;"
while Mr. Quincy, equally staunch, has favoured me
with " Retrospect of the Glorious Revolution, and Reflec-

tions on the landing of king William the Third :" Both these edifying and entertaining pieces are withheld. *Illacrymabiles urgentur.*

On looking onward, I anticipate with grief the close of my existence. On looking over the list of my fore-fathers, I should say, that Griffin was a very great man: Courtenay was a great man too: Grildrig was a tolerably great man, but trod somewhat closely in Griffin's foot-steps, which, however, he did not quite fill. I myself have been, perhaps, a more singular being than any. I have outdone Proteus and Vertumnus in the changes I have undergone. But even if I am not a worthy follower, I am at least a devoted admirer, of my great predecessors.

Now while I confess that the benefits arising from intervals of reflection are incalculable ; that, by devoting a portion of our time to them, though we give up all hope of pleasure or of wealth, of dignity or of power, though we leave others to seek splendor, yet we seek, and find, contentment ; I cannot but reflect with anxiety on the motives which caused my deserting, in my own person, what I am so vehemently endeavouring to recom-mend to others. Sometimes, indeed, I cannot help condemning my temerity, but I am more frequently inclined to applaud my courage.

There are those who have ventured in as daring a manner, who have run as singular a course, who have gained the victory they sought, and reached the goal they strove to win. But there are also luckless wights, who have exhausted their whole stock of goods in the trade of authorship, and who find themselves equally destitute of actual property, and credit which might supply

its place. They suffer the usual fate of ruined men
among their friends ; they call on the Muses, who are of
course " not at home ;" and on touching the strings of
their lyre, they hear it return, astounded and stupified,
the discordant twang of a hurdy-gurdy.

If this is destined to be my fate, let me bear it with
patience ; if not, let me avoid it with diligence. A peep
behind the curtain, a more accurate and particular
account of the circumstances which attended my birth,
would, I believe, astonish all those who are acquainted
only with my smooth exterior ; who deem me as regularly
formed and set together as my own types, as neatly
arranged as my own title page, as elegantly dressed as
my own compositions. The tale must soon be told ; and
I, like many another criminal, must at the expiration of
my existence, give over my body for analyzation. As
yet, however, I have not proceeded even to my " Last
Dying Speech," and my readers must wait with patience
till the appointed time.

ADVERTISEMENT

Lost, somewhere in the vicinity of Eton College, some time during
the month of October, the soul of David Ap Rice, esquire, of Twly
Upwhlly. 'Tis of a middling height, and fiery complexion, having
clothed itself in an unowned carcass ; it has a savour of toasted cheese.
It is a merry and good-humoured, though testy, creature, and may
easily be discovered both by the leeks which are entwined with its
garments, and by its constant references to its genealogy. *

Whoever will bring or send the same (carriage paid), free of damage,
and sound in wind and limb, to Mr. Ingalton, bookseller, of Eton,
shall be handsomely rewarded.

---

* It has been found that Mr. David Ap Rice is *not* descended from Owen
Glendower, notwithstanding his positive assertion to that effect, on his last
appearance.

THE VICTIM.

The north wind breaks the deep midnight,
　　Borne with the sound of flame,
And, riding on its wings of might,
　　The voice of Battle came,
That distant voice in thunder spoke
　　Above the bending trees,
And every Indian maid awoke
　　To catch the fateful breeze,
As if the wind which, in its flight,
Swept o'er the dark and changeful fight,
Had burst the forest depths, to show
The Indian's triumph o'er his foe.
Alas! e'en England's native swords
Were vain against those vengeful hordes.
While, all around, each leafy screen
　　Was echoing with the dreadful yell
Of foes unnumber'd and unseen,
　　Her eagle spirit droop'd and fell.
Though England's blood was streaming fast,
Her sons fought bravely to the last.
Now bursts the shriek of triumph out,
　　In those wildly thrilling tones,
Oh! In the pauses of that shout,
　　Hear ye not their dying groans?
More solemn than all the wild rage of the strife,
Are the sounds of that last farewell to life.
But once upon the startled ear
　　The mingled accents fell,
The sinking of those sounds of fear
　　That had its tale to tell.
It told, that all of British birth
Lay slaughter'd on the streaming earth,
Save one, and he without a tear
Gaz'd on his brethren's bloody bier;
He deem'd, in truth, each gallant breast
'As noble slaughter'd nobly blest'

For not in mercy—no, in hate
They saved him for a darker fate;
He lay imprison'd, and alone,
   To think on death in all its gloom;
His weary mind was overthrown,
   His body seemed its living tomb.
There is no light in that dark eye,
Which kindled at the battle's cry;
Alas! that fair and open brow
Is scar'd with livid paleness now,
As if despair had serv'd to drain
The life-flow of the youthful vein.
Although that bursting heart was brave,
   His soul seem'd wrapt in flame,
Whilst crowding thoughts, like wave on wave,
   In thick confusion came,
Until at length, from all her woes,
Exhausted nature sought repose.
He slept—and o'er him bends a form,
With eye as bright, and heart as warm,
As ever beat in joy or woe,
To lend the smile its sunny glow,
Or bid the ready tear-drop flow.
When England's baffled heroes fled,
   Yet proudly conscious of their might,
Her lov'd and only brother bled,
   When foremost in the doubtful fight;
And well she knew that, from that hour,
The laws assign'd to her the pow'r
   To save or to destroy .
She hail'd her privilege to save
The stranger from an early grave,
   With all a woman's joy:
She came as woman should, to bless,
   And pleas'd with novel power, to save,
And bent in holy tenderness,
   With brow as sweetly, softly, grave,
(When in his dreams the victim smil'd,)
As a fond mother o'er her child.
She left him with a beaming eye,
And softly sigh'd, "He shall not die."

That parting word the silence broke,
He caught it, started, and awoke.
There was a darkness on his soul,
A phantom which deceiv'd control,
A sense of undefined ill,
Which on his heart weigh'd deep and chill ;
Till like the wild electric flame,
The startling flash of mem'ry came,
And drooping with a heavy sigh,
He knew that he was doom'd to die.
But those long hours of deep repose,
Had nerv'd his soul to bear its woes ;
The memory of his island sires
Relum'd his eye with wonted fires :
The memory of the brave who bled
When Cressy's battled legions fled,
And all the trophies which they bore
From hard fought fields in days of yore.
He thought on these, and, as he ponder'd,
To distant scenes his fancy wander'd,
Where deep'ning in the pure moonlight,
Arose the abbey's moss-grown height.
He thought on the hour when he was there,
And beneath him the dust of the brave and the fair.
When he call'd on his fathers who slept below,
In the pride of his spirit's youthful glow ;
When he call'd upon them, his vow to hear,
Never to tremble, never to fear ;
Whether early or late, by land or by sea,
To die like the son of the brave and the free.
" It was not thus my fathers fell,
    Their spirits proudly soar'd away,
The trumpets rung a thrilling knell
    Over the hero's senseless clay,
And nations grateful to the brave,
Sounded a requiem o'er their grave.
But I, defeated and alone,
With none to mark my dying groan,
I that have drawn my with'ring breath,
And thought on torture and on death,

Till fainting nature reel'd, and sunk,
And e'en this boasted courage shrunk,
With none to see, and none to heed,
Must nerve my soul to bear and bleed,
And hear the foes insulting cries,
To mock my dying agonies.
Yet will I die in spirit free,
They shall not wring a groan from me.
'Tis hard that one so lov'd should fall
Unnotic'd, and unknown to all ;
That, when these limbs have ceas'd to feel
The tortures of their eager zeal,
And from their hands this mangled form
Is yielded to the milder worm,
There are no sympathies, to tell
My father's children how I fell.
They cannot think, they cannot know,
That we shall meet no more below.
That while the wolf, in the forest gloom,
Growls o'er the scarce-concealing tomb,
My father's house may bend in glee
O'er lines late gaily trac'd by me;
Nor think how soon the tale may be told,
That this hand is stiff, and this heart is cold.
But I must rudely tear apart
These gentler feelings from my heart,
Mine ear, with a prophetic dread,
Hath caught a close and heavy tread ;
And I with brow serene and high,
Must show them I have learnt to die ,
Must still my troubled breast, to hide
All feelings in the rush of pride "

Through the forest wilds, at the dead of night,
    They led him slowly on,
By the torches' red and waning light,
    They mark'd the stranger's son,
As o'er the tree of death he leant,
On him each fiery brow was bent ;

His answ'ring eye, serene and proud,
Glanc'd calmly o'er the savage crowd,
His soul enshrin'd in deep repose,
Just mark'd the malice of his foes;
Then turn'd from all surrounding things,
To dwell in its own imaginings,
As, raising high the choral song,
They bound him there, that eager throng:
They bound to the stake his senseless clay,
For the light of the spirit was far away.
Whilst high the brandish'd torches shone,
His soul unconscious ponder'd on;
His fiery spirit in him wrought,
With such intensity of thought,
That soon in Fancy's vivid hue,
The present parted from his view,
And, as before his dazzled eyes,
His father's moss-grown turrets rise,
He thought that all around him mov'd
The fairy forms of those he lov'd;
He saw them, and he seem'd to hear
Their voices murmur in his ear;
All things that glide around him, seem
Too clear and vivid for a dream,
As rising on, distinct and near,
The scenes of time long past appear;
What graceful beings around him press
In the light of youthful loveliness?
In lively mirth they seem'd to stray,
And laugh the careless hours away;
He saw them visit each well-known spot,
And marvell'd that they knew him not.
He saw, distinct enough to trace,
Each lovely sister's form and face;
He heard repeated all around,
Their cheerful laughter's ringing sound:
He heard them speak, and could almost tell
Each mutter'd word, as it carelessly fell ·
Whilst all around them, he could see
Each well remember'd tower and tree

The fair broad river seem'd to rush,
As it flow'd away, in a fuller gush;
And the near chapel's taper spire
Glow'd with the sunset's living fire:
He started and look'd up, around,
The dark and stately cedars frown'd,
Their overhanging branches made
A murky and eternal shade;
For many a hundred years before,
   Time had seen them as he pass'd,
Swinging slow, with sullen roar,
   To the cold and stormy blast;
And still in their majestic age,
They seem'd to spurn its futile rage.
He gaz'd in doubt—where at his side
Those fairy forms appear'd to glide,
A thousand torches brightly shone,
A thousand warriors swell'd the tone
Of the wild war-song, as it rose
From that fierce circle of his foes.
And those dark features which he saw,
Whilst anger mingled with his awe,
Through the red and smoky light,
Gleam'd like the phantoms of the night.

Now the warlike bands advance
In their wild and mystic dance,
Now they wave their swords on high,
Soon to wear a deeper dye.
How the deadly weapons glitter!
Oh, that sudden start was bitter!
From all the joys that fancy gave,
It recall'd him to the grave,
And but another moment's giv'n
To prepare his soul for heav'n.
He mark'd, the calmest of them all,
The circled falchions flashing full,
With eye of light, and steady breath,
He gaz'd, alone unmov'd, on death.
They rais'd the sword—but Linda came,
Swift as the lightning's darting flame;

Though, when she met the startled glare
Of all the chieftains gather'd there,
The warm blood sprung with a quicker rush,
And deepen'd in her cheek the blush ;
The beam of her eye was proud and bright,
Transparent with her pure delight,
As, braving every dreaded eye,
She cried, " My brother shall not die !"—
It was a wondrous thing to see
How sunk at once their savage glee ;
How all those chieftains, stern and wild,
Abash'd before a trembling child,
Stood gazing, till again on high
The maiden cried, " He shall not die !"—
A thousand voices join'd the cry,
And spread like cloud on cloud around,
The forests echo'd to the sound.

ON ELOQUENCE.

Gratia facundi quanta sit eloquii !

I shall consider myself richly repaid for any pains
which may be expended in the composition of this paper,
should my readers derive from it half the amusement
which I have enjoyed, in tracing the various ramifications
of Eloquence through their separate channels to their
common fountain-head.   It has been usual in this country to divide this great art into three portions only : and
to reduce all under the heads of the Senate, the Pulpit,
and the Bar.   Further investigation will suggest to an
inquiring mind many additional subdivisions : which,

though they may not assume so lofty a character, nor
boast so widely-extended an influence, have a legitimate
claim to be considered by him who undertakes to descant
on this subject

The Eloquence of the Bar is certainly, to a youthful
and ardent mind, not the most inviting of the three great
branches. It is connected too strongly in the imaginations of most of us, with dusty folios and midnight lamps;
with hundreds of treatises to be perused, and thousands
of cases to be registered in the memory; in short, such
Tartarean horrors are to be encountered before even the
possible attainment of the Elysium of legal eminence,
that we are usually content to decline the bargain "*in
toto*" rather than to pay the price "*in limine.*"

The Eloquence of the Pulpit is not as much admired,
or as carefully studied, as its nature and subjects imperatively demand. It has indeed been long acknowledged,
and long lamented, that the acquisition of this most
noble gift has not been properly estimated in the formation of schemes of education. Nor has the deficiency
any where been more painfully felt than among the
learned and venerable class of men who in this country
are orators, as well as priests, by profession. Certain it
is, that no topics can be better fitted than those which
they are accustomed to handle, to rouse the energies and
stimulate the powers of the speaker. They are more
lofty, they are more wonderful, they are more extended,
and yet they are more simple, than the subjects supplied
by the range of affairs merely terrestrial. As their office
is one of the most exalted utility, so it ought to be an
object of the highest, and the most refined ambition:

and incalculable would be the good which might be
effected by a more universal transformation of the cold
and unanimated lecture into the fervent and glowing
exhortation.   Checks have been imposed on our forefathers, indeed, by the disadvantages and deficiencies of
their education . but it is the duty, as it should be the
pleasure, of the rising generation to lay hold on the increased and increasing means of improvement, which are
generally within their reach, and to exert themselves to
the utmost in striving to attain what is so eminently
calculated to make them both useful and distinguished
members of the professions to which they are to belong.

The ambition of the most ardent and aspiring minds
is usually directed towards St. Stephen's.   The τὸ καλὸν
of most of those who are at all disposed towards oratorical
pursuits is situated within the walls of the House of Commons.   Visions of joy and honour open on their enraptured sight.   A successful debût—an offer from the
minister—a Secretaryship of State—and even the Pre-
miership itself—are the objects which form the vista
along which a young visionary loves to look.   But there
is a barrier to pass, and an ordeal to endure : there are
such articles as maiden speeches, sometimes calculated
to act more generally and more forcibly on the lungs of
such an audience than the most violent or the most
cutting of all the breezes which Æolus can boast.   There
are such things as roars of coughing, as well as roars of
cheering : and the man ought to be endowed with a considerable share of fortitude and presence of mind, in
addition to natural and acquired powers of eloquence,

who allows his hopes of the one to overcome his fears of the other.

· The first which it is my intention to notice among the less celebrated kinds of oratory, is that of Auctioneers. This is indeed a depraved and vitiated branch : yet it may claim the lofty title of *creative* eloquence, with undeniable propriety.   Truth, reason, and consistency, impose restraints on many descriptions of the speaking art : here those vain and troublesome restrictions are entirely unknown, and the imagination of the orator is at liberty to soar into the clouds, or descend into the sea, to traverse the earth, or search the heavens, for materials to adorn his discourse and his lots.   Few have been able to resist the temptations offered by such liberty as this.   Poets might once have claimed, on the score of prescription, the sole and exclusive privilege of speaking falsely by licence : but the Lords of the Hammer have intruded on their province, and have apparently succeeded in making good their possession of the acquired territory. However, we must remember that an Auctioneer actually disburses hard cash to the magistrates for his licence ; whereas it is usual among Poets to obtain them *gratis* from the Muses themselves.   But the latter are confessedly outdone.   What Poet could ever change sour sloe-juice into ". Fine Old Bottled Port ?" transform a bare rock, or an unfathomable bog, into a " Desirable Freehold ?" or clothe a leaky, mud-walled, straw-roofed, or rather roofless hut, with the inviting denomination of a " Romantic Villa," and an " Elegant Retreat ? "

There is also an Advertising, and a Bill-Sticking

Eloquence. There is a Shop-keeping, and a Sight-puff-
ing Eloquence. There is one scheme of oratory in use
among those who love to sell dear; and another, its
antagonist, equally beloved by, and equally valuable to,
those who love to buy cheap. Two adverse professors
of these rival descriptions will frequently engage in, and
continue a contest with, such equal and such admirable
abilities, that they might well be exemplified by the
poet's simile of two bulls, whose foreheads remain fixed
firmly and obstinately against each other, each resolving
to be the longest to endure, and the last to yield. * In
their contest, too, there is an exact parallel to the long,
though speedy, course of the combatants in tournaments;
who, commencing their career with a considerable intervening space, rapidly approach the scene of actual war:
Thus these two equally determined antagonists will
begin, the one, by offering five shillings, the other, by
demanding a guinea : a fall to fifteen is met by a rise to
ten, and somewhere about mid-space the mighty cham-
pions engage in the arduous struggle—which we will
here leave them to conclude as they best may.

We have, too, an Eloquence of Beggars. . The Eloquence of Distress must always be touching : and when
Nature and Truth are the prompters, the tongue of man
is seldom deficient in the powers of supplication and
complaint. But the eloquence of Beggars is not always
the eloquence of distress.

I think no incentive to Eloquence, little as it has been
mentioned or esteemed, can be considered as superior,

---

* Classical—ὃ δὲ τρὼ.—I might adduce innumerable precedents.

perhaps; I might say, as equal to that afforded by the
sight of an impending rod, a stern visage, and a powerful arm.   Truly, the tale with which our friend Herodotus
entertains his readers respecting the eldest son of Croesus,
would have possessed a fairer claim to confidence, had
he placed the youth in the common situation of a delin-
quent school-boy, about to suffer the reward of his evil
deeds.   Then it is that the tongue vies with the eyes in
their lamenting streams, and the hands in their suppli-
cating attitude : these are clasped, and those are flowing :
while the little organ of speech is vigorously exerted in
pouring forth, congregated and united confessions of guilt,
protestations of repentance, intreaties for mercy, and pro-
mises of amendment.   Eloquence has been defined as
the art of persuasion ; never was definition less applicable than such a one in the present instance. . Persuasion ! alas ! how few whippings have been escaped by
means like these !   Though the voice be honeyed, the
attitude graceful, the expressions appropriate—though no
requisite of the perfect orator be wanting, the uplifted
hand descends in chastisement, and the cruel twigs perform their office.

    I must request the kind indulgence, and the particu-
lar attention of my Etonian readers, while, in winding
up this paper, I earnestly endeavour to impress on their
minds another, a more serious, and a more familiar
topic.   I allude to the existence, the importance, and
the condition, of the Debating Society established here.

    It may amuse the gay to laugh, it may gratify the nar-
row-minded to rail, at such an institution.   The proud
may spurn it—the thoughtless may deride it—the male-

volent (if such there be—I believe there are not such among us) may hate, may traduce, may injure it; but it *has* endured, and it *does* endure, and it must continue to endure, as long as the liberal and indulgent spirit of our superiors shall continue to foster those aspirations of legitimate ambition, to mature those buds of opening ability, which are, I rejoice to say, so abundant in the minds of those whom it is my pride and my pleasure to call by the homely, yet endearing, name of school-fellows.

To such cavillers as I have mentioned above, no answer need be given, for no satisfaction would probably suffice. To the candid reader, to the fair and unprejudiced inquirer, facts like those which I have to mention, may demonstrate the utility, and the efficacy, of such institutions as that which I am striving to recommend. *Scarcely any one* of the great orators of this country has risen to so proud a distinction without previously trying his strength, maturing his faculties, and remedying his defects, in a *private Debating Society*.

But I may here be met by a triumphant assertion, that they were not societies of boys which have thus contributed to form our orators and statesmen. I am happy to have to adduce what, I believe, is a strikingly powerful and conclusive answer.

Of the very few distinguished young speakers in the House of Commons, as it exists at present, (altogether, perhaps, not more than four or five,) three, and those perhaps the first—I mean Lord Morpeth, the Hon. E. G. Stanley, and Lord Castlereagh—have been members of the ETON DEBATING SOCIETY ! that Society which affords such abundant room for ridicule and contempt: that

Society which has struggled with, and overcome, ridicule, and contempt, and prejudice, in its birth and in its growth—that Society which has, within no very long time back, exhibited buds of very great promise within its walls—that Society, which deigns not to apologise for its merits to the multitude, and which may condemn by disapproval, or may honour by assent, this, the to them unknown attempt of their humble and unworthy vindicator. From that Society, three of the few young men now distinguished as speakers in parliament have proceeded.

To the good sense of Eton and Etonians I fearlessly commit its hopes and its prospects. Embracing subjects as various and as interesting as propriety will admit of, it bestows, I will venture to assert, an *additional* advantage on the store which Eton already possesses. It may suffer through my feeble advocacy : I may lose the small estimation which it is my happiness to enjoy in its cause. That loss shall be cheerfully endured, if I have the honour of feeling that it has been caused by such an endeavour as this. I am well aware that I am going against the grain, as regards the inclinations of many of my readers. They may find here nothing witty or amusing : they may find something troublesome. But I feel and know that I am now doing a far greater, if not a more acceptable, service to my fellow-citizens, than if I yielded to their prejudices, or than when I have endeavoured to amuse their imaginations. If there is to a humble and unknown writer like myself any truly just and legitimate object of ambition, it is that of being known as one who feared not the tide of popular prejudice, or the gale of popular displeasure; whose wish it was, to do service even to the unwilling, and to have his name connected with that of an Institution which will ever be applauded by Candour and Justice, as it has ever been calumniated by Folly and Misrepresentation.

THE SHIPWRECK.

Vainly, o'er the rippling sea,
Ye speed your course right merrily;
Vainly ' on th' horizon's verge,
O'er the line of dark'ning surge,
Blows the swift and stormy blast,
　　And howls in gloom around,
Clouds in its train their burthens cast,
　　And pealing thunders sound.
Behold the murky diadem!
　　Behold the Spirit's form!
In vain! In vain! ye may not stem
　　The fury of the storm.
The thunder, pealing o'er ye then,
May never peal on you again.

Above the sea, and stormy gale,
There rose one loud and piercing wail;
Above the howling of the blast—
Ah, me! that wailing was the last!
No pow'r of earth might hope to save
The sailor from his ocean grave!
None o'er thy cold and silent bier
Might pour the tribute of a tear,
None sooth'd thy dying agony,
　　'Mid the widely-swelling foam;
The tempest was a dirge for thee,
　　And the deep abyss a home;
And, mingled with its roaring, rise
Thy pray'rs for mercy to the skies.

Now all is hush'd and calm again,
O'er the wide earth and silent main ;
The breeze is soft, the sky is bright,
And glowing with ethereal light ;
The zephyrs, o'er thy wat'ry bed,
Hymn the soft requiem of the dead ;
And many a wide and swelling sail
Spreads its broad bosom to the gale.
Yet there hath been, that sky beneath,
A scene of terror and of death ;
Few fragments yet remain to tell
What hap the wretched band befel ;
No sound of human voice is there,
No, not the death-shriek of despair ;
No ! all beneath the swelling foam,
Have found their sad, their common home.
Calm be their rest ! may gentle peace
Embalm them in their dwelling place :
And, hov'ring round them, dewy sleep
Guard the cold chambers of the deep !

Yet there is one, whose tearful eye
    And heaving bosom show
He was not, 'ere his flight on high,
    Forgot by all below.
In him was center'd all her love,
    In him her hope, her fear ;
For him her plaintive accents move,
    And flows her silent tear.
Full often, on the sea-beat shore
    She watch'd the coming sail ;
And, trembling, heard the tempest roar,
    And the howling of the gale.
Around her heart froze terrors chill,
    And the sickness of delay,
The rays of Hope, that cheer'd her still,
    Fell silently away.
The clouds of terror and affright,
    In thick'ning gloom and darkness roll ;
And day on day, and night on night,
    Fall sadly o'er the victim's soul.

Bloom from thy youthful cheek hath fled,
And left the paleness of the dead ;
And health, and grace, and beauty, fly,
And fades the lustre of thine eye :
Save that the heaving breast is there,
And lips that move in suppliant pray'r—
Else might the pitying gazer deem,
    Thou hadst breath'd thy parting breath ;
As, bound in wild and fleeting dream,
    Thou tread'st the path of Death.
Poor child of Sorrow ! Woe can fly
Swift as the breezes of the sky ;
Those breezes, low and mournful, bear
The tale of anguish to thine ear.
Those clasped hands are loosen'd then,
    Those lips are mov'd no more ;
That breast may never heave again,
    For the strife of pain is o'er :
Yes ; kindly Death hath brought relief,
And burst in twain the bonds of grief ;
In *his* bath seal'd *thy* mournful doom,
And bound thee in the silent tomb.
And many a tear, of youth and maid,
Flows where thy drooping head was laid ;
And bids the simple flow'ret wave
Its foliage o'er thy lowly grave.

LETTER FROM THE COUNTRY.

Barnton Park, Oct. 17, 1827.

My dear Bouverie ;

I certainly do not think that you will much regret that
you could not accept Frederick Thornton's invitation to
accompany me hither, unless it be that you may miss the

opportunity of gaining a little information about dogs
and horses. I arrived here yesterday afternoon ; and, if
I may judge from the commencement, I am immured in
a place inhabited only by fox-hunters and barbarians.
On my arrival, I found the family waiting dinner for me,
which I had particularly begged them not to do; but it
is one of their established maxims to think that they
must know what a person likes better than he does himself. I begged them to go to dinner, but the 'squire said
he was in no hurry, which was immediately re-echoed by
his wife, and both agreed that it would be more comfortable for me to change every particle of my dress. They
accordingly ordered dinner to be kept back ; but, alas !
their kind intentions were frustrated by the non-arrival
of my trunks, and I was obliged to wait near an hour
before I could get a mouthful of dinner, during which
time I amused myself in examining the furniture of the
best parlour, and in watching the motions of some silver
pheasants, which were feeding on the lawn. In due
time the hostess appeared, and made me many apologies
for having left me so long to my own meditations. I
could hardly keep my eyes open while I assured her I
had been very well amused. She immediately proceeded
to the weather, and observed, that the rain had been so
hard, that the 'squire had been prevented from hunting.
In a short time in came Frederick, and gave me a
hearty welcome, and apologized for his brother's absence,
who, he told me, was gone to a neighbouring estate of
the 'squire's, to get a little pheasant-shooting. He
desired to be remembered to you, and to all his old Eton
friends ; he is very much pleased with the commence-

ment of his college life, and has at last determined to
go into the church, while his brother is to spend his
life as a country 'squire. I found him the only person
in the house who had any information on subjects more
abstruse than dogs, horses, and guns. You know how
often he has told us of his father's attachment to field
sports; but I had no idea that he carried it to such a
pitch. Dinner was at last announced, and I was requested
to hand my hostess into the dining parlour, and was
placed at her right-hand, with the 'squire at my side—he
having resigned the bottom of the table to his two sons.
He was remarkably courteous to me; and, before the fish
was removed, he had entered upon a most interesting
account of some men whom he had found nutting in
his woods, and whom, I afterwards found out, were
discharged without any punishment; upon which the
'squire had quarrelled with all the justices in the vicinity.
He had got through half his story, when he started from
his seat, and darting to the window, immediately desired
the servant to bring him his hat and stick, and rushed
out of the room. I, who had no idea of the cause of
this sudden movement, sat perfectly astounded, while
the butler, laying down my plate, instantly followed his
master. As soon as I had recovered from my surprise,
I ventured to ask Mrs. Thornton whether any thing was
the matter. Oh, no! said she, my husband only heard
a dog barking in the woods, and, on these occasions,
never trusts any one but himself. I hope he will discover the rascals, for they disturb us every day by their
poaching practices. This, as Frederick afterwards told
me, was a common occurrence with his father; who,

although he was rather hard of hearing on other occasions, could, nevertheless, distinguish the bark of a dog
at a great distance. After some time the 'squire returned,
rather out of humour at not being able to discover the
offenders, and vented his spleen in sundry invectives
against the mal-administration of the laws, ignorance of
country justices, &c. &c. When the cloth was removed,
my hostess retreated, and the bottle circulated very
freely. I am, as you know, no great advocate for hard
drinking, especially after a journey, and accordingly
made my escape, by saying that I was excessively tired,
and wished to go to bed. I was shown into a room,
such a one as you may have read of in the Mysteries of
Udolpho, or in any romance in which ghosts form a
prominent part. It was hung with tapestry, which was
not, as you may guess, in very good repair, and, in short,
bore evident marks of being the state room. Whether
ghosts do not frequent this apartment, or whether sound
sleep prevented my observing them, I do not know ; but
I did not meet with a single adventure, out of which I
could manufacture even a six-penny pamphlet. Early
this morning I was awakened by a chorus of dogs in the
yard, who were running about as if they were mad. But
I did not regret the interruption, as my window looks
out upon the most beautiful country you can well imagine.
While I was admiring the prospect, I was informed by
the breakfast-bell that I was waited for, and therefore
hurried down stairs, and found the 'squire breakfasting
on beef-steaks and ale, which he strongly recommended
to my notice. But, as I am not training for a prize-fight,
I preferred a plain cup of tea. The 'squire took my

refusal very quietly, although I saw by his looks he
thought me a great fool. Immediately after breakfast I
was hurried out to see the stables and dog-kennel, and
was forced to hear, from the 'squire's own mouth (who,
by-the-bye, I am told is a very good judge in these matters), the pedigree of each horse, and the merits and
demerits of every dog. My whole morning was wasted
in this intellectual employment, for it was two o'clock
before I had got through the whole stud, and then we
went to luncheon. I asked Frederick whether he would
take a walk, but I found, not a little to my disappointment, that he was engaged to go with his father to call
on a gentleman who had a pointer to sell. The 'squire
told me that he would be very happy to introduce me,
adding, that he had one of the best dog-kennels in the
country, and that it was built on a new plan; but, as I
felt no inclination to see either the gentleman or his
kennel, I excused myself on the plea of a head ache;
and, since I did not know what to do with myself, I
determined to give you an account of the commencement
of my fortnight's visit, and to send you my most hearty
congratulations on your not being with me. We are
going to have a grand dinner-party in a day or two,
from which I hope to derive some amusement, and of
which I will send you an account, if this long letter does
not sicken you of the diary of this place. I am afraid
I have tired you already, so, with best wishes for the
success of No. VIII,

I remain,
Your's truly,
P. M.

P.S. By-the-bye, send me the Seventh Number; it
will be some little relief to me.   The 'squire desires me
to say, he is very sorry that you could not come down
with me.   I hope, for your sake, that the regret is not
reciprocal.

THE SLAVERY OF GREECE.

> The Isles of Greece! the Isles of Greece!
>   Where burning Sappho lov'd and sung,
> Where grew the arts of war and peace,
>   _ Where Delos rose and Phœbus sprung !   *Lord Byron.*

It is the hour of even—and the sun
  _ Shines in autumnal splendor o'er the deep,
The orb of light his course hath nearly run,
  And the long waves majestically sweep
On the cool breeze, and glist'ning in the spray,
Reflect the glories of the parting day.

Bright is the prospect, and those Grecian Isles,
  Like sea-born giants, spring from out the flood;
Thus were their haughty summits deck'd with smiles,
  When the proud Persian ting'd with Asia's blood
The deep, indignant in his blushing waves
To hold a tyrant's minions, Syria's slaves.

Soft blow, ye gales, ye zephyrs gently breathe,
  These *were* the Isles of liberty and Greece,
Here laurell'd freedom twin'd her fairest wreath,
  Here flourish'd arts and arms, and dove-wing'd peace ,
All, all are fled !—Yet, ah, forbear to tell
Not how Greece flourish'd, but how Grecians fell.

Mute is the voice of triumph, and the sound
  Of the hoarse trumpet from mail-fronted war,
And meagre want, and pallid care, around,
  And Desolation's havoc, reign afar
'Tis silence all—the lover's silvery lute,
And the fair virgin's plaintive song, are mute.

No more with generous animation glows
   The free-born spirit of each warrior chief;
But the lone widow'd breast conceals its throes,
   In secret pines, and vainly seeks relief;
Then left, as if by earth and heav'n accurst,
The grief-tost heart must sorrow till it burst.

The sun's bright beams their beauties freely fling,
   O'er hill and dale the wild stag freely roves,
And Philomel, if captur'd, would not sing;
   Uncag'd, she freely warbles in the groves.
Yon rocky shores th' unfetter'd ocean laves,
Yes '—all are free—and ye, oh heav'n ! are slaves.

And are the spirits of old ages dumb,
   Of Sparta's heroes, of Athenæ's line ?
And shall no remnant of those warriors come
   Who fought the Persian o'er the billowy brine ?
It cannot be !   Their sad, their silent doom
Is the cold slumber of the marble tomb

Could but the shadows of those patriots arm
   Bewilder'd Greece '—alas, each hope is gone '
Vain ev'n the potency of freedom's charm,
   The power that conquer'd, and the light that shone.
Yet 'mid this wreck of all, oh ! might there be
One soul, that fears not death, lost Greece, for thee.

Yet one there was—but he has pass'd away
   Like the faint glories of a summer's dream;
He was a noble minstrel,* and his lay
   Cast, like a comet, one bright fervid gleam ;
His touch could almost rouse the dead, his lyre
Warm ev'n those icy hearts with patriot fire.

His voice is whisper'd 'mid the forests now
   That rise umbrageous o'er the tempest's shock ;
I saw his name on Sunium's marble brow,
   In characters of light, upon the rock—

---

* Lord Byron

* 'Grav'd with an iron style—Oh ! who shall sever
That record from the stone ?—It lasts for ever.

It is the hour of even—gentlest hour,
    That calls the wearied traveller to his rest ;
(When the soft twilight creeps from flow'r to flow'r,
    And nature's peacefulness becalms the breast),
That knits our souls in heavenliest sympathies,
And bears the soaring spirit to the skies.

Farewell,—farewell—the mountain torrents fall,
    Re-echoing deeply round from shore to shore,
And the rough billow's angry splash, are all
    The sounds that break this silence—but no more—
Still ever-swelling roll the foamy seas
Mid the wan splendor of the Cyclades.   PHILACHÆUS.

ON THE NATIONAL PROPENSITY TO FEASTING.

Sir ;

Your correspondent Impransus has humorously insinuated that the grand rallying point of Englishmen is a dinner ; and in truth, not without reason, for upon reflection we must acknowledge, that on every pretence, however slight, on every occasion, however trivial, our countrymen expect a feast.

Thus cabinet ministers form schemes of economy, and project plans of retrenchment in the junior parts of their offices, while they, the heads, are carousing. Thus on the anniversary of a Dispensary, the friends of the institution love to meet, and drink wine, perhaps not much better than the physic which they themselves give. Thus

---

* *Vide* Job Ch. 19, v. 24. They were graven with an iron pen and lead in the rock for ever.

commissioners of a road, or guardians of a minor, assemble as it were only to differ; but thinking it wrong to part from each other in ill will, they drown their disputes in a bottle of wine, at the expense either of the public, or the ward.   But yet there is really no evil to be dreaded from this propensity; though certainly at some dinners the wit is so appalling, that if I was disposed to speak in heroics, I should boldly assert that it made my blood run cold in my veins.   A moderate man can put up with bad wine, or a bad dinner, but bad wit is in its consequences so dreadful, that a tax ought to be laid on every old pun, conceit, or quibble.   Thus at a Dispensary dinner the jokes are so technical, that we almost fancy ourselves patients.   To give the reader some idea of my meaning, let us imagine this conversation.   Two apothecaries disputed, and the following dialogue passed between them :—

A. Sir, your wit is all puns.

B. Sir, your puns are not all wit.

A. Sir, your jokes are strong emetics.

B. Sir, your's by use have lost even that effect.

An apothecary joking, is like a cat playing with a mouse previous to killing it.   But if your muscles obstinately refuse to relax into a smile, the son of Galen gives a grin, as much as to say, "For this I'll be the death of you."   To give the reader some idea of the manners of the people at public dinners, let us record this anecdote.   A gentleman helping the soup, said to a man opposite, "Sir, shall I have the pleasure of giving you a little soup?"   To which the disciple of Chesterfield replied, "No, give a good deal !"

But in private there is the same relish for a good
dinner; for when a young heir comes of age, he is
expected to give a dinner to all his friends and tenants.
The latter class invariably, when requested to pass the
wine, help themselves in the middle. On the birth-day of
the head of the family, he is required to give a grand
feast to all his relations ; and, should he lately have succeeded to a large fortune, some general, in the person of
an aunt, whom he never before saw, leads on to the attack
a battalion of cousins, whom he never before heard of.

Some Cynics, indeed, find fault with the luxury of this
age, and books are constantly published, shewing the
way to live to an old age, by observing a proper regimen ;
but the fact is, that those who give us such judicious
advice, are themselves the best livers, like captains of
militia, who brag most of the hardships of a military
life. We have, indeed, heard of a doctor, who said that
his constitution was weak, and his system required support, and so prescribed for himself turkey and chine,
mild ale, and old port ; while, on the other hand, he said
that his patient must be lowered, and confined him to
water-gruel.

Were I a physician, and accused of being an epicure,
I should answer in the words of a *Bon Vivant* of my
acquaintance :—" Why, truly, I prefer a good to a bad
dinner." This answer suits every purpose, it at once
precludes every suspicion of sensuality or affectation, and
shews that you neither gormandise like an epicure, nor
fast like an anchorite.   B.

MANLIUS OVER THE DEAD BODY OF HIS SON.

My child, my child, now all are gone,
   The fountain of my tears may flow—
One long last look, my gallant son !—
   Thou canst not see thy deadliest foe,
Who bends in writhing o'er thy bier,
And prays in mercy for a tear.

They will not flow, they will not flow !—
   Who dar'd to slay the Consul's son '—
I bend to kiss thy pallid brow,
   And the red gore flows slowly on '—
That dreadful witness * does not err—
I was—I am—thy murderer !

Thanks for these tears, to my despair
   They bring, if aught can bring, relief :
Oh, no—my spirit cannot bear
   This change from madness into grief.
Though madness be a bitter curse,
This horrid consciousness is worse.

Yet have I done a Roman deed—
   An act of Roman justice—what !
I that have doom'd my son to bleed —
   I cannot mock my grief with that.
I can but be in sullen gloom,
And wither slowly to the tomb.

---

* I have taken a poetical licence, in transplanting the old Gothic superstition of the blood of the victim flowing afresh at the approach of the murderer.

My brave !—my beautiful '—farewell '
  My salt tears wash thy ghastly wound—
They come—I know those sounds too well—
  To lay thee in the cold, cold, ground !
And I must learn to hide, and bear,
The gnawing canker of despair !

F. J.

WRITTEN ON A WOODY DELL, AT ——

Much admired for its romantic situation, and beauties.

Stranger, whosoe'er thou art,
Whom fate decrees to play thy part
In the busy scene of life,
'Midst of bustle, 'midst of strife ;
Shoulds't thou desire to quit that scene,
For one more tranquil, more serene,
And live awhile from troubles free,
In silence and tranquillity ,
Ask'st thou where those blessings dwell ?
Seek them in the woodland dell.

Thou, whom the Muse hath taught to sing,
And strike the Lyre's melodious string ;
Who lov'st in gay poetic dream,
To wander by Castalian stream,
Or Pindus' sacred top to gain,
And listen to celestial strain,
And quit, with laurel-circled brow,
All meaner thoughts of things below,
Ask'st thou where the Muses dwell ?
Seek them in the woodland dell.

Thou, whom th' unartificial sight
Of Nature's charms can more delight,

Than princely towers, and cities plann'd,
And rais'd by Art's laborious hand—
Who lov'st hill, dale, and mead, to see
Mingled in sweet variety—
And when the sun with ray serene,
Smiles upon the spangled green,
Perch'd upon each leafy tree,
To hear the birds' soft melody—
Bid all the pomp of art farewell,
And welcome to the woodland dell.

Here Phœbus shines with mildest ray,
And songs arise from ev'ry spray ;
Nature her fairest form assumes,
And ev'ry flow'ret brighter blooms.
Here oft with eager steps I run,
When sinks beneath his hills the sun.
Oft I ascend that chalky brow,
That beetles o'er the mead below ;
Or when the clouds pour down their streams,
Or Phœbus darts his fiercest beams,
Then to those friendly shades I fly,
A refuge from th' inclement sky :
Nor, from those shades, when doom'd to part,
Will soft remembrance to my heart,
(When time hath quick pass'd o'er my head,
And youth and all its pleasures fled),
Recall a place I lov'd so well,
So truly, as the woodland dell.

A GOTHIC FRAGMENT,

After the Recipe in the possession of A. HEAVISIDE, *Esq.   With notes critical and explanatory, by* B. BOUVERIE.

* The nocturnal Deity had expanded her sable wings over the terrestrial globe, and had enveloped towers,

---

* Being translated, " It was night." It is an indispensable rule to begin

forests, and seas, in her dusky mantle.—The bellowing thunder * rolled along : ever roaring with its hollow reverberations, and the ever-and-anon-flashing lightning served only partially to shew by its fitful gleam, a castle which had long since been mouldering in decay, and where the owls and bats alone held solitary vigil; the rain poured down in unceasing torrents, the only cover from which was the gloomy foliage of the umbrageous cedars, which were now rapidly succumbing † to the indescribable cataract of rain which was precipitated on them. — The Conte Rodolfo Agostino Raimondo della Ineffabilla-Vomica ‡ was travelling, accompanied by his

---

with night, inasmuch as it is a good old ready-made wear and tear beginning, and will equally fit any story; and secondly, such are the deeds of horror which are to be perpetrated, that it is of the highest consequence, that

> " thick night
> Should pall her in the dunnest smoke of hell,
> Nor heaven peep through the blanket of the dark,
> To cry hold ! hold !"——
> " Taking the present horror from the time,
> Which now suits with it."—

The reader cannot be mad enough to expect to understand half that is said, but he must always suppose that there is something very sublime or witty couched under every incomprehensible sentence.—As, indeed, of course there is.

* Over and above, it is beyond every thing expedient, that the night be hugely rainy and stormy, for the ruined castle (which is a first rate ingredient) cannot be shown off to better advantage than by lightning, which gives a horribly imperfect and imperfectly horrible idea of its appearance and situation, meant to be highly poetical. Rain is necessary in order to compel them to take shelter in it.

† A *Goth* always refines on his ideas, so as to make them as incomprehensible as possible. A simple Bombastes would have said only " yielded." However, there is nothing like stretching a metaphor pretty well.

‡ Now for the hero : he must be Conte or Marchese (Count or Marquis

sturdy and faithful follower, Gasparo, round the skirts of
the dark forest which has been delineated, and the tarry*
and horrible aspect of the night, was, as has been mentioned, only temporally dispelled by the illumining
coruscations of the electric fire, which discovered to the
all-astonished eyes of our travellers the moss-covered
and overgrown battlements of a castellated ruin.

The Conte imposed a check on the precipitate rapidity
of his quadruped, and addressed to his follower these
most impressive words.—" O faithful of all faithful †
servants, art thou not of opinion that it would be the
most advisable plan to seek shelter in the adjacent walls
of these turreted fragments. Thou beholdest," continued
he, looking dolorously at his servant, " that we are soaked
almost to death,‡ that our hats are as sponges, and our
breeches as spiders' webs, to keep off this pitiless water-
spout. What thinkest thou, then ?" His devoted attendant responded to this question by a single, short, em-

---

would spoil all), with as many names as an Hidalgo of a thousand years
standing : all the Christian names to end in o, or i, and to be at least
of three syllables, with good sesquipedal surname, to finish up all like a
cannon at the end of a roll of musquetry. A *faithful attendant* also is in
general useful, to be frightened here and there ; to be talked to, and to
perform divers little offices not at all consistent with the dignity of the
hero.

  * Pitchy darkness, and why not tarry.

  † Is this derived from the language of the Athenians, or from that of the
Sausage tribe ? From ἀλλᾶντ᾽ ἀλλάντων, or from " Sausage of all Sausages ?"

  ‡ N. B.—The object in Gothicized language is, as may be seen here, and
throughout the tale, not to strike out any new or magnificent idea, and
but chiefly to dress out every-day thought in the most roaring and unintelligible words, for example, the "drowned rat" just below, is far from
a new, or a fine and poetical idea, but is, by dint of small changes and
lengthenings, metamorphosed into a most sublime passage in a Gothic
tale.

phatic, and decisive, " Eh?"—" Dost thou not behold,"
again returned the Conte, "that I am similar to a rat
immersed in water even to drowning, and that deprived
of immediate succour I shall inevitably contract a
rheumatic disorder?" Gasparo again answered by a
still more impressive grunt of discontent.—" Insensible
animal," exclaimed his iracund lord, " feelest thou not"
——" Feel " snorted out the *　　*　　*　　*　　*
　　*　　●　　*　　*　　*　　*　　*　　*

The blue light [vide recipe] at last moved taciturnly on :
the Conte for some time hesitated whether or not he
should pursue this mysterious appearance. The indescribable perils, into which he would precipitate himself,
rushed in horrible array on his staggered mind ; he might
be entrapped into a fathomless abyss, in which he might
from starvation undergo the most excruciating dissolution, deprived of the solace of the resplendent reflection
of a looking-glass for his Gordian neckcloth, or of the
wonted Macassar oil † for his ambrosial mustachios. He

---

* The asterisks in a Gothic story should be frequently introduced, and
in large bodies, and should always follow the two words, "replied the,"
or something to that effect. Delightful asterisks ! what worlds of trouble
would be saved both to writers and to readers, if modern custom had
not so infamously slighted these expressive little gentlemen ! Asterisks,
too, excel equally in the pathetic, the sublime, the terrific, or the ludicrous, style , and equally outshine every other mode of expression, in
every species. Who has not been penetrated with the most heart-rending
emotion in viewing the formidable squares of Asterisks in the Giaour .
or to pass to greater things, who has not quivered with terror and anxiety
as conning over those of the "Goblin of the Vault," or of the "Banditti
of the Black Cave."

† The Emperors of Russia and Japan, as well as the Cham of Tartary,
use Macassar oil, according to the newspapers, those infallible registers of

might be absorbed in a quagmire, or be dashed headlong
from a time-broken turret. The intrepidity, however, which
was bestowed lavishly upon him by propitious nature, hurried him on, and he dauntlessly dashed into the midst of
perils. The blue light, after leading him through a long
range of ruinous aisles and corridors [*vide* recipe] at last
grew stationary, and assumed a more livid hue, and the
Conte could distinctly behold a small death-coloured figure
rise from the ground before it. This hobgoblin had no
sooner emerged from its subterraneous mansions than it
began rapidly to grow larger, till at last he increased to
so enormous a size, that the astonished beholder, on looking upwards, could only see as high as the top of his
instep : the rest of his body being utterly beyond the
reach of human vision.*

The Conte, all-courageous, as he was, was beginning to
sink under this soul-overwhelming † prodigy, when he
took from his bosom, where he preserved as an invigorator
under all phantasmiacal horror, a small phial of salts,
which, applied to his nasal orifices, by its superhuman
assistance, soon recreated his languishing courage.—He
replaced his salts in his bosom, and drawing forth his

---

all that is remarkable and *true*, and why not the hero of a Gothic
romance ?

* The consummation of Gothicism ; the prince of all ghosts has now
appeared, the acmè of hobgoblinism is attained. The genius of the
Arabian Nights frightened a poor hunchback almost to death by magnifying
himself from a cat to a buffalo ; and what was he to this fellow? How
many thousand buffalos would the mere foot of this quondam pigmy make
well sliced up ?

† As many compound words as possible give a most desirable effect to
the sentence. It signifies not whether they are sense or not, so as they
are long, and have one or more hyphens in the middle.—N. B. "All" is a
convenient little expletive to place at the head of adjectives, as in all-
coura one, all the truth, &c.

sword, made so desperate a thrust at the near end of this
awful being's great toe, that he buried not only the weapon but the whole of his arm in the limb.   Immediately
repeated peals of the most overwhelming thunder, mixed
with demoniac shrieks, rent the vaulted arches of the
celestial concave, and the lacerated toe was rapidly lifted
up so high as to be entirely invisible to the ocular powers of any mortal; then came it down with such earth-
crushing violence as to be buried up to the knee in the
earth, within a few feet of the adventurous hero, who,
fired with the spirit of salts, had dared to attack it—The
fragile globe trembled and groaned under such a before-
unfelt shock; its caverned entrails quivered to their fundamental basis.   The vivid expanse of the glassy ocean
was borne back upon its own terrified surface, and a thun-
dering and destruction-spreading avalanche was hurled,
by the earthquake attending it, from its station on the all-
over-topping crags of Switzerland.

The high-souled and nothing-daunted Rodolfo again
plunged his glittering weapon into the enormous knee of
the earth-begotten phantom; again an infernal yell filled
the whole ethereal space, and the gigantic limb was suddenly upraised to its former station before the noble
Conte had time to disengage his sword and arm; so that
adhering to the incision he had made, he was snatched
up with the limb, and found himself within a few feet of
the silvery orb of the pallid moon.

Our hero, with a presence of mind peculiar to his
illustrious race, drew from his breast a small pocket-pis-
tol, and hastily discharged his tube* into the grisly

---

* Vide a most beautiful specimen of this style, price three-pence, or (1

thigh of the soul-appalling monster. Instantly thick volumes of smoke obscured the blackening atmosphere: the rubicund* lightning darted forth its triple tongue in fiery abundance through the murky shroud of the all-around-ruling obscurity. The Conte was suddenly buried in a death-like stupor, and when he was awakened to the full use of his senses, found himself entombed, uninjured, in the frowning recesses of the castle-dungeon, amid broken and disjointed fragments of bones, now mouldering in the dust.—He lay for several minutes as it were benumbed by this melancholy situation, when suddenly a sepulchral groan, issuing from a spot where a dubious ray of light shewed him where lay a ghastly skeleton†, grated on his ear. This horror-breathing sound, and sense-appalling spectacle awakened him to a knowledge of his situation, and infused a supernatural terror through every fibre of his inmost soul, at the same time inspiring him with an invincible resolution to make his escape, if any exertion could do so, from this loathsome scene.

After a long and diligent search he discovered a small door [*vide* recipe again], which he with some difficulty opened, and rushed forward, brim-full of the most ecstatic rapture at having regained his liberty, when he suddenly felt a cold and clammy hand placed on his eyes, and heard behind him   *   *   *   *   *

---

do not wish to undervalue it,) it may be six-pence, where a person speaks of "the discharge of his tube," *i. e.* pistol.

* Rubicund I allow to be rather more frequently applied to the nose; however this passage is the more original.

† Only one is taken of the two prescribed by Mr Heaviside—that one being considered a quantum suff.

THE PRAYER OF JUDITH.

The star of day was sinking low, and ev'ning slumber'd still,
And incense fill'd the breath of Heav'n from Sion's holy hill ,
It was the solemn hour of pray'r, when pious Judith rose,
And sought the succour of the Lord, for vengeance on her foes;
Her tender limbs in sackcloth clad, and ashes on her head,
She cried aloud unto her God, and thus the widow pray'd :—

" O Lord on high, the God who gav'st thy sword's avenging might,
Who mad'st my sire of strength to help the cause of injur'd right,
When Israel's foes with spoiling came, and seiz'd the virgin maid,
And for chaste honour's spotless name, disgrace upon her laid .
But Thou against the deed hadst sent thy death-denouncing word,
And woe to them that lightly scorn the threat'ning of the Lord !

" Thy children cried on thee for aid, with holy zeal inspir'd,
And well thou heard'st their cry, and soon thy righteous wrath was
    fir'd ;
For lo ! thy vengeance from above by Simeon's hand hath sped,
The ruffian spoiler lieth low, the conqueror hath bled,
The lords upon their thrones were struck, their wives for prey are
    given,
The spoil of victory is shar'd by Israel, lov'd of Heaven !

" Thou heard'st thy children when they cried, and mad'st them to
    rejoice,
O God, in mercy hear thou now a widow's suppliant voice ·
For thy right arm, in every age, hath deeds of glory done,
And Thee the future and the past alike their ruler own ;
Thy will controls events far off conceal'd from mortal sight,
Thy judgments wait their destin'd hour, then spring to life and light.

" E'en now, great Lord ! th' Assyrian hosts are glorying in their pow'r,
The mountain pours her thousands forth, to plunder and devour ;

They come with chariot and with horse, their wheels are thund'ring
   nigh—
With shield and spear, and bow and sling, thy children they defy :
These are their boast—but vain their strength—they know not Israel's
  . might—
The God that breaks the battle-spear, the Lord that rules the fight !

" They come with sword of steel to rend thy altar's sacred horn,
To spoil the resting-place which thou in Glory dost adorn :
But, Lord ! let vengeance fiercely rise and smite their impious host, ,
And grant a widow strength to quell the rebel chieftain's boast.
Oh ' let the nations warning take from haughty Assur's fate,
And see, by woman's hand o'erthrown, their princes and their state !

" For thine is not as mortal pow'r that trusts in armed bands,
Thou vauntest not thyself in might of thousand warrior hands ,
'Tis thine in mercy to uphold the weak that call on Thee,
To help the lowly when oppress'd by wrong and injury ;
'Tis Thou that art the Saviour, Lord, of all that are forlorn,
The God that bids affliction cease, and gladd'ning hope return.

" O Lord of Heaven and of Earth, Creator of the waters,
Thou God of Simeon, send relief to Israel's mourning daughters ,
O hear the pray'r of her who calls for vengeance on the foe, .
The foe that comes thy house to spoil, on Sion's hallow'd brow ;
Then shall the nations own that thou art God of pow'r and might,
That Israel wants not sword or shield, while God protects her right !"

ON TEA.

Do not think, Mr. Bouverie, that the inestimable compound of dried leaves, milk,* sugar, and hot water, is
the subject of my present discourse ; I am not going to
entangle both you and myself in an elaborate dissertation

---

* Milk at Eton ; in other places, cream.   B. B.

on the virtues, or ill-effects, of the above-mentioned beverage, nor to inform you with arithmetical precision the exact number of years, during which it has continued to grace British tea-tables. I intend, in the best manner I am able, to say a few words in praise of that meal, which, with us mortals, generally succeeds to dinner; but more of its social and comfortable qualities, than of its sensual pleasures and epicurean delights. There is nothing at my tea-table, Mr. Bouverie, which can please the fastidious palate of the *bon vivant*. In Summer I am content with bread and butter, and in Winter I desire no delicacy beyond my simple toast or muffin. But, Mr. Bouverie, when I sit down before my tea-tray, I feel that all the labours of the day are over, and that now nothing remains to me for the remainder of the evening, but rest, tranquillity, and my arm-chair.

At breakfast my mind is disturbed by the harassing thoughts of what I have to do, directly it is swallowed; of the drudgery of turning over the leaves of my *Lexicon*, and writing down my *derivations*; and whatever your ingenious friend, Impransus, may say as to the virtues of a good dinner, I am ready and willing to defend my own cause, and to discuss the merits of the rival meals, any evening he pleases, over a warm fire, and a social cup of tea. If I entertain my friends for the evening, I have always found (as you no doubt have, Mr. Bouverie) how much more agreeable this time is than any other. When they first arrive at my house, they (and the shy ones in particular) are so over-polite and ceremonious, so full of what is called "*palaver*," that the time passes away in a very irksome and disagreeable manner. This sometimes continues through dinner; but when, the happy hour arrives at which we are summoned to the ladies, and the tea-table, every body seems to have become suddenly sociable and unceremonious, and those who, a short time before, were dull and reserved, seem miraculously to acquire new life and animation.   Now, Mr. Bouverie, I cannot but persuade myself that the tea-table has a kind of innate power of imparting to all who approach it the magical effects I have just mentioned.   If I am not deceived in this opinion, I think it would be by no means a bad plan, if people would more often dispense with the ceremonious practice of "asking to dinner," and be content with inviting their acquaintance to partake of the pleasures of the tea-table, which, by way of experiment, it is my own intention to do.   Your's,

THEAPHILOS.

CHORUS

From the " Hecuba" of Euripides.—v. 893.

STROPHE I.

Ilion! on thy desert shore
Sounds of joy are heard no more;
See the Grecian foemen's cloud
No more unconquer'd Ilion shroud!
The spear, the spear, hath laid thee waste,
    Thy splendor and thy glory shorn;
Black'ning tow'rs, and gates defac'd,
    Humbled pride and honours torn!
Hapless Ilion! never more
May we tread thy silent shore!

Antistrophe I.

'Twas dead of night, and silence deep
Buried all in dewy sleep,
For feast, and dance, and slaughter done,
Soft slumber's season had begun.
The lyre was hush'd, the altar cold,
   ' The sword, the lance, all bloodless lay ;
My husband, softly resting, told
     The toils and dangers of the day ;
No longer watching for the foe
Sworn to lay proud Ilion low.

Strophe II.

I strove my flowing hair to bind
With many a festal chaplet twin'd ;
The mirror's rays of glitt'ring hue
Betray'd me to my virgin view,
Hast'ning to rest.   Then peal'd on high
O'er Ilion's walls the victor's cry ;
Troy heard the shout that sounded then,
   " Dash'd down the turrets of the foe,
" Shall sons of Greece again, again,
   " To home, and rest, and glory go ?"

Antistrophe II.

I started from the nuptial bed,
To mighty Dian's temple fled ;
With vest that Spartan virgins bear,
I sought, I found not, safety there !
I saw my warrior in his grave,
And, hurried o'er the salt sea wave,
Look'd back on Troy, my own no more.
   The ship began its homeward way,
And torn from hapless Ilion's shore,
   I left in woe the light of day ,

EPODE.

Yet gave to curse, to ban, to death,
  The sister of the sons of Jove;
Yet doom'd to woe, with failing breath,
  Th' Idæan shepherd's traitor love ;
No love ! but Furies' vengeful ire
  Hath torn me from my father's home ;
Hath given Troy to raging fire ;
  For ever may she hapless roam
A wand'rer o'er the swelling main,
Nor see her sire's abode again.*

FRAGMENT.†

Yet, while I mourn with low and feeble strain,
  The dearth of children of the lofty lyre,
And while I weep for that Parnassian plain,
  Where wont to gleam the Poet's noble fire ;
Where old Mæonides sublimer sings,
Than e'er on earth, of heroes, sages, kings ;
Where Virgil quaffs the waters of the blest—
The sacred bands in seats of gladness rest—
Yet let my Muse her humble tribute pay
To Canning's Eloquence, to Canning's lay.
Say not the flow'rs of poesy are dead,
While the Nine wreathe with laurels Canning's head :
Say not the fount of eloquence is dry,
It springs from Canning's lip, and sparkles in his eye !

---

* It is particularly requested of my readers, that, on the perusal of this Translation, they do not refer to the original ; it will dispel the illusion, as the critics say.

† Written, as the reader will perceive, long ago ; its date is January, 1825.

Yet, ah! the bright but evanescent fire
Burn'd but to die, and gleam'd but to expire!
The buds of Poesy the Muses gave,
Neglected lie, and wither in the grave.
Far other tasks his patriot care demand,
  Far other thoughts his ardent soul employ;
The helm of England needs his guiding hand,
  A nation's wonder, and a nation's joy.
He is the pilot that our God hath sent
To guide the vessel that was tost and rent!
Exalt thine head, Etona, and rejoice,
Glad in a nation's loud acclaiming voice,
And 'mid the tumult and the clamour wild,
Exult in Canning—say, he was thy child.

THE DISASTERS OF A BALL.

Dear Bouverie;

There is nothing I like better than a ball, not only
from an innate love of dancing, but from all the conco-
mitant circumstances which usually shed lustre round a
ball-room. I am rather fond of a little secret satire, as
I walk about the rooms appropriated for dancing and
flirting; and do not dislike a quantum sufficit of secret
Champagne, as I walk about the rooms appropriated for
eating and drinking. There is something exceedingly
agreeable in the sudden stop which the carriage makes
after the terrible impetus of its whirl round the last
corner, and the hall resounding with all imaginable
modifications of your name. There is one thing, however, which generally strikes me, that ladies are much
longer in putting away their cloaks, than there is any
necessity for. I hate to stand pottering there for at least
ten minutes, to put away cloaks and handkerchiefs, when

one would serve as well, as they are never to be found
at the close of the ball, and by that means you would
have nine minutes clear gain.   I always put my hat down
on the first place where there is sufficient room for it, and
I never lost it but once ; then, indeed, I am ashamed to
say, I took another : I was visited by some severe scruples
of conscience, but I was alone, a perfect hermit in the
ball-room, having outstaid the rest of my party ; and
had to walk nearly half a mile to the nearest hackney
coach stand, and the night was raw and rainy.   Common
sense suggested imperatively, that this walk could not be
effected without a hat ; Conscience suggested, why not
by me, as well as by the owner ?   Sophistry suggested
he might have a carriage, conscience suggested he might
not.   Still, however, a hat was necessary, absolutely
necessary, and I wandered about disconsolately in the
vain hope of finding my own beaver, to save me at once
from cold and dishonesty.   It would not do : I still
walked round and round, vainly pondering what to do.
Peter Shlemel, when he lost his shadow, was not more
disconsolate than I when I lost my hat.   But having
for the third time disturbed an old lady, who was sitting
on the bench under which I had placed my own hat, and
the other gentleman had placed his, which was soon
about " *permutare dominos, et cedere in altera Jura ;*"
she rose with the greatest asperity of politeness, exclaiming, " are you looking for your hat, Sir? is it under here?"
I gathered energy from despair, and reduced the matter
to a syllogism.   Somebody has taken my hat, he cannot
have gone away with two, therefore if I take this, his
hat will still remain for the other unfortunate gentleman,

and every body will be suited; if I leave it, there will be a vacant hat at the end of the ball, which I might just as well have carried off. I seized my prize, and rushed out as if pursued by the avenging furies, nor did I think myself safe till I reached Bond-street. It is perfectly useless to make a noise about it, as I *have* seen a lady do, who, on the strength of having lost a *very* handsome cloak, as she gave every body to understand, flew as if she were famished, upon the unfortunate mass of vestures, and made her way through the press, *vi et armis;* one cloak flying out at the door, another on the stairs, and the lady herself holding forth in a style of female eloquence, which I did not quite admire. I should have been tempted to laugh had it been a gentleman looking for a lady's cloak, at the air of resolute fury with which she set herself at every other person's garments, which flew right and left with a velocity which reminded me of Baron Munchausen's mad dress, which bit and lacerated his wardrobe in the most terrible manner. As, however, I particularly dislike a virago, I turned into the street, rejoicing that I had never seen such a public exhibition of temper but once, and hoping that I never should see it again. Thine,

F. J.

*** The Prayer of Judith comes under the same class of compositions as Ada, and the rest of those mentioned in the Seventh Number. B. B.

ETON MISCELLANY,

No. IX.

INTRODUCTION.

Veluti in speculo.

IT is impossible to doubt, that the public must always have.been, and still .continue to be, extremely anxious to know something of the character of one, with whom they have so long been .acquainted, as their humble servant who now addresses them. . It is a formidable and an invidious task to depict one's own disposition; formidable, in spite of the much celebrated, but little practised, γνῶθι σεαυτὸν of antiquity, and " know thyself" of. modern times; invidious, .notwithstanding the calmness and impartiality, with which all philosophers are supposed to examine and delineate their own frame of mind.

When, on first introducing myself to the public, I enlightened them with a brief account of my origin and life, I did not inform them .what a quaint, pragmatical, old-fashioned, bachelor-like looking personage I was; how early I was honoured by the title, and how fre-

quently I was saluted by the appellation, of a " Quiz:"
how many and how various were the appendages affixed
to my back by the hands of my malicious play-mates;
how they, having learned from their school-books that
poetry and madness were nearly allied, perceiving in me
already infallible symptoms of the one, prophesied that
I should soon display some decided tendency towards
the other. In spite of my assurances of my own
modesty, they declared I had so much of the "*frons
urbana*" about me, that I could not long remain contented without showing my (they said, ugly) physiognomy to the world.

I have constantly been considered generous—to myself; have proved myself affable—to customers who had
unpaid bills; and have always strenuously refused to
vend my conscience, except to a very high bidder: and
this on the undeniably sound principle, that my conscience, being a first-rate best-London-make water-proof
one, ought, in reason, to fetch a tolerable price, and not
to do a dirty job even for a friend, without, as Isaac
says, " a consideration."

I am, I may say, made of ambition. But I am
usually—at least, so say the malicious—as anxious for
success, as certain of failure. Jealousy, however, I
never feel; excepting, indeed, when one of my contemporaries excels or rivals me in any of the accomplishments which I pride myself on possessing. To censo-
riousness I have always had a vehement dislike; a dislike,
which has operated with peculiar energy since I became
an author, and a fair butt for the arrows of rebuke or
criticism. I am positive of my being charitable, from

actual inward experience of the emotions occasioned by that most excellent quality; for I have never even been able to conceive, how people can possibly grudge their shillings. And after having thus set forth some of my own peculiar properties of mind, the paper speaks for itself, in one remaining point ; and it is totally unnecessary for me to hint in a side-wind, or add in a postscript, that I am perfectly, purely, and inviolably, modest. I am not without fear, that my " I need not add," like that of my betters, here prefaces what I am in reality most anxious to insinuate, and most determined to declare.

My readers have long ago understood, that Mr. Jermyn is a poet, Mr. Quincy a radical, Mr. Heaviside a John Bull ; and that my friends have generally some one .or more peculiarly marked characteristic. They, having no doubt formed great expectations, will, however, look in vain for traits like these in me. The public, in fact, positively assure me of my being utterly guiltless of so horrid an act as the perpetration of poetry ; my conscience is indignant at the charge of radicalism; and my lank appearance, peaked nose, and parchment-coloured physiognomy, satisfactorily acquit me of any relationship to the Bull .family. Mr. Willoughby walks unbewildered in the labyrinths of British politics, as does Mr. Montagu in those of Greek choruses. But I can adduce pretty good presumptive evidence of my inability to perform the feats of the first, and have excellent positive testimony to my ignorance of the favourites of the second, in the frequent chastisements, and still more frequent rebukes, which have so often served at once to certify and to punish my deficiencies. Of being

a wit or a philosopher, I have never yet been accused;
and should be less surprised, at hearing myself branded
as a footpad or a pickpocket.

But, finding myself now indicted for the crime of
Book-making, at the awful bar of Public Opinion, I
gallantly show myself the man,

" Qui juris nodos, et legum ænigmata solvit"—

who disappoints the expectations of all clerks and under-
workers—who cruelly blasts the fair visions of fees and.
briefs which adorn and sweeten the waking as well as
the sleeping dreams of our barristers and attornies—
astounding at once judge, jury, witnesses, and audience,
by simply pleading " Guilty." I crave, however, to be
allowed to call witnesses to character; and by their
evidence it will satisfactorily be proved, that I am a
harmless and innocent drudge—not fond of running into
mischief of my own accord, though, perhaps, easily
deluded into it by others—neither a robber of orchards,
nor a picker of pockets—one whose genius can condescend, instead of galloping over the plains of Parnassus,
to take a quiet walk along the Slough road, and whose
appetites are of the humble cast, which relish humble
barley-broth as fully as imperial turtle soup.

. Thus, then, most noble public, you have before you—
expressa ad vivum—the Bartholomew who has so long
eluded you. He waits for your sentence—and, if it be
that of death—he begs the day appointed may not be
nearer than the third of December next, by which time
he expects to anticipate Jack Ketch, and save him the

trouble of performing his office.   Even then, he trusts, he shall still enjoy a posthumous existence.

Meanwhile, my nine Numbers must certainly become in the estimation of men the

          " —— Aonii turba novena jugi."

I positively *will not*, in compassion, read them out in public at any of our assemblies, lest the enraptured audience should rob the temples of Herodotus to crown the locks of Bouverie : and should declare our lúcubrations far more worthy than those of the Father of History, to bear the names of the Pierian damsels.

Behold, then, the pragmatical Quiz, the modest nondescript, while he yet remains before you.   Behold him, forced as he has been into the world by an extraordinary birth, and discordant parents.   And, when you have dubbed his nine literary children with the names of the Muses, he still hopes that you will be kind enough to add a tenth to the number, if it be only for the purpose of bestowing it on his next, and positively ultimate progeny.

THE LADDER OF THE LAW.

As once I mus'd on man's terrestrial state,
The wheel of Fortune, and the nod of Fate,
Wrapp'd in the mantle of a dream, I saw
The grand ascent, the Ladder of the Law.
  And thou, my Muse ! assist mine infant wing,
And teach to write, the Bard that may not sing ,
Although Parnassus, and its blest retreat,
Are full e'en now, and few can find a seat—

When mills and men make paper scarce enough
For all our Prose, our Poetry, our Stuff;
When all must publish—some from humble press,
Some bright and proud, and clad in gorgeous dress;
When daily journals boast their daily rhymes,
From Globe and Sun, to Chronicle and Times;
Give too to me—to others 'tis allow'd—
To try my fortune in the scribbling crowd;
Although, to see our wits, should strangers come,
We answer straightway, with a "Not at Home."
Although ho Butler's gems, no Milton's fire
Beam in my page, or flashes from my lyre;
My bark's unmoor'd, I venture from the shore,
Set all my sails, and ply my joyous oar.
 Nay, those that rhyme not, fear not to do worse
In sleepy Epic and in slow blank verse;
Not that we speak of poets; 'twere a crime
To chain a Milton in the bonds of rhyme;
As well enslave a nation of the free,
And lavish fetters on the swelling sea
Yet, where is nought to captivate the mind,
Th' expanding soul in pleasing thrall to bind,
There, there, at least (chime in, ye makers, chime!)
The ear is captur'd by the sounds of rhyme.
But, ho! my Muse! so soon, so far, astray?
When scarce begun our long and toilsome way?
In themes like ours, digression is—a flaw,
Return, and sing the Ladder of the Law!
 Th' ascent, which thousands in their course sustains,
Rests its broad foot on wide-extended plains;
Form'd by the labours of a by-gone race,
Profound in depth, and measureless in space.
An hundred voices of Stentorian sound
Too few to tell the makers of the ground;
Cases on Cases, and disputes on Law—
Report and Trial—Summons, Writ, and Flaw—
All, all, combine to form th' extended plain,
And dim the visions of the toilsome train.
 Ah! happy they who hail the setting sun,
Their bodies weary, yet their labours done.

Let not the haughty arrogance of pride
The humble blessings of the meek deride ;
By them no midnight lamp is dimly fed,
No dusky tome in midnight silence read ;
And Heaven hears the poor man's lowly pray'r,
And Peace, and Health, and Innocence, are there.
  Some o'er the plain all light and joyous skip,
Swift their career, but frail and slight their ship ;
Youth on their cheek, and lightness in their eye,
They live for pleasure, and by pleasure die.
Amid the thousands buried in their toil,
They course, unheeding, o'er the pond'rous soil ;
No weapons they to pierce its bosom bear,
Self is their god, and Idleness their snare ;
They sport and gambol round the Ladder's base,
Nor seek the prize, nor run the doubtful race. .
  Yet some to Fortune and to Cunning bend,
And deem the means made holy by the end ;
Behind—below—in silence, on they creep,
Climb o'er their honest neighbours on the steep ;
They seek a new and hidden path, and leave
The dull and just to labour and to grieve :
By stealth and plunder find a swifter flight,
E'en to the summit of the Ladder's height.
But when, that summit of the Ladder nigh,
They dare look downward with exulting eye ;
While they the harvest of their labours reap,
In plenty revel, or in leisure sleep—
Then, then, ye rash, ye valiant, who shall dare
The path to question, which hath led them there ?
  What if the waves of adverse Fortune roll,
The haughty threaten, and the strong control ?
Shall Heav'n's vindictive Justice suffer all ?
The bad to triumph, and the good to fall ?
A little while your tyrant course pursue,
Despise the humble, and revile the true :
Your quiv'ring bands in conscious guilt shall part,
And vainly seek to 'scape th' impending dart :
Riches have wings ! could you but on them fly,
And seek a dwelling 'neath a milder sky !

The word has sounded, and the bolt has sped—
The base are prostrate 'mid th' unhonour'd dead.
As thickest darkness treads on clearest light,
Their fall is deepest from their loftiest height.

  Ye few, who soar on Virtue's gladd'ning wing,
And serve your God, your Country, and your King,
Ye who have learn'd to scorn the base man's wile,
The tongue of Flatt'ry and the lip of Guile ;
If aught avail one feeble voice's praise
The pealing thunders of acclaim to raise—
Blest be your labours, and your fortunes blest,
Your joys unceasing, and your cares at rest.
Go ye triumphant on your onward way,
Still Honour's children, Virtue's surest stay ;
Each one, sustain blind Fortune's impious rage,
And pass unblemish'd on, from stage to stage ;
And ne'er to guile, to fraud, to falsehood, trust,
Nor deem expedient what thou doubtest just.

  Turn we to see the wan and haggard eye,
To watch the bosom heave in many a sigh ;
To see bright Health, and Beauty's angel grace
Fled from the care-worn and emaciate face ;
Where, young in years, but old in stage of life,
Fame spurs her destin'd victim to the strife.
Yes ! he, poor youth, a phantom to pursue,
Gave up the homely and the tranquil view,
No charms for him had soft domestic bliss,
The plains of Leisure and the stream of Peace.
He fled from all, and, hapless, fled to be
A wayward wanderer on a stormy sea
One, one faint light, that glimmer'd from afar,
He fondly dream'd a kind, a guiding, star ;
Yet little knew how many a surge would rise,
And toss his fragile vessel to the skies ;
And little deem'd, that, those dread perils past,
Yon meteor light would vanish in the blast.
The fairy vision, that Ambition spread—
The beaming torch, that kindly Hope hath fed—
All, all have vanish'd from the troubled air,
And left him woe, and darkness, and despair.

At the deep tolling of the midnight bell,
A little while he'd leave his 'custom'd cell,
Far from the tumult and the hum of men,
He stray'd by desert rock, and silent glen;
By gentle stream, or unfrequented wood,
He pour'd the musings of his pensive mood;
Now in deep thought and forward prospect lost,
Now by the waves of Care or Sorrow tost,
And 'times, in thought of brighter, happier years,
Beam'd the soft smile amidst the mourner's tears.
With upward gaze he'd wring his hands and sigh—
Bold was the cast, and hazardous the die;
Pursuing Fame from first to latest breath,
He sow'd for Glory, but he reap'd in Death!

In broken health and broken spirit sad,
He mourns the prospects that were fair and glad.
Mourns all his dreams of fleeting honours gone,
Unown'd, uncherish'd, silent, and alone;
He sees Oblivion wrap in murky gloom
His humble mem'ry and unhonour'd tomb;
His darling idol, vainly-worshipp'd Fame,
Snatch'd from his grasp, a vision and a name;
Smiles his last smile, and sighs his latest sigh,
And seeks his cot, to linger and to die.

He spoke not, wept not, murmur'd not: for he
Bent meek and lowly to high Heav'n's decree:
Yet, as the rising Spirit strove to fly,
And claim its birth-right in the realms on high,
Cast one faint look around, 'mid dark'ning gloom—
Saw none to weep the dying Victim's doom—
To bend in sorrow o'er his lowly bed—
To cheer him living, or to mourn him dead—
To cool his parch'd lip with Affection's stream—
To shed around him Hope's effulgent beam—
His manly bosom heav'd one parting sigh—
" 'Tis this," in agony he cried, " to die,
" With none to succour, and with none to save,
" To stay the hunger of the rav'nous grave,
" And yet 'tis mine—I sow'd the deadly seed,
" I struck the blow, I did the murd'rous deed,

" Then be it mine to bow beneath the rod,
" And still to cry, ' Thy will be done, O God ! ' "
   And there are those whose hearts are gentle, those,
Whose tears flow freely for another's woes ;
Seek they, the kind, the merciful, to know
His binding spell, and destiny of woe ?
His failing frame forbade th' unceasing toil—
Dark was the strife, yet mighty was the spoil ;
That spoil was doom'd to grace another's breast,
That strife, to give him to his house of rest.
Youth, Health, and Life—yes, all he fondly gave,
Self-doom'd, self-driven, to an early grave.
Fame was the curse's spring ; the foe, the dart
That cleft its passage to the victim's heart ;
Fame was the spell, the deadly spell of ill—
A beauteous idol, yet an idol still.
   Let gentle Mercy weep the Suff'rer's doom,
And dark'ning foliage twine around his tomb ;
Bind ye for him the early cypress wreath,
Mourn for the child of Sorrow and of Death !
O ! bid his ashes blest and tranquil sleep,
Nymphs of the grove, the fountain, and the deep !
For you he lov'd, for you he'd fondly gaze,
The fancied partners of his wand'ring ways,
Where the wild herb and op'ning flow'ret spring,
Where the gay lark expands his joyous wing ;
Where the dark forests of the mountain wave,
Where stormy blast and ocean surges rave ;
Or where the silence of the spreading grove
Charms the rapt soul to harmony and love.
   He rests amid the dust that gave him birth,
And stilly moulders in his mother Earth ;
The graven stones, and rustic sculpture tell,
How Fame's poor Victim struggled, droop'd, and fell.
   " Stranger ! here lie the crumbling limbs of one
" Whom Death cut off, ere Glory had begun ;
" O ! if on thee the gifts of Heav'n be shed,
" Weep, 'mid the mansions of the silent dead ;
" If Beauty's glow, and Talent's fire be thine,
" Snatch the bright gems from mad Ambition's shrine ;

" Lest thou, like him, cut off from joyous bloom,
" Tread in his path, and wither in his doom.
" Here the cold clay his ashes lightly press'd,
" Here we have borne him to his balmy rest ;
" May Pity's tear o'er him, the Mourner, flow,
" And all around the earliest flow'rets grow ;
" And yon dark yew its shielding branches wave,
" O'er Virtue's, Sorrow's, and Affection's grave."

ON THE IDLENESS OF AUTHORS.

"———— Non sat idoneus
Libro ferebaris————"

This, gentle reader, being the sum of Mr. Bouverie's
accusation against me, I have religiously determined to
sit down and begin writing immediately, though my
brain be as dry as a lemon-chip, and my fancy as barren
as a senior wrangler's. I am afraid, however, my dear
Public, that I am not writing this essay to amuse or
instruct you, but merely to fill up a certain number of
pages in the Ninth Number of the Miscellany, and therefore I think I may as well endeavour to vindicate myself
from the charge of idleness which has been alleged
against me, by my much-esteemed and respected friend
at the head of our undertaking. I must acknowledge
that I have begun three several articles, and burnt them ;
that night after night I have spoiled a new pen by dip-
ping it in the ink, and a clean sheet of paper by scrawl-
ing figures of all sizes and sorts upon it, one more hideous

than the other, to encourage myself to begin, and that all this has been in vain. I have yawned and bitten my lips, I have pulled off my neckcloth, coat, and waistcoat; but I have put off my labours day after day, and am now commencing an article when it ought to have been ready for the press: but I deny that I put it off for the gratification of my own laziness, but my respect for that worthy and enlightened part of the community, who are in favour of Catholic Emancipation, and who buy, and, I hope, read, the Eton Miscellany, is so great, that I could not bear to dedicate any but my brightest moments to an attempt at their amusement.

On the first day, therefore, shortly after tea, I descended to my narrow dwelling with a full intention of writing unmercifully. Having lounged about in the luxury of solitude for some time, I determined upon writing poetry, but not feeling mad enough for that very excellent intention, resolved to read Lord Byron. Accordingly, I began at " Childe Harold," and forgot every thing about the Miscellany, till I came to the end of " Manfred;" it was then nearly ten o'clock, and although the enthusiasm which I had desired and read for, so long and so earnestly, was certainly kindled, yet it was kindled to such a degree, that I could not bear a line of my own; so I seized the poker, and walked about the room, brandishing it with such enthusiasm, that I did nearly as much damage to the walls as the trunk-maker in the upper gallery, in the " Spectator;" and spouted the " Siege of Corinth," till I went to bed. Was this idleness? No! I gained from it a good deal of useful knowledge, which I will impart to my readers, namely, never to read Lord Byron instantly before they wish to poetize; and a great deal of pleasure, which I intend to keep to myself.

Tuesday.—I began to think that my fits of stupidity were, like the appearance of the Miscellany, periodical, and that they always came just when they should not, which is, I hope, very unlike that excellent publication. Read the "Spectator," and was beginning to write, when my new Sporting Magazine arrived. Struggled manfully on against time and inclination, when I recollected that I wanted to see whether they had reported the St. Leger correctly. So I despatched my article, and read the Sporting Magazine, returned to the Miscellany, read my composition over, did not think it good enough, particularly as I recollected that it would be an ungrateful return to be negligent because the public was indulgent, so I gave it *emendaturis ignibus.* Was this Idleness? No! it was respect.

. Wednesday.—Read the "Etonian" for a hint, and grew very angry at finding it so much better than the Miscellany; determined to write furiously, that I might surpass Gog. As it was to be a great undertaking, I considered long and deeply for a suitable subject, till at last it suddenly struck me that I should not be able. Was this Idleness? No! it was emulation.

Thursday.—Felt rather dull; gymnasticized for half an hour; found I was not in a humour for writing: so I took up the Miscellany, and endeavoured to console myself by reading my own productions—fell asleep; was this Idleness! No! it was accident.

' Friday, Mr. Bouverie, I was engaged, ' deeply
engaged. I am sorry, very sorry, Mr. Bouverie, but I
have bolted my door; I am reading hard, very hard. I
am deaf to the voice of an Editor; I am reading Walter
Scott's new novel.

Saturday.—I am at last writing this plain narrative
under every disadvantage, with a bad fire and a vacant
coal-box, with a great noise around me, and a fourth-form
boy doing his verses. I am writing, my dear Public,
with the melancholy consciousness that the stupidity
which has clung to me like a night-mare, ever since I
finished the " Victim," seems to possess the monotonous
regularity of a ticking clock, and to threaten the awful
durability of a trade-wind. Pity me, my dear Public, I
feel as dull as a prize ox, or a prize poem, if indeed the
latter ever has any feeling at all; and yet when, in defiance of all these horrors, I continue to write an essay,
which I am afraid, if the Miscellany is able to stand the
test of time, will only immortalize me as an ass, I am
stigmatized as being idle. I appeal to you, if indeed you
will listen to, or rather read my defence; whether I have
been so or not; and as it is contrary to the rules of justice
to condemn a man unheard, I should certainly recommend
you to acquit me at once. If I may judge from my own
feelings, although among the faults which I have the
misfortune to possess, I must confess that I am not in the
least deficient in vanity, yet I sincerely pity the reader of
this, conceiving, by a very palpable syllogism, that what
has been written with many yawns, will not be perused
without many more. But I must just go and see what

horses have won at Newmarket, and then I will come back and finish this directly.

NOTE BY BARTHOLOMEW BOUVERIE.

Coming into Mr. Jermyn's room at a time when his compositions ought to have been ready for the press, I found the room empty, and this unfinished essay on the table, where, I was informed by a lower boy, who came in whilst I was there, it had lain ever since the morning. As the Number was very late, and as this vindication itself affords a good practical apology for my accusation of Idleness, which Mr. Jermyn seems so bitterly to resent, I sent it off as it was, without waiting for the return of its volatile author.

GUATIMOZIN'S DEATH SONG.

No longer sounds the battle cry,
   The sword reposes in its sheath ;
No longer peal the rocks on high,
   With shouts of strife, and woe, and death :
The chain is on my red right hand,
Another wields my father's brand ;
And, in mid space, 'twixt life and death,
Receive my brief, my parting breath.

The hand is bound, the sword is cold,
   The warrior hastens to his grave ;
Yet ere the fleeting time be told,
   Hark to the death-song of the brave !
I could not do the villain deed,
I could not see my country bleed ;
Nor buy the splendor of a throne,
With widow's curse, and orphan's moan.

Go, tyrants ! seek your distant home,
   And traverse back the swelling main ;
Yet, never, o'er its plains of foam,
   Behold your country's hills again :

Let wind and storm in fury rise,
And darken round the azure skies ;
Nor ocean wave, nor earth, nor air,
The villain and the traitor bear ;

Or bear ye back to curse and ban,
    To stain with blood your father's land ;
The pest, the hate, of Gods and man,
    To bring the vengeful Furies' brand.
Away ! ye bear the seeds of war,
That Guilt hath purchas'd from afar,
And many a harvest, rich in woe,
Shall spring from that ye proudly sow.

Then, when the dales of verdant Spain,
    Resounding with the widow's cries,
Shall hear the battle-shout again,
    In thunder to the heavens rise
Look back along the stream of Time—
Behold the blot of dark'ning crime—
Behold the dust ye bleed to win,
The fountain of your country's sin.

Ye men of blood, of iron heart,
    Unfeeling as the swords ye wield,
Ye knew my swift unerring dart,
    Ye knew me in the bloody field ;
Ye knew me in the battle-shock—
I met it like the tow'ring rock ;
Ye knew me, when my country's shore
Was redd'ning with the Spaniard's gore.

Yet, did this bound and tortur'd hand
    Still feel the strength it felt before,
Still wield my father's glitt'ring brand,
    Still hurl the dart it hurl'd of yore—
Some victims on my tomb should fall,
Some mourners bear the fun'ral pall ;
And tears of friends, and tears of foes,
Bedew me in my last repose.

And yet I deem'd another fate
  Was riding on the breeze's wings,
And other destiny should wait
  The children of an hundred kings,
Than that the malice of my foes
Should mock my parting spirit's throes,
And Spaniard's sword and lance should wave
In triumph o'er the warrior's grave.

I felt the breeze that fann'd your sail,
  I saw ye on the eastern wave ;
Would that the wild and roaring gale
  Had plunged ye in an ocean grave ;
Would that my heart, in wisdom steel'd,
Had warn'd ye from our battle-field,
Nor met ye on the swelling seas,
With hand of love, and kiss of peace.

Pure is my soul, and pure my fame ;
  Then pure depart my dying breath,
And welcome, dread and raging flame,
  And welcome, agonies of death !
Far sweeter than the roses' bed,
Lead to the mansions of the dead ;
And bid my spirit wing its flight
To regions of ethereal light.

Ye Gods, who guard my father's throne,
  And watch the coming of its foes,
Avenge my country's wrongs—my own
  Leave to Oblivion's deep repose ;
Then rest upon the Spaniard's head,
The ban and vengeance of the dead ;
And ill on ill, and woe on woe,
Light on the villain and the foe !

ON FLATTERY.

Sir;

I cannot, for the life of me, conceive, why this most useful and agreeable talent should every where be so unmercifully mauled : it is really quite disgusting to hear the way in which some surly rascals abuse it, who, because they themselves never either said or deserved a civil thing, think it proper to dignify all gentle eulogiums with the names of lying stuff, fulsome nonsense, &c.; though they must themselves be conscious that they would leap as eagerly at the most despicable attempt at a panegyric, and swallow it down with as much greediness, as a half-starved cur would the wing of a chicken, or a half-starved author a good beef-steak.

But, lest these gentry, who frankly tell you their mind, and so kindly "inform you as a friend," that you are the veriest fool in the universe, should fall martyrs some day to their considerate and affectionate openness, I would recommend to them to take a small lesson from a hero, hight Daniel O'Rourke, if they are acquainted with him, if not, to form the acquaintance as soon as possible. "'Why, then,' says I, very civilly, because why? I was in his power entirely, 'Sir,' says I, 'plase your honour's glory, and with submission to your better judgment,' "—and so forth. It is quite delightful to contemplate the perseverance with which he, under every circumstance, "thinks it best to keep a civil tongue in his head any way." Poor man ! that so much urbanity should meet so little return !

I will try, however, for the benefit of those who are not blinded enough to slight this estimable pursuit, to draw up a few rules, and right well shall I be pleased, if I aid in the slightest degree any young aspirant after these honours.

In the first place, flattery may be well divided into two great branches, the practical and the colloquial. And now first for the practical.

. This species of flattery requires hardly any of that ability, without which the colloquial sinks into nothing ; the chief requisite is an imperturbable patience. It consists chiefly in permitting the intended gull to win in every trial of skill, strength, or learning, which may be proposed ; particularly, of course, on those points of which he is, justly or unjustly, vain. For example ; if he be a gentleman of the fancy, you must, with unshrinking fortitude, put on the gloves with him, as long and as often as he pleases, and must bear, like any martyr, the head-aches and bloody noses which will be the natural consequences of your exhibition, always taking care to display just as much skill as you can without foiling him. If he pique himself on being an excellent pedestrian (for these trifles are of course the things in which he is to be indulged), and, with intent to prove his prowess, takes you a walk of a few miles, you, on your return, must throw yourself eagerly in an arm-chair, declare you were never so " done " before in your life, that you never felt such a fagging walk ; seasoning the whole (though this belongs more properly to the colloquial), with suitable compliments to his own "iron frame" and "indefatigable powers."

'It is the second *genus*, however, which calls forth all your powers; the first is, in fact, a matter of course, and nothing more than a kind of conciliatory introduction to the second. Some little skill is perhaps necessary, in order not to yield too clumsily, for a clumsy compliment is far worse than nothing. The blindest dolt will soon be palled by a repetition of "You don't say so!" "Good heavens!" "How wonderful!" wound up, perhaps, by, "But then you are so clever!" The greatest fool must soon be tired of a fellow who roars out a horse-laugh at the wrong part of a good story; compliments a hypochondriac on his good looks, and pays his court to a lady of "a certain age," by remarking how well she wears.

The first, easiest, and most obvious branch of the colloquial kind, is flattery direct, as when you tell Miss ———— how beautifully she played that last air; or remark, with what extraordinary skill Dowager ———— managed to gain the odd trick. This, however, is so very easy, that it is almost worn out; so that, however high you may carry your panegyric, you will scarcely get any thing by it, as there is always somebody ready to out-lie you.

The second is the oblique, which is not quite so thread-bare as the first, and certainly has a most insinuating way about it, and a wonderfully disinterested appearance withal. A student in this line will, in company with a miser, lay great stress on precise economy; revile generosity of any kind as impiously throwing away the gifts of Providence; swear, that if he had a son, whom he suspected of spending sixpence a-year

more than was necessary, he would cut him off with a
shilling. He will relate, with the highest encomiums and
the most extravagant enthusiasm, an anecdote of the very
man to whom he is speaking, and, finally, will draw the
gull's character, or what he, blind and miserable wretch,
conceives to be such; and declare that he considers that,
as all that can be desirable for a friend or acquaintance.

The third, I shall adopt another person's expression in
calling the argumentative flattery: which is, the talent
of entering into a discussion with your *flatté*, and suffering yourself gradually to be convinced by his arguments;
of course your apostacy must not be too rapid, and it is
necessary to say something, in order to give your opponent an opportunity for refuting it. This serves the two
purposes, first, of impressing him with a good opinion
of his own oratorical talents, and thus bringing him into
a good humour; and secondly, of displaying your good
sense in appreciating his powers, and your candour in
yielding to them.

The fourth, or deferential kind, operates most readily
on persons of the busy-body and Lady Bountiful cha í
racter. This consists in asking your friend's opinion on
every subject, however trifling; listening to it with the
greatest possible respect; expressing your *unfeigned*
admiration of the same, and exclaiming at your happiness in having received it, and your pleasure in following
it. *Mem.* Always to reserve to yourself the privilege
of not acting up to your promise, in case the advice be
bad.

The last that I shall name, the comparative flattery,
is a powerful auxiliary of the oblique; though I hardly

know whether that ought to rank as flattery, which chiefly consists in depreciating others. For instance, in company with a blue you must blame the superficial studies of the present age, and contrast the solid acquirements of Hebrew, Chaldaic, Chinese, Arabic, and Kamschatchan, with the flimsy accomplishments now in vogue; and compare the mind of a modern Miss to the froth on the top of a trifle, which, on tasting, melts to nothing, and the other's fathomless stores of knowledge to the depth, solidity, and sweetness of the cream at the bottom. Unhappy he, who is delighted with the despicable and trivial pursuits of music, dancing, &c.

"Olli cæruleus supra caput astitit imber. "

The blue will soon burst on him in a furious volley of argument and learning.

And now, Mr. Bouverie, I take my leave, hoping that what I have said may perchance profit some junior professor of the art; and believe me,

Sir,

Ever yours,

MACSYCOPHANT.

P. S.   If at any time you should be in want of a puff, or a panegyrical advertisement, I am your man.

MY MISTRESS.

IN IMITATION OF ANACREON.

Master of the graphic art,
Paint the mistress of my heart;

Paint her, if thy pencil can,
Less a woman than a man ;
Seek not model true to find,
In the rest of woman-kind ,
Figure to thy mental view,
The *ne plus ultra* of a shrew ;
Paint thy utmost skill to try,
The matchless rancour of her eye ,
Paint her angry light that flashes,
From the cloud of sable lashes ;
Paint a brow the eye-lids crowning,
Furrow'd with eternal frowning ;
Paint in part and whole the organ,
Such as would become a Gorgon ,
Then with hair the temples rig,
Snaky as Medusa's wig.
Draw her face distent with fury,
To which Xantippe was an Houri ,
Colour not her face with pink,
But mingle violet with ink ;
Paint for her complexion's hue,
Blended tints of black and blue ;
Paint with India's reddest drug,
Nose sarcastically pug ;
Lips that grin with fury keener
Than the never-tam'd hyena ;
Draw with outline free and bold,
Form of Amazonian mould ;
Strong and sturdy as Thalestris,
Active and alert as Vestris ;
Quick and strong in vengeful mood,
Slow and weak in doing good ,
Paint her dress a torn capote,
Once 'twas muslin, but 'tis not.
On her wrist a cambric ruffle,
Torn in matrimonial scuffle ;
Gown and bodice that display,
Signs of yesterday's affray ;
But if thy art delights in scandal,
Paint her with a golden sandal,

In dress for queen of Lydia meet,
And me Alcides at her feet :
Or paint me as the Attic sage,   -
And her Xantippe in a rage ;   ,
While, after rain from pitcher flung,
He bides the thunder of her tongue ;
And more and more she growls unruly,
To see her husband take it coolly.

Master of the graphic art,
Well hast thou perform'd thy part ;
Lo, I see the fury rise,
I see it sparkle in her eyes :
She seems with inward rancour stung,
And venom rankles on her tongue—
Hold ! audacious artist, hold !
Soon the canvas' self will scold

THE TERRACE.

If music's voice can make the mournful gay,
And charm, enchantress-like, our cares away,
Sure ne'er had grief such cause as now to fly,
To seek a gloomier, more congenial sky.
The radiant sun hath set , with martial sounds,
Thy Castle, Windsor, Britain's pride, resounds ;
All ranks, all ages, to the scene repair,
To strut an hour away, and banish care.
'Tis not for me—I cannot, will not, tell,
Who ranks the smartest beau, the fairest belle ;
For all too well can please—too well all know
Their power, nor want the will t'inflict the blow.
Unwonted lustre boots and eyes acquire—
One shines with blacking, one with Cupid's fire ;
Red coats resistless steal each lady's heart,
The sons of Mars are proud such charms t'impart ;
Each with the other pleas'd, conspire to show
What music, mirth, and officers, can do.

Here struts th' apprentice, just from toil let loose,
Laughs at his betters, and affects jocose,
Thinks that all eyes are fix'd on him alone,
And counts his equals few—superior, none.
There, link'd with John the footman, arm in arm,
The simpering *femme de chambre* strives to charm ;
Should conversation flag (converse they must),
Rails at " the plaguy heat," " the plaguy dust,"
Asks if that's Eton in the distant view,
Perchance her dwelling, and her birth-place too.*
Alas ! how hard must John his bosom prove,
If all should fail to wake him into love !   .
Thrice happy fair one, who can now insure
(Such beaux aren't quite so easy to procure)
Some young and handsome captain of the Guards,
With whom to flirt (her smiles his sole rewards),
Whilst rustics, open-mouth'd, look back and stare,
Envy the soldier, and admire the fair.
O Goth ! O worse than Goth ! whom joys like these,
Joys felt by all who feel, refuse to please,
Whom cannot force to seek this festive scene,
The love of seeing, or of being seen.
Nor are Etonians wanting to complete
The motley group which hither weekly meet.
To France, to Spain, to Germany repair—
Go north, go south—yes, go the deuce knows where ;
Still an Etonian stares one in the face,
A friend, a welcome friend, in every place.
Ye, who can sympathize, with me lament
That winter comes such pleasures to prevent,
Lament that ev'nings festive now no more,
Bring not those harmless joys they brought before.

---

* This is almost a matter of fact : a countryman and his wife had met
some acquaintance on the terrace ; after the usual how-d'-ye-do's, a dead
silence ensued , they stood staring at each other quite at a loss what to
say, till one of the ladies, whom I remember as an inhabitant of this place,
broke out with " Isn't that Eton ?" pointing at the same time with a
finger, which convicted its owner of having made a good use of the needle.

EXTRACTS FROM BARTHOLOMEW'S DIARY.

" ———Pueri DIARIA poscunt."—MARTIAL.

My motto will, by means of a very slight exertion of
their excellent powers of mis-translation on the part of
my worthy school-fellows, completely justify my favouring
my readers with some curious and interesting extracts
from my Diary. And this exertion they surely will not
hesitate to make; seeing that they have, times without
number, made much greater for no such obliging purpose,
and with far more pernicious effect, as they have no doubt
felt from woeful experience. To all the lovers of *antiquity*
(and we are in duty bound to hope that they are numerous
within these venerable walls), I need offer no apology for
thus offering them a specimen of their favourite species
of composition.

Monday, June 4, 1827. Twelve o'clock. Walked out. Saw a little boy
—evidently a novice. Resolved to sound him. Asked him, if it were
true that a new periodical had that day commenced. He had heard of
some such thing, he replied. I asked, if he had read it ? " No." Did
he mean to read it ? " No." I perceived, fortunately, that the animal
was spinning a cock-chafer: and I beat him as he deserved—of course
for his cruelty to the poor creature. His passion rose high ; and when
I charged him with torturing the insect, he said, he had indeed been
torturing two brutes at a time ; but he could guess which of them it
was I felt for !

June 7. Saw a boy with what I thought an intelligent countenance.
Asked him how he liked the Miscellany, by Bartholomew Bouverie,
of Eton College ? " The what ?" " By whom ?" " Of where ?" said
he. The veriest lout and dolt that I ever saw in the whole course of
my existence—you might read it in his, or *its*, countenance.

June 16. Found a person who had read the Miscellany. Inquired
what he thought of it. " Without doubt, Sir," replied he, " it is very

well"—"Certainly Sir," I rejoined—" very well printed!" he resumed;
" but 'tis pity the writing is so contemptible !"

One scratched his head for five minutes, before he could conjure up,
in answer to my earnest inquiry, a recollection that he had heard one
Bartholomew Bouverie mentioned by a boy, some days ago. Another
boy was well aware that such a thing had been set on foot, but, being
very *blue*, said, "it was decidedly peregrine from, and integrally uncon-
genial to, literary consectations."

September 29. Complaint from printer that my compositions were
illegible in manuscript; from a customer, that it was extremely
difficult to read them in print. Publisher says my accounts, readers
say my wits, are deranged—or that those are employed in fire-lighting,
while these have gone a wool-gathering.

October 1. Proof-sheets came down. Wish some ingenious person
would get a patent for proof-sheets, and keep them all to himself.
Asked a boy if he knew what Tartarus and Elysium were ? He
responded in the affirmative. " What," I asked, " are the employments of their respective inhabitants ?" He said, he supposed that in
the one there were nothing but holidays and half-holidays, while the
horrors of the other consisted in a perpetual *Friday's business*. Surely,
I thought, there must be proof-sheets there too. Corrected them. At
last, my brain swam, and went round as fast as Ixion's ; I filled my
inkstand as often as the Danaides did their urn; and found, when I
had once waded through, that my labour was still, like that of Sisyphus,
to be begun again. My case therefore appears to be a sort of combination and consolidation of the miseries of all their's.

October 3. Wrote a light comic article. Happened to lay it on my
bed. Violent night mare when I fell asleep—tremendously oppressive.
Woke in a perspiration, and found my article lying just over my chest.

Mr. Quincy told me, that if I had adhered to his notions of equality,
and not placed this directly over and upon me, the misfortune would
never have happened.

October 4. Read a few pages of " The Eton Miscellany." Violent
head-ache, accompanied with nausea, after it. What can have been
the reason ?

October 5. Purchased two-penny-worth of snuff. Seeing the man
wrap it up in printed paper, had the curiosity to examine it ; after
exercising in the search more industry and ingenuity than the most
lynx-eyed collator of manuscripts ever displayed, deciphered, amidst
the fragrant dust, the name—*horresco referens*—of " The Eton Mis-

cellany." The man assured me it was by far the cheapest paper he could purchase; and that the author, printer, and publisher, had gone to the dogs together. I lifted up my hand in alarm to discover whether my head was on my shoulders, and was unspeakably gratified by ascertaining the fact through actual *digital* demonstration.

October 8   Asked a stranger, casually, what he thought of the last Number. " Why, Sir," answered he, " Mr. Bouverie has succeeded in proving one point to our satisfaction; this is, that there is in literature as in Pandæmonium,

'———in the lowest deep a lower deep :'

in short, that he could produce something worse than his fifth Number, which nine out of the ten or eleven people who read him, were either sceptically doubting, or unequivocally denying "

October 20. Inquired into my own character. I found myself, according to the reports of my various respondents, " floundering"— " mad, quite mad"—" a disgrace to Eton"—" a sullier of the glories of my worthy ancestors"—" a poor creature"—" a failure"—" fitter for Grub-street, London, than for High-street, Eton"—" an upstart" —" a plagiarist"—" one too proud to learn from the writings of his ancestors"—" a complete censor"—" a milk-and-water do-no-good"— *Cum multis aliis, quæ nunc perscribere longum est.**

Thus, alas! has my laudable curiosity, my ambition to learn what was my own condition and reputation, been repaid by my ungrateful informants.

Thus, gentle reader, in endeavouring to carry into effect the wishes, and to illustrate by example the precepts, of those who have in all ages bid men know themselves— thus have I been greeted! Thus, surrounded by the mysteries of hieroglyphic manuscripts, and the horrors of infinite proof-sheets—by hungry duns and indolent contributors—by epigrams without point, essays without maxim, tales without incident, and miseries without end; thus it is that, having hitherto survived and endured the

---

* Classical reader, bow in reverence to a quotation from—" The Latin Grammar."

whole, I intreat that, by your friendship and affection, the
brow of my publisher may be rendered something less
black than the ink with which I am writing ; that my *ten
or eleven* readers may be increased to *twelve or thirteen ;*
that I may not eat my own butter off my own philosophy,
or find my snuff enrolled in my wit ; then, indeed, if not
till then, endowed with the most pungent qualities, and
enabling itself at length

" ———virûm volitare per ora "

ODE TO THE SHADE OF WAT TYLER.

Shade of him, whose valiant tongue
On high the song of freedom sung ;
Shade of him, whose mighty soul
Would pay no taxes on his poll ;
Though, swift as lightning, civic sword
   Descended on thy fated head,
The blood of England's boldest pour'd,
   And number'd Tyler with the dead !

Still may thy spirit flap its wings,
At midnight, o'er the couch of kings ;
And peer and prelate tremble too,
In dread of nightly interview !
With patriot gesture of command,
   With eyes, that like thy forges gleam,
Lest Tyler's voice, and Tyler's hand,
   Be heard and seen in nightly dream.

For, scratching oft his bullet head,
The stout and swarthy warrior said,
" 'Tis hard, 'tis wondrous hard, to pay
" For toil and trouble day by day !
" For what art thou, my poll, to me,
   " Save work and labour for my hand :
" I will not pay a groat for thee,
   " At king's or parliament's command !

" What man of mettle pays a groat,
" For what with half one might be bought '
" His folly he shall deeply rue,
" Who four shall give, where needs but two.
" And I had been a dolt and calf,
    " To render four-pence for a brain,
" That never had been worth the half,
    " For use, or ornament, or gain.'

Our father delv'd, our mother span ;
And who was then the gentleman ?
We ne'er have known ; but this we wot,
That thou, most valiant chief, wert *not* !
For thou had'st vow'd a righteous vow,
    Had'st nobly sworn to level all ;
To plunge the proud and haughty brow
    In humble and deserved fall.

Then should the lordly giant stoop,
To stature of the dwarfling troop ;
The dwarfling sprout afresh, to raise
His honours to a giant's praise.
And thou had'st done it, but that fate
    The tissue of destruction spread,
Cut down thy carcass desolate,
    And sever'd, carcassless, thine head !

Could gentle Straw, and Miller too,
And Carter, Wat's disaster view ?
Yes ! Miller, Straw, and Carter—all
Beheld their warrior-Vulcan fall.
Yet still shall Tyler's glory live,
    And Tyler's verdant chaplet bloom,
While patriot forge and anvil thrive,
    Untam'd, unconquer'd by the tomb.

I hymn the gallant and the good
From Tyler down to Thistlewood ,
My muse the trophies grateful sings,
The deeds of Miller and of Ings ;

She sings of all, who, soon or late
  Have burst subjection's iron chain,
Have seal'd the bloody despot's fate,
  Or cleft a peer or priest in twain.

Shades, that soft Sedition woo,
Around the haunts of Peterloo !
That hover o'er the meeting halls
Where many a voice Stentorian bawls !
Still flit the sacred choir around,
  With " Freedom" let the garrets ring,
And vengeance soon in thunder sound,
  On church, and constable, and king.

And still the weaving race regale,
On patriotic beer and ale !
Or let them quaff the dingy stream
To " Tyler, Liberty, and Steam !"
And, weaving, let them dream they form
  A banner for the bold and free,
To ride amidst the raging storm
  In brightness and in majesty.

And whether you to spy it please
A cotton-spun Demosthenes ;
Or whether, from the shuttle's throw,
Come forth a weaving Cicero ;
Or whether, midst of smoke and steam,
  Some youthful Tyler's buds expand,
His race from thraldom to redeem,
  And level, yet exalt, the land ;

Still mid the cotton and the flax
Warm let the glow of Freedom wax :
Still mid the shuttles and the steam,
Bright let the flame of freedom gleam !
So men of taxes, men of law,
  In alley dun, and murky lane,
Shall find a Tyler or a Straw,
  To cleave the despot's slaves in twain !

OLIVER QUINCY.

THE DEATH OF THE ATHEIST,

A Fragment.

’Εχθρόν γε θνητοῖς, καὶ θεοῖς στυγουμένον. EURIP.

—————————— Loud blew the angry blast ;
The midnight storm was hurtling in the air,
And all was dark and desolate : the moon
Refus'd her wonted solace, and withdrew   .
Her train of starry satellites ! and all
Was buried in the fearfulness of night.
No light shone in the firmament, save where
The lightning flash'd across the traveller's path
In transient splendour, which but serv'd to show
The dangers and the horrors of the way.
All nature was convuls'd : the elements,
So lately sleeping in one happy calm
Of heav'nly peacefulness, now burst their bounds,
And seem'd one universal war to wage.
Loud burst the thunder-crash ; and each man look'd
Into his neighbour's face, as if to ask   ˆ
If that night were his last ? for it did seem
As if the Almighty Angel had dissolv'd
The charm of Death ; and that dread hour had come
Which borders on Eternity, when all
Must wake from the omnipotence of Death.   ˋ
   The horse had thrown his rider   his wild eyes
Seem'd starting from their sockets , he burst forth
Heedless and masterless; and with each flash
Rear'd his proud neck, and stood aghast with fear,ˋ
So terrible and awful was that night !.   ˎ
   But who was he, who, in that fearful hour,   ˙
Unknown and friendless, 'neath a stranger's roof,
Had found a cheerless welcome, but to breathe
His last farewell in frightful agony ?

'Twas the stern Atheist¹ in whose guilty face,
Death was too deeply stamp'd : within his breast
Tumultuous passions rag'd, more horrible
Than the proud elements, which round him pour'd
Their wrath in each loud thunder-crash, as if
Revolting at the actions of that man.
Fix'd was his glazed eye and motionless ;
His glance was terrible : upon his brow
A thousand crimes were trac'd, and on his lineaments
Despair, Disease, and miserable Death !
He turn'd to former deeds, and if perchance
Oblivion would disperse them, and produce
One gleam of sweet forgetfulness ; too soon
Remembrance would awake, and o'er him burst
In one long fearful groan of misery.

The thunder roll'd above him ; and more near
The lightning flash'd—oh ! surely in that hour
The Almighty wrath was kindled, for if aught
Did whisper of repentance, he would curl
His lip in bitter scorn.   Upon his brow ·
Sat the big heat-drops—and his voice howl'd forth
Wild and unmeaning sentences, which spoke
Of murder, sacrilege, and fearful deeds.

And now the thunder roll'd more awfully ;
All objects faded round him, and a film
Spread o'er his fixed eyes ; for Death held forth
His last and darkest terrors · in his throat
Th' unutterable words were chok'd, which breath'd
Curses and blasphemies , he heav'd his breast,
Gasping for breath—and gave one shriek—and died !

ON AMBITION.

Errori nomen virtus posuisset honestum.

· There are some·qualities·of the human mind, which
· though originally of doubtful merit, are generally con-

sidered as rather belonging to vice than virtue, because
their dependance upon the spirit in which they are implanted by nature is, so great, that it is this which ele-
vates or debases them to its own level, instead of their
having that effect upon the soul. Of this number is
ambition, which, certainly, if it shoot up in a mind which
is unable to check or direct it, is generally productive of
dreadful consequences. But surely it is unfair to assume,
that any abstract essence of the human mind is absolutely vicious, because it is frequently debased and
adulterated by the mixture of grosser passions, and
thereby rendered subservient to vice; when we see that
the same feeling, if it be awakened in a virtuous and
elevated soul, may produce great and beneficial effects;
particularly as it must be confessed that there is not one
single virtue which may not be so overstrained and misapplied, as to degenerate into a vice. It is certainly
very true that these passions, of which ambition is one,
are, if perverted, the main causes of crime. But in
allowing this, we must not forget that when properly
subdued, and directed to their real ends, they are also
the main springs of virtue, as without them the soul would
be utterly stagnant, and unconscious of any impulse,
either towards good or evil. The soul of man is naturally weak and sluggish, and the passions were bestowed
upon it by Divine Wisdom, in order that the perpetual
hurry and excitement in which they contribute to keep
it, might counteract the natural propensity to sloth and
inaction, and elevate it to those sublimer aspirations, in
which it seems to attain some portion of the future grandeur, which is marked out for it on a release from its

earthly imprisonment. It is but too true, that these pas-. sions must be originally kindled in a noble spirit, and even then, if not directed by judgment, and controlled by religion, they may be prostituted to meaner uses, and by an alloy of baser feelings, degraded into the character of appetites ; but is it from hence to be inferred, that they are. in themselves ignoble and vicious? Surely not.

Among the first and loftiest of these is the pure passion of ambition. I am not speaking of that petty selfishness, that mean avarice of false glory, which incites men, whose highest hopes are centered in the gratification of a despicable vanity, to attempt actions which are commonly considered great, that they may awe the vulgar into admiration, and shine forth the temporary wonders of the world ; not that base envy which, desiring nothing greater than the destruction of some hated rival, does not hesitate to wade through crimes of the deepest dye, to wrest fame or authority from the hands of his rival; not that mad ambition which will sacrifice every thing for the acquirement of glory, and heedless of blood and slaughter, of imprisonment and death, cares not what it may overthrow in its mad career, and would rather obtain renown by the destruction of a noble edifice, which had long been the admiration of the world, than rest contented and forgotten in honest obscurity ; but that real and pure desire of glory, which scorning the blandishments of sense, and the sordid bribery of the world, is cherished by a generous spirit, and aspires to the almost celestial object of nourishing and bringing to perfection all those numerous virtues

and talents, the seeds of which have been implanted by
nature in the deep recesses of the human mind, in order
that its energies may be exerted, and its invention exhausted, for the improvement and happiness of his fellow-
creatures.   It is impossible, when a being of this description
tion has, by the force of this pure ambition, obtained
those great objects which he originally proposed to himself, to gaze upon him dispensing blessings to his fellow-
men, without a feeling of veneration.   His mind seems
to have pierced through the clouds which envelop the
human understanding, and to stand aloof like a being of
a superior race.   These minds, indeed, are few ; but still
those whose ambition has been directed to great, though,
perhaps, unlawful ends, are as superior to men utterly
devoid of the excitement, as the mountain torrent, whose
strength and magnificence we admire, even whilst we tremble at its fury, is to the still pool whose waters stagnate
unobserved by all.   Many, indeed, are the absurdities
which ambition produces, when it has taken root in a
soul unable to bear the weight of so powerful a passion.
The man, who throws away his fortune and character, is
actuated by the desire of being considered a fine-spirited
fellow, in the estimation of those of his own stamp.   He
feels that by disdaining the voice of reason, and the
suggestions of his conscience, he may obtain applause
and admiration, and he has not sense enough to distinguish that it is not worth his acceptance.   The man who
determines to eat himself into renown, must do it in defiance of the dictates of human reason, and a human stomach.
But he feels himself impelled by a violent appetite for
fame, and therefore gorges himself like a hog.   Another,

who considers himself to have attained the height of fame
when he is able to swallow liquor like a sponge, fancies
that his mouth is parched with a thirst for true glory.
These ambitious fancies of a low mind are indeed truly
ridiculous, and show themselves in a thousand different
ways ;   they generally,   however,   bring their   own
punishment with them, as none but spirits of a superior
order can appreciate the value of this passion, and direct
it to its proper objects ; for ambition is like the sun, which
though his light be common to all, will suffer nothing
but the eagle to gaze upon it undazzled.

F. JERMYN.

THE BROCAS.

Where father Thamis rolls his glistring tyde,
  With sedgy bankes and willow frayle y-dight ;
  And many a lithsom boat is seen to glide
  Along the christall surface fleeting light ;
  Where many a barge-horse in full weary plight
  Against the streame his taske hardly dothe drag ;
  And many a bargeman, stout and sturdy wight,
  Doth sware, and curse, and baste the tired nag,
Ne spares ne oath ne stick to make him harder fag ;

Here, where magnificke Windsor's lordly towres
  O'erlook the sylver streame so haughtilye,
  And laugh at all old Time's mightiest powres,
  Rearing their heads in scornfull maiestee,
  A goodly heape and wondrous for to see ;
  Here stands Etona, learning's mother kynde,
  And here right many a lasie urchin bee,
  Trifling and geering still with emptie mynd,
Whilome in hateful school, by hatefull taske confyn'd—

Here too for Eton's sonnes a muddy lane,
  Spreds its blacke masse of durt and filth displaide;
  Most loathsom, fowle, and full of vildest staine,
  Of bull-dogges, and of pigges, blood that there laide :
  O'er this ill place a dark Tartarean shade,
  Great Sol doth alway hide, and alway lowre,
  Tartarean smoke is with its dust dismaide,*
  As black with thickest fog and sootie powre,
It spreds a murky night in summer's brightest howre.

And through this darksom dredd and glooming den,
  Receptacle accurs'd of mudde and night,
  (Which nye too pois'nous is for living men,   ·
  Save whom long use of filthe and custom's might,
  Woe teach to dwell in this most filthie plight,)
  Through this blacke hole, a plaine you may beholde,
  Renoun'd for badger-bait and bull-dogges fight ;
  Here too is many a batter'd boat and olde,
And many a subtle varlet, brasen-faced and bolde.

A bargeman wight was pricking† on this plaine,
  Y-cladd in ierkin olde and shoes worne out,
  With sturdy face, whereon did still remaine
  The blackened markes of many a bloody bout,
  And blood-shot eies and blow-distended snout ;
  In his right hand a smarting whip he had,
  And in his left a cudgel thick and stout,
  Quarrelsome wight, I wot, he was and badde,
And nothing did he dread, but ever was y-drad.

A peareless elfe was he in boxing ring,
  And heaped blowes lyke yron hammers strong,
  And joyed in fiersest brawle and ryoting,
  And for contention eagerly did long ; ·
  Ne ever right did love, but alway wrong.

---

* Faery Queene, I. iv. 4, 5.—" The purest skye with brightnesse they dismaide."

† Vide beginning of the Faery Queene.—Some commentators read, " whipping," for " pricking," but with no manuscript authority.

It chaunst that then a little childe did pas
Under the horses nose that waie along,
And ror'd, and roll'd about upon the gras :
A durtie littel bratte, and impudent he was.

Him then with smarting lash the bargeman wight,
As thus the teme he squalling did effraye,-
Harshly and roughly on the face did smight ;
" Thou durtie littel urchin, goe thy waie,
" Ne fraye the nags," quoth he, " ne longer stay."
And moe he would have added, but the childe
Smarting with paine, eftsoones did ronne awaie,
With grones, and screeching, and with clamour wilde ;
Whereat the motlie throng the bargeman much revyl'd.

One yong and lusty elfe above the rest,
Full lowdely cryde, " Thou villen vild and base,
" Thou wicked raskall, ruthless and unblest,
Thou caitiff, merciless, sans good or grace,
" Why strak'st thou thus the urchin in the face ?"
" Fool," quoth the other most uncourteously,
" Take heed lest thou too rew." " If such the cace,"
Then aunswered streight the first with boldened eie,
" Come fight, and thou eftsoones on muddye erth shalt lye."

As when two lyons dredd or rugged beares,
In some lone woode doe battle o'er their praie,
Each the other gryps, and with his teethen teares
His mangled sydes in this contentious fraye ;
Ne this ne that his enimy may slaye,
Ne either one will yeld the slaughtered hart ;
But ever doe in horrible affraye
With yre and dolour ever howle and smart,
The whyle the ruddy blood doth streame from every part ;

Thus they with murd'rous fystes doe engage,
Whyle all arownd the crowde them doth admire,
How eache doth ever hitte, and ever rage,
And bruze the other's face with deadly yre,
And gard, and hurtle rownd in warlike gyre ;

And then they smott and thondred mighty blowes,
Inflamed much with baleful anger's fyre :
Blacke is each eie, and bloody is eache nose,
Such dreddfull battel doe these wroth and furious foes.

Eache stricken strykes, and felling each is feld,
  Till that the champyons did so fiercely fight,
  That they their fystes coulde hardly longer weld ;
  Yet still the crowde doe showte with strength and might,
  Ayding their rage and vengeable despight ;
  And still with handes and feete most greedily
  (In sooth, I wote, it is a goodly sight)
  Doe squeeze and kycke and shove, them for to see ,
While to Dan Sathan eien and limbes devoted bee.

But now, aye me ! the skye with clowdes doth lowre,
  And lightning eke doth flashe, and thondre rore ;
  Notus and Boreas stryve in wrathful stowre,
  And streaming torrents of thick raine doe poure ;
  And dryve the hers foes from the drenched shore ;
  Ne conquered either is, ne conquer may ;
  But all must flee, ne ought can stand before
  The pelting streame, but all doe ronne awaie,
For drowned, drowned will they bee, if they doe staye.

Thus rainy streames and stormy thondre wylde,
  Ended this cruel fyght and furor madde ;
  Drave off the champyon of the durtie childe,
  And the stout wight in ierkin olde y-cladd.
  Pity it is and misadventure sadde,
  Combat so fiers should end so shamefullye ;
  Pity and eft disgraceful want and badde,
  That elfes so brave should lack of victoree ;
But I am sleepy, gents, and, certes, so are yee.

ON PRIDE OF BIRTH.

Sir;

It always appeared to me that nothing was so absurd, or so ridiculous, as pride of ancestry; and in truth it is seldom seen, except in those, whose fortunes having long since decayed, their titles remain an useless weight, an unprofitable honour, and only tending to show what their ancestors were, and what they are. For it is notorious, that in poor Lords this haughtiness is chiefly found; a certain class of people are always glad to substitute etiquette for wealth, and pomposity for power. Thus we find a laudable similarity between German Princes and Scotch Noblemen, as they are in general very poor, and very proud. In Germany every cottager is an Elector, and every pig-driver a Prince; the Irishmen in their humblest cabins, are nothing to them. And in Scotland, all

> "The bootless host of high-born beggars,
> Mackays, Mackenzies, and Macgregors,"

though they may only possess a slip of land, which never bore any thing but thistles, think themselves on a par with the first Duke in England. In the poorest nobility is this absurdity chiefly found, just as the ugliest (or more politely speaking, *plainest*) women dress in the gayest colours.

How miserable it is to go to the house of one of these

falling columns ; every thing around has the appearance of poverty, and formality. How we are startled on entering the porch,

> " Where the gaunt mastiff, snarling at the gate,
> Growls at the beggar, whom he longs to eat."

Every thing looks meagre and desolate. Green baize pinned down for carpets, prints of old " Running Horses," the property of some one long ago deceased ; few chairs in the room, and those worn out ; and then the master of the house is treated by his few servants, and expects to be treated by his guests, with great reverence, though they may be by far his superiors in wealth, power, and merit. And though certainly, *cæteris paribus*, men of good family are to be preferred, it must only be in that case. For my part, I care little who a man's ancestors were, before his grandfather; for surely we are to be estimated by what we *are*, not what our forefathers *were*.

I never shall forget the inimitable reply of the Lord Chancellor Thurlow to the Duke of Grafton, who let drop some insinuations about the lowness of his birth. Lord Thurlow rose from the wool-sack, advanced several steps into the House, and said something to this effect to the trembling Duke :—" When I look round this House, I see its brightest ornaments, who have obtained their honours by their own virtues, and not through the winding-sheet of their fathers."

We shall find that two of our greatest Statesmen commenced their public lives as commoners—Sir Robert

Walpole, and the Earl of Chatham, while some of our weakest were noblemen, as the Duke of Newcastle, and Lord North.

A most just and witty remark was made on this subject by Sheridan, and will serve for a conclusion to this Paper: "Nobility," he said, "ought to be burnt, like a Japanese widow, on the funeral pile of the estate."

Your's, faithfully,

B————.*

TINTERNE ABBEY.

Amid yon Abbey's vaulted aisles,
Amid yon Chapel's ruin'd piles,
Where ivied walls their towers raise,
The monuments of prouder days—
Where is the chaunt's melodious breath?
    Where is the Monkish power old?
The Minstrel's voice is hush'd in death,
    The Monk himself in the grave is cold!
Beneath yon chapel's ruin'd heap,
The fathers of the Abbey sleep.

And though no chaunt, no organ's sound
Re-echoes o'er the hallow'd ground,
'Tis yet a pleasure to survey
These ruins cas'd in stern decay.
And still the Vaga's wandering tide
    Rolls on its murmuring wave,
It sooth'd the abbot in his pride,
    It now flows by his grave.
And still the waving forest's gloom
Hangs o'er the lonely monkish tomb.

No torch gleams o'er the mould'ring stones,
Where rest the mitred abbot's bones:

---

* My Correspondent must answer for his own sentiments.

Scarce can the moonlight's placid beam
Through the ivied windows stream :
Each ruin'd arch, each noble hall,
Only mark how great its fall.

It seems as though, in some airy dream,
We float on Time's departed stream,
And when we see this beauteous spot,
The graves of men long since forgot,
Some inward feeling seems to bind
Our hearts to all now left behind.
No graven stones enshroud their bones,
    No hallow'd masses sound ;
This ruin's gloom frowns o'er their tomb,
    And casts a spell around ;
A spell which in our thoughts entwin'd,
Casts a deep pleasure o'er the mind.

[We extract the following Stanzas from a Correspondent's communication]

ON THE DEATH OF EMMA.

*   *   *   *

But no—the clay-cold earth has chill'd
    Thy fair and lovely breast ;
The icy hand of death has clos'd
    Thy lips in endless rest.

O sad and grievous was the hour,
    When they laid thee on thy bier !
And many a youth and maiden dropp'd
    With me the glist'ning tear.

*   *   *   *

No shouts, or martial trump was heard,
    That grace the soldier's tomb ;
No clarion shrill, or muffled drum,
    Broke through the silent gloom :

No sound was heard, but sounds of woe,
    As they laid thee in thy bed ;
Save the deep-ton'd and solemn dirge,
    The anthem of the dead.

Ah ! weep ye brooks and grassy meads,
　　Where, wand'ring side by side,
We view'd the sun's departing beams,
　　Reflected in the tide :

And talk'd of joys too soon, alas '
　　Dissolv'd, and pleasures lost,
For, as a flow'r, you died away,
　　Nipt by the wintry frost.

　　*　　　*　　　*　　　*

My hand thy grass-green tomb shall deck—
　　(Bound by Affection's ties).
And many a flow'ret's hue shall mark
　　The spot where Virtue lies.　　　W. P.

ON COLERIDGE'S POETRY.

The fond and unmixed love and admiration which is the natural and graceful
temper of early youth.—COLERIDGE.

Sir ;

When a young man writes and sends forth his writings
to the public, he requires a certain allowance to be
made for his youth, which older and more experienced
judges are willing to grant, for fear of crushing, by ill-
timed severity, the promise of maturer years. Pardon
for his faults is all he can hope, and without that he
dies. But when a young man assumes the office of a
critic, and presumes to blame the works of men of superior years and understanding, he not only arrogantly
judges before his judgment is matured, but forfeits all
claim to that indulgence of which he is so much himself
in need, and may bitterly rue a decision which he probably may afterwards change, and which he now puts forth
as insolently, as he had hastily assumed it. I was led
into this thought by seeing how much it is the cant of
the day to abuse certain authors of our own time, but par-

ticularly the writer from whom my motto is taken; not
that I believe his fame will be in the least injured by the
cry which Envy, or the Fashion, or whatever it be, raises
against him, but that I am sorry to observe that cry
reiterated by those whom it least becomes, and who, if
they are unable to look with admiration, should contemplate, at least, with respect, a man who has passed fifty
years of a laborious life in the pursuits of literature, and
who is as far above those who rail against him, as light
is above darkness.

But as I am eager to hope, so am I willing to believe,
that this judgment has been hastily assumed, and will
as quickly be repented of; for though I am by no means
unwilling to confess that there are many passages in the
author of the Christabel which do not meet my notions
of exalted poetry, yet there are many which show that
vigour of imagination and expression which have scarcely
been surpassed, in my opinion, in the present day; and
I think there are few who can appreciate genuine poetry,
that will not admire that splendid composition of Kubla
Khan, nor shudder at the masterly picture of the soul's
agony pourtrayed in the "Pains of Sleep." I would
instance briefly this passage:

> "But yesternight I pray'd aloud
>   In anguish and in agony,
> Upstarting from the fiendish crowd
>   Of shapes and thoughts that tortur'd me.
> A lurid light, a trampling throng,
> Sense of intolerable wrong,
> And whom I scorned, those only strong!
> Thirst of Revenge, the powerless will,
> Still baffled, and yet burning still!
> Desire with loathing strangely mix'd
> On wild and hateful objects fix'd," &c &c.

I would also bring forward one passage from the Christabel : not with any vain desire of lauding a man, whom, I feel to be as far above the praises of the world as he is, careless of its censure, but with the wish, and I hope not a vain one, that some, who, perhaps, had not seen or regarded these lines, may be struck by their beauty, and confess that such a passage alone is enough to stamp the author a poet of the highest and most exalted cast. I allude to that part concerning the quarrel of lord Roland and sir Leoline :—

> " Alas ! they had been friends in youth,
> But whispering tongues can poison truth ;
> And constancy lives in realms above ;
>   And life is thorny ; and youth is vain ;
> And to be wrath with one we love,
>   Doth work like madness in the brain.
> And thus it chanc'd, as I divine,
> With Roland and Sir Leoline ;
> Each spake words of high disdain,
>   And insult to his heart's best brother ;
> They parted—ne'er to meet again !
> But never either found another,
> To free the hollow heart from paining—
> They stood aloof, the scars remaining,
> Like cliffs which had been rent asunder :
>   A dreary sea now flows between,
> But neither heat, nor frost, nor thunder,
>   Shall wholly do away, I ween,
> The marks of that which once hath been."

I do not expect, nor do I hope, that the admirers of the sickly trash which is now so prevalent, should admire with me the nervous vigour of this passage. Those who delight in that which is now called poetry, that mixture of effeminate sweetness which has no thought beyond coronets of flowers; languid light, azure skies, sunny seas, the Day-god, and the Honey-bird, to compose which, costs not a 'moment's thought, and is within the reach of any would-be-poet of fourteen. The effusions of girls and of children, with which our daily and weekly publications teem, I leave to revel in a·sweetness which may touch the sense, ·but cannot penetrate the heart; nor ·would I have them praise what I am sure they cannot appreciate, nor do I fear forfeiting all claim to lenity from them for my own faults, since I would rather have their censure than their praise, and " *Discipularum inter jube plorare cathedras.*"

Your humble servant,

F.

I believe that much of' the warmth displayed in the letter of my Correspondent might have been spared, without any disparagement thereby occasioned to the merits or the reputation of Mr. Coleridge. Byron has railed at him ; but few will, I fear, agree with my worthy friend, in thinking Mr. C., according to the sweeping assertion contained in the letter, as far superior to his lordship, " as light is above darkness." Whether it be perfectly fair to put Mr. C. on a level with poets " of the highest and most exalted caste," my Correspondent is perhaps fitted—I most certainly dare not consider myself so—to determine. But I believe, that neither my voice nor his, however loudly raised, however frequently exerted, can have much effect on the present opinion entertained, not by partial friends on the one hand, and prejudiced enemies on the other, but by the public at large, of the merits of Messrs. Wordsworth and Coleridge. I may venture to say, it is pretty generally understood, that the sentiments of their judges are pretty much fixed·on the subject ; and the complaints which are raised against them have for their basis, not an assertion of want of genius on their part, but a remonstrance and protestation against the manner in which they have chosen to use the bright and precious gem, which they are on all hands allowed to possess.

B. Bouverie.

*** In the Ninth Number, two compositions, namely, the Death of the Atheist, and that on Coleridge's Poetry, are the work of Correspondents, my contemporaries, but not now Etonians.

ETON MISCELLANY,

No. X.

INTRODUCTION.

[HÆC decies repetita placebit.—Hor.

MOST of those who are at all interested in the matter are probably of an opinion, to which I myself beg leave to subscribe, that my readers and I, such as we are, are now by far too intimately acquainted to require an *Introduction*. And, moreover, as my literary, or scribbling, existence has now nearly reached its termination, I beg to refer all those of my friends who have the least curiosity to investigate the characters, or learn the fates, of my companions and myself, to the conclusion of this Number, where they will actually perceive the destined boundary—the bourn from which poor Bartholomew, at least, never shall return.

I shall, therefore, at present, content myself with presenting to them, for an occupation, if not an entertainment, an Epistle which effectually redeems itself from any charge of obsequiousness, which the idle or the

malignant caviller might be disposed to cast upon it—
an Epistle which must, at least, be allowed the credit
of one strong evidence of impartiality; namely, the
undeniable fact, that it is not *partial*.

A METRICAL EPISTLE

To one BARTHOLOMEW BOUVERIE,

ON THE MERITS OF A PUBLICATION CALLED "THE ETON MISCELLANY."

——— Opus teneras mordaci radere vero
Auriculas.——PERSIUS.

Most potent, grave, and rev'rend sage,
Father of the prosy page!
Valiant hero, king of men,
Wielder of the inky pen!
Or, if it suit thy lordly will,
Sov'reign of the grey goose-quill!
Whether "Bartle" please thine ear,
Or "Bouv'rie" you delight to hear,*
Hear thy vot'ries, sad and few,
Most excellent Bartholomew!
See thy mourning children, see,
Most high and mighty Bouverie!
First in the van let Quincy come,
With blast of trump and beat of drum;
The cap of Freedom on his head,
Himself with Freedom's victuals fed—

---

* Sive tu Lucina probas vocari,
Seu Genitalis.—HOR.

For trump and drum shall surely see
That gentle youth's catastrophe,
Where headsman's axe pours forth the flood
Of Freedom's veins, in Quincy's blood !
  'Gainst Willoughby and Rice I'd weigh
The hundredth of an author's pay,
And fear the shavings of a feather
Would overbalance all together.
Then, given to the public view,
Comes modest Mr. Montague ;
Yet prithee, sith so modest, why
Join'd he the Bouv'rie fox-hounds' cry ? ,
And, sith so kindly, why translate
Things worthy of a milder fate ?
  Nay, friend, your Poet, Mr Jermyn,
Is, to my mind, but sorry vermin ,
And future ages will, 'tis said,
For Heaviside read Heavyhead—
If future ages e'er shall see
The works of Bartle Bouverie.
  Behold the line ! the goodly band
As waiting for their sentence, stand.
Mark Antony—and David's bump,
That Cambro-Plinlimmonian thump ;
Next let the Critic, judge-like, rise,
With stern judicial wand and eyes ;
To rake and search the scribblers' mine,
From Number One to Number Nine.

  " ' No doubt my readers wish to see
Who is this Bartle Bouverie :'
Thus thou beginn'st, audacious elf,
With puff oblique upon thyself ;
Yet might the truth be told—you stare—
Your readers neither know nor care.
And grant, thine head above the wave,
Thy trunk is in the wat'ry grave—
And *sans* a trunk, a man must be
Nor more nor less than *Nobody.*

" In Dull Clubs does thy genius shine?
No club is duller, friend, than thine.
In thee Hibernian readers spy
' Prediction,' *sans* a prophecy;
And Bulls for member of their clan,
Shall hail the ' parchment-colour'd' man.
Who half so fit to tell of thee,
Fair Nothing, as this Nobody ?
And yet the tale, though worn and old,
Might, *certes*, have been better told.
 " If Homer's close be lame a few,
One foot, say—thine is lame of two ;
Yes—thou may'st climb for life, and still
Stand low on the Parnassian hill
Thy modest tongue reveals thy state,
' A poet not so very great'—
Yet soon the thin disguises fall,
And show that thou art—none at all !
Hark, friend ! thy list of crimes is large,
But none lay *this* one to thy charge !
They who thy parting line obey,
And hie to vender's shops away,
Shall swiftly find their fare the worse,
And wish their shillings—in their purse.
 " For ' many' things we find but few
And scant, to praise in Number Two.
Go, seek from Bear and Blacking brood
A tongue to tell thy gratitude ;
Well would they thine occasions fit,
And put *some* polish on thy wit !
And whence this Letter ' On Ennui ?'
Behold its model, friend, in thee ;
Let him, who wills to feel her pow'r,
Indulge in thee for half an hour.
Thy ' Patriot' takes a deeper trace
Of rage in 's-brandy-glowing face ;
And yet, ye gods ! the cunning knave
Amidst this rage ' his wrongs forgave !'
On ' Gifford's Ford' we say, good sooth,
'Tis Gifford's Ford in deed and truth ;

For Ford and Gifford, noble pair,
In copious Extracts figure there.
Then, Measter Ploughtail's mother-wit—
For thee a Correspondent fit—
But wherefore thus from page to page
Drawls on the Critic's vengeful rage ?
Or wherefore should so cruel doom
Molest thine essays in their tomb !
Yet Justice owns, that ' Peter Puff,'
And ' Philomyst,' are good enough.
But though Utopia *nowhere* dwells,
With magic wisdom Bartle tells,
Some find it 'mid the groves and trees,
And some amid the swelling seas ;
And truth if Orange standard be
Fair Britain's only ' panoply,'
Through silken armour many a dart
Will make poor Britain's sides to smart.
And, prithee, what thyself dost deem,
With ' Mushroom Gentlemen ' for theme ?
For all shall see, who Bartle scan,
A Mushroom—not a Gentleman.
If Virgil breath'd our upper air,
He came to little purpose there ;
Thy ' Postmen ' are a bitter pill,
And Master Pleadwell pleadeth ill.
The Monarch of the Lion-heart
Hath perish'd by ignoble dart ;
For thou hast kill'd him—or hast tried,
By badly singing how he died.
But hail, Conclusion, Labours done !
Thou brightest gem of Volume One !
But brightest—be my reason pass'd—
Brightest—because thou wert the last !
    " In Number Six doth Bartle dare
Ancients with Moderns to compare ?
Yet who will judge, that hath not read,
Or speak malignly of the dead ?
We'll freely own we skipp'd the bout,
And left them there to fight it out.

Yet, 'mid the whole Reciping school,
Where are ' Specifics for a fool ?'
For none could better teach the art,
Than who so oft had play'd the part.
But how ? what's here ? Misnomer sad !
' Good Writing ' is but writing bad !
Thy lips would water, as thine eye
Did yonder words, " On Dinners," spy ;
Your ' Ada ' sits in shady bow'r,
Where cabbage springs, and cauliflow'r,
And soothes her woes by homely means—
With thoughts on Raymond—and on greens !
Good Bartle, too, his reader woos
With lines from Beelzebub and Shoes ;
Fit reading for the fry that dwell
In Mother Eton's holy dell !

  " See Introduction's threat'ning phiz,
And ' Victim,' that no victim is :
Shipwrecks of Hope and vain desire
Are wrecks that best befit thy lyre ;
Let thistle bloom, and nettle wave,
O'er Bouv'rie's, Jermyn's, Quincy's grave !
Next, ' Letter from the Country,' see ;
Far happier had it been for thee,
If, since produc'd, 'neath rural shade,
Still in the Country thou had'st staid !
And canst thou dare to write ' On Tea,'
Most milk-and-water Bouverie ?
Yet whence should ' Gothic Fragments ' come,
Save from the brain of Gothic chum ?
If Jermyn dreads disastrous ball,
Why show his visage there at all ?
For giddy ball, and senseless rout,
Can manage well to do without ;
Yet still, perchance 'tis there he'll see
His best and fittest company.

  " Bright picture of the sapient youth,
All Wisdom, Innocence, and Truth !
That greets our fond, but weary eyne,
On threshold-stone of Number Nine !

Beware, beware ! lest raptur'd Muse
Should Bartle for her husband choose ;
The loving pair together fly,
With billing, cooing, vow, and sigh ;
He, riding on the airy wind,
She, on a pillion snug behind.
To Idle Authors deal we praise—
And be they idle all their days !
Pray we the gods, such idle be,
As Jermyn, Rice, and Bouverie !
And prithee what has bright Ambition
To do with Bouverie's condition ?
His proudest wishes dare not soar
Beyond a dozen or a score ;
And, truth, say creditable men,
His readers are but nine or ten.
　　" O never soil thy sterling worth,
Bartle most dear, with ' Pride of Birth ;'
With half an eye we see, and know
Thy parents were but poor and low.
　　" Let truant Rice nocturnal stray
By sylvan dell and old Abbaye ;
Let Quincy live by Freedom's laws,
And die a martyr to her cause ;
For strawberries' and melon's fate,
Let Fred, the Speaker, legislate ;
Let Phil, the Classic, pine away
O'er Chorus, Particle, and Play ;
Let Jermyn dance, till scarce he feels,
If topmost be his head or heels ;
And sapient Heaviside descry
Th' impending storms of Popery ;
Do thou, arch-scribbler, swiftly come
To darkling Pandæmonium ;
And struggle on, thyself to save
From Lethe's dim and murky wave ;
Though bankrupt, still, or soon or late,
Thou'lt pay one debt—the debt of Fate."
　　He spoke the doom ; the audience cry,
' Away, away with Bouverie ;'

And urchins toss their caps, and shout
In triumph o'er the hapless lout.
   ' The best fall first,'* the ancients said ;
His brains, who spoke it, were of lead ;
The test of time proclaims, the worst
Shall fall into oblivion first,
Then soon, for he's the worst of all,
Shall vainly-struggling Bartle fall ;
And lest he seek Lethæan strand,
Ere our epistle ' come to hand,'
I, Mordax, his most faithful friend,
Here bring my labours to an end.

MORDAX.

THE DEATH OF RICHARD CŒUR DE LION

Writhing with pain, those pangs too proud to show,
Cursing the vengeful hand that gave the blow ;
His eye-balls gleaming with tempestuous fire,
Mute, but expressive symbols of his ire ;
By Death unalter'd, by Despair unbent,
Richard expiring lay beneath his tent.
" Let him," he cried, " who sought this life, draw nigh,
" And view at once his king and victim die.
" Bertram de Gourdon nam'd, whose trait'rous dart
" Hath pierc'd, and e'en may quench, this ' Lion Heart.'
" To God, who knows what motive wing'd the steel,
" Alone for pardon must the wretch appeal ;
" But ne'er can I his dark designs forgive,
" He must not hope, he must not sue to live."

In fetters bound the noble archer came,
His brow bespoke no fear, nor sense of shame ;
A frown sat there, which seem'd at once to brave
The death, the tortures, he so lately gave ;

Optima prima ferè manibus rapiuntur avaris.

His step was firm, his eye, that told of woe,
With glance repaid the glances of his foe.
"Seek'st thou," he said, " my reason for the deed,
"By which thou bleed'st, and I perchance may bleed?
"Ask thine own conscience—who but thou hast torn
" (Ought else without a murmur I had borne!)·
" Torn from me all I lov'd, or valued most!
" My sire, my brothers twain—for ever lost?
" Their shades for vengeance call'd, nor call'd unheard,
" T' avenge their death, my own have I incurr'd;
" With fatal aim the fatal arrow flew
" Its reeking barb with thy best blood t'imbue;
" And whilst it quiver'd rankling in thy breast,
" My sire's, my brother's wrongs, and mine, redress'd.
" Think not that I your royal mercy crave,
" Think not I dread the dungeon or the grave;
" What though I stoop to justify the deed,
" What though for me the ties of Nature plead,
" It is not fear—it is, that all may know,
" Not unprovok'd, I laid my monarch low.
" Now, tyrant, do thy worst—I stand prepar'd;
" Torture, or chains, or death, are nought compar'd
" To that delight, that feeling of content,
" Which to this breast revenge appeas'd hath lent;
" Glad to have honour'd him who gave me birth,
" Glad to have swept a tyrant from the earth."

He ceas'd; the monarch heard, and felt, and sigh'd,
Forgave his murd'rer, and, forgiving, died.

A TALE OF THE COURT OF FRANCE.

It was in the reign of Philip le Hardi, immediately after the death of his son by his former wife, that the whole of Paris seemed in motion, and the eye of every man was fixed upon his neighbour with a wild and penetrat-

ing anxiety of expression, and the voices of thousands
arose with a hoarse and rustling murmur, as if the whole
city were engaged in the discussion of some deed of
mystery and horror ; every countenance wore an expression of curiosity and deep interest, checked by a timid
caution, from the uncertainty and dangers of the report
which, either insinuated by some emissary of Pierre de la
Brosse, the artful and unprincipled minister of Philip, or
perhaps casually dropped by some more indifferent person,
had circulated like wild-fire among a populace ardently
attached to the young Dauphin, and burning with a
desire to be revenged upon his murderers (for that he
was murdered seemed certain), that the young Queen
herself, the beautiful Marie de Brabant, had been guilty
of the murder of her step-son, in order to remove the barrier between her own infant and the throne of France.
But all seemed doubt and conjecture, so suddenly indeed
had the illness of the young prince been followed by the
annunciation of his death, that the people of France were
not yet sufficiently recovered from the horror which had
seized them at the moment of his dissolution. They
could hardly yet believe, that the prince, whom but a
few short hours before they had themselves seen a
living and a breathing man in all the glow of youthful
spirit and knightly enterprise, the young, the brave, and the
generous, the love of ladies and the theme of song, had so
suddenly fallen a victim to some savage and cold-blooded
assassin, who, intent on some scheme of self-interest, or
self-aggrandizement, had not scrupled to destroy the
hopes of France in the person of its future sovereign.
But the shaft of calumny had been skilfully launched,

and the public mind, when stretched to a painful degree of tension by the sense of its bereavement, had been seized upon by the minister with great art, and diverted to the advancement of his wishes. He had from the first objected to the marriage of his master with the princess Marie from the consciousness, that if the young queen obtained any very strong hold on the affections of her husband, his own influence must be essentially diminished. This, however, he had failed to prevent, and the increase of the young queen's power having, as he expected, been attended by the gradual diminution of his own influence, his dark and ambitious spirit was continually employed in endeavouring to devise some means by which he could overthrow his unconscious rival; therefore, having artfully caused it to be insinuated that she was guilty of the death of the Dauphin, whom he himself had privately poisoned, he had entangled her in a net from which she, utterly unconscious of the storm that was brewing against her, would find it difficult, if not impossible, to escape. To do him justice, even his dark spirit had at first recoiled in horror from the means which offered themselves for the completion of his project. He loved his young master much, but he loved power more; and after long and severe struggles, his crafty spirit had decided upon sacrificing his affection and the hopes of his country to his resentment and his ambition. Cruel, indeed, must he have been, who could bear that such a spirit should be quenched, that the light of that soul, which had served to rekindle the drooping energies, and reanimate the courage of his subjects, like a beacon on the hill-top, should be ingloriously extinguished, that his own base interests might be urged to their completion over the dead body of his lord.   He had already unfolded to the king his suspicions; who, though at first he had turned from them with proud confidence, yet began to fail when the artful minister skilfully contrived to bring in with merciless accuracy, many trifling, yet, at the same time, connected circumstances; and when he promised, if he would but hear him advance his accusation, to prove it to his own satisfaction.

It was a lovely evening, and the young queen sat musing over the loss sustained by the country, in the death of its future sovereign.   She had been able to appreciate the high qualities, which, had they been allowed to come to perfection, would have been well fitted to adorn a throne; and had deeply lamented his untimely death.   She also was a spirit of a kindred mould, and she mourned him as a brother.   She had wept deeply when the cloud of death, and the still more savage hand of man, extinguished those glorious energies before they were permitted to unfold themselves for the benefit of mankind; though it would be too severe on the frailty of human nature to inquire whether the thought that she was the mother of the destined king of France did not contribute to insinuate rays of hope and of splendor through the darkness of that universal sorrow which attended upon the death of the Dauphin. She was sitting silently in her own apartments, attended only by two of her favourite maidens, and conversing with them freely and affectionately, when the king entered suddenly.   He appeared excessively agitated, and there was an expression in his eye which betokened more than grief, as he addressed the queen; and his

voice, though perfectly calm, appeared almost as if it
were not his own. The queen felt surprised at the
sound, and almost started as he spoke to her. It
might be only that from the excessive agitation
marked on every feature, the studied calmness of his
voice and manner, appeared strange, and even fearful;
and the matter of his speech, which was indifferent, and
even gay, sounded still more terrible. "This is the first
time, Philip," she exclaimed, "that I have been forbidden to share your griefs. I have been accustomed to
consider myself as the partner of your sorrows, as well
as of your splendor; do not then refuse me the dearest
privilege of a wife, when the hand of sorrow is heaviest
upon you." Philip seemed to hesitate, but he turned
suddenly away, and appeared to struggle with some
internal emotion; and then, as he again turned to address
her, the queen observed, with a mixture of sympathy and
terror, that although the words were kind, they were
delivered with a conviction of fierce and withering
scorn, in his manner of addressing her, though she
thought that it seemed involuntary; and that though
they were gay, even too gay, considering the recent
tragedy which had deprived him of a son whom he had
idolized, she saw that the big drops were standing on his
brow, and the stain of blood upon his lips as he replied.
"Why should my fair wife conceive me to be so overcome
with grief? It is true," and his brow darkened as he
spoke, "that I have lost a brave son; it is true that his
spirit seems to call for vengeance on his murderers, and
by the living God" he continued, grasping her arm with
a violence of which he himself was perhaps unaware,

" if·I can but discover who they were that planned that
deadly deed, I will takë the deepest revenge that was
ever yet taken by a king and a Christian"—There was a
deep·pause—and he resumed in a tone of bitter irony,
" But the hour that has bereft me of ·my son, ·has proved
to me how tender and faithful is my wife, who can sympathize with her husband in-the death of his first born,
even though it should elevate her to the dignity of the
mother of the Dauphin." The queen gazed in astonishment for some time, half doubting whether excessive
grief had-not injured his usually powerful understanding;
when suddenly the extent of his unjust suspicions flashed
across her mind : for a moment· she appeared overwhelmed by the enormity of the alleged crime, till the
pride of virtue and of birth came to her aid, and turning
with dignity to Philip, she said, while her cheek reddened
with honest indignation, and her eyes kindled· as she
spoke, ·" I see, Philip, whither·these insinuations ·tend ;
you have dared to imagine (and may God pardon you
the injustice of your thoughts), that you are indebted to
the wife of your bosom, for the murder of your child. I
will not ask you to bring forward your witnesses, for no
witnesses can justify you in the belief. I should have
thought, that the confidence of Philip· in me was ·too
deeply rooted to be shaken by the representations ·of artful and designing men ; if, however, he can think vilely
and falsely enough of the woman whom he has selected
as a queen, to believe that such mean and paltry motives
as he has dared to impute, could possibly influence her,
even to think without horror of so foul a crime, it matters little whether she be guilty or not ; if he does her no

wrong in supposing ·it possible that she should do so, the woman, be she a king's daughter, is unworthy to be the wife of the poorest gentleman in France. If he do her wrong by that supposition, as I call God·to witness he now does, though he be the mightiest ·of Europe's monarchs, is unworthy to touch the hand of the meanest peasant girl in his wide dominions." The pride of innocence unjustly aspersed, had supported her so·far, but oppressed by a variety of conflicting emotions, she sunk into a seat, and found relief in a flood of tears. The king appeared considerably affected, and turned away, exclaiming, "Oh, if I could believe the truth of her honest indignation|! But I cannot ; the deepest villain that ever breathed, would not have had the audacity to forge an accusation against so lovely a creature. He warned me, too, not to be entrapped into a belief of her innocence, by her assumption of ·surprise and indignation. But yet, it is impossible that one so beautiful and virtuous should have committed a crime so deadly! I will not—I cannot—believe it!" He turned round as the queen was vainly endeavouring to overcome the feeling of the moment; threw himself at her feet, exclaiming, ·as he raised her hand to his lips, "I believe you—upon the honour of a king, and a gentleman, I believe you—only say once more 'I am innocent.' "—" No," she replied proudly, as she dried her tears, " I will not owe my life to the feeling which ·a moment has kindled, and ·a moment may extinguish ; I am confident in my own integrity, and I will defy the malice of my enemies, trusting in heaven to overthrow and confound their designs." She retired hastily as· she concluded, and Philip departed to join his minister, who had

promised to bring the proofs which should establish the
guilt of the queen. He entered the room, and weaving
together artfully much trifling circumstantial evidence,
proceeded to call the servants of the queen, whom he
had corrupted to perjure themselves against their mistress. The king, no longer under the influence of her
tears, was, with much difficulty, persuaded to believe
the guilt of his consort; and exclaimed, "I will see the
base wretch once more; I will upbraid her with her
perfidy and dissimulation, and stab her with my own
hands; the spirit of my slaughtered son calls on me for
vengeance, I cannot wait for the slow forms of law!"
"My gracious liege," interrupted the wily minister, "do
not again trust yourself within the influence of her fasci-
nations; remember, that she almost made you believe
her innocence." Finding, however, that the king seemed
resolved to persist, and dreading lest the queen should
be punished in this summary manner; he resolved, however he might wish ultimately for her death, to stand
between the infuriated sovereign and his destined victim; and making a forcible appeal to the nobler feelings
of his master, he succeeded for the present in tranquil-
lizing his excessive agitation : "Son of a race of kings,
be not in the hour of trial unkingly; if you stain your
royal hands with the blood of this woman, murderess
though she be, you are degraded to her level. God
knows, that since the blood of my royal master rests upon
her head, her death were more welcome to me than her
life. But it is not to glut the passing hatred of a moment, that a king must break through the eternal laws of
justice; think how will it sound to the ears of posterity,

that Philip murdered the woman whom he had first wrongfully accused—that is,'' he exclaimed (endeavouring to correct the expression in the heat of his address), '' whom they will say was proved innocent, by what was in reality the punishment of her guilt. Not so must the spirit of your son be avenged by the murder of a defenceless woman; let her die according to law and justice.'' The king acquiesced moodily; and, throwing himself on a chair, leant his head upon his hands in a paroxysm of mental agony; the tears actually forcing their way through his fingers as he wept. The minister, who really did feel an attachment to his master, whatever his other crimes might be, stood irresolute, as he muttered, brushing his hand across his eyes, " I half repent me of the deed; but I have thrown for a high stake, life or death, power or ignominy, and I must not now fail, whatever be the feelings which assail me in the course of the game." Both remained in deep silence, when Philip started suddenly up and seized him by the throat. "Villain, thou hast slain my son! and now, now you wish to deprive me of my wife, that I may be a widower, as well as childless." The villain, who had grown pale at the commencement of this attack, rallied his spirits, and exclaimed in a bold tone, which was fearfully belied by the pale expression of horror and despair which yet stood upon his features; "I the murderer of my young lord! my gracious liege, be yourself; suffer not these chimeras to exert the pernicious influence of insanity over your understanding; retire to your chamber, my lord; and endeavour to tranquillize your spirits, for the trying scenes which we must go through to-morrow."—"Aye,

my good and faithful servant," answered Philip, recovering
himself, " I did thee wrong ; but believe me it was under
· the influence of grief, which prompted me to attack thee,
scarcely knowing who thou wert.   Evil indeed must that
influence have been that could prompt me to doubt thy
fidelity; yet, alas! I once thought myself equally sure of the
truth and tenderness of my wife.   Fare thee well."   The
king retired privately, and the minister, wrapping his cloak
around him, reached his palace, where, throwing himself
on a couch, he endeavoured to gain a short oblivion of his
guilt.   For a long time he was unsuccessful; visions of
splendor, darkly relieved by the horrors of crime, floated
before his eyes in terrible succession, and the thickening
fancies came over him in wild confusion, and frequently as
· he was dropping into a sort of fevered sleep, he started up
with a gasp of agony, appalled at the form of the murdered
prince as it flitted slowly before him, and laid its cold hand
on his burning brow.   Even as he woke and sat upright on
the bed, he seemed to see it slowly retiring through the
draperies of the ample room, and then, cursing his weakness, again endeavoured to compose himself to rest, and
at length succeeded ; which, however, was but an increase
of the intensity of his feelings, and the agony of his
remorse, as the same figures flitted slowly before him, and
the sleep he had so long coveted, only deprived him, as it
came deeper upon him, of the power of breaking the spell
by starting from his slumbers.   His young son, the brave
Auguste, who had been the intimate friend of the
unfortunate prince, and who nearly resembled him in
the chivalrous gallantry of his disposition, had been much
in the habit of living on terms of almost equal friendship

with his young lord, and having been captivated by the
charms of the young queen, who, with the grace that
never deserted her, had been particularly attentive to the
friend of her step-son, had dwelt upon this dangerous
subject, till it became an essential part of himself; and the
grief which he felt at the death of his friend, his brother
in arms, and his prince, was almost drowned in the overwhelming horror and indignation which he felt against
those who had dared to cast so foul an imputation upon
the honour of the queen.   He was awake in the adjoin-
ing chamber, fevered with honest indignation, when his
quick ear caught a broken exclamation of his father's .on
the subject which lay next his heart, he caught the name
of the queen, and with a wild laugh, the sleeping villain
exclaimed; " Innocent! yes—I know you are so! But
you will nevertheless die! Do I not know that I poisoned"
—a strong shudder passed over his features, and he
almost instantly resumed, bursting into a laugh of·wild
and demoniac triumph, " But that which I did it for is
mine."   As these sounds reached him, considering the
internal interest which he felt in the guilt or innocence
of the queen, it was not in human nature not to listen,
and, cautiously opening the door, he stole into the room,
and bent in dreadful anxiety over the couch of his guilty
father, whose sleeping remorse soon wrung from him the
confession of the plot which he had laid, and disclosed
the depth and extent of his guilt to his unfortunate son.
Yet the first feeling which came over his mind, was joy
at the establishment of the queen's innocence; it was
almost instantly succeeded by a sense of deep and terrible
·humiliation, as he reflected that the unhappy being who

lay before him with a mind lacerated by remorse, the worm of the mind that never dieth—who was stained with the deadliest crimes that it is in the power of man to perpetrate—was nevertheless his father. He could not suffer the young queen, rich in all the graces of beauty and innocence, to perish, through the subtle and savage machinations of a hoary traitor—but then that traitor was his father. And to bear the name of parricide!—He could not, would not live as the murderer of his father. The struggle was powerful, but his noble spirit prevailed: " I can yet," he said, " save the queen by dying for her. It is indeed hard to die, to go down into cold obscurity, when we have scarce entered life in all the glow of generous feeling and youthful happiness! It is yet harder to take upon myself the guilt of a crime at which my soul revolts, and to leave that name, which I once fondly imagined was to shine in the annals of my country, as an object of generous emulation to the heroes of posterity, to be remembered, when the hand of time should have laid me in the unbroken slumber of the grave among the old warriors of our line, whose deeds are sung by minstrels, to incite the young, the brave, and the generous, to imitation, a name which should now only be mentioned in execration, as the dark and midnight assassin, whose revenge came in the hour of darkness like a deadly blight upon the hopes of France, and left them to weep over the promise of youthful virtue unaccomplished, and the youthful pledges of glory unredeemed. But it is yet harder to see her in all the pride of innocence, led forth to an ignominious death; it is yet harder to bear the mark of Cain upon my brow, and to be pointed at in fear and wonder, as the murderer of my father. He left the room hastily, and having first gone to the servants of the queen, who had been corrupted by his father, and whose names he had gathered from the broken exclamations in his sleep, and explaining to them the manner in which he had discovered the guilt of his father, told them that they might yet save their lives if they would swear secrecy, and do as he commanded them. "Go, then," said he, "to the king as if ye repented, and I hope ye do repent, the part ye have had in this foul business, and say that ye had been corrupted by me; as if I had murdered the prince, and place me as the principal instead of my father." They did so; and immediately after, as if it were done spontaneously, and without knowing their motions, he went to throw himself at the feet of the king; and protesting the innocence of the queen, avowed himself as the murderer of the prince, which he said he had wished to lay to the charge of the queen; but finding that the innocent blood was heavy on his soul, he came and delivered himself to death; and demanded one boon as the reward of his voluntary confession, "And what boon, villain," said the infuriated king, "can the murderer of the Dauphin have to ask of the king of France?"—"That my death may be private and instantaneous."—"No," answered the king, "not for worlds shall the murderer of my son escape. Ho, guards! seize this traitor and bear him to the deepest dungeon, while his tortures are preparing to glut my revenge!"—"Thus, then," said the youth, drawing his dagger and stabbing himself, "I die, I can bear death, but not the execration of the multitude. For the last time, I protest, the queen is innocent." He

fell to the ground on saying this, and almost immediately
expired.   His unfortunate father soon after came, and
seeing the body of his devoted son, remained for a short
time stupified with agony.   " He thought to die for me,
he wished to save both his father and his queen!   But
it was I, not he, who was the murderer, and I must
expiate my crime on the scaffold or the wheel."

THE RETURN.

How oft, in many a distant place,
　　Beyond the foaming sea,
I've wept to think, how vast the space
　　Betwixt my home and me .
I've thought, beneath a foreign sky,
　　(Nor e'en from tears forbore,)
How long must be the time, ere I
　　Could see my native shore.

But still, whene'er my mind was sad,
　　When dimm'd my eye the tear,
One thought my heart could always glad,
　　One thought my spirit cheer ·
For, from my mind Hope's heav'nly light
　　The gloom could clear away,
And bid my soul, when wrapt in night,
　　Be brighten'd into day.

I hop'd my native home, once more,
　　And all I lov'd, to see ;
And there to dwell, my wand'rings o'er,
　　In long felicity.
Those thoughts how vain, that bliss how short,
　　Alas ! I little knew ;
Nor yet had sad experience taught,
　　That Hope could prove untrue.

And time, indeed, hath pass'd away,
    But ah ! how slowly pass'd ;
Arriv'd is now the long-wish'd day,
    And I at home at last.
But where are those fond dreams of joy,
    Hope's visions, where are they ?
No more my mind those thoughts employ,
    They all have pass'd away.

An exile in my native land,
    A home have I no more ;
Against me now a stranger's hand,
    Hath clos'd my father's door.
And where are they who gave me birth,
    More dear than all beside ?
My father in his bed of earth,
    My mother by his side.

If e'er an hour of bliss I knew,
(And mine, alas ! have been but few)
'Twas when I reach'd my native shore,
My griefs forgot, my wand'rings o'er ;
I plac'd my foot upon the sand,
And knelt, and kiss'd the long-wish'd land,
Look'd back exulting o'er the sea,
And wept in boundless ecstasy ;
I thought of parents and of home,
Of sorrows past, and joys to come ;
Of friends, and ev'ry tender tie,
And scenes long dear to memory ;
I ne'er had felt such bliss before,
And ne'er, ah ! ne'er shall feel it more.

Fair was the summer's eve ; the sun
Was sinking slow, his journey done.
When homewards I with hurried face,
And panting heart, and joy-flush'd face,
Through scenes well known in younger day,
My native village, bent my way ;
Unchang'd, unalter'd, as before,
It still the self-same aspect wore :

But oft strange faces met my view,
And memory could recall but few—
The aged, whom I once had known,
Now slept beneath their burial stone ;
I look'd around, but none could see
Whom I had known in infancy :
So chang'd were those by lapse of time,
Whom I had left in youthful prime.

And now my home was just in view,
As quick I pass'd the church-yard through ;
Where many a new-rais'd mound might tell,
That death had done his office well.
One stone there was, whose marble fair,
Show'd that no vulgar dead lay there.
One side-long glance I careless threw,
It could not be—I saw not true—
Again I look'd with phrensied eye,
And saw the appalling certainty ,
I saw—and stood in mute despair—
My father's name was graven there !

R.

THE DEATH OF MONTGOMERY.

Calmly he lay ; from that young side,
Ebb'd forth of life the gushing tide ;
Clos'd were those eyes, where erst the flame
Flash'd at his injur'd country's shame ;
And still, and nerveless, was that hand
Which, waving high his patriot brand,
Had bade the British despot feel,
Columbia's charging front of steel.
Yes, he, who in her deserts wild,
Fair Freedom view'd her fav'rite child,
And taught the storms of war to brave,
By wild Niagara's torrent wave,

Has fallen ; he who wont to brood,
In forest depths of solitude,
Had heard the wild birds shrilly screaming,
Had seen the Indian watch-fire gleaming,
And felt his free-born spirit soar
On lone Oswego's desert shore.
Yet, Britain, know, for him, who dies,
Millions of kindred souls shall rise;
Go, and pour forth thy purchas'd horde,
The refuse of some German Lord;
And mingle with the British cry,
The Indian howl of victory.
In vain, in vain, these hirelings bleed,
Beneath the free Virginian's steed ;
And true, too true, that sulph'rous flame
Tells of the rifle's deadly aim,
And dying heroes, as they fall,
Prove the unseen, th' unerring, ball.
Will savage force, will Hessian spear
Check the Columbian's fierce career ?
No, though this heart in death be chill,
A thousand patriot bosoms thrill,
A thousand hands will point the way,
From Europe's chains, and despot sway ;
And fair Columbia's shore shall be,
The refuge of the brave, and free.

OLIVER QUINCY.

ON PUNCTUALITY.

Tantum de medio sumptis accedit honoris.

There are, amidst the chequered shades and infinite
varieties of terrestrial feelings and passions, certain quali-

ties of an indifferent and negative nature in themselves ;
qualities which, though they do not display any feature
from which we can discover in them a direct or immediate
tendency to the nature of Virtue or of Vice, are nevertheless found, in the degree of influence which they exercise
upon our habits of life and rules of action, to be firm,
though humble auxiliaries of the one, and though the
mere outworks and projections of the fortress, still, in their
measure, bulwarks to oppose the progress of the other.

Thus we have heard, that Cleanliness is next to a
Virtue, and Debt next to a Vice. The former of these
propositions is much more easy to swallow than the
latter ; and, fortunately for some of us, Reason here
appears to agree with inclination. For, as the preservation of health is certainly a duty, and as cleanliness
is a powerful accessory to such preservation, it may herein
be placed on a footing different from that of its brother
thesis : since the moral merits or demerits of debt must
entirely depend on the accompanying circumstances,
under the influence of which such and such responsibilities
are incurred. There are for instance, many occasions on
which it is sinful—some, on which it is meritorious, to
incur a debt. The man who contributes, by borrowing,
to cause even the possibility of the embarrassment or the
ruin of a fellow creature, voluntarily renders himself liable
to at least the guilt of a contingent injury towards his
neighbour. But he who for a lawful or a generous end,
borrows that which he has good reason to suppose it will
be in his power to repay—reason, founded not on capricious or interested suppositions, but on sound circumstantial evidence—such a one, surely, may rather have to claim

our commendations than to deprecate our reproaches. Yet, notwithstanding such examples as these, the maxim is, as a general one, good ; and the rule of our actions ought to be, a general unwillingness, not only to indulge in that which, however differently viewed among men, in the eye of Justice is simply theft—borrowing without a prospect of the power of repayment—but likewise to run the slightest risk of involving our fellow creatures, for the sake of our own extrication, and bringing upon them that which of right falls upon ourselves. Perhaps substituting Neatness for Cleanliness, might bring the two propositions more upon a parallel, for Neatness is, if not a moral, at least a social duty, which we owe to the feelings, the tastes, and the habits, of those around us.

The cardinal Virtues and Vices have long been the constant objects of unremitting praise or assiduous reprehension. Were I gravely to assure my readers that Truth was lovely, and Falsehood odious ; that Revenge was wicked, and Mercy equally excellent and delightful ; I certainly should show my regard for Truth, by speaking it in uttering these words, but should not display much Mercy towards my readers, by dinning into their ears what they must before have heard times without number, set forth with far more power, and enforced with far more authority.

No doubt my readers have by this time begun to doubt and to inquire what the subject of this paper may be. As their desire is, to tell the truth, a reasonable one, I shall endeavour to gratify it ; and hereby do declare, that I espouse the cause and proclaim myself the champion of the much abused, and much neglected, but homely and useful

damosel, yclept Punctuality. She is one of the most
desirable, and has been one of the most despised, of the
qualities which I mentioned, and I have gallantly determined to break a lance in her defence with any knight
who may choose to encounter me—be he Sir Tristram
himself.—"Bartholomew Bouverie against all comers."

But if I proceeded in this martial way, however congenial to my valorous temperament, I might find an enemy
nearer home than I could wish; I should perceive my
friend Jermyn, mounted on the winged Pegasus, equipped
by Passion, and squired by Negligence, rushing at full
speed against me. Such an apparition would be any
thing but pleasant, considering the affection which I entertain for that worthy gentleman. Therefore we will endeavour to discuss and illustrate the question in a more
peaceable manner.

We may in general observe that the useful class of
qualities are pretty liberally praised, though somewhat
sparingly acted upon, among mankind. Here the case
however, is the reverse; every gentleman deems it a point
of honour to leave punctuality to tradesmen: these worthies are now in their turn becoming ashamed of it, and
we, as customers, can testify that many of them have
utterly dismissed it from the precincts of their establish-
ments, to seek humbler adherents among a lower class of
human beings. In other case people preach, but do not
practise; in this they neither preach nor practise. This
most excellent and steady-going time-keeper is now like
a damsel wandering through the streets, with "nobody
coming to marry her," as the old song says. Buffeted on
one side, and re-buffeted on the other; abused by many,

and defended by none; contemptuously commanded to
seek a mate among husbandmen or menials, as unworthy of the society of a reputable person; she looks
back to those days of old, when she was an inmate of the
mansion, and a governor of the days and nights of Alfred
the Great; when she was courted by the noble, the
wealthy, and the powerful; when she governed the motions
of the general and the *gourmand*, and was equally conspicuous in the life of the philosopher and the fashionable.

While we revile and reject her, we tacitly, and as it
were involuntarily, pay a manifest tribute to her sterling
worth. Pedagogues love punctuality in boys, ministers
in messengers, mistresses in servants, customers in trades-
people. But should we turn the tables, and say that
tradesmen love punctuality in customers—servants in mistresses—messengers in ministers—school-boys in pedagogues—all would be of no avail; there might indeed be
an abundance of the will to procure, but there would be
a lamentable deficiency of the power to enforce, the
exercise of this most valuable and most calumniated
quality.

To illustrate by example what I have advanced in precept, let us for a moment suppose—(so improbable a supposition should not be continued longer)—that I, Bartholomew Bouverie, being, as we all trust, a gentleman,
should be minded to claim to myself the undoubted privilege of my station, and for once be a little neglectful of
punctuality. What would be the consequences? Dreadful beyond measure—though the measure should chance
to be the new Imperial one—and pernicious beyond ex-

pression. A crowd of customers would assault my worthy
publisher's windows and shopmen; attack his goods and
his brains, and cost him more in the invention of excuses
than he has gained by the sale of the Eton Miscellany.
Such, in our neighbourhood, would be the consequences
of the Number's not being out to its day. The dismay
of the London, country, and foreign Booksellers, I need
not attempt to depict.

There are indeed men of narrow and unenlightened
minds, who seek to endow qualities of this description
with a weight and a merit which I am far from wishing
to ascribe to them. There are men who think, that unless
our motions are performed with the monotonous accuracy
of the clock, they must be governed by no rule, and consequently productive of little advantage. There are men
whose whole souls are centered in pounds, shillings,
pence, counting-houses, and punctuality; who condemn
as a cheat the man who keeps them waiting for five
minutes beyond the appointed time; who set down for a
reprobate and a cast-away the hapless youth who does not
get out of bed in the morning, and into it at night, as
the clock strikes a certain hour; who would consider a
fraud, provided it be committed in the way of business,
or a lie, if told to cheat a customer or an exciseman,
a far more slight dereliction of duty, than the most
trivial aberration from their darling punctuality. Such
men, however, are little seen, and less respected; and
if their opinion be pernicious, its sphere of operation
is limited. We need not, at least, fear falling into this
extreme, till we have effectually removed ourselves from
the other.

But thus it is—it has been remarked a thousand times, and shall now be remarked for the thousand and first— thus it is that the perversity of man transforms good into evil. Hence it arises, that Economy and Generosity, which ought to be, and in their nature are, most faithful friends, are perpetually at logger-heads with one another; hence our Courage bubbles into Temerity, or sinks into Cowardice; hence our Piety is sublimed into Enthusiasm, or cooled into Indifference. Hence, to descend a few steps, Neatness and Simplicity are frequently associated with Dandyism and Dirt, (query, which preferable?) and hence, lastly, it is, that the friends of Punctuality exalt her into Virtue, while her enemies degrade her into mean- ness; voluntarily widening the breach already formed between their opinions, and each increasing the difficul- ties, and lessening the probability, of his own and his opponent's reclamation.

The prevailing bias is certainly, at present, against Punctuality. The few who practise her in secret, dare hardly espouse her cause in public. She will not appear so unimportant as we are prone to consider her, when we consider how often the want of Punctuality in our various relations towards one another produces mutual irritation, and engenders mutual offence. If its practice often lead to narrow-mindedness on the one hand, and its neglect to idleness on the other, why should we therefore either worship her with blind veneration, or revile her with even more absurd disgust, when it is her corrupted, and not her pure and proper, form, which is the subject of discussion?

Why should not Punctuality regulate the hours of the

gentleman as well as of the shop-keeper? What is the ingredient in her nature, which renders her advantageous to the one, but hurtful to the other? She is the companion and the friend of diligence and accuracy; the opponent of sloth and negligence. The division of time produces almost as extraordinary effects as the division of labour. It facilitates our exertions, regulates our conduct, gives wings to the heavy, and takes them from the rapid, hours; it employs our time without burdening it, and it is equally subservient to our own, and our friends' accommodation.

Expelled, however, from the fashionable world, Punctuality is still cultivated amidst the seats of learning. Who has not wondered how exactly and how regularly our citizens of Eton, after having dispersed themselves into every quarter of our little world, gather together almost to a minute?

But the printer's devil calls, and not being minded to cause the calamities I have described above, I must send my article to the press.

RECOLLECTIONS.

[Upon my soul a Lie.—SHAKSPEARE.]

Though thrilling tones so wildly sweet,
When the voice and harp notes lightly meet,
Might force the sternest heart to weep,
   As they rise in silver swell;
There is not in music a pow'r so deep,
   As the sound of the rolling bell;

Which, gently o'er the spirit stealing,
Enthrals it in the chords of feeling.

I stood, when all around was gay,
And heard their soft tones float away;
To swell the widely-spreading gale,
    With Music's holy voice,
To bear on its light wings a tale,
    That bade us all rejoice,
Unmindful of the bitter grief,
That well repays a joy so brief.

Then, whilst a young and lovely bride
Mov'd gently at her lover's side,
With happy smiles and happier tears,
    I stood in silence there,
To drink within my thrilling ears,
    The music-mingled air ;
Whilst, open'd by surrounding glee,
My heart beat joyously and free.

Ere sunk those notes so softly gay,
I went in happiness away ;
I did not see her beauty fade,
    As with a deadly blight,
Nor sorrow fling its dark'ning shade,
    Upon that brow of light ;
Which, whilst the heart was yet untorn,
Beam'd brighter than the fresh spring morn.

Yet often thought on that fair form,
That brow with love and fancy warm,
Those eyes of soft and changeful hue,
    In my spirit's youthful lightness ;
Till she rose before my boyish view,
    In her beauty's living brightness ;
Nor would I leave th' ideal chains,
For the softest heart that yet remains.

The bells rung forth—I did not start—
Their sound sunk deep into my heart,

As I came again at night, alone,
    And heard that she was dead—
It was enough that life was gone—
    I ask'd not how it fled.   .
The soul, that warm'd that beauteous clay,
Had burst on wings of light away.

Through ev'ning's chill and falling gloom,
I went to seek her in the tomb ;
I wish'd, I know not why, to say
    One echoless farewell !
The guide that marshall'd me the way,
    Was the dirge note of the bell ;
How chang'd, since last their merry sound
Breath'd love and joy to all around.

I saw with light, and holy song,
Assembled there a friendly throng ;
I waited, for I would not go
    Within that sacred aisle,
That those might meet in deepest woe,
    Who parted with a smile :
I waited till again the gloom
Roll'd back upon the silent tomb.

I waited till I saw them go
In all the solemn pomp of woe,
The death-peal through the rising storm,
    Still spoke in sullen swell,
As bending o'er her prostrate form,
    I breath'd a sad farewell !
The ivy, round the pillars twin'd,
Wav'd slowly to the passing wind.

Oh I have sought thy darken'd tomb,
    To weep in silence there,
This marble's cold and massive gloom
    Suits not a thing so fair ;
The fresh green turf, with roses spread,
Were meeter couch for Beauty's head.

Yet why for thee should nature's birth
  Her flow'ry tribute rear ?
Alike to thee the bed of earth
  · And the cold marble bier :
Thy spirit ceas'd its mounting flight,
Amid the quenchless springs of light.

Yet, as a source of happier dreams
  The fresh green turf appears,
To us the sullen marble seems,
  To chill the rising tears ;
To choke the soft and kindly flow,
In cold solemnity of ·woe. ·

I came to see thy face once more ;
  They say thy tomb is there,
I brought a fresh and lovely flow'r,
  To deck thy shining hair ;
I can but fling it down to weep,
And fade o'er Beauty's dreamless sleep.

FRAGMENT.

Say'st thou that human glory can endure ?
That ought of earth affords foundation sure ?
Say'st thou that empire, dignity, or fame,
Shall live for ever—flourish on the same ?
Gaze on each temple, on each lofty dome,
Gaze on the ruins of imperial Rome !
Can the proud city, or embattled tow'r,
Contemn old Time, and set at nought his pow'r ?
Gaze on the ruins—nay, go seek the spot,
Where high and haughty Babylon—is not.
Snakes of the fen, and lions of the wood,
Possess the spot where she, proud city, stood.
Her gates of brass—her gold—her silver—all
Have perish'd in the universal fall ;
No frail memorial is left to tell
Where stood the stronghold of the impious Bel.

Yet mark—there is a city that shall be
Strong and unmov'd to all eternity.
No sun illuminates that city bright—
No moon is there, to cheer dark dismal night—
No night is there—GOD is its beaming Sun,
Its Light the Lamb—the Holy Three in One.
What city thus shall cank'ring age contemn ?
No earthly work—the New Jerusalem !

DINNER OF THE DULL CLUB,

November 15, 1827.

Mr. Ignoramus took the chair precisely at half-past six. He was supported on his right-hand by Mr. Bartholomew Bouverie, who has been some time admitted as an honorary member of the Club. The dinner passed off with the most uninterrupted apathy ; and, indeed, throughout the whole evening no circumstance occurred to disturb the equable temper of the company. When the cloth was removed, the President, without leaving his seat—for to rise would be derogatory from his dignity—proposed as a Toast,

"The Goddess of Dulness, Patroness of the Club ;"

which was drunk with becoming *sang froid*, and in silence.

RECITATIVE.*

Adagio.—Queen of the murky brow, black, gloomy, solitary,
        Stalk forth from pitchy Erebus, and darkly-flowing Acheron,
        Thou dwellest not in grove where all blest spirits tarry,
        Nor in the meads of Asphodel, nor in the νῆσοι μακάρων,

---

* The reader will understand that this was composed and sung by professional gentlemen, and not by any member of the club. All the members are ready to make affidavit to that effect, if it should be thought necessary.

For thee no virgin hands the myrtle bough prepare,
　Nor twine the purple hyacinth, nor beautiful geranium,
The night-shade's deadly tendril is wreathed in thy hair,
　And poppy and mandragora surround thy *pericranium*.
Thy subjects are the fenny snake, and cavern-loving toad,
　And in thy cloister'd dungeon, thou rul'st with power
　　despotic,
And all around that dungeon, where'er thy foot has trod,
　Waves the soul-dead'ning plant, n d blooms the flower
　　narcotic.

ARIA.

Goddess ! o'er thy votary's head
Soporific influence shed ,
By the hall, where, round thy throne,
Flits the bat and hums the drone—
Descend, thou slumber-soothing guest,
To eyes with idleness opprest.
Silence ! silence ' she is near,
Let no profane one enter here ;
Her soothing tongue shall cure our ills,
The tongue that laudanum distils
She comes, she comes, (beware ! beware !)
Lolling in an easy chair ;
The chair that drowsy donkies draw,
Hark ! I hear them, he ! he ! haw !

At this moment the arrival of the goddess was announced
by the barytone modulations of Mr. Lernill's olfactory
organ ; the company hailed the omen with as much
satisfaction as the ancients did another faculty of the
same organ, viz , sneezing ; and in a short time the melodious diapason included every nose in the company,
except Mr. Bouverie's ; who, being a bit of a wag, when
the fit was on him, though dull enough at other times,
winked to the fiddlers and drummers who were in attend-
ance, and in a minute Haydn's Surprise Symphony was
begun : softly and soothingly did the music steal upon
the minds of those members who were not already fast

asleep. Every head nodded in cadence; suddenly out thundered the Surprise, the Chairman started upon his legs, overturning the punch-bowl into Mr. Sloman's lap ; Mr. Dolton tumbled backwards in his chair upon the leg of a fat turn-spit, the property of the Club; Mr. Lernill rushed to the door, followed by as many of the Club as were on their legs ; and such a squeeze took place among these corpulent patrons of inactivity, as had not been known since the first institution of this Society.

When the tranquillity was restored, which was not for a considerable time, on account of the *vis inertiæ* of the Club, to speak scientifically, the President again rose, and after lamenting the unfortunate circumstance which had disturbed the usual tranquillity of the meeting, proposed the following toasts :

" The March of Dulness and the Muses' Town-house."

Song.—" Such a genius I did grow."

" The Pleasures of Society."

Song —" We're a' nodding, &c."

" Mr. Bartholomew Bouverie, the Editor of the Eton Miscellany."

Mr. Bouverie returned thanks in a neat and appropriate speech :—

Gentlemen ; I feel it the more incumbent upon me to declare my sentiments upon this occasion, as I am now about to conclude a work which has conferred upon me the distinguished honour of a seat on your benches. If in the conduct of that work I have satisfied the members of this honourable Society, why should I regard the opinion of the rest of the world ?

" Satis est equitem mihi plaudere."

(Cries of !" Order ! No Latin !") If I have ever deviated. from the line of dulness, I assure you that I did it by mistake, and not from any desire of currying favour with the vulgar, in opposition to the interests of this Club; and in conclusion, I beg leave to return thanks to the members here present, and to assure them that my most listless apathy, and my most strenuous inertness shall always be devoted to their service. Gentlemen, allow me to propose the health of your honoured President, Mr. Ignoramus.

Mr. Ignoramus.—Gentlemen; if I were to thank you as you deserve, I should exert more energy than is consistent with my dignity, therefore, as in duty bound, I must suffer the laws of the Club to curb the impulse of my heart. I, Gentlemen, am an example of the true " otium cum dignitate." (Cries of " What? What?") I beg pardon of the Club—of a President sitting in an easy-chair— some Presidents there are who sit upon thorns, through the violence and ungovernable spirit of their members, but I, to your credit be it spoken, have never even been awakened, except on that memorable occasion when Mr. Lernill's nose was so deplorably out of tune.

But with respect to the general interests of the Club, I have to congratulate you all on the prospect of its becoming fashionable. I collect this from the following signs : Firstly, that we are to have three universities instead of two, portending an increase of dulness by one-half : Secondly, that one of the greatest writers of the age has published a *dull* novel ; a new and portentous prodigy ! Thirdly, that one of the greatest orators of the present time writes about what he does not fully understand; a sure promoter of ignorance in those who read him. These are the signs that lead me to suppose that dulness will at length have its day, in spite of the vain endeavours of the *literati*, and of those whose abilities are even now directed to the ruin of *our* cause, while *their own* seems daily verging to destruction.

Gentlemen, I have nothing more to say, except to inform you, that I have received the following donations for the use of the Club :

1. Twenty-five pounds of Opium from the Porte, the present of a Russian gentleman.

2. Ten green Night-caps, made up in the form of Turbans, the gift of Lieut. R Ignoramus, R. N.

3. Five Egyptian Hammocks, very narcotic, with Smyrna Coverlets, from the same.

4. One dozen pair of blinkers, of Russia leather, designed to promote sleep, by excluding the view of side objects.

Soon after the speech of the President, the company separated.

TO ———

Oh ! sweetly bloom the hopes of youth
  While joy is on the wing ;
While Fancy wears the garb of truth
  In Pleasure's revelling ,
My spirit had a gentle dream,
That threw a visionary gleam
  Upon my young life's spring ;
It was a bright and gladd'ning view,
Alas ! and I believ'd it true.

I know not when that cheering thought
  First dawn'd upon my mind ;
My young remembrance tells not aught
  But hath that thought combin'd

Before my memory 'twas born,
Gilded my childhood's early morn
    With.visions undefin'd ;
Oh ! seldom in so young a breast
Hath Love securely built his nest

For it was Love—if that be Love
    Which lives for one alone ;
And seeks all restlessly to prove
    Devotion to that one.
I meant not love—but did delight
In gazing on thy features bright,
    My lost companion :
Ne'er in my absence thee forgot,
Nor felt full joy where thou wast not

There was a time, when ev'ry joy
    Of thine was shar'd by me ;
And freely I, like artless boy,
    Gave every thought to thee :
And often would our young hands meet
In walk, or sport of childhood sweet,
    And oft in guileless glee
Were names exchang'd, which one, alas !
Deem'd fondly time should bring to pass.

Oh ! thou wert lovely in thy prime
    Of life , and thou art lovely yet :
My raptur'd eye from earliest time
    Hath seen all graces in thee met ;
And aye, when song or story tell
Of bright and beauteous damozel,
    My mind on thee is set ;
For blended with thine image warm
Were my first thoughts of Beauty's form.

Yet was it not thy loveliness
    Of feature that I lov'd ;
Nor smile of joyous playfulness,
    Nor eye that glancing rov'd ;

But dearer, dearer far to me
Was thine own spirit, fair and free,
    That o'er those features mov'd :
For thy soul's purity and grace
Found portraiture in thy sweet face.

Thy years were springing fresh, and ah '
    I thought they bloom'd for me ;
And made thee as the guiding star
    That rul'd my destiny :
And oft, when angry storms arose,
I calm'd my passions to repose
    By memory of thee ;
And precept mov'd me not so well
As thine example's holy spell.

O ' tell me not that they have lov'd,
    Who say 'tis idle all ;
Who speak of talents unimprov'd,
    And genius held in thrall .
Love lights high thought in warrior's breast,
And slumb'ring spirits wakes from rest
    With soul-enliv'ning call ;
Love bids the gen'rous mind explore
Fair Virtue's ways, and Wisdom's lore.

And I lov'd on, and thou didst grow
    In Beauty's fairest mould ,
And now soft looks alone might show
    What oft my tongue had told ;
And rip'ning years brought jealous care,
With gloomy feelings of despair,
    And fears, lest friendship cold
Should end my cherish'd hopes, and mar
My heart's first dream, and prospect fair.

And now no longer did one breeze
    Fan both upon one spot ;
In fields, 'neath shade of wonted trees,
    I walk'd, and saw thee not ;

And sad thoughts told me that the years
Of partnership in smiles and tears
    Would now be all forgot ,
That worthier hand would take from me
The flow'r I watch'd so faithfully.

Yet, though thy visions melt in air,
  Fond dreamer, why complain ?
The sailor wins not Heav'n's bright star,
    That guides him o'er the main.
Then be thou, fair one, still at hand,
Thy spirit still with sweet command
    Within my breast shall reign ;
I would not change thy sov'reignty ;
I would not, if I could, be free.

ON CRITICISM.

Fiet Aristarchus.—Hor.

From the earliest period of the reign of Science, there
has existed no class of writers, in all the numerous
branches of literature, so generally dreaded by those
who court the Muses, as the Critics. So strong is the
feeling of fear and envy, that the lash of the Critic has in
all ages given birth to, that the "Fœnum habet in cornu,
longe fuge," of Horace, is still, we are afraid, applicable
to many members of this unfortunate tribe ; and the
example of the ill-fated Zoilus, is perhaps, not unparalleled, even in this land of liberty and learning. The
unmanly attack inflicted upon Dryden by the resentment
of Rochester ; and in still later times, a similar assault
upon the author of the Mœviad, may serve to shew, not
less than the cross of Zoilus, how rancorous and malig-

nant a spirit prevails against the censor of the literary
world.   It is, we must own, a degrading, an invidious
task, to blast, though justly, the hopes of a youth, who,
like the courser starting from the barrier, ardently pants
for literary fame, to damp at once the breast beating
high with mingled fear and hope, with disconsolate
anguish.

Yet the rugged ways of this seemingly baneful and
unprofitable art have been honoured and adorned by
the names of Aristotle, the father of Criticism ; of Aristarchus, the loss of whose voluminous commentaries
we have to regret ; the truly-sublime Longinus, and the
elegant Quintilian, among the ancients : and in later times,
Boileau, Addison, Johnson, Porson, and the lamented
Gifford, have deigned to apply their talents and their
learning to this unlovely branch of writing.   We should
from the authority of these distinguished writers,
naturally conclude, that criticism is not devoid of advantage to the interests of the literary world.   Let us, therefore, in the first place, though it may be a disquisition
useless to many, and uninteresting to most, of my readers,
endeavour to point out those acquisitions which may
arise from criticism to the cause of learning, when aided
by talent and sound judgment.

It may be objected to us, what advantage can arise
from an art, no less irksome to the censor himself, than
to the unfortunate object on whom his thunders are
destined to fall ?   We allow, that the hopes of many a
youthful mind may have been abandoned, by too severe
an exercise of the powers of criticism ; that many an in-
experienced author may want resolution to confront the

withering thunders of the Critic's brow; yet certain it is, that by the dread of that disgrace, which the Critic's thunders would inevitably bring upon a failure, the literary world is free from an unceasing torrent of bad writing and nonsense, by which it would otherwise be in danger of being deluged; while, on the contrary, the praise and encouragement of the Critic, has often brought into the favour, and even friendship, of the learned, a man of unaided, native genius, who might have been born to " sing unseen," but for the friendly help of a being whom he thought would be the last to lead him to the paths of that renown which he so ardently desired.

We have always considered the proverb, which teaches us, " that we should not scorn to take advice from any one," to be a maxim full of good sense and candour; which is happily expressed by Ovid; " Fas est at ab hoste doceri." This advice might be followed with advantage by the writer, who, while smarting under the lash of the Critic, breathes nothing but fury and revenge against his censor. He forgets the motives of justice and candour that actuate the Critic to give praise to whom praise is due, blame to whom blame; and in his anger and fruitless indignation, he utterly loses sight of all reason and improvement; and himself becomes infinitely more culpable than he supposes the unfortunate object of his wrath to be. By such conduct, he causes his own and the Critic's labour to be entirely thrown away; for the want of candour and equanimity is no more excusable in the author than in the Critic. A man of patience and industry will extract honey, instead of gall, from the criticisms of his censor; he will survey his own faults

with an unprejudiced eye; and, convinced of the justice of
the Critic's blame, will lay aside all thoughts of anger and
resentment, and thus profiting from an apparent misfortune, will ensure to himself that success, which perseverance never fails of obtaining. Thus, in another point
of view, the task of the Critic becomes productive of the
most salutary effects to the cause of literature.

. The Critic should, above all, engage in the sacred cause
of religion, with no less zeal and ardour than in that of
learning. All impiety, every word tending to profane its inviolate sanctity, should be peremptorily
and effectually discountenanced ; and the critique should
be as firmly attached to its cause, as the pulpit. Addison boasted of having transplanted philosophy from
the studies and libraries of colleges, into cities and coffee-
houses ; but here, criticism becomes an instrument in the
hands of good men, for diffusing religion through pamphlets and journals.

· Let us now consider those qualities which give dignity
to the character of the Critic, which may render him
respected by all around him. The art of criticism may
be made alternately the medium of the most salutary
effects, or the most baneful injuries to the cause of learning. In the hands of an unbiassed and just man, it
diffuses a spirit of equity, and liberality of candour and
learning through the world ; a bad man, on the contrary,
renders it productive of the basest party-spirit, the gross-
est injustice, and of the blindest prejudice and ignorance.
Candour, and a mind utterly void of that littleness and
meanness of soul which are too truly objected to many
of this class of writers, are the first requisites to the man,

who may wish to be revered for his goodness, as well
as to be admired for his talents in this branch of literature.
Without this virtue so necessary to form the character of
a good man and a good Critic, the censor will not only
incur the contempt of the good, and the hatred of the bad,
but will give full reason, for the justice and impartiality
of his criticisms deservedly to be impugned. A good
Critic should at all times act the part of a just judge ;
his censures should not be written in blood, as were the
laws of Draco of old, but rather, in the true spirit of equity
which characterized the milder regulations of Solon,
should temper justice with mercy. The noble sentiment
of Terence, " Homo sum, humani nil a me alienum puto,"
should be ever present to his mind ; and he should constantly bear in view, the respect due to all his fellow-
creatures· from him, not as their censor, but as a ,man.
The Critic will thus command the reverence even of those
whom he condemns ; and his praises will be received
with the more delight and gratitude, because they bear
with them the marks of sincerity and truth:

The Critic, though the censor of others, should lay the
severest restrictions on his own pen, and should pass the
most rigid judgment on his own actions. The caprice of
a moment, the slightest portion of rancour or harshness,
which may hastily flow from it, will yield sufficient
ground to his enemies (for who are there ·among the
great and good that have not enemies ?), to deface his
fair· character, with imputations as frivolous and ill-
founded as they are foul and malicious. The censor's
bearing towards all men, should·be as conspicuous for
mildness· and affability, as his writings for equanimity

and moderation. No arrogance towards his equals, no
haughtiness to his inferiors, should leave a stain on the
character of the Critic. He should be as averse to resent,
in a manner unworthy of his dignity, as he should be to
inflict, an injury. Such a man will never fail to command
the respect and secure the esteem of all.

But, as Shakspeare finely observes, "men's vices live
in brass, their virtues we write in water;" so the bad
part of mankind prevail over the good. It is with regret,
we must confess, that there are, in the republic of letters,
many, too many Critics, who are unworthy of being
ranked with Aristotle and Longinus, of Addison and
Johnson. There are Critics, whose hearts are full of
bitterness and envy; whose minds are puffed up with
pride, or sunk with narrow prejudice; who, like the
cynic, snarl at all around them; and who are equally
indifferent to the fall of friend or foe. Such are the
individuals who have thrown a foul stigma on an useful
and salutary art; who have covered a multitude of good
men with base aspersions which belonged solely to themselves. These have no share in the fame of learning, nor in
the more excellent renown of justice and virtue; they spread
indeed for a time, their baneful influence, like the mist of
the night, but like it, are finally dispelled by the radiant
beams of the sun of science and truth.

Candidus is a Critic endowed with genius, learning, a
classical taste, and the soundest judgment. His opinions
are regarded as oracles by those who cultivate the art of
criticism, and over all of whom he maintains undoubted
superiority. Yet this high distinction, has neither
altered in any respect the affability of his demeanour,

nor the equanimity and moderation he constantly displays
in his criticisms. He is neither haughty nor arrogant,
neither invidious; nor resentful. His renown in the
literary world has been gained solely by his own talents,
and his own persevering industry ; yet he is as remarkable
for his modesty, as his learning and his merit. In the
judgments which he passes upon those writings which
he reviews in the character of a censor, he is ever ready
and indefatigable in praising every word that merits commendation ; but a censure, though given with decision,
is given painfully and reluctantly. The only author, who
dreads the censure of Candidus, is the impious scoffer at
religion, who disdains every thing that is sacred, and
scruples not to profane every thing that is holy. In short,
Candidus is the model of a good and great Critic ; one,
whose deserts are fully equal to his recompense ; whose
praise is never tainted with flattery, nor his censure with
envy ; a man who is above all littleness of mind ; who
unites the talents and the virtues which do honour to the
Critic and the man.

Mævius, though possessed of a good understanding,
and excellent talents, is a character totally opposite to
Candidus. His talents are sullied by rancour and envy,
and his judgment is perverted by the prejudices of a little
and narrow mind. Mævius makes the science of criticism
wholly subservient to his own secret purposes and designs.
The pages of his criticism are defaced by the worst passions that harden the heart, or debase the understanding.
In his praise he is actuated by base motives of interest
and selfishness, and his censures are a vehicle of rancour
and malice. Mævius is, I allow, the terror of Grub-

street, and the dread of all the tribe of poetasters that inhabit its garrets; but he is hated by the bad and despised by the good; and must undoubtedly, sooner or later, sink into that state of oblivion from whence he arose.

MERCUTIO.

TO MEMORY.

Nymph array'd in robes of light,
   Twin sister of Regret;
Restorer sweet of visions bright,
   Forbidding to forget;
What though thy smiling cheek the tear
   May dim, sweet nymph, awhile,
That tribute is to sadness dear,
   And softens still thy smile.
Then Memory come, on lyre and spirit breathe,
And with thine emblem flow'rs my temples wreathe.
Few may be those o'er whose dark features steal
Crime's burning stamp, or sad misfortune's seal;
Whom fate regarded with portentous lour
E'en at their birth, and childhood's playful hour
Mock'd with a sneer, so nipp'd the op'ning flow'r.
For them no former joys (like islands green,
O'er the parch'd waste of desolation seen),
For them no dreams of time that once was bless'd,
Afford a refuge to a mind distress'd.
Dark was their life, and darker still to trace
The scenes where Mem'ry to Remorse gives place.
Not such the view, nor such the tainted gale
Which Mem'ry wafts to me; hail, goddess, hail!
Peace on thy wings, and honey in thy smile,
No phantoms haunt thee, and no crimes defile!
As 'neath the morning mist, yet undefin'd
The landscape rests; till now the sun inclin'd

From some bright mountain pours his flood of light,
Straight wreath on wreath adown the neighb'ring height,
Rolls the bright veil of nature, till display'd,
Village and flocks and winding streams are laid :
So o'er my raptur'd soul those visions glide,
Dim shades at first, till Mem'ry by my side,
With retrospective art my fancy warms,
And bids the past to glow with Recollection's charms.
From what slight causes, goddess, can thy pow'r
A lasting pleasure draw ! a kiss, a flow'r,
A look of love from eyes unsunk by care,
Stamp'd on the heart, will live for ever there !
Then in soft melancholy's twilight hour,
Seek the lone grot, or overhanging bow'r,
Nor let ambition in your thoughts be found,
A bright allurer, and an empty sound.
Thence o'er th' Atlantic borne on Mem'ry's wing, }
Roam to the lands where spicy forests fling   }
Unceasing odours to eternal spring.   }

K. L.

A ROMAN SKETCH.

It was on a fine evening at that period when Sylla,
after a series of sharp contests and the most wily in-
trigues, was considered to be on the point of entering
Rome in triumph for the last time, that two persons of
the Marian faction, which was now rapidly decaying,
were walking together at a quick pace from the forum,
towards the Tiber.   The quiet, firm, and yet sorrowful,
manner, and the plain and soldier-like dress, of the elder
of these two, formed a striking contrast with the studied
and perfumed eloquence which shone over the person of
the younger, and with his agitated and unequal gait.
The first seemed about forty years old, and one who from

his youth had been inured to all the labours and chances
of war; and from being perpetually a spectator of its
dangers, and a sufferer under its inconstancies, seemed to
have acquired a kind of subdued calmness, which still
supported and elevated his mind; and yet, as the veteran
looked around on the palaces and gardens which he was
quitting, the forum in which he had remembered such
noble and venerable characters, and the capitol, where
he had beheld so many a glorious triumph, he seemed
fully and deeply to feel, that he was looking on them for
the last time. The younger was not much above twenty;
his dress was most like that of a young debauchee prepared for a banquet, but the expression of his flushed,
animated, and still commanding, countenance, the bright
and piercing eyes, and the grace and easiness of his
whole demeanour, instantly shewed that he was far, far
above the common herd of libertines and profligates.
The first was Quintus Sertorius, the second Caius Julius
Cæsar.

They walked together in silence till they reached the
banks of the Tiber, where a small vessel was waiting for
Sertorius. "Farewell, Caius," said he, pausing for a
moment on the bank, "farewell; this will soon be no
place for Marians; however, we may still make head in
the provinces; and, by Diana, if there are a thousand
true Romans in Spain, I will engage to keep the tyrant's
hands employed for some years; we have Perpenna in
Sicily; Carbo, if he fails here, in Africa; myself in
Spain; Sylla's fortune cannot last for ever, and then"—
"Aye, and then"—echoed Cæsar eagerly, his face
brightening as he spoke—"then the proud murderer

shall be crushed as he deserves! Then Rome shall be again Rome; the mistress of the world! Then she shall have again her heroes, her senate, and her laws." Sertorius smiled mournfully at his companion's warmth, "And, I fear, always a master! Degenerate Rome!"—"At any rate, he shall not be such a one as Sylla; she shall have a master wise and brave, who will fight her battles, conquer for her, and die for her! She shall have a master like "—"Like yourself, perhaps, you mean, 'my good Caius?'"—"And what if I do mean so," returned Julius, quickly, and reddening as he spoke, "that is, I mean "—"No matter; may she have as good a one as you will be to her, young man; but for our own private affairs; whither are you bound, when Sylla, as I fear he must, comes to act his butcheries here?"—"I will await the tyrant," said he, energetically, " I will await him in the midst of his assassins and legionaries; I will beard him while he is wading through blood to the dictatorship or the throne. I will be a basilisk to his eyes, and a lion in his path; he shall feel that the spirit of Marius has not all died with him! He shall feel what one courageous heart and determined spirit can do! Murder me! He dare not do it! I feel that here (touching his breast) which bids me hold at defiance Sylla, and all the mercenary dogs who lick up the offals which he throws to them, and who will destroy their patron, father or brother, if he give the nod; and him too, if they thought they could gain two talents by it. I will await him here."—"Dear Cæsar, would you rush into certain destruction? Think you that he would permit the nephew of Marius, and the son-in-law of

Cinna, to live one day longer, while his power could prevent it? Come with me, I beseech you, and secure at once your safety and your independence in Spain, with me, and with the poor remains of the Roman Senate."—"I have told you I will await the blood-thirsty tiger here, in his den! And besides," he added, gaily, "you know my cousin Marius gives his parting banquet to-night; all that is fair, and all that is brave of Rome, is to be there, and some half dozen of my loves among the rest, and would you have me turn infidel to them, to Chian wine, to the dice, and to Marius? I am no such Scythian, Quintus. By Bacchus, and Venus, and all that is mirthful, there I must be, so farewell, Quintus, farewell."

PHILIP MONTAGUE.

HISTORY OF A HACKNEY COACH.

Mr. Bouverie;

A few days ago, being caught in a shower, I called a hackney-coach; the one which came appeared to have seen better days, being very neatly built, although much injured by time. I seated myself, and was considering what changes it must have undergone before its final transformation into a hack, when all at once, a part of it began to shake in a very odd manner, and methought I saw a roll of paper, which, having seized with avidity, I opened and found to contain the following history:

"I was brought into existence twenty years ago at a great coach-maker's yard, and was sent to a gentleman of great celebrity in the sporting world, who took me to races, theatres, parties, and all other places of amusement; in which service I was sometimes upset, sometimes had my wheels broken, and met with a variety of other accidents which there is no occasion for me to relate. This gentleman, however, was soon ruined by his extravagance, and I fell into the hands of a sober citizen, who went to church on Sundays (if it did not rain), and in the afternoon took me out in the park : I did not, however, like my situation, for during the week I was kept closely shut up, and when I did get out, was loaded with my master, his wife, and five children ; at last, however, my mistress died, and my master, turning economical, dismissed me, as the first step towards retrenching his expenditure. Being now put up to auction, I was purchased by a young man with a moderate fortune, who used me well, and neither shut me up all day, nor wore me out with hard work; this was the best of my situations, and I should, perhaps, have staid much longer, had not my master gone abroad, when his establishment was broken up, and I was again exposed at an auction, and purchased by an old dowager, who was excessively pleased with me, until one of my wheels broke down, at which accident she was so frightened, that she immediately gave me away to one of her acquaintance, who in a short time sold me to my present owner, with whom my life is a scene of constant vicissitude : not long ago I carried the duke of ———, who was succeeded by a drunken sailor. I have carried a lover, who whined and groaned incessantly ; and a soldier who, with the greatest cruelty, poked me with

his sword and " punched me full of deadly holes." No
one, perhaps, has known more changes than I have;
I have carried an alderman to a feast, and a thief to the
gallows; I have conveyed a bride to church, and a sick
man to a hospital, but although some years ago, Hackney-
coaches were considered of great importance, we are
now so degraded, that there is scarcely a reputable
tradesman who will enter one of us, but I, being so
worn out with labour, do not expect to be long a spectator of the miseries of my friends, and have, therefore,
taken this opportunity of informing the world through
you of the adventures which I have experienced."

Such, Mr. Bouverie, is the account which I received,
and which I send to you; if you should think it amusing,
insert it, but if not, burn it.

P. T.

SONNET TO A REJECTED SONNET.

Poor child of Sorrow ! who did'st boldly spring,
   Like sapient Pallas, from thy parent's brain,
   All arm'd in mail of proof ! and thou would'st fain
Leap further yet and, on exulting wing,
Rise to the summit of the Printer's Press '
   But cruel hand hath nipp'd thy buds amain,
   Hath fix'd on thee the darkling inky stain,
Hath soil'd thy splendour, and defil'd thy dress !
Where are thy " full-orb'd moon," and " sky serene ?"
   And where thy " waving foam," and "foaming wave ?"
All, all are blotted by the murd'rous pen,
   And lie unhonour'd in their pap'ry grave !
Weep, gentle Sonnets ! Sonneteers, deplore !
And vow—and keep the vow—you'll write no more !

[I extract the following lines from a Poem with which a Correspondent has favoured me, entitled "THE SEER." B. B.]

Now is the time, the peaceful hour,
To stem th' assailing squadron's power—
Sound the charge, and from afar,
Urge the courser to the war—
Grasp your blades and, fir'd with rage,
Spare not aged, youth, nor sage—
But hark ! the rolling tempests lour,
　The livid flashes blaze,
And gleaming through the midnight hour,
　The fiery columns raise.
Now the spectres, rais'd from hell,
Howl around with murd'rous yell,
And rushing on 'midst haggard death,
Claim the slaughter'd victim's breath.
See—the iron-mingled show'r
　Hurtles in the darken'd air ;
Rages fierce the Tyrant's pow'r—
　Sons of Liberty, beware !
Confusion seize the coward heart,
The fearful gaze, the sudden start—
But ever hail ! ye chosen few
Who dare the battle's strife renew,
And, born to conquer or to die,
Disdain to tremble, yield, or fly.
Fall all around in death-like gloom,
　Soldier and chieftain, friend and foes :
They fall to meet an early tomb,
　While faster still the life-blood flows,
And louder rings the battle's shout,
The signs of death, and fearful rout :
Through the black clouds the pale moon flies,
Now hid—now flashing through the skies.

ON FALSE CANDOUR.

Candour, which loves in see-saw strain to tell
Of acting foolishly, but meaning well.—CANNING.

Of all the falsities which mankind adopt, either to feign virtues which they have not, or to conceal blots which they have, there is no one species of affectation so odious as False Candour. He who conceals his real opinion under this loathsome veil is like the general who, fearing to put forth manfully his whole strength, has recourse to a shifting system of manœuvres. The professors of Candour are divided into two classes— those who pretend to cloak what is true ; and those who are (as they express themselves) constrained to assert what is false.

The first class can often be recognized in those who, meeting you, will say, " I do not think our neighbour's affair so very bad ; to be sure, no woman should admit any one in the absence of her husband ; but then her case allows palliation :" Or, " Well, really I think there are uglier persons than our friend So-and-So," though he may happen to be one of those

In whom all human beauties flourish fair,
In his thick lips, flat nose, and flaming hair.

Now these persons think, or pretend to think, that, by this mock liberality, they do a great service to the person mentioned; whereas, to defend a man from the imputation of imperfections which are palpable to every observer, is like a ruined spendthrift pretending to keep up his appearance, and to deceive his already-awakened creditors. If a man has faults, let them be borne, and let not the remedy, by an attempt at an excuse, become worse than the disease.

For my part, I do not love to beat about the bush, when my object must be known; and, although there is no necessity for raking up a man's blemishes, it is still worse to expose them by an injudicious defence.

The next class are those who say, "Well, really, I must say that you are the most hideous personage I ever saw; I am sorry to say any thing harsh, but the truth must be told." Then, if you mention it to a mutual friend, he will tell you, that the Candid gentleman is a person who will speak his own mind. It is very well for Pope to write,

> I love to speak out all my mind, as plain
> As honest Shippen, or downright Montaigne.

The truth is, that though politeness, in its modern sense, has weakened the natural simplicity of manners, it has, at the same time, blunted the edge of bitterness; if it has destroyed the warmth of friendship and genuine kindness, it covers the coolness of indifference, and smothers the turbulence of animosity. Conceive the disturbance which would be caused in female society if every one spoke that which lay nearest her heart. How many who thought themselves amiable, young, and beautiful, would be hailed by the complimentary appellation of an " Ill-natured old Crump."

In a professor of Candour we never can distinguish whether they are friends; for on one side they are masked under whining hypocrisy ; on the other, under pretended independence. They are not your real enemies, but those concealed under the appearance of friendship, who are so uncontrolled in their strictures. Gay has warned us against both parties in the couplet,

> An open foe may prove a curse,
> But a pretended friend is worse.

And another eminent writer has enlarged on the idea in these lines, which serve as a conclusion to my paper :—

> Give me th' avowed, th' erect, the manly foe,
> Bold I may meet, perhaps may turn his blow.
> But of all ills, good Heav'n, thy wrath can send,
> Save me, O save me, from the Candid friend.

B.

P.S. My readers will perceive that I have kept to the Horatian maxim, " Servetur ad imum, &c.," for the same author furnished my motto and conclusion.

THE CAPTIVE MINSTREL'S COMPLAINT.

> Shall I, amid my prison gloom,
> Be buried in a living tomb ?
> Doom'd here, unfriended and alone,
> To moulder on the dungeon stone ?

My very keepers seem to me
To shun the child of misery.
They've bound my limbs, they cannot bind
The secret workings of my mind;
And though they snatch'd my joys away,
They barr'd me not from the light of day:
They could not mean to cheer my cell,
They play the keeper's part too well.
Perchance they wish'd to hear me sigh
O'er spots endear'd by days gone by;
They thought, that if they let me see
All round my prison glad and free,
I then might feel my misery;
Might wish to break my chain, and share
The freedom of the purer air.
Ah ! when upon the vale I gaze,
The happy scene of youthful days,
A thousand thoughts upon me rush,
A thousand sorrows o'er me gush.
What would I give for one lone hour
Of rest, within that peaceful bow'r '
Which, smiling on this dark recess,
Seems to mock my wretchedness.
Ah ! sweet I ween is the fleeting gleam
Of hope's refreshing light;
Like summer ray on wintry day
It beams through clouds of sorrow's night.
And though that beam is twice as fleet,
Yet still, I trow, 'tis twice as sweet,
To one o'er whose distracted soul
The icy waves of sorrow roll.
Yet e'en in hope there is some pain;
Our sorrows will return again:
And, like the bridled charger's course,
Rush on afresh with double force.
Is there a man so cas'd in grief,
Whose mind in hope hath no relief '
And said I then that hairs are grey ?
I trust to see a better day.

And spoke I of my wither'd fire?
I trust again to strike the lyre.
And though my heart is low with sorrow,
I still look forward to the morrow;
I know not why : perhaps in death
I long to spend my parting breath ;
Perhaps some innate dread of fate
Has made me love what most I hate—
Though 'twere not half so desolate.
Though 'twere not half such pain to die
As mould'ring mid these walls to lie ;
Yet hope, whom still I love too well,
Sometimes dissolves the fatal spell
Which, round my inmost thoughts entwin'd,
Has cas'd in grief my sorrowing mind.

OMNIUM GATHERUM.

Omnia novi.—JUVENAL.

A press of matter, naturally attending the close of my labours, must be my excuse to my worthy Correspondents for my giving only a partial and obscure kind of insertion to Compositions which might, under other circumstances, have obtained, as they may have deserved, a better fate.

To all who have encouraged and aided me ; to all who have looked with a favourable eye, whether active or passive, on my undertaking, to my Correspondents and Supporters in particular, let me here express my hearty and sincere gratitude. If they have not met with the encouragement they deserved, I have to ask their pardon   To old Etonian Contributors, in particular, I would wish to state, that I have been desirous, as much as possible, to confine the Eton Miscellany to those who have been actually at the time inmates of our classic walls.

From the communication by the Author of the ' Stanzas to Mary,' I extract the following stanzas,

TO THE MEMORY OF A YOUTHFUL FRIEND.

*   *   *   *   *   *

Teach us what few brief hours may roll away,
   'Ere we may meet thy Spirit where 'tis fled ;
When each survivor of this mournful day
   Shall lie beside thee in thy lowly bed.

And ye, the young, the thoughtless, and the great,
   Who breath'd for him the momentary sigh,
Hear the stern dictates of unalt'ring fate,
   Think how he liv'd, and learn like him to die !

Pale as the shroud which wraps his mould'ring clay,
   Cold as the stone above his youthful head,
Too soon that form in indistinct decay
   Must mix its dust with the unhallow'd dead.

For now, while seated on that lonely spot
   Where we, in early youth, were wont to meet,
The Zephyrs sigh, the dew-drops mourn thy lot,
   And fall, like tears of sorrow, at my feet.

From E. H. I can only extract the following stanzas.

NEY, AT HIS EXECUTION.

*   *   *   *

The ruddy drops that warm'd my heart
   In battle's fiercest cry,
Still glow—with these from life I part,
   And e'en proud death defy.

Am I the traitor ? who to save
   The falling crest of France,
Was once the bravest of the brave,
   To couch my quiv'ring lance.

And when I'm gone, and in the tomb
  My mould'ring limbs shall lie,
Some will lament the hero's doom,
  And heave the willing sigh.

* * * *

Can I, as one of many left,
  A wish for life disclose,
Of well-won laurels thus bereft
  To see my country's woes ?

A thousand deaths to life were sweet,
  Forgotten and forlorn,
And forc'd to live in dark retreat,
  Unpitied and in scorn.

Oh sing to me of broken vows,
  Of faithful love by scorn requited ;
Yet no—'twill but recall my grief,
  Whose heart is stung, whose hope is blighted.

Then sing of all the joys that flow
  From hearts in mutual faith united
Yet that were mock'ry of my woe,
  Whose love is torn, whose hope is blighted.

Then sing not of or joy or pain,
  'Twill but recall love's fitful fever—
I would not even dream again,
  Of that too beautiful deceiver.

But sing a sad and solemn strain,
  But yet not all to sorrow given,
That tells of what doth 'yet remain,
  A higher, purer, love of heaven.

F———.

Perhaps some learned friend can inform the *Writer on Anomalies* why, though duelling is unlawful, a defendant is allowed in our courts to challenge any Juryman! and on what pretence any poor curate can complain of an insufficient stipend, when he certainly possesses a *Surplus!*

In the Tenth Number, the Stanzas to the Memory of a Youthful Friend, those signed F.——, and those To——, come under the class of Ada, &c. &c.

METEMPSYCHOSIS AND CONCLUSION.

Ὥρη ἀποβλώσκειν, μὴ πρὶν φάος ἠελίοιο
*Δύῃ ὑποφθάμενον.——————————*APOLLONIUS.

Suspended between hope and fear, divided between confidence and hesitation, once more, and that for the last time, do I come forward to address my friends. I cannot help feeling that there has now been continued, for at least a sufficient period, an exhibition which, even if Mercy can pardon, Justice may yet condemn; an exhibition which, having perhaps been made in thoughtlessness, and certainly received with indulgence, we are now at least called upon to close. With the full and admitted consciousness of many deficiencies, of many errors, of many faults, we yet claim to ourselves the humble commendation of an acknowledgment that, however weak in their nature, however capricious in their exertions, however impotent in their effect, our efforts have, at least, not been such as to betray a disposition on our part to forfeit the pledge which we voluntarily gave, of striving with humble yet constant assiduity to pay our tribute of veneration to that foster-mother whom we then did, and whom we still continue to honour and revere.

The voice of duty sounds in my ears (to indulge, for the last time, in the darling sin of quoting poor Horace),

> "Tempus abire tibi est; ne potum largiùs æquo
> Rideat, et pulset lasciva decentiùs ætas."

The aim and nature of the sentiment which these lines are intended

to convey, may perhaps render adducing them a more venial delin-
quency than those I have before been guilty of, as conveying an
assurance of my consciousness, that I am called upon to depart from
a station I am unworthy to fill, and to relinquish that literary
sceptre which my hand is unable to wield with due efficiency.

But I feel and acknowledge, that the subject which I am now
commenting upon, that namely of leaving Eton, and, what is more,
Etonians, is one which is to me at least a topic of powerful but
melancholy interest : it is one which would lead me, did I not
restrain its impulses, into many a lengthened lamentation, which,
however truly it might depict my own feelings, could not in fair-
ness be expected to produce any sympathizing effect on those of my
readers. I will, therefore, without further delay, betake myself to
my task; and endeavour to describe the fate of the Spirits of my
coadjutors, while, in this our present and last Number, their bodies
are finally committed to the press. Long, long may those spirits
continue to animate the frames of those to whom they rightfully
belong, to animate them with the combined and united glow of
Taste, Genius, Virtue, and Religion ; to animate—not the visionary
and fragile limbs which boast alone of paper for flesh, of printer's ink
for blood ; but those substantial and vivacious carcasses, to which they
rightfully belong.

None of my friends need be alarmed at my relapsing into the
erroneous doctrines of the heathen Philosophers. Mr. Bouverie
enacts the part of the Pythagorean for this day only; and indulges
in a species of literary Paganism alone. Nor on the present occasion is he less obedient to truth than to convenience ; his motive
being to restore to their lawful owners certain spirits which he has
for some time past abstracted from their bodies, for his own use
and benefit ; to dissolve the charm which has bound them in their
constrained state of existence, and, after a long and faithful service,
to grant them the discharge which they require.

As soon, therefore, as the Tenth Number of the Eton Miscellany
had been composed and arranged, my coadjutors, supposing that their
labours were now at an end, assailed me in my humble habitation. They
were not satisfied with a release from their occupations, but demanded
rewards in addition I thought to soothe them with fair words, and
hoped, between giving a little and promising a great deal, to get fairly
out of their fangs. I told them, however, plainly, that I could not very
easily give what I had not got . that one soul could not well be divided

between two bodies ; that I would immediately deliver to all who could produce legitimate testimonials of their pretensions, the spirits which I at present held under my magic thraldom.

They pressed upon me on every side with increasing violence ; those, who had Spirits in my hands, eagerly asserting their claims to them ; and those who had not, declaring that they would revenge themselves on me, and lacerate me limb by limb, till each had obtained his legal share of me. In how piteous a manner I was mangled, I will not relate, till I have gone through the list of those whose demands I was able to satisfy, by parting with my stock in hand.

GEORGE AUGUSTUS SELWYN led the van, and conducted this formidable array of duns to the attack. He held in one hand the Second Number, and with the other pointed to the character of ANTONY HEAVISIDE. While, by a tremendous exertion of his voice, he convinced me of the propriety of his claim to that gentleman's lungs ; he threatened me, in case of a refusal on my part to do him justice, with a most positive and palpable proof of his possessing his " physical force ;" and, to tell the truth, my own sense of justice, such as it is, directed my attention to the " Art of Conversation," the " London University," and many other excellent contributions, and thereby convinced me of his full title to all the encomiums which had been pronounced upon the abilities of the person, whose spirit he came forward to claim.

Accordingly, I performed the magic ceremony, and dismissed the spirit of Mr. Antony Heaviside. It migrated, with as much regularity as if Pythagoras himself had directed the movement, into the body of its lord ; leaving behind it none of its appurtenances mentioned in the description of it, and specially taking care not to lose one single scruple or grain of Mr. H.'s " Hatred to the Pope."

The soul of MR. AP RICE was no where to be found, notwithstanding the "handsome reward " offered.* This shows, at least, that whoever has found him, considers him too valuable to be parted with, even for a " handsome reward."

Next, therefore, in order to the last-mentioned individual, came FRANCIS HASTINGS DOYLE. " Am I not Jermyn ?" quoth he—"Hath he not an unpolished superficies ? And is this my neckcloth tied by mathematical ordination ? Doth he not love Mamaluke and Pega-

---

* See Advertisement, No. VIII.

sus? And do I not alternately admire and mount the one and the other? He has an unhappy constitutional risibility; and did not I, in days of yore, by laughing in my preceptor's face, double the force with which the birchen rod descended on me? He 'was not intended to carry messages,' and was I? did not I, when thou didst give me the manuscripts to convey to the publishers, deliver them to the house-maid? And when thou desiredst me to correct the proof-sheets, transfer the office to my fag?" My excellent friend's modesty prevented his proceeding to remind me that "The Prediction," "The Victim," and their companions, invested him with a far more brilliant claim to all the commendations which poor Bartholomew did, or could, confer on the spirit which he now demanded.

Next, therefore, was dismissed Mr. Francis Jermyn. With a species of regular irregularity, the representative pursued its somewhat circuitous course towards the represented. They appeared perfectly well acquainted, and Mr. J. migrated into Mr. D., without the slightest difficulty It was found, however, that the portrait was scarcely a fair substitute for the original, and that sundry great and conspicuous merits had been omitted in the former, which acted with peculiar efficacy in the latter.

After a short interval had elapsed JAMES MILNES GASKELL commenced an eloquent address, in which, he said, he hoped to prove to the satisfaction of the House, within the space of a few hours, his legitimate claim—

MR QUINCY's spirit here interrupted the hon. Gentleman. Legitimacy was a mere bug-bear—it had been the source of much evil—the people ought to choose a sovereign—the British Constitution—Mr. Q. was at length stopped, after having disregarded my repeated cries of "Order"—

Mr. Gaskell proceeded. He could afford us ocular demonstration of his inability to feather an oar or handle a bat He would, if we pleased, offer a few observations on Sir Robert Walpole and his successors, down to the present day. He did not mean to depreciate Homer or Virgil. The former, in fact, had reported the debate between Achilles and Agamemnon, and the latter, that between Turnus and Drances, extremely well—except that they had not been careful to observe in what parts of the speeches there was cheering from one, and disapprobation from the other side of the House. This was wrong. Virgil's speeches smelt of the lamp. But Homer, he really thought, would do credit to St. Stephen's.

During the whole of this time, MR. WILLOUGHBY evinced an ardent desire to embrace the speaker. He became unmanageable; he cheered furiously; he clapped his hands in ecstasy; and when released from my custody, rushed immediately across the room to Mr. Gaskell, and became merged and hidden in his body.

MR. JOHN HALSEY LAW came forward, and said, that he would exercise his privilege as a citizen, and lay claim to Mr. Quincy. He thought the Ode to Wat Tyler worthy of an American Laureate; the feeling allusion to the immortal Ings had delighted him inexpressibly. He had never bowed to a despot. His voice was for the people. He had taken his passage by the next packet for America. He *had* broken a constable's head. Robespierre was an injured man: He— We assured Mr. Law that his case was most invulnerably complete; and immediately delivered over Mr. Quincy's spirit. The "*vox populi vox Dei*" of the one, was answered by the other with—

> ———— ita Di jubeatis, et istum
> Nulla dies a me, nec me seducat ab isto.

They joined in the most amicable manner.

The now sole remaining spirit, that of MR. PHILIP MONTAGUE, was unanimously declared to belong to FREDERIC ROGERS. The acquaintance did not, however, appear so intimate as might have been expected. The former had not any thing in which the latter was deficient, but was wanting in many of his attributes. My beliefs have been confirmed, and my assertions established, by the test of time. The spirit recognized the substance—and, a reciprocal recognition not immediately following, classically began—

> 'ὦ πόποι, ἦ μέγα θαῦμα τόδ' ὀφθαλμοῖσιν ὁρῶμαι.

On our adding, however, to the spirit, a large portion of Humility and Good Temper, with a scruple or two of Idleness intermixed, freeing at the same time from a good deal of his *exclusive* attention to classics, the resemblance appeared complete, and the junction, or in Mr. Willoughby's language, the coalition, instantly took place—

> Neutrumque et utrumque, videntur.

Many, however, the chief of whom was ARTHUR HENRY HALLAM, still remained unprovided for. The as yet unsatiated reader (if such there be) may consult my list of contributors for an account of them.

My angry assailants resolved to satisfy their rapacity at the expense of my unhappy person. Mr. Hallam seized a leg, Mr. Pickering an arm, and so forth , and, what was worse than all, they vowed that the greater part, if not the whole, of my brain belonged to them. Judge then, gentle reader, how wretchedly my hastily-formed and ill-compacted body was lacerated, by the vehement efforts of my merci-less enemies ; once con-, now dis-tributors, of poor Bartholomew Bou-verie. When each had carried off his limb, or his portion, of the trunk, nothing positively remained, save the fingers of the right hand, which have contrived to write this Conclusion, and a small portion of the brain—perhaps my readers may incline to think, none at all. These three fingers, however, whether accompanied or not so, by any portion of the spirit, taste, genius, or industry, of the great Bartholo-mew, are the property of WILLIAM EWART GLADSTONE. It may be said that he is an unworthy representative of the Editor of the Eton Miscellany , and I am confident he will not attempt to deny it. He awaits, with those around him, the sentence of his judges ; yet humbly advances this plea, if not a title to acquittal, at least a claim to mitigated punishment—the plea, that his own will did not bring him before the world, or urge him to expose to the scrutinizing eye of all beholders efforts, which, like the mean and lowly plants of the impe-netrable thicket, may indeed sustain their obscure existence, and bud forth their humble vegetation, beneath the shade and protection of darkness and oblivion, but which wither, droop, and die, when they feel themselves exposed to the penetrating rays of a noon-day sun.

Such is his apology for his individual offences. The crimes of his companions have not been so extensive, and may not equally require extenuation. Let him, and all who once were mine, retire ; and if their literary efforts be doomed to the grave, let there be said to each at least,

" Sit tibi terra levis."

And now, most worthy Public, I have come to the painful, the brief, the necessary duty, of bidding farewell to my foster-parent. If any one should think my Metempsychosis a clumsy machination, let them in common charity attribute it to my orthodox unwillingness to appear too perfect and experienced a Pagan.

My sorrow, in real truth, is too big to find utterance in the flimsy phrase of an Epilogue. The Dying Swan, and *Memnon Vespertinus* are established and orthodox similies for a *Vale* Such I cannot use. We are all aware of the extreme, the almost unequalled, strength and durability of Parental Affection. Even where the progeny is unworthy of the progenitors, the attachment, on the part of the latter at least, usually remains. As in Nature, so in Literature. *I* am attached to my literary children, and, indifferent as the public may consider them to be, I dismiss them with unfeigned regret. Let the kindly reader judge, how rapidly and how powerfully that regret is heightened and increased, when I find myself vanishing too from the scene of my early hopes and early joys—their counterparts I need hardly mention, for the fears of an Eton boy are few, and his griefs, none.

But I am indulging in lamentations which I promised my reader to spare. The feeling, however, which dictates them, is generally allowed to be praiseworthy ; and its excess may, from that consideration, be esteemed venial.

Then, though my benedictions be such as Eton does not stand in need of—though my efforts may have been such as to tinge the cheek of her presiding spirit rather with the blush of shame than with the glow of exultation—still let them be uttered—May Time in his course never deprive her of her present glory, but continually enrich her with accumulated honours. May generation after generation rapidly and steadily increase the proud catalogue of her Generals and Statesmen, her Divines and Philosophers, her Poets and Scholars ; may the foundation be Religion, Taste, and Learning—while the Superstructure, rising in splendour equalled only by its stability, shall abound in all that can adorn the mind, in all that can strengthen the faculties, in all that can improve the heart, and command the legitimate veneration, of mankind.

For those whose charge it has been, and is, to train up the denizens of our little world, in true, substantial, and never-fading Wisdom, may it be their destiny to exercise it long, with equal honour to the teacher, and advantage to the taught.

It may be a duty—it certainly is a difficult one—to add a few words regarding HIM under whose care, and by whose unceasing exertions and honest solicitude, we have been thus far happily conducted along the path of life. It is not to offer praise which it would be in me equally needless and impertinent to pronounce, but to seek a protection which none can despise, and which I for one do not undervalue, that he is here introduced. May the merits, if any, of the Eton Miscellany, bear their fruits, as they owe their origin, to him—may the faults, however great, remain with ourselves. Our course has hitherto been strown with flowers, it may, and it must, henceforward, be beset with thorns. That Peace and Joy, whose benignant influence hovers as a guardian angel round the head of the Eton boy*, no longer bestow on him such undivided attention, or foster him with such affectionate assiduity, after his transformation into the Oxford or Cambridge *man*.

Under the influence of feelings such as these, is it otherwise than natural that poor Bartholomew should be desirous to place the name of his Instructor as a shield in defence of his literary offspring; knowing, that if it be doomed to the darkness of oblivion, his approbation may, if any can, avert the miserable destiny; that if, on the contrary, to use the glowing expression of one of the greatest orators of the day, "my name have buoyancy enough to float upon the sea of time," it may there be associated with that of one, whose rebukes we have often merited, but whose approbation it will be our pride and our pleasure to receive.

BARTHOLOMEW BOUVERIE.

---

* Often does the Etonian, indignant at the appellation of "boy," strive to substitute "fellow" for the obnoxious monosyllable. When he is asked if he knows a *boy* named ———, he answers that he has heard of such a *fellow;* but boy he is, and boy he must be considered: and the best parting advice I can give him is, to bear and delight in a title which he will infallibly be sorry to lose.

CONTRIBUTORS

TO

"THE ETON MISCELLANY,"

VOL. II.

(Some unowned articles in Vol. I. are here included.)

INDEX

INDEX

TO THE

SECOND VOLUME.

END OF VOL. II.

T C. Hansard, Paternoster-row Press, London.

Lightning Source UK Ltd.
Milton Keynes UK
UKHW021504021218
333216UK00015B/2820/P

9 781355 952596